PRESIDENTS AND PRIME MINISTERS

PRESIDENTS AND PRIME MINISTERS

Conviction Politics in the
Anglo-American Tradition

Patricia Lee Sykes

UNIVERSITY PRESS OF KANSAS

© 2000 by the University Press of Kansas
All rights reserved

Published by the University Press of Kansas (Lawrence, Kansas 66049), which was
organized by the Kansas Board of Regents and is operated and funded by Emporia State
University, Fort Hays State University, Kansas State University, Pittsburg State University,
the University of Kansas, and Wichita State University.

Library of Congress Cataloging-in-Publication Data

Sykes, Patricia Lee.
    Presidents and prime ministers : conviction politics in the Anglo-American tradition/
Patricia Lee Sykes.
       p. cm.
    Includes bibliograpical references and index.
    ISBN 0-7006-1017-0 (alk. paper)
       1. Presidents—United States—History—Case studies. 2. Prime ministers—Great
Britain—History—Case studies. 3. United States—Politics and government—Case studies.
4. Great Britain—Politics and government—Case studies. 5. Political leadership—United
States—Case studies. 6. Political leadership—Great Britain—Case studies. I. Title.
E176.1.S98 2000
321.8'0941—dc21   99-089938

British Library Cataloguing in Publication Data is available.

Printed in the United States of America
10 9 8 7 6 5 4 3 2 1

The paper used in this publication meets the minimum requirements of the American
National Standard for Permanence of Paper for Printed Library Materials Z39.48-1984.

For my friends on both sides of the Atlantic,
especially Margaret and Marsha

CONTENTS

PREFACE

When Margaret Thatcher and Ronald Reagan won the elections of 1979 and 1980, they shocked social scientists and puzzled political pundits on both sides of the Atlantic. As prime minister and as president, these overtly ideological, controversial leaders promised to pursue their radical convictions in nations that had been known to govern by consensus and enact only incremental change. When they threatened to reverse the twentieth-century trend toward increasing state intervention in the economy, their aspirations appeared absurd. Moreover, the fact that this remarkable phenomenon occurred in the United Kingdom and the United States at the same time seemed a strange coincidence. Throughout the 1980s, many observers continued to view Thatcher and Reagan as aberrations and remained convinced these leaders would leave no enduring legacy. Then in the 1990s the opposition parties returned to power in the British government and the U.S. presidency—but only after they embraced and espoused essential aspects of Thatcher and Reagan's neoliberal public philosophy. At the end of the twentieth century, Prime Minister Blair's Labour government and President Clinton's administration rendered the most convincing evidence that Thatcher and Reagan had made possible what had seemed impossible. Defying conventional wisdom and political predictions, Thatcher and Reagan altered the national agenda and transformed the nature of political discourse in the U.K. and the U.S.

Perplexed by their success, I began this book in order to explain why and how Reagan and Thatcher, as self-proclaimed conviction politicians, managed to achieve their goals, but the scope of my project quickly expanded. Employing a historical lens that scanned two hundred years in the U.S. and the U.K., I discovered three significant aspects of presidents, prime ministers, and conviction politics. First, conviction-style leadership constitutes a recurrent feature of political development: As presidents and prime ministers, conviction politicians have achieved fundamental change at critical moments in history. Second, conviction-style leaders appear in the U.S. and the U.K. at roughly the same junctures, creating transatlantic waves of change and demonstrating links in political development that extend across the Atlantic. Third, these leaders articulate similar ideas, ones that adapt liberal ideology to suit changing circumstances. This book became a larger study than originally intended: Now it attempts to explain why and how leaders have altered liberal ideas and institutions within the Anglo-American tradition by practicing conviction politics.

To conduct my study, I relied on a number of sources, including the speeches, diaries, and memoirs of leaders and their contemporaries, newspapers and periodicals, secondary scholarly accounts, public opinion data and election results, and elite interviews. From 1990 through 1994, I conducted interviews with more than fifty politicians, their assistants, media consultants, party officials, and journalists in the U.S. and the U.K. I spoke with as many members of the Reagan administrations and Thatcher governments as I could. Interviews took the form of lengthy and informal conversations rather than rigid question-and-answer sessions. Most lasted more than an hour, and in many cases, I spoke with the same person more than once. In chapter 7 on the media, I also used interview data that I collected in the 1980s while conducting research for an earlier study on British politics. I would like to thank everyone who generously agreed to be interviewed for their time and their insights.

Throughout the process of research, writing, and revision, I enjoyed several special opportunities. A summer research grant from the National Endowment for the Humanities enabled me to start this project. The results of that research and a version of chapter 6 on parties appeared in the spring 1993 issue of *Studies in American Political Development*. I wish to thank the journal's editors, Karen Orren and Stephen Skowronek, and the anonymous reviewers for comments and suggestions that improved my article and informed my subsequent research. I completed final revisions on the manuscript as a Fulbright Senior Scholar at Trinity College Dublin during the 1997–98 academic year. I would like to express my gratitude to the Fulbright commissions in the U.S. and in Ireland and to Karen Adams, the senior program officer for Europe at CIES. Of course any opinions expressed in this book are mine and not necessarily those of NEH or Fulbright. I also wish to thank the department of political science at Trinity College, especially Michael Laver, Michael Marsh, Yvonne Galligan, and Kathie Young, a visiting lecturer from the University of Glasgow. They taught me a great deal about Irish politics, helped me to start a new research project while I completed the old one, and ensured that I enjoyed a wonderful year in Dublin. I also had the chance to present the research for this book when Niamh Hardiman invited me to speak to the faculty and graduate students in the department of politics at University College Dublin, and I thank them for their warm welcome and helpful comments. When I returned to American University, the new dean of the School of Public Affairs, Walter Broadnax, provided funds to facilitate the publication of this book, and I greatly appreciate his support. Finally, I thank my former dean, now Provost Neil Kerwin, who encouraged me to apply for the NEH grant and then made it possible for me to secure a leave to receive the Fulbright fellowship.

While I was writing this book, the University Press of Kansas made the project a joy when the task might otherwise have become a burden. As my editor, Michael Briggs provided constant encouragement, showed great patience, and repeatedly rendered decisions that revealed his excellent judgment and his wide-ranging knowledge. I also thank the reviewers of my book proposal, Bert Rockman and Colin Campbell, whose suggestions helped shape the project and improved the original research design. For many years, I have been fortunate to benefit greatly from the wisdom and guidance of David Mayhew and David Butler, and I was pleased to learn that the press chose them to review this book before its publication. David Mayhew's meticulous reading resulted in several corrections, while David Butler's suggestions improved the clarity of my argument. Their keen insights and constructive comments reminded me of the exceptional qualities that have made them both such accomplished political scientists and distinguished scholars. Of course any substantive mistakes that remain are my own responsibility.

Many other people have provided various kinds of valuable assistance. I wish to thank the following colleagues, students, and friends: Andrea Agathoklis, Roseanna Bess, Melissa Deckman, Christine Degregorio, Cynthia Enloe, Jeff Fishel, Cindy Focht, Graham Hacche, Steve Kelly, Barbara Koziak, Greg Lewis, Jack Loughney, Jenny McGough, Alan Metelko, Amy Oliver, Laurie Rhodebeck, Robert Scigliano, Reg Stichbury, and Laurie Strayer. I would also like to thank Adrianne Lucke at ASL Business Services in Adams Morgan for supplying all the services of an efficient, well-equipped office, while also contributing to the congenial atmosphere of our neighborhood.

Finally, I wish to thank my family in the U.S., in Bradford, England, and in Kiltibo, County Mayo, Ireland, and my friends on both sides of the Atlantic. Special thanks go to my mother, who has always inspired and encouraged me and who in recent years provided the support I needed to finish this book. I am also especially grateful to Marsha Rabe and Margaret Stichbury for providing decades of dear friendship. It is reassuring to know that on either side of the Atlantic, I remain close to home and never far from the best of friends.

TIME LINE

1800

1828 Jackson elected
1832 Jackson reelected

1834-35 Peel's 1st brief
ministry
1841 Peel becomes prime
minister
1846 Peel resigns

1868–74 Gladstone's 1st
1868–74 Gladstone's 1st
govt.
1884 Cleveland elected
1880–85 Gladstone's 2nd
govt.
1888 Cleveland loses election
1886 Gladstone's 3rd govt.
1892 Cleveland elected
1892–94 Gladstone's 4th
govt.

1900

1912 Wilson elected
1916 Wilson reelected
1916 Lloyd George
becomes pm
1918–22 Coalition govt.
with Lloyd George
as pm

1980 Reagan elected
1979 Thatcher's 1st govt.
1984 Reagan reelected
1983 Thatcher's 2nd govt.
1987 Thatcher's 3rd govt.

2000

1

INTRODUCTION

"I am a conviction politician," Margaret Thatcher boldly declared in the 1979 general election. "The Old Testament prophets did not merely say, 'Brothers, I want a consensus.' They said: 'This is my faith and my vision. This is what I passionately believe. If you believe it too, then come with me.'"[1] Her resolute remarks won enthusiastic applause from Ronald Reagan, who immediately adopted her label as his own. As self-described "conviction politicians," Thatcher and Reagan promised to provide strong leadership, establish new national priorities, and restore fundamental principles to politics. Inspired by lofty vision and spurred by high ambition, they tried to transform their nations by restructuring the state and society and advancing a new public philosophy. In launching their bold assault on the existing regime, they supplied a sharp contrast to their immediate predecessors, but Thatcher and Reagan were not unique. They represent only the most recent examples of leaders who have practiced conviction politics in the Anglo-American tradition.

This study compares Reagan and Thatcher with six other conviction politicians: Andrew Jackson and Sir Robert Peel, Grover Cleveland and William Gladstone, Woodrow Wilson and David Lloyd George. The analysis that follows employs a two-tier historical approach that examines recurrent features of leadership while tracing the evolution of ideas and institutions. Comparisons across time reveal the capacity of conviction-style leaders to achieve fundamental change, although constraints and opportunities vary at different stages of political development. Comparisons across the Atlantic show that developments in the United States and the United Kingdom have been closely linked and that politics in the two nations have been more similar than generally recognized.

Initially, the leaders in this study were chosen because of their similarities, and among these the most significant is their style. All eight succeed (in different degrees) in demonstrating strong leadership based on pursuing principle, directing national policy, and infusing political discourse with meaning that transcends "politics as usual." They clearly constitute a minority of leaders in the history of the U.S. and the U.K., but studies that focus on the experience of most leaders tend to neglect conviction politicians and, instead, emphasize the obstacles leaders usually encounter. To appreciate

1

fully the capacity of presidents and prime ministers to change their environment requires not only a wide historical lens but also one that zooms in on the rare yet recurrent cases of conviction-style leadership. Then the picture that develops allows us to view leadership as a critical factor (rather than a residual variable) in the dynamics of political change.

This study in political development also highlights striking similarities in the ideas espoused by conviction-style leaders in the Anglo-American tradition. Within each pair, the leaders promote parallel principles as essential features of their public philosophies. In doing so, they reveal ideological waves that extend across the Atlantic throughout political development. Several factors link the two countries. First, they share a high degree of interdependence that grows stronger throughout history. Furthermore, a great deal of interaction takes place between reformers—intellectuals and activists—and, in the twentieth century, contact increases among members of the political elite. Perhaps most significant, the U.S. and the U.K. enjoy a common legal and philosophical tradition, with liberalism as the dominant ideology in both countries. In fact all eight leaders articulate principles that fit squarely in the liberal tradition. Differences that evolve over time reveal the adaptation and revision liberalism has undergone and the role leaders have played in those transformations.

Finally, institutional differences of two types emerge: across the Atlantic and across time. Cross-national comparisons reveal the impact of different institutional structures on executive leadership, but as this study shows, those differences diminish over time. The erosion of institutional integrity and constitutional viability that takes place in both countries helps to explain the convergence between the two political systems. As in ideological transformation, conviction-style leaders play a critical role in institutional evolution.

Of course any study of this historical scope confronts limitations and merits qualifications. Many prominent presidents and prime ministers have been excluded because they are not conviction politicians. Franklin Delano Roosevelt might have been paired with Clement Attlee, for example. Yet FDR held few firm convictions; instead, he succeeded largely as a result of his creative pragmatism and his charisma.[2] On the other side of the Atlantic, the postwar Labour government created the modern corporatist state, but Attlee presided over the creation as a chairman of the board, not as a conviction-style leader. As the cases of FDR and Attlee indicate, conviction politicians are not the only agents of change.

Furthermore, this study's set of conviction politicians is not inclusive. The focus on Anglo-American developments led to the exclusion of the consummate conviction politician Abraham Lincoln as a case study. Other presidents and prime ministers might fit the description of conviction politicians: Rather than address all the possibilities, I encourage readers to apply the label to other leaders. If it sticks, they might see those leaders in a new light and acquire a different perspective on the nature and impact of their leadership.

The leaders who have been included provide good (if not the only) examples of conviction-style leadership, and they create the basis for reasonable cross-national and historical comparisons, even though some of the choices might seem surprising. Admittedly, no leader completely or consistently fits the ideal type, and no pair is a perfect match.[3] Among other factors, personality affects each leader's adherence to conviction, especially when the circumstances call for a degree of flexibility. Cleveland, Gladstone, Wilson, and Thatcher emerge as the most rigid adherents to conviction, while Jackson, Peel, Lloyd George, and Reagan prove much more adaptable. Institutional religion or strong paternal influence seems to have produced a profound impact on the four most rigid leaders. On the other hand, the fact that such dramatically different personalities adopt the same leadership style and pursue common ideological goals indicates that personality provides only a secondary explanatory factor in the study of political leadership. The following analysis remains sensitive to the personal and contextual differences among these leaders but emphasizes the similarities in the style and substance of their leadership. As conviction politicians, all eight leaders demonstrate the potential power of presidents and prime ministers to shape the development of popular ideas and political institutions.

The Recurrent Pattern: Conviction-Style Leadership

"Conviction politics" is a phrase employed in public discourse, even though the concept does not lend itself to precise analytic definition. Ordinary citizens are likely to apply the label "conviction politician" to a strong, decisive leader whom they admire, and they seem to grasp the meaning of conviction politics when they use the phrase. No U.S. citizen would invoke it to describe George Bush or William Clinton, but it frequently emerges in remarks about Reagan. What Justice Potter Stewart said of pornography could apply to conviction politics: A citizen might simply say, "I know it when I see it." Perhaps Thatcher came closest to reaching an analytic understanding when she drew the distinction between conviction and consensus politics.

Conviction-style leadership can provide a useful contrast to the consensus-style leadership that usually prevails in British and U.S. politics. Both conviction politics and consensus politics are simplifications, but like any models they can serve to highlight central features of the phenomena they represent. Of course, conviction politicians occasionally compromise, and consensus leaders sometimes show conviction. (It is even possible for a consensus leader to be a conviction politician, as the British Labour party leader Hugh Gaitskell was, but such leaders will not produce substantial change.) For the purpose of this analysis, what matters most are the dominant features of the two leadership styles, which differ in three fundamental respects: their goals, their strategies, and the conditions conducive to their success.

To a great extent, conviction politicians challenge the notion that leaders seek power as their ultimate goal and not as the means to achieve some other objective.[4] When political scientist Anthony Downs asserted politicians "are interested in gaining [and maintaining] office per se, not in promoting a better or an ideal society,"[5] he described the typical consensus-style leader. Conviction-style leaders call into question this basic assumption when they proclaim as their objective the fundamental transformation of their regimes. Thatcher summed up the position of conviction politicians in her memoirs when she described politics as "philosophy in action."[6] For conviction-style leaders, public office does provide the place to promote their notion of the ideal society.

Conviction politicians aim to achieve ideological change, while consensus politicians generally seek and maintain power by avoiding controversial issues. Consensus politicians are likely to articulate ideas only when it proves functional: when it serves to reinforce the status quo, preserve the existing regime, or augment their personal power. For conviction leaders, the goal is primarily ideological: The expansion of power provides the means to promote ideas and does not serve simply as an end in itself. Long before they assume the executive office, many conviction leaders promote the same principles that they advance throughout their careers. If they develop a conviction while in office, they are often willing to sacrifice their influence for the sake of preserving their principle. In the practice of conviction politics, conviction generally precedes or excludes strategic calculations about how to achieve and expand power.

Reagan and Thatcher illustrate the point. If ideas had been merely functional for them, they would have articulated only those views that reflect popular opinion. Instead, early in their careers, both delivered speeches that disturbed many members of the political elite and failed to appeal to the general public.

Consider Reagan's well-known speech "A Time for Choosing," which he presented on national television on October 27, 1964, just as Barry Goldwater headed for defeat in a landslide election.[7] Initially, Goldwater himself was reluctant to include Reagan's speech as part of his own national appeal because his advisors considered it too radical. Despite the Goldwater campaign's reservations, Reagan launched an aggressive attack on the modern welfare state, and he did so on the eve of Lyndon Johnson's Great Society.

At the very start of his speech, Reagan wasted no words in proclaiming his convictions. "I am going to talk of controversial things," Reagan alerted his audience and added, "I make no apology for this." Immediately, Reagan rejected "a kind of safe middle ground," but he also envisioned "no left or right, only an up or down"—"up to the maximum of individual freedom consistent with law and order, or down to the ant heap of totalitarianism." The conviction critic of the welfare state voiced two basic objections that he would repeat throughout his career: The welfare state's authority subverts individual choice, and its size invites inefficiency and incompetence. Moreover, the need for tax reform figured prominently in Reagan's proposed alternative to the welfare state, a conviction that would determine his priorities as president. He also linked the domestic and the international with a warning against creeping socialism: Using language that foreshadowed his assault on the "evil empire," Reagan labeled socialism "the most evil enemy of mankind." In conclusion, he returned to defend what he was doing (as well as saying) when he urged, "We must have the courage to do what we know is morally right." The goal in his message is clear: to pursue ideological objectives or, in Reagan's own words, to do "what is morally right."

Four years after Reagan's speech, Thatcher offered a similar choice to the British when she delivered a lecture on behalf of the Conservative Political Centre at the party conference in Blackpool.[8] Thatcher chose to address fellow Conservatives and not the general public—in part, a reflection of the structural differences between British and U.S. politics. Despite different audiences, Thatcher's message struck a chord similar to Reagan's in both style and content.

Like Reagan, Thatcher began her speech with a critique of consensus politics at a time when the pragmatic Harold Wilson acted as prime minister. Immediately, she exposed what she considered the electoral ploys of consensus politicians: Such leaders attempt to maximize their appeal by making promises to the majority in exchange for their votes. In contrast, Thatcher declared, "I believe that parties and elections are about more than rival lists of miscellaneous promises—indeed, if they were not, democracy would scarcely be worth preserving." In substance as well as style, Thatcher resembled Reagan as she proceeded to attack the welfare state with a warning against its negative impact on "the outlook and approach of our people." According to Thatcher, the modern welfare state nurtures dependency and undermines individual autonomy, while bureaucracy breeds official irresponsibility. The combined effect or the "result of the democratic process has therefore been an increasing authoritarianism." Thatcher recommended a shift away from the control of incomes to the control of the money supply, reduced rates of taxation, and fewer social services; in other words, the same restricted role for government in managing the economy that she would advance as prime minister. The conviction leader concluded her appeal with a dire warning: "There are dangers in consensus; it could be an attempt to satisfy people holding no particular views about anything. It seems more important to have a philosophy and a policy which because they are good appeal to sufficient people to secure a majority." Not a program, she might have added, that was good simply because it appealed to the majority.

As these speeches indicate, conviction-style leaders communicate two messages to the public: On one level, they articulate and promote a public philosophy or set of principles; on another, they define (as they pursue) its distinctive approach. Reagan and Thatcher instructed their audience that leaders should "talk of controversial things" and expound a philosophy and a policy "which are good." As they advocated conviction-style leadership, they also articulated specific convictions and then adhered to their principles even when the electorate initially rejected them. In their words and in their deeds, Reagan and Thatcher revealed a second difference between conviction leaders and consensus politicians—namely, the strategies they pursue.

As candidates, consensus politicians tend to shun ideological extremes and situate themselves at the center of the political spectrum, where most voters are assumed to be located. Avoiding issues and uttering platitudes, they try to master the art of ambiguity and develop the craft of compromise. Once in office, such leaders often prove preoccupied with reelection and consequently continue to avoid declaring controversial positions. In an environment where politicians allow public opinion alone to determine their strategy, the roles reverse and the leader becomes a mere follower. (Thatcher once derided German chancellor Helmut Kohl for his practice of consensus politics. "He's a very peculiar man," she remarked and then explained, "He leads by following.")[9] By contrast, conviction leaders promise to pursue their own beliefs and persuade the public to follow their lead. They set the agenda and then seek to mold public opinion. Circumstances can also convince conviction politicians to compromise, but they rarely sacrifice the principles that define the purpose of their leadership and provide the core of their public philosophy.

When conviction politicians promote the notion that leaders must seize the initiative, define objectives, and act decisively, they articulate a concept of leadership that assumes a floundering followership: Democracy lacks direction, and the public looks for strong leadership to solve the problems that plague the polity. In practice, the state of the public and its opinion varies, and the variation points to a third distinction between the conviction and the consensus styles: The conditions conducive to successful leadership differ, and public opinion can prove decisive.

Conviction-style leaders can emerge when the public expresses as its salient and central concern the desire for "strong leadership." The leaders' conviction conveys strength and determination, which supplies a crucial component of their support. British citizens frequently remarked, "I don't always agree with Maggie, but at least we know where she stands." In the view of U.S. voters, Reagan's strong leadership conjured up the image of John Wayne: The president stood as the Western world's cowboy, prepared to fight evil forces on any frontier, including space. Even when voters disagree with the substance of the convictions, the leadership style can win their admiration and their support.

At such junctures in political development, citizens no longer perceive the benefits of the type of leadership they have come to reject. Consensus politicians can forge and maintain national unity by bridging ideological gaps and negotiating compromise. They tend to emphasize the importance of procedural fairness and honor the guidelines for policy implementation, which often constitute their preoccupation. Compared with conviction politicians, their leadership is more inclusive and safer: No radical reform threatens interests or institutions. Usually, their policies preserve stability and lend continuity to political development, but changing circumstances can transform these strengths into weaknesses.

When public opinion proves uncertain and obscure on specific issues, the consensus-style leader who seeks to follow the public appears weak and indecisive. In search of a center that no longer exists, the leader as follower fumbles and fails to fill the void left by the breakdown of consensus. When the public demands strong leadership in the absence of consensus, conviction-style leadership can supply a successful strategy. Fragmented public opinion provides a window of opportunity for conviction politicians. In these circumstances, leaders can shape their strategic environment so that the ideological proves to be the pragmatic and conviction becomes a rational choice.

The public can matter in yet another way. Dissatisfaction with the existing regime usually includes allegations of widespread corruption. (In the U.S. special interests often appear as the culprits, whereas in the U.K. class bias tends to constitute the cause for concern.) Majority opinion might not have formed to endorse a particular remedy, but social and intellectual movements do struggle to advance specific reforms. In most cases of conviction-style leadership, the leaders tap one or more of these movements, while they can also blunt the appeal of or undermine other challenges to the regime. The ideas they espouse rarely originate with the leaders themselves, but presidents and prime ministers can determine which ideas will win a national forum.[10]

When they take up a particular cause, they facilitate the formation of majority support for it. In choosing the cause, they exercise wider discretion with fewer constraints than the consensus politician who brokers among many groups.

These two leadership styles are rooted in different concepts of democracy and governance. In its legislative or policy-making capacity, consensus leadership satisfies the basic requirements of representative government in the Lockean liberal tradition: The leader expresses the collective judgment or the "public good" as the accumulation of private (individual or group) interests. Conviction leadership more closely resembles the role of Rousseau's "legislator," who plays an active part in formulating the "general will," whose sum is greater than the parts. As a conviction-style leader on the British left put it, conviction politics holds that "democracy must have a leader to inject into the public mind some understanding."[11]

As an executive, the conviction politician possesses authority that is less "ambivalent" than the leader's "power to execute" in the Lockean liberal tradition. Locke's constitutional executive is both weak and strong, forced to act out of necessity but able to exercise discretion and show assertiveness through executive prerogative.[12] Like Lockean liberal leaders, conviction politicians are strong because they possess substantial discretion, but they can also choose their goals and alter structures to shape their circumstances. To maintain their authority, consensus politicians do what they must; to achieve desirable (albeit not necessary) ends, conviction politicians do what they believe they should. Political contingency and necessity restrict consensus politicians; normative values and opportunity invite conviction-style leaders to innovate.

The Changing Context: Ideas and Institutions

Liberal principles constitute the central convictions of presidents and prime ministers in this study, and adapting those principles to suit changing circumstances is one of the essential ways they innovate.[13] The leaders return to the fundamental problem that Lockean liberalism attempted to resolve: how to design a government that would maximize individual freedom and, at the same time, serve the "public good." Locke concluded that the only legitimate form of government would be one that is limited in nature and operates with the consent of the governed. When conviction politicians redefine the limits of government (and the meaning of rights), they employ Lockean reasoning: The need to secure individual freedom delineates the realm and justifies the activity of the state. Of course, consent is essential for all political leaders who wish to wield power in liberal, democratic societies, but public support proves critical to conviction politicians, who are more inclined than consensus politicians to tap extra-institutional sources of authority. Although conviction-style leaders play an active role in the formation of public opinion, the public can also place constraints on the practice of conviction politics.

As they attempt to revise and reinvigorate liberalism, the conviction politicians examined here generally neglect (if not reject) the assumptions and goals of republicanism.[14] These leaders do not attempt to advance a notion of community, encourage participation, or nurture civic virtue. Nor do they usually employ the language of civic humanism, a critical component of republican thought. (Civic humanism provides the republican solution to its central problem: how to reconcile absolute virtue with the contingency of a secular republic.)[15] The style and substance of these conviction politicians certainly affect republican institutions and values, but their assumptions and goals are essentially liberal ones.

Indeed, the role these leaders have played in the liberal tradition indicates why and how liberalism has needed to adapt to endure and why it has required conviction politicians to facilitate change. It is not surprising that a seventeenth-century philosophy would need adaptation to guide nineteenth- and twentieth-century politics; yet some of the limits of Lockean liberalism would be addressed not only by the substance of subsequent revisions but also by the style of conviction politics.

Among other things, Lockean liberalism failed to solve the problems posed by the concentration of wealth and influence that accumulates with evolving class or "special" interests. Attacks on class or special interests as the source of corruption have usually provided the impetus for change. Conviction politicians embrace the cause of reform and promote or adapt liberalism in ways that appear to restore its integrity and sustain its relevance.

In the first transatlantic wave, Jackson and Peel advanced a type of "democratic liberalism." Both leaders objected to government activity that served the interests of the elite and neglected the needs of the wider public, including the disadvantaged. When Jackson vetoed the charter for the National Bank, he alleged that "the rich and powerful too often bend the acts of government to their selfish purposes." According to Jackson, the state serves to "make the rich richer and the potent more powerful," while it neglects the interests of "the humbler members of society—the farmers, mechanics, and laborers."[16] Peel sent a similar message when he addressed the House of Commons and urged repeal of the Corn Laws "for the benefit of all classes": "The mere interests of landlords . . . are subordinate to the great question— what is calculated to increase the comforts, to improve the condition, and elevate the social character of the millions who subsist by manual labor, whether they are engaged in manufactures or agriculture?"[17] Jackson urged the government to adhere to equal protection of the laws and "shower its favors alike on the high and the low, the rich and the poor," while Peel promised "legislation [framed] upon the principles of equity and justice." Jackson and Peel attempted to alter the relationship between the state and society by limiting the scope of government in critical areas of economic policy. When they succeeded, they institutionalized liberal principles, while they also muted more radical calls for change that threatened the liberal tradition.

In the late nineteenth century, William Gladstone and Grover Cleveland advocated "classic liberalism" to meet renewed challenges to liberalism. As new groups—the Welsh, the Irish, and the Dissenters—clamored for political recognition, Gladstone embraced liberal reforms that addressed fundamental issues of national identity, including disestablishment of the church and home rule for Ireland. In the U.S. Cleveland responded to economic distress and social dislocation by attacking the corrupt Republican regime for its "sordidness" and "selfishness" and promoting liberal remedies of civil service reform and tariff reduction. As Cleveland and Gladstone carried out their crusades to promote classic liberalism, they resolutely resisted the most serious challenge to it. For liberalism to survive the twentieth-century challenge of socialism, their successors would need to accommodate the demands of organized labor and other reformers.

By the early twentieth century, social, economic, and political factors again supplied the impetus for change, which conviction-style leadership could facilitate. World War I placed new demands on the state for the mobilization of resources, but even earlier, the Progressive movement in the U.S. and the Labour movement in the U.K. raised fundamental questions about the existing regime. Wilson and Lloyd George responded to charges of unfairness by regulating labor and farm conditions in ways that redefined the relationship between the state and society: The state started to play a positive role in social and economic life and assumed greater responsibility for the public welfare. Wilson and Lloyd George promoted the notion that society should be organized for collective action in the public interest, an idea that eventually replaced nineteenth-century individualism. Their "new liberalism" maintained that government must exist to secure equal rights, but such security required an expanded role for the state.

In the 1980s Reagan and Thatcher harked back to nineteenth-century individualism as the basis for a new relationship between state and society, while they also hoped to alter the relationship between their states and the rest of the world. Tax reform and deregulation or privatization were critical components of their "neoliberalism," an ideology that once again advocated limited government involvement in the economy. Through lofty moral rhetoric Reagan and Thatcher attempted to elevate political discourse above the interplay of entrenched special interests associated with the welfare state. At the same time, their agendas for change nurtured new nationalism and promised to make their countries "great again." Despite their emphasis on the need to restore individual liberty, threats to freedom—from communism, international terrorism, and domestic crime—provided the rationales they needed to expand state authority in new ways.

By the late twentieth century, Thatcher could boast about her government's efforts to combat terrorism and boldly declare, "We do sometimes have to sacrifice a little of the freedom we cherish in order to defend ourselves from those whose aim is to destroy that freedom altogether."[18] Her remark provides one reason why liberalism might need to adapt to endure, but it also indicates that such adaptation can dilute the original meaning of liberty and undercut the individual rights that liberalism was designed to secure.

From Jackson and Peel through Reagan and Thatcher, conviction politicians have attempted to sustain liberalism by the style as well as the substance of their leadership, but their impact on liberalism in this regard also proves problematic. Conviction politicians elevate the modest safeguards and practical considerations of liberalism to the level of an ideal: Liberal principles provide the core of their vision and lie at the heart of national identity. The leaders infuse Lockean rationalism with passion, and in doing so they initially fuel and then seek to satiate a public longing for politics imbued with meaning. Locke explicitly rejected high-minded or lofty visions in favor of a philosophy that was low (designed to protect property) but secure. The founder of modern liberalism would have feared that passionate pursuit of the ideal could overwhelm rational regard for the constitution and the institutions that are designed to secure individual rights. Subsequent developments suggest that such fears might be well founded.

Conviction politicians operate in a structural context that changes substantially throughout the nineteenth and twentieth centuries. In general, the political environment evolves from one conducive to consensus to one that gives freer rein to the practice of conviction. As in the transformation of ideology, the innovations of conviction politicians frequently facilitate change — in the development of political parties, media politics, the relationship of the executive to other national institutions as well as the state, and global affairs.

Contrary to conventional wisdom, throughout Anglo-American history, parties frequently present one of the most significant obstacles to change. (To a great extent, the strength of parties in the late nineteenth century limited the success of Cleveland and Gladstone, while the weakness of parties at other junctures facilitated the leaders' ability to pursue their principles.)

Strong parties can prove incompatible with conviction-style leadership and the pursuit of change for several reasons. In pluralist societies with two-party systems, each political party comprises multiple interests. The need to satisfy diverse interests can force leaders to compromise and follow strategies based on ambiguity and equivocation, not principle. Furthermore, parties primarily exist to win elections, but conviction-style leaders attempt to pursue fundamental change. Distinct objectives can create a clash that pits principled leaders against their own political parties. In contrast to many contemporary party theorists, conviction-style leaders understand the limitations imposed by their parties, and many of them consciously attempt to circumvent or alter party constraints.

To pursue their goals, conviction-style leaders generally prefer to rely on the media rather than parties, and in this respect they prove to be more Machiavellian than Lockean. They emphasize the importance of appearance and cultivate their image as a way of shaping their "reality," and as a consequence, their relationship to the media acquires special significance. Of course, as institutions weaken (and the link between the executive and public opinion strengthens), the mass media become more important, but the press have always played a critical part in the practice of conviction politics. Perhaps unwittingly, reporters endorse conviction politics because its characteristics conveniently coincide with news values (which often stem from commercial pressures). Several aspects of conviction politicians create a "good story," especially their strong leadership, the pursuit of change, their passionate rhetoric, and populist appeals. For this reason, they are more likely than consensus politicians are to win favorable news coverage.

News values change very little, but other developments in the twentieth century do affect the media's depiction of conviction politicians. With the development of the state, reporters acquire the role of "explaining" public policy to the public. At the same time, their place in the political order becomes institutionalized in the form of the White House press corps and the British lobby system. Nevertheless, these institutions allow little independence: Reporters are removed from their news organizations and situated within the structure of government. Their physical proximity to officials combined with their need for information creates circumstances favorable to media manipulation or "news management." Late-twentieth-century conviction politicians seize the opportunity created by these conditions, while they also incorporate the advantages of the televisual age into their news management strategies. In general, the spectacle they create dazzles the press and the public, producing an effect that becomes even more spectacular when they perform on a global stage.

In addition to the changing nature of political parties and media politics, substantial institutional developments occur that alter the place of conviction-style presidents and prime ministers within the government and in relation to the state. Institutional constraints can explain executives' failure to achieve change (along with parties, Congress and cabinet restricted Cleveland and Gladstone), but other leaders manage to alter their structural environments in significant ways. Moreover, when these leaders adopt institutional innovations, they often expand the scope of authority for their successors. In the U.S. a system structured for consensus politics becomes more conducive to conviction leadership as executive supremacy replaces legislative dominance. In the U.K. conviction-style leaders struggle with a succession of consensus mechanisms until it becomes possible to make their position more independent and autonomous. Power shifts first from Parliament to parties and later from cabinet to Number 10 Downing Street. (Admittedly, fluctuations occur within these developments, especially when the absence of strong executive leadership creates a vacuum.) Ultimately, several factors contribute to institutional change, but conviction politicians play an important part: They adopt and promote innovations to free themselves from institutional constraints as they seek to strengthen the link between the executive and the public.

In many instances what the leaders say proves as significant as what they do. While they advance reform, many of the leaders critique the institutions that preserve consensus. They argue against the notion that consensus is democratic because it embraces the concerns of many groups and guards against concentrated power. Instead, conviction politicians allege that consensus and its supporting structure preserve the status quo and protect entrenched interests. To advance their goals, conviction politicians insist they must break the mold in terms of institutions as well as ideas.

In fact, conviction politicians not only seek structural change; the leadership style of conviction politics itself can facilitate the decline of constitutional limits and alter widely accepted norms. To expand their authority and bypass institutional restrictions, successful conviction-style leaders often rely on populist appeals. By linking the expansion of executive authority to popular aspirations, they advance new notions of legitimacy. The process of institutional decline enables executives to practice conviction politics freed from many traditional constraints, but much more important, the style itself further weakens these institutions.

As these leaders attack the legitimacy of traditional institutions, another type of change takes place. Lockean liberalism in its original, undiluted form provides a procedural blueprint: In theory equal opportunity and equal access produce decisions and policies that serve the public good. In practice, however, liberal processes fail to ensure liberal outcomes. (Even if everyone votes or participates in debate, the result can benefit one class or interest more than it does others.) Similarly, to achieve liberal ends might require departures from liberal means, as conviction politicians are quick to point out. At the same time, liberal procedures can be slow and inefficient. Impatient with the process (and increasingly dissatisfied with it), the public demands results and conviction politicians promise to deliver. Gradually, the emphasis in both the public's demands and the leaders' promises shifts from means to ends. Although they largely operate outside the republican tradition, these leaders do accept the popular maxim attributed to the founder of modern republicanism: The ends justify the means. Ultimately (though not explicitly), conviction politicians in this study invoke Machiavelli to realize Locke.

The global context provides an even more auspicious arena for conviction-style leaders to argue that the ends justify the means, and the world in which conviction politicians operated in the late twentieth century created unique circumstances and opportunities for Reagan and Thatcher. They benefited from an unusual "special relationship" that was based on ideology, interest, and personality. More significant, they confronted and facilitated the imminent collapse of the communist superpower, and as a result, Reagan and Thatcher were able to practice conviction politics on a grand scale, unparalleled by their predecessors. At home they reaped the political rewards of their achievements abroad, but some of their activities on the global stage also called into question the viability and integrity of constitutional democracy in the late twentieth century.

The account that follows explores in greater detail each of these aspects of conviction-style leadership and its changing context. Part I comprises chapters 2 through 5: Each chapter focuses on a pair of conviction politicians, examining their leadership style and the role it plays in the liberal tradition. Part II analyzes the changing environment: It includes chapter 6 on political parties, chapter 7 on media politics, chapter 8 on executive authority, the political system, and the state, and chapter 9 on global affairs. Throughout this study the experience of conviction politicians reveals a paradox that provides a persistent theme: As conviction politicians pursue their liberal principles, they increasingly undermine the liberal regime they seek to secure.

At the start of the twenty-first century, the danger posed by conviction politicians might not be readily apparent, but one astute nineteenth-century observer delivered an early warning against leadership that is inspired by lofty vision and spurred by high ambition. Addressing an assembly in 1838, Abraham Lincoln identified the threat to "the perpetuation of our political institutions." "If it ever reach us," Lincoln warned, it would not come from foreign invasion but "it must spring up amongst us." After considering the danger of "the mobocratic spirit" that leads citizens to take the law into their own hands, he addressed a more subtle, and perhaps more serious, concern: The U.S. Constitution had survived because the fame and ambition of great men depended on the success of the experiment, but circumstances had changed. "This field of glory is harvested, and the crop is already appropriated," Lincoln told his listeners. "But new reapers will arise, and they, too, will seek a field." Then he alerted his audience:

> It is to deny, what the history of the world tells us is true, to suppose that men of ambition and talents will not continue to spring up amongst us. And, when they do, they will as naturally seek the gratification of their ruling passion, as others have so done before them. The question then, is, can that gratification be found in supporting and maintaining an edifice that has been erected by others? Most certainly it cannot. Many should undertake, many ever be found, whose ambition would aspire to nothing beyond a seat in Congress, a gubernatorial or a presidential chair; but such belong not to the family of the lion, or the tribe of the eagle.[19]

Lincoln's choice of metaphor was apt, for he identified the national symbols of Great Britain and the U.S., and his message was prescient. As Lincoln understood, any powerful leaders who seek glory pose a threat to the liberal polity, but conviction politics renders an especially effective tool for strong leaders who strive to dismantle old structures and construct a new edifice. After Lincoln observed Jackson's presidency, perhaps he could foresee the soaring heights that would be reached by conviction-style leaders and hear the thunderous roar of conviction politics that would echo through centuries of the liberal tradition.

PART I
LEADERSHIP AND CONVICTION POLITICS
IN THE LIBERAL TRADITION

2

DEMOCRATIC LIBERALISM:
ANDREW JACKSON AND SIR ROBERT PEEL

When Andrew Jackson and Sir Robert Peel practiced conviction politics, they institutionalized liberal principles in ways that responded to democratic pressure for change. Early in the nineteenth century, on both sides of the Atlantic, the public grew increasingly dissatisfied with regimes they regarded as privileged and corrupt, and as a result, conviction politicians could tap several sources of discontent. Through strong, decisive leadership, Jackson and Peel focused national attention on a single issue that served to define their new political order. Jackson eagerly rode the wave of democratization whereas Peel slowly succumbed to the changing tide, but both leaders supplied conviction-style stewardship when their nations called for it.

Admittedly, no special relationship ever linked Jackson and Peel. Jackson disdained the British and held them responsible for several deaths in his family, including those of his two brothers and his mother.[1] Peel frowned upon Jackson's crude appeals for popular support even though the British prime minister admired aspects of the democratic spirit that elevated Jackson to the presidency. To a great extent, the leaders' perspectives simply reflected the dominant views of their people and revealed the tension that continued to characterize Anglo-American relations long after the Revolutionary War.

Throughout the nineteenth century, the difference in status between the United States and Great Britain obscured their common interests and frequently brought them into conflict. A major world power, Britain shared a border with the young U.S., and in trade disputes, the character of the conflicts often exposed the impetuosity and insecurity of the youthful nation. For example, when Jackson tried to reach a trade agreement with Britain that would open West Indian ports to U.S. ships, he threatened to impose a boycott on trade with Canada if Britain failed to make concessions. Although Jackson secured his goal, his bluster and bluff reinforced international opinion that the U.S. remained a mere child among the mature nations of the world.

Cultural and psychological factors proved as significant as economic interests in shaping the nineteenth-century relationship between the U.S. and Britain. The liberal tradition linked the two nations in political development, but in the early nineteenth century, the young U.S. struggled to establish an

19

identity separate from its "mother" country. Like a child struggling to assert its independence, the U.S. often rebelled against the authority of old-fashioned English manners and customs. In Jacksonian America, the new democratic ethos clearly clashed with the old aristocratic tendencies of Britain.

Politics within the U.S. and Britain also differed more at this juncture than at any time since. The identity of the interests in government and the structure of the two governments were sufficiently distinct to conceal some significant similarities between the leaders. Indeed, the distinct contexts in which they operated help to explain some of the ideological and political differences between them.

During the first half of the nineteenth century, the nature of entrenched interests differed dramatically in the two countries. In Britain, the landed aristocracy dominated Parliament, while in the U.S., commerce created a moneyed aristocracy with special influence. As a consequence, when the leaders leveled assaults on the privileged position of the aristocracy, Jackson promoted agrarian interests, while Peel challenged them. Both Jackson and Peel attacked the status quo and advanced the cause of newly enfranchised voters, but the leaders represented and rejected distinct groups, reflecting the unique character of their countries.

The contexts of reform movements also differed. In the U.S. no significant national mass movement mobilized to challenge the existing regime, but in Britain the government confronted increasing domestic "pressure from without" from several sources, including the radical, working-class movement known as Chartism. With no national force organized to his left, Jackson appeared to speak for a wide array of discontented voices when he promised to pursue radical reform. In contrast to Jackson, Peel advanced his liberalism while fending off the ultras within his Tory (or Conservative) party and halting the extraparliamentary threat from the left. The British context of reform (and the fact that Peel officially led the Tory party) made him appear more conservative than he actually was, while it also obscured the liberal, transforming nature of his leadership.

In addition, the institutional structures of the two nations differed, and structural constraints had a significant impact on leadership in the nineteenth century. Jackson benefited from the democratization of the political system that was already under way when he became president in 1829, but Peel operated in an environment of "politics without democracy."[2] Before the Reform Bill of 1832, Parliament represented only the aristocracy and the gentry, and mere shades of difference existed among parliamentary groups. Even after the 1832 legislation, local interests and the mass public were largely excluded from parliamentary representation. Moreover, until 1841, the prime minister was selected by and accountable to the Crown, not the

Commons. Both Jackson and Peel redefined the roles of president and prime minister, initiating changes that would provide the foundations for modern executive leadership, but Peel started from a position obstructed by structural barriers that made the task of reform a more formidable challenge.

Distinct environments only partially explain the differences between Jackson and Peel: They also held different perspectives on and adopted different approaches to the task of reform. Jackson took a simple and absolute view of democratic liberalism: Government should be extremely limited, and policy should be based on majority rule, unobstructed by any institution. Influenced by utilitarianism as well as liberalism, Peel believed that changing circumstances made liberal reform increasingly necessary, while he also insisted that political institutions and enlightened statesmanship should regulate the pace of change and steer its course. The result rendered a difference that amounts to one of radical versus moderate reform, but the difference also reflects their distinct attitudes toward their nations' constitutions.

Notwithstanding these distinctions, similarities between Jackson and Peel reveal the role conviction politicians started to play in the evolution of liberal ideas and institutions. Both Jackson and Peel acquired reputations for strong, determined leadership early in their careers, and although neither one articulated precise positions before taking office, that reputation helped propel each of them to the office of president or prime minister. (Generally, elections before Jackson and Peel did not empower leaders or render policy "mandates," but their leadership started to change that.) Moreover, in both cases the call for strong leadership came at a time when the public was divided and mass opinion fragmented. Widespread disenchantment with the status quo created opportunities for Jackson and Peel to seize the initiative and pursue their convictions. When they succeeded, they redefined the relationship between state and society, while they also infused politics with the meaning of democratic liberalism that identifies their age.

Andrew Jackson

In 1824 Jackson's "chivalric character, his lofty integrity, and his ardent patriotism" impressed the French observer Michel Chevalier. "His tactics in politics, as well as in war," remarked Chevalier, "is to throw himself forward with the cry of *comrades follow me*."[3] At the time, several factors encouraged people to turn to the "Old Hero" of the Battle of New Orleans for strong national leadership.

Substantial economic and technological change took place in the 1820s that sparked widespread public apprehension. Financial panic from 1819 until 1822 fostered social and economic tensions and provided the backdrop to the class conflict that set the stage for Jackson's dramatic gestures on behalf of the masses. Furthermore, early developments in transportation and communication rapidly occurred in the 1820s. U.S. citizens witnessed the completion of the Erie Canal, the building of the first steam locomotive, and the patent of the internal combustion engine. As the decade drew to a close, the Pony Express transported information about these and other developments, while the early typewriter and Morse's telegraph promised to facilitate communication in new and surprising ways. The nature of these changes helps to reveal some of the appeal of Jackson's leadership. When Jackson described the National Bank as a "monster"—both unnatural and unjust—he found a "way to damn the unfamiliar, threatening, sometimes punishing elements in the changing order by fixing guilt upon a single protean agent."[4] Much of Jackson's rhetoric harked back to an agrarian age of innocence and restored a romantic vision of the individual linked to the land, threatened only by the greed and avarice of a new acquisitive class.

Jackson's romantic rhetoric quelled the fears fueled by rapid economic and technological change at the same time popular culture embraced the twin values of individualism and equality that lie at the heart of his vision. People in the Northeast started to reject customs associated with British high society and adopted instead manners and habits that were more direct and egalitarian. As the steamboat fostered the development of towns in the West, expansionism promoted frontier values. Urban centers grew in the North, and only the South retained a paternalistic social structure. As Alexis de Tocqueville observed, the popular taste for individual freedom and the experience of relative equality made the abstract principles of liberalism and democracy concrete in the U.S.

In a country increasingly devoted to freedom and equality as social values, Jackson's rhetoric and his convictions struck just the right chord. As he led the people into battle against the "aristocrats," he extolled the virtues of ordinary people—planters, farmers, mechanics, and laborers. Jackson believed only common citizens, not sectional interests or parties, could produce the "public good."[5] Yet the task of unifying the mass public of the 1820s presented Jackson with a considerable challenge as well as an unusual opportunity.

Various sections of the country cherished the values of equality and individualism, but regions proved deeply divided on several specific issues: the tariff, land policy, internal improvements, slavery, and banking. New England shipping interests demanded free trade, while the manufacturing sector that dominated the Northeast preferred protectionism. The South favored free trade for its overseas sales of cotton, while the same issue split the West. The Northwest urged protectionism for hemp, while the Southwest sided with cotton interests in the South. Land policy also divided the country: The North and South wanted land to be expensive, while the West wanted it to be cheap. Internal improvements also became increasingly important after 1820, but the country could not agree on the source or nature of funding. Slavery largely remained a local issue, but to the limited extent that it became national, it provided another deeply divisive issue: The North opposed, the South defended, and the West tended to support slavery. (The West sold products to the South, and most settlers emigrated from the South.) Finally, the second National Bank, which was created in 1816 and corrupt from the start, created yet another source of cleavage. Clearly the nation needed a national unifier.

Jackson did not attempt to resolve all these issues or mediate among the various groups to achieve a national consensus. Instead, he adopted two strategies characteristic of conviction-style leadership. First, he tried to focus national attention on his agenda, which attacked corruption created by the economic and political elite. He worked to ensure that his priorities—destruction of the bank and the pursuit of political reform—would also become the nation's central concerns. Second, although he compromised on many issues, he rejected a conciliatory approach to achieving his central goal. Instead, Jackson attempted to muster majority support by launching a moral crusade and using his conviction to cast a clear line between his supporters and his enemies.

In addition to the economic and social factors conducive to Jackson's conviction politics, the political environment also proved ripe for the rise of a popular, national hero. Extension of the franchise, direct selection of presidential electors, and the decay of the old two-party system created new opportunities for leadership. By Jackson's first administration, the U.S. had virtually achieved universal white male suffrage. In all but two states—Delaware and South Carolina—direct election produced delegates to the electoral college. At the same time, for several reasons, the old party formations had fractured: The Federalist party disappeared during the administrations of James Madison and James Monroe, and in the absence of a single enemy, factionalism flourished within the Republican party. (Furthermore, as a party with a philosophy hostile to government spending, the Republicans proved unable to unify during the War of 1812.) Last but not least, the lack of leadership drive and ability in Thomas Jefferson's successors made it difficult to maintain his legacy in leadership or principle[6]—until President Jackson promised to fill the void by supplying strong, conviction-style leadership.

Jackson inherited Jefferson's mantle soon after the 1824 presidential election, although the result and not the character of the campaign made him the heir apparent. During the campaign, Jackson won popular support as a result of his military record and substantial anti-incumbent sentiment, but essentially the race represented a contest between personalities. Both candidates declined to address significant issues that might have alienated voters.

When the campaign concluded, however, the outcome proved significant in at least two respects. Despite Jackson's plurality in popular and electoral votes, John Quincy Adams won the presidency when he secured the support of Henry Clay and a majority of the states in the House of Representatives. When President Adams later appointed Clay as secretary of state, the move led to charges that the two had struck a "corrupt bargain" during the election. To Jackson's supporters, the outcome of selection in the House defied the notion of popular sovereignty and exposed the special interests of the elite. Furthermore, when President Adams pursued an ambitious federal program of internal improvements, his critics alleged he was trying to overturn the Jeffersonian "revolution of 1800." Jackson's loss then assumed even greater symbolic significance.

In the next presidential election, Jeffersonian images featured prominently in Jackson's campaign against the "corruption of manners in Washington." "Issues, programs, policies" found no place on the electoral agenda, but corruption provided the broad, central theme of the contest.[7] The *U.S. Telegraph* depicted the Adams administration as "depraved, venal, and corrupt"[8] and expressed the hope that Jackson would "reinvigorate and cement the great Republican party" in pursuit of change.[9] By contrast the administration's newspaper, the *National Intelligencer,* attacked Jackson's behavior and warned against the threat posed by military leadership.[10] Throughout the campaign, Jackson advocated only one specific "reform"—the spoils system, which he depicted as a "program for democratic America."[11] In general, however, character assassination and lies overshadowed serious considerations. As a consequence of the nature of the campaign, Jackson emerged victorious, without a policy mandate of any kind, but with the invitation to supply strong leadership and restore integrity to government.

For a conviction politician, Jackson's campaign commitments were unusually vague and ambiguous, and yet he was widely perceived as a strong leader who would initiate change. To some extent, the absence of issues in the campaign can be explained by the norms and expectations of the period: Elections were not intended to render policy mandates in the early nineteenth century in the U.S. or Great Britain, and neither Jackson nor Peel secured a mandate before taking office. Yet Peel established a distinguished record of government service and political reform, which provided the basis for his national reputation as a strong leader. For Jackson, his heroic military feats more than compensated for his somewhat limited experience and extremely low profile in national politics. As Jackson's case indicates, a candidate can cultivate the image of a conviction politician before declaring any clear convictions if that candidate is also a distinguished general.

Despite Jackson's evasion during the campaign, the president seized the opportunity to declare his convictions once he took office. As Jackson revealed in his inaugural address, Jeffersonian philosophy did inspire and inform his core beliefs. In his first speech as president, Jackson identified his convictions as the following "principles of action": to revive federalism,[12] to initiate fiscal retrenchment, to guarantee "equity" in matters of revenue, and to reform the political system. The president's public philosophy was summed up by the masthead of the Jacksonian newspaper, the *Globe*: "That government is best which governs least."

Jackson quickly returned to his one specific campaign pledge and placed the principle of rotation in office at the center of his agenda. According to Jackson, "[T]he recent demonstration of public sentiment inscribes on the list of Executive duties, in characters too legible to be overlooked, the task of *reform*."[13] Rotation in office, otherwise known as the spoils system, was his top priority in the task of reform. Jackson presented spoils as a bold new initiative that promised several benefits to the public and the president. Of course, the practice of spoils was not new, although no substantial turnover in administration had occurred in a long time. Furthermore, Jackson's new appointments constituted less than 20 percent of government officials. What mattered more than these facts, however, was Jackson's ability to convert an old practice into a new principle. His rhetoric advancing the principle of rotation in office made it seem that he was pursuing one of the central convictions on his reform agenda.

Jackson's leadership style and his determination were not always sufficient to allow the president to define the national agenda, and among the issues he was forced to address, none threatened to enfeeble his presidency more than the tariff. Jackson tended to favor free trade, at one point declaring the liberal view that "commerce [should be] allowed to flow in those channels to which individual enterprise, always its surest guide, might direct it."[14] Yet tariff revision did not constitute one of Jackson's top priorities. Initially, he tried to downplay its significance—noting that the tariff had failed to hurt commerce or help agriculture as the opposition alleged, blaming the unfair trade practices of foreign countries, and acknowledging the need to compromise "to harmonize the conflicting interests of our agriculture, our commerce and our manufactures."[15] Jackson called for "higher and purer motives" than partisan conflict, but he knew the issue deeply divided his own party. Despite his best efforts to evade the subject, Jackson failed to avert a national crisis caused by this critical issue.

Logrolling repeatedly produced "support" for protectionism in the legislature. Northern and western agricultural interests dominated Congress, and high duties were placed on raw wool, hemp, flax, and liquor in the 1828 "Tariff of Abominations." After a second tariff revision in 1832 failed to satisfy South Carolina, the state responded by passing an Ordinance of Nullification. When Jackson threatened to use force to ensure that South Carolina would comply with federal law, the state backed down and a compromise on the tariff was reached. Although Jackson was prepared to compromise on the tariff, he took a firm position to preserve the Union.

Throughout his first term, Jackson searched for a mechanism to capture control of the agenda, and he believed he found the essential tool in presidential veto authority. Indeed, the president's threat to South Carolina proved convincing only because it followed his bank veto and his subsequent reelection. That election rendered a personal endorsement of Jackson's leadership and produced a clear mandate for him to pursue his central purpose as president: the destruction of the National Bank. As the bank battle increasingly came to dominate the national agenda, the issue Jackson wanted to avoid—the tariff—declined in significance, although it would reemerge to play a critical role in conviction politics fifty years later.

In Jackson's battle against the National Bank, the president proved able to tap a broad base of discontent: Both the bank and its president, Nicholas Biddle, had many enemies. Some of the bank's opponents simply distrusted paper money. Others included small bankers (who were kept from lending freely), people in the West where money was scarce, and New York City bankers who resented the control from Philadelphia. Still others objected to the bank because they viewed it as a monopoly. The bank did have a monopoly of funds, and it was managed by a private citizen and controlled by a handful of wealthy men. Biddle's personal wealth and social position further exacerbated popular resentment.

Nevertheless, Biddle had his own base of support, which he built by offering advantageous loans and retainers to sympathetic politicians and newspaper owners, while also cultivating a special relationship with Henry Clay and the National Republicans. Clay and Daniel Webster convinced Biddle to renew the bank's charter before the 1832 election, although it would not have expired until 1836. Initially, they hoped the issue could defeat the popular president, but Jackson welcomed the electoral challenge. (In fact, in his first annual message, Jackson had urged Congress to consider the bank's charter.)[16] Congress approved legislation that renewed the charter in July 1832, and Jackson immediately vetoed it. Rather than skirt the issue before the campaign, Jackson seized the opportunity to declare his conviction and then embarked on a popular crusade to promote his principles.

In his veto message (and later during the campaign), Jackson made the bank the symbol of concentrated power and privilege. In stating his constitutional objections, Jackson charged that the bank had subverted the rights of the states and the liberties of the people. More significant, for the first time a president defended the executive's role as interpreter of the Constitution by asserting that all three branches have equal authority and legitimacy in the review of national legislation. Even more important, President Jackson broke new ground when he opposed the legislation for political as well as constitutional reasons. In his own language, Jackson revealed his political objections to the bank's re-charter: First, "it embodies a forceful influence which may be wielded for the agrandisement [sic] of a favorite individual, a particular interest, or a separate party"; second, "it concentrates in the hands of a few men, a power over the money of the country, which may be perverted to the oppression of the people."[17] With the aid of Amos Kendall, Jackson's final message employed more dramatic and eloquent language:

> It is to be regretted that the rich and powerful too often bend the acts of government to their selfish purposes. Distinctions in society will always exist under every just government, . . . but when the laws undertake to add to these natural and just advantages distinctions, to grant titles, gratuities, and exclusive privileges, to make the rich richer and the potent more powerful, the humble members of society—the farmers, mechanics, and laborers—who have neither the time nor the means of securing like favors to themselves, have a right to complain of the injustice of their Government. There are no necessary evils in government. Its evils exist only in its abuses. If it would confine itself to equal protection, and, as Heaven does its rains, shower its favor alike on the high and low, the rich and the poor, it would be an unqualified blessing.[18]

For Jackson, the outcome of the bank battle would fundamentally redefine the relationship between state and society.

When members of the Jacksonian press sent the bank veto message to the masses, they employed sensational and inflammatory rhetoric. Even before Jackson's official action, the *Richmond Enquirer* predicted that the president would follow through on his threat to destroy "the oracle of the 'ancient dominion' of Great Britain." The paper argued the issue would not jeopardize Jackson's reelection, but in any event, "If there be a man in this country who would not turn his heel to save his office, Andrew Jackson is that man."[19] The *Globe* hailed the veto message as a "second Declaration of Independence"[20] and welcomed Jackson's rebellion against "the titled Aristocracy in England and the moneyed Aristocracy of America."[21] The veto message defined political alliances: the chief magistrate with "the people" against corrupt special interests in Congress.[22] Whereas Jackson's supporters applauded his conviction, his opponents condemned his method and his leadership style.

Two-thirds of the press sided with the bank against Jackson.[23] The *Baltimore Chronicle* argued against Jackson's allegation that all three branches were equal in their judgment of legislation. Instead, the *Chronicle* insisted that when representatives in Congress have spoken, their judgment constitutes the final word of the people.[24] The *National Intelligencer* repudiated Jackson's expression of his political views and argued that constitutional objections provide the only legitimate basis for the veto.[25] The opposition press also quoted at great length the remarks rendered by Jackson's opponents in the Senate, especially Clay and Webster. Clay reminded his listeners that the veto "is a feature of our government, borrowed from a prerogative of the British king." According to Clay, Jackson defied constitutional design and practice: The president departed from the veto's proper use as dictated by the constitution (designed to halt "precipitate legislation") and attempted to alter constitutional arrangements by promoting the notion that the president is equal to other branches.[26] Webster also compared Jackson with the king who exercised "despotic power." More important, according to Webster, presidential power became "primary power, the power of originating laws." Attacking Jackson's veto as demagoguery, Webster warned, "We have arrived at a new epoch."[27]

The debate between Jacksonians who embraced the substance of the veto message and opponents who warned against executive tyranny continued throughout the 1832 election campaign. Jackson's personal popularity and the bank were the only "issues." Against the opposition's fear that Jackson would establish the "dominion of one man,"[28] Jacksonians portrayed Jackson's reelection as a victory of the people against privileged interests.[29] When Jackson defeated Clay by more than 150,000 votes (219 to 49 in the electoral college), his victory did symbolize a "new epoch"—the triumph of democratic liberalism facilitated by a popular president.

Despite Jackson's triumph of leadership and principle, the demise of the National Bank produced dire practical consequences for the economy. Jackson did not fully understand banking, and to a great extent he adhered to his conviction out of ignorance, perhaps captivated by the moral tone of his own crusade. He could have reformed the bank,[30] but he preferred to destroy it, and its destruction immediately ignited speculative mania. In response to the financial crisis, Jackson finally issued his "species circular" in the summer of 1836 (which required purchasers to pay for public land in gold and silver), but abolition of the bank continued to intensify swings in the business cycle, fueling a depression that lasted until 1843. The experience serves as a warning about the danger of conviction-style leaders who adhere to their conviction out of blind faith, undeterred by concrete constraints or changing circumstances.

Jackson's crusade had negative short-term consequences for the economy, but it otherwise succeeded in achieving the president's goals. In fact, his opponents' style and strategies changed in ways that attest to Jackson's success. The Whigs maintained their limited view of executive authority but adopted other aspects of Jackson's appeal and approach. In the 1840 presidential election, Whig opponents portrayed Jackson's successor Martin Van Buren as a remote figure and the embodiment of special interest,[31] just as Jackson had described Adams.[32] The Whigs promoted the cause of the ordinary citizen with General Benjamin Harrison, and when Harrison died, he was followed by John Tyler, a former Democratic states rights advocate (albeit one who opposed Jackson's use of executive power). Shortly after Jackson's presidency, his opponents embraced elements of his democratic crusade, although they continued to reject his expansion of executive authority.

Furthermore, cloaked in conviction, Jackson had successfully challenged the legitimacy of political as well as economic institutions that mediate or obstruct the will of the majority. In his battle with Congress concerning the removal power of the president, Jackson responded to the Senate's censure (after he removed his secretary of treasury) by attacking that institution's authority to reprimand the president, who "is the direct representative of the American people."[33] On an issue unrelated to the bank battle, in 1832 Jackson clashed with the Supreme Court and refused to endorse its decision. (In that case, Jackson opposed the Court's ruling in favor of the Cherokees, a move that revealed his disdain for Native Americans and the limits of his liberalism, though it served to bolster his support from a public that shared his prejudice.) Immediately after he took office, Jackson proposed a change in presidential selection to "remove all intermediate agency in the election of the President and Vice President."[34] Perhaps the only constraint on this "tribune of the people" was imposed by his own liberal conviction, expressed in the motto "That government is best which governs least."

Ultimately, Jackson's most profound, enduring legacy comes from the link he established between executive authority and democratic aspirations. Herman Melville could mock the "Spirit of Equality," the "great democratic God"—"who didst pick up Andrew Jackson from the pebbles; who didst hurl him upon a war-horse; who didst thunder him higher than a throne."[35] But that democratic spirit not only lifted Jackson to the presidency, it elevated the stature of his office. Indeed, Jackson's majestic display of conviction politics provides an early indication of the soaring heights U.S. presidents can reach when they take the public under their wings.

Sir Robert Peel

Across the Atlantic, British observers of Jacksonian democracy drew various lessons from the experience. Parties across the political spectrum expressed interest in Jackson and the conditions in his country. Whigs and Tories as well as Radicals closely watched developments in the U.S.[36] Each group tended to interpret the practice of U.S. democracy in a way that would advance its own principles and interests. In general the Tories emphasized how the U.S. experience demonstrated the dangers of laissez-faire, but in this respect Sir Robert Peel proved to be no typical Tory.

British knowledge of the U.S. rapidly increased in the 1830s as a result of several factors. As transatlantic travel became more convenient, the British press expanded its coverage of the U.S., and an outpouring of new travel literature appeared. In 1835 alone, a half dozen significant works on the U.S. were published in England, including the first part of Alexis de Tocqueville's *Democracy in America,* translated by Henry Reeve, a critic and editorial writer for the *Times.*

Of all the observers of U.S. democracy, Tocqueville had the most profound influence on British opinion after 1835. His book won the praise of John Stuart Mill in the *London Review,* and Tocqueville made frequent visits to England. In 1835, Tocqueville gave evidence before the Select Committee on Bribery at Elections, and Peel used this testimony five months later in the Commons debate. Throughout the late 1830s, in his public speeches Peel frequently referred to Tocqueville's warnings about the mediocrity of democratic politicians, their habit of pandering to the masses, and the subsequent danger to liberty.

Tocqueville's description of Jacksonian democracy seems to have affected Peel's approach to reform, alerting him to its dangers but also convincing him that democratization was inevitable.[37] Without enlightened statesmanship to direct the nature and pace of reform, Peel feared, the masses might turn to demagogic leadership that would undermine the British constitution and endanger individual liberty. As Mill observed, Reeve had exaggerated Tocqueville's negative view of democracy, and consequently Peel had "praised it, and made the Tories fancy it was a Tory book."[38]

On the other hand, in a significant way Peel and his followers disagreed with the dominant Tory view of "democracy in America." Most Tories shared Tocqueville's aristocratic distaste for the economic behavior and social habits of Americans, but Peel admired the Americans' enterprise and industry. Tories generally believed in patriarchy, but the Peelites endorsed the economic individualism, minimal government, and enterprise economy that Tocqueville described in the U.S. As the "real friends of America in Tory ranks," Peel and his followers approved "of its atomistic society and emphasized economic links which bound England to the Union."[39] While the Tories tended to attack the social values of the acquisitive society, Peel declined to condemn the new middle-class values. In a way that set them apart from traditional Tories, Peel and his followers promoted the economic principles and social values of democratic liberalism.

Peel saw the spirit of laissez-faire flourish in the U.S., and he believed that many liberal principles could also be employed to address the changing economy and society in Britain, a situation encapsulated by the phrase "the condition-of-England question." From 1815 to the 1830s, rapid urbanization and industrialization took place in England, while enclosure of the land created a "new gentry" and increased the number of paupers. By 1832, England started to change from an agricultural nation ruled by squires, parsons, and wealthy landowners to an industrial nation dominated by industrial expansion and commercial enterprise. The new classes had the "spirit of the age" on their side: When at first Peel and later Gladstone promoted liberal principles, they embodied "the aspirations of the new order."[40] But Peel needed to do more than appeal to the new industrial and commercial classes. A severe trade depression and industrial decline from 1837 to 1842 created the "hungry forties." "To give earnest and diligent heed to the condition-of-England question," Peel would also need to consider "the miserable condition of the labouring poor."[41]

Peel believed his liberal convictions and the policies that stemmed from them would address both the interests of the new middle classes and the needs of the poor. Liberal economic policies would free industry and commerce from many traditional constraints. Lower tariffs were expected to lower the price of food and consequently benefit even the neediest members of society. Reintroduction of the income tax would compensate for lost revenue and, at the same time, shift the bulk of the burden to those most able to bear it: the landed aristocracy. The new industrial and commercial classes constituted Peel's natural constituency, but his liberal policies also promised to produce benefits for many who were more seriously disadvantaged.

Changes in economy and society combined with technological developments to increase pressure for political reform. Rapid advances in transportation played an important role in exposing the unfairness of political inequality. In the new era of railways, steamships, and improved roads, one observer concluded while traveling, "Parliamentary Reform must follow soon after the opening of this road. A million persons will pass over it in the course of this year, and see that hitherto unseen village of Newton; and they must be convinced of the absurdity of its sending two members to Parliament, whilst Manchester sends none."[42] Ideas and information spread quickly in the 1830s and 1840s, as a result of improved transportation and with the creation of the penny post. In addition, throughout this period, mass meetings and popular oratory attracted large crowds across the country. Peel repeatedly expressed concern about the consequences of popular protest and mass politics, but extraparliamentary pressure for political change was part of the environment that proved conducive to Peel's strong leadership and his pledge to pursue moderate reform.

In general, Peel's relationship to the popular reform movements of the period is complex. On the one hand, he believed that members of Parliament should resist external pressure and exercise independent judgment to discern the public good. On the other hand, throughout his political career, his convictions were frequently determined by changing material circumstances (in which the threat of civil unrest often figured prominently) and the persuasive arguments articulated by the leaders of reform movements. There were limits to these types of influence—Peel resolutely resisted radical reform—but in several cases he embraced and implemented change that had been advanced as a popular democratic cause.

In the 1820s, for example, the utilitarian campaign for law reform found a champion in Peel when he served as the Duke of Wellington's home secretary. Peel established the first metropolitan police force in London (hence the nickname for the police, "the Bobbies"). His move was largely a response to changing circumstances—in particular, the riots and crime that followed urbanization and passage of the Corn Laws in 1815. From today's perspective, Peel's effort does not appear to be a progressive social reform, but his initiatives actually improved the situation of the masses. (Previously, the military was used to break up mobs.) Peel shifted the emphasis in crime control away from punishment to prevention, and his method for funding the police linked crime and poverty as social problems. When Peel first established the police force, he faced antagonism toward this new form of official authority, but he managed to convince the public it would ease repression and enhance the safety of the community. As in tariff reform, the impact of Peel's efforts extended across the Atlantic: In 1845 New York City adopted Peel's model for its metropolitan police force. Peel also reformed the criminal code, abolished the death penalty for more than one hundred offenses, and made other punishments more humane. His record as home secretary established Peel's reputation as a man of reform.

One of Peel's next daring moves was an attempt to extend that reputation to his party. The Tories had dominated politics from 1806 to 1830, but after they opposed the Reform Bill of 1832, they suffered a devastating loss and were reduced to being the third and smallest party. The Whig government had passed the Reform Bill for purely pragmatic reasons, not out of conviction or commitment to the middle-class groups who demanded change. The 1832 legislation maintained the representation of property, although it did reform some of the worst abuses of the old system by establishing a ten-pound householder franchise in parliamentary boroughs and giving separate representation to some of the large industrial towns. After the Reform Bill, the new industrial wealth gained the opportunity to govern with the landed aristocracy. The new parliamentary franchise also gave Peel a unique opportunity to demonstrate his leadership and reinvigorate his party in the 1835 election.

Peel called the 1835 election within weeks of becoming prime minister of a minority government. (In the fall of 1834, the king had dismissed the Whigs and invited Peel to form a new government.) Attempting to secure a majority, Peel issued the first party manifesto as a popular declaration of principles—addressed to his constituents in Tamworth but publicized to the country through the national press. In the document, Peel announced that he and his party would accept the terms of the Reform Bill, which he had once opposed. Then Peel went even further, explicitly identifying his party with the cause of "moderate reform." Although the Tories failed to win a majority until 1841, they decreased the Whig vote in the 1835 and 1837 general elections, while increasing their own base largely through appeals to the middle class and the promise to pursue reasonable reform.

Peel's campaigns for moderate reform took place in an environment where pressure was mounting for much more radical change. In 1836, William Lovett established the London Working Men's Association, and in 1838, he and Francis Place drew up the "people's charter," which called for universal male suffrage, equal electoral districts, removal of the property qualification for members of Parliament (MPs), payment of MPs, secret ballot, and annual general elections. The petition gave voice to several sources of popular agitation and inspired a dynamic working-class movement.[43] Although the Chartists failed to secure any of their radical reforms, the size and intensity of the movement did reveal the extent of dissatisfaction with the status quo.[44]

At the same time as Chartism, a largely middle-class movement formed in opposition to the Corn Laws. The first Corn Law passed in 1815, and in 1828 a sliding scale of import duties replaced the original absolute prohibition. A poor harvest and depression in manufacturing increased opposition to the Corn Laws, which many people blamed for economic distress. To campaign for complete repeal, in 1838 Richard Cobden and John Bright founded the Anti–Corn Law League. Leaders of the movement tended to come from the classical free-trade school of thought. Peel accepted many of its free-trade principles, but he refused to acknowledge or respond to pressure from the mass movement.[45] Yet when he eventually announced his decision to repeal the Corn Laws, Peel admitted that the arguments made by Cobden in the House of Commons had helped to convince him.[46] Nevertheless, in the 1841 election that put him in power, Peel kept his distance from the league and declined to declare any conviction on this critical issue.

To a great extent, Peel's victory in 1841 resembled Jackson's in 1828. In both cases, a substantial negative vote registered against the incumbent created an opportunity for new leadership. Just as significant, like Jackson, Peel had acquired an extensive personal following. As J. W. Croker wrote on July 20, 1841, "The elections are wonderful and the curiosity is that all turns on the name of Sir Robert Peel."[47] In the election that year, Peel's party secured a majority of 76.

The *Times* identified the public's disillusionment with the Whig government and its confidence in Peel's leadership as the critical factors in the election.[48] The paper contrasted Peel's party and its campaign to its previous record: The party had failed in the past because it was based on expediency, not on principle, it concluded, but now "we cannot refuse him credit for what he has done." Peel was described as great not only because he was a "strong leader," but also because "he made his party strong by giving it principles."[49] In articulating those principles, Peel remained rather vague, committing himself only to the "moderate reform" he had first espoused in the Tamworth Manifesto.

Despite the absence of policy debate during the campaign, the result of the election proved to be a watershed in British politics. For the first time, the electorate rejected a majority government and transformed a minority party into a new governing majority. Even more significant, when Peel took office, he established the constitutional principle that the executive should be accountable to the Commons, not to the Crown: The monarch must appoint the first leader to command a majority in the House of Commons. Peel, the great guardian of the British constitution, had managed to alter the constitutional balance of power in a fundamental way. He permanently changed the place of the prime minister in the political order from "minister of the crown" to leader of the legislature.

What Peel would do as the new prime minister only started to become clear after he took office. Shortly after the election, he declared his "independence" and indicated he would chart a new course. As he instructed the House of Commons, "If I exercise power, it shall be upon my conception—perhaps imperfect—perhaps mistaken—but my sincere conception of public duty. That power I will not hold, unless I can hold it consistently with the maintenance of my own opinions, and that power I will relinquish the moment I am satisfied that I am not supported in the maintenance of them by the confidence of this House and of the people of this country."[50] Shunning extraparliamentary pressure for radical reform, Peel continued to identify his leadership with moderate change, which he insisted would be dictated only by his conscience.

Peel's first dramatic move as prime minister was both a matter of conviction and a response to increased popular agitation. In his 1842 budget, Peel revived the income tax (imposing a charge on incomes that exceeded 150 pounds). In 1830 as home secretary, Peel also promoted the income tax to lessen the burden on the poor, but then his aristocratic cabinet colleagues defeated him. As he remained unpopular with his parliamentary colleagues in 1842, Peel's move to reintroduce the income tax in peacetime showed substantial courage and appealed to the middle class. He believed the income tax was necessary to balance the budget and desirable as a measure to achieve greater social justice.[51]

Restoration of the income tax enabled Peel to pursue yet another policy based on his convictions. With an alternative source of revenue, Peel could repeal old restrictive and wasteful duties. He always believed in steady employment and cheap food as remedies for human misery and social unrest, and deteriorating economic conditions increased his conviction that he should lower the tariff. In his budget of 1842, Peel reduced the tariff on 250 articles; the budget of 1845 achieved even further reduction. By 1846, all duties were removed on exports, almost all raw materials were admitted free, and tariffs on other imports were slashed. Tariff reform provided the core of Peel's liberal economic policy.

Other reforms show that Peel was much more willing than his U.S. counterpart to employ and extend the authority of the state. (In the nineteenth century, there was much more "state" to employ in Great Britain than there was in the U.S.) Peel promoted and secured factory legislation, long before it was possible to do so in the U.S., where judicial interpretation restricted congressional powers. The Mines Act of 1842 prohibited the employment of boys under ten and women and girls. The Factory Act of 1844 restricted women's hours to twelve and children's to six and a half. In 1844 Peel also secured passage of the Bank Charter Act, which limited the issue of bank notes, stimulated trade, and reduced inflation. Of course, the bank lacked the symbolic significance it possessed in the U.S.: Commercial interests in Britain were newly enfranchised, not entrenched or privileged as the landed aristocracy was. Yet these measures do indicate that Peel was willing to use the authority of the state in ways that he believed would serve but not detract from the public welfare.

During this period, church and state supplied the only subject that rivaled the economy in significance, and in this area Peel also made several surprising moves. As the Duke of Wellington's home secretary, Peel initially opposed

Catholic emancipation, but he came to support it when the government faced the threat of public disorder (even though he continued to hold a low opinion of Irish Catholics). To a great extent as a result of Peel's efforts, Parliament passed the Roman Catholic Relief Act in 1829. More significant, in 1845 Peel delivered a serious affront to Protestantism when he proposed to increase the grant to Maynooth College, a Catholic seminary in Ireland. The intraparty split on the Maynooth grant vote in 1845 foreshadowed the cleavage that would appear on repeal of the Corn Laws in 1846.

Peel's decision to repeal the Corn Laws was clearly his most significant initiative, comparable to Jackson's bank veto. The Irish famine in 1845 provided the immediate catalyst, but Peel had already become convinced by Cobden's persuasive arguments. Several factors played a role in shaping Peel's conviction that the laws should be repealed: the success of the 1842 budget (which lowered the duty on corn); his understanding that the level of wages did not fluctuate with the price of food; his belief that expanding markets and increased productivity, not protection, would enhance prosperity; and his fear that public hostility toward the Corn Laws threatened the constitution.[52] In 1845 the *Times* reviewed Peel's accomplishments but admonished his government to address the nation's "one dark spot": "The nation thrives but the people deteriorate. The Irish peasant and the English labourer have not seen this year any remission of their wretchedness."[53] Peel hoped his initiative would soon render some essential relief.

In June 1846 the prime minister introduced his bill to secure repeal of the Corn Laws. In his speech on the third reading, Peel faced his intraparty critics and defended his move: He feared the continuance of the Corn Laws would create "a desperate conflict between different classes of society."[54] Acting out of "the conviction that the policy we advise is correct," Peel explained that repeal would benefit all the people, not only the Irish. According to Peel:

> The real question at issue is the improvement of the social and moral condition of the masses of the population; we wish to elevate in the gradation of society that great class which gains its support by manual labour. . . . The mere interests of landlords—the mere interests of the occupying tenants, important as they are, are subordinate to the great question—what is calculated to increase the comforts, to improve the condition, and elevate the social character of the millions who subsist by manual labour, whether they are engaged in manufactures or in agriculture?[55]

Peel admitted he had once defended the Corn Laws but denied he had only recently adopted the principles of free trade. His speech concluded with a moving statement about his objective: "My earnest wish has been, during my tenure of power, to impress the people of this country with a belief that the legislation was animated by a sincere desire to frame its legislation upon the principles of equity and justice. . . . I wish to convince them that the object has been to apportion taxation, that we shall relieve industry and labour from any undue burden, and transfer it, so far as is consistent with the public good, to those who are better able to bear it."[56] Repeal passed the Commons with the support of the Whigs, the Irish, and the free traders of the Tory party. It passed the Lords largely due to the Duke of Wellington's loyalty to Peel's government. On the night of passage, vengeful Tories joined the Whigs and the Irish to defeat Peel on the Irish coercion bill and force his resignation.

As the *Times* described it, Peel's repeal constituted a "great concession of aristocratic prejudice to public necessity."[57] In the peroration upon his resignation, Peel revealed what he expected would be his legacy:

> In relinquishing power, I shall leave a name, severely censured I fear by many who, on public grounds, deeply regret the severance of party ties. . . . I shall leave a name execrated by every monopolist who, from less honourable motives, clamours for protection because it conduces to his own individual benefit; but it may be that I shall leave a name sometimes remembered with expressions of good will in the abodes of those whose lot it is to labour, and to earn their daily bread by the sweat of their brow, when they shall recruit their exhausted strength with abundant and untaxed food, the sweeter because it is no longer leavened by a sense of injustice.[58]

When Peel secured the repeal of the Corn Laws, his liberal principles provided a democratic force for change, while his policy based on those principles permanently shattered the old order.

By defeating protectionism, Peel altered the public ideology of nineteenth-century Britain.[59] Repeal of the Corn Laws signaled the victory for laissez-faire liberalism over protectionism and established the predominance of industry over agriculture. To achieve this momentous victory, Peel had employed autocratic methods, which aroused deep resentment from the ranks of his own party and fueled the revolt that had been ignited by his conviction politics. Even though his move ended his career as premier, Peel adhered to his conviction and won the policy argument.

Repeal not only ruined Peel politically, it put Benjamin Disraeli in the leadership, split the Tories into two factions, and led to two decades of Whig-Liberal rule, but others maintained Peel's legacy. After 1846, the Peelites joined the Whigs and formed the core of the Liberal party.[60] Moreover, his former opponents accepted many aspects of his policy and his public philosophy. As the *Times* had predicted in 1846, the new Whig government needed to maintain, not reconstruct, for "We cannot be always undoing, or nothing will remain to be undone."[61] Peel introduced the age of liberalism, and his successor in conviction politics, William Gladstone, governed at its zenith.

Peel's contemporaries acknowledged the role he played in setting the course of political development. Always sympathetic to Peel, the *Times* encouraged and applauded his leadership in 1846:

> If it be, indeed, a new era that dawns upon us, if that is the solution of our embarrassments and the excuse of our inconsistencies, surely that era must be one of honesty and truth. Surely Sir Robert Peel, as Minister of this new era, and interpreter of our new destinies, is bound to rectify those original vices of the old regime, antigua vestigia ofendis. The new year must be one of explicit declarations and of honest convictions. Let neither party be deceived, nor conscience belied; and let the multitude of the ignorant poor or the interested rich learn to venerate the unwonted magestry [*sic*] of political truth.[62]

The following year, the *Times* rendered another laudatory judgment on Peel's leadership and explored the historic and global implications of his "moral revolution." No one "who has seen the progress of the commercial idea throughout Europe, and the development of commercial power, [can] reconcile himself to the notion that the change which England has been the first to introduce into her economical system, and her great family in America the first to imitate, can be without momentous consequences to every nation in the civilized world."[63] The report correctly concluded that Peel's legacy in liberal economics would endure.

When Peel attacked protectionism and defended his liberal convictions, he delivered a roar that would reverberate across the Atlantic. Indeed, the history of laissez-faire reveals the reciprocal influence that frequently characterizes Anglo-American developments. Scottish philosopher Adam Smith supplied the theory of laissez-faire; conditions in the U.S. proved conducive to the spirit of its principles; Peel made those principles official government policy in Britain; and his success encouraged free traders in the U.S. to press for further reform.[64] After the Civil War, the tariff would return as a critical issue in the U.S. Echoing many of Peel's sentiments, another conviction politician—Grover Cleveland—would attempt to make it the defining issue of his leadership and his era.

Peel's legacy was not limited to the public philosophy he advanced: To preserve the constitution, Peel had substantially altered it. His legacy of executive leadership made the prime minister directly accountable to Parliament and situated more closely to the people. As the next leader in the family of lions, Gladstone would reach outside Parliament for popular support, a step Peel himself declined to take but one that his leadership made possible.

Both Jackson and Peel demonstrated strong leadership based on principle; focused national attention on a critical, defining issue; and altered their ideological and institutional environments. Though they often appeared oceans apart, the sources of difference between them would soon start to dissipate. In the late nineteenth century, classic liberalism would construct a much stronger ideological bridge between conviction politicians in the U.K. and the U.S.

3

CLASSIC LIBERALISM:
WILLIAM GLADSTONE AND GROVER CLEVELAND

In the second half of the nineteenth century, conviction-style leaders again demonstrated strength and determination as they advanced liberal principles on both sides of the Atlantic. When William Gladstone and Grover Cleveland altered the national agenda and established new priorities for public policy, they capitalized on the renewed public desire for moral leadership and tapped the support of several reform movements. For most of their careers, they enjoyed personal popularity and public admiration, although institutional and ideological factors set severe limits on their ability to act as agents of change.

As Gladstone and Cleveland set out to find new pathways in political development, they also followed in the footsteps of Sir Robert Peel and Andrew Jackson. Gladstone was clearly a disciple of Peel: The Conservative prime minister brought the young member of Parliament into his brief 1834–35 government and later appointed Gladstone to the Board of Trade, where he played a critical role in tariff reduction from 1841 to 1845. Cleveland considered himself a Jacksonian Democrat and explicitly drew a comparison between his struggle for tariff reform and Jackson's battle against the National Bank.[1] Conviction politics links these leaders across time as well as across the Atlantic.

Gladstone and Cleveland never had any direct contact, but each admired the other's leadership. Gladstone believed Cleveland's civil service reform made him "the noblest man that has filled the presidential chair since Lincoln."[2] Upon receiving a copy of John Morley's *Life of Gladstone,* Cleveland wrote to the gift giver, "I desire to thank you for it from the bottom of my heart. Somehow I don't get much chance to read now-a-days; but this book I shall read."[3] Several factors would have discouraged direct contact between Gladstone and Cleveland, including the tense climate that continued to characterize Anglo-American relations through the nineteenth century. Cleveland was particularly sensitive to this: During his presidencies, he was subject to frequent Republican attacks that he was an Anglophile who put British financial and diplomatic interests ahead of those of his own country.

Anti-British popular sentiment made it a serious liability for any politician to be perceived as pro-British, as Cleveland learned in his 1888 election campaign. When he retaliated against Canada for its unfair treatment of

U.S. fishing,[4] Republicans suspected it was merely a measure calculated to court the Irish vote. To expose Cleveland's presumed ploy and portray him as essentially pro-British, a Republican sympathizer wrote to the British ambassador and tricked him into endorsing Cleveland. What came to be known as the "Murchison letter" (the pseudonym used by the letter's author) and the ambassador's response were widely publicized and might have cost Cleveland some of the Irish vote in the election. Long after the United States and the United Kingdom established a special relationship, presidents have needed to balance the preferences of ethnic voters and the interests of the Anglo-American alliance.[5]

Throughout the nineteenth century, the threat of Great Britain loomed large in the American imagination. When President Cleveland tried to return the Hawaiian monarch, Queen Liliuokalani, to her throne,[6] Britain played a role in two seemingly contradictory ways: The English press urged the U.S. to share "the white man's burden" and annex the islands.[7] At the same time, however, the U.S. press expressed the fear that the English would invade the islands if the U.S. returned them to the monarch and withdrew the treaty of annexation. The *Commercial Advertiser,* for example, warned "that the Hawaiian Islands shall be tossed as a prize into the arena of international strife, for which the Japanese, the English, and heaven knows who else may scramble and quarrel."[8] Britain often appeared as the evil empire of the 1800s, even when it was urging the U.S. to pursue its own imperialist interests.

Later in the same term, President Cleveland tried to check British imperialism in the Western Hemisphere when he attempted to settle Britain's boundary dispute with Venezuela. As Cleveland saw it, he needed to preserve the integrity of the Monroe Doctrine (which he clearly construed very broadly) and protect the interests of a weak southern neighbor against an aggressive world power. His secretary of state, Richard Olney, sent a belligerent message to Britain in which he attacked British claims and declared that three thousand miles of ocean makes "any permanent political union between a European and an American state unnatural and inexpedient."[9] Olney justified his forceful language by explaining that "In the English eyes the U.S. was then so completely a negligible quantity that it was believed only words the equivalent of blows would be really effective."[10] In fact the message had little effect on Lord Salisbury, who responded by providing instructions on the proper, strict construction of the Monroe Doctrine.

After receiving Lord Salisbury's response, Cleveland and Olney drafted a firm and fiery message to Congress, which was delivered on December 17, 1895. In it, the president requested that Congress authorize funds for a commission to determine the boundary, whose decision the U.S. would enforce. Guided by liberal principles of self-determination and sovereignty, Cleveland originally hoped to preserve the territorial integrity of a vulnerable neighbor; instead, his words served to spark warlike enthusiasm and ignite imperialist sentiment in Congress and in the country.[11] Nevertheless, the nations reached a settlement in 1899; and even earlier, in response to Cleveland's message, signs of support for Britain started to emerge in the U.S.[12]

Despite continuing tensions between the U.S. and the U.K., by the late nineteenth century, the two nations had grown more alike. Increasing interdependence forged a single transatlantic economy: Britain relied on the U.S. for many raw materials, and the British textile industry flourished as the nation sold goods to the expanding U.S. market. At the same time, British political culture became more open and egalitarian; revolution in transportation, communication, and economy continued to fuel political reform. The social and political differences that distinguished the U.S. and Britain in the age of Jackson and Peel had substantially diminished by the late nineteenth century. Gladstone and Cleveland gave voice to a "transatlantic persuasion," which reflected the changes that had taken place and established new links in Anglo-American development.[13]

Not only did the two nations become more alike: The substance and style of conviction leaders were much more similar than during the days of Peel and Jackson. Cleveland and Gladstone shared many classic liberal positions: tariff reduction, civil service reform, economy in government, international cooperation, and self-determination. Both believed that strong independent leadership could (and should) mold public opinion, and both promoted their policies with religious zeal, infusing their rhetoric with passionate moral sentiment. Finally and perhaps tragically, both Gladstone and Cleveland concluded their careers by clinging to their convictions while failing to achieve their most cherished goals.

Gladstone and Cleveland were principled politicians but by no means pure ideologues. Cleveland rarely engaged in abstract thought or employed theoretical reasoning. Except for the Bible, no text or philosophy significantly shaped his views. As with Jackson, instinct and experience largely determined Cleveland's convictions. By sharp contrast, Gladstone was a serious scholar, whose views were influenced by a wide range of sources—including the Homeric Greeks, Plato and Aristotle, and several theologians. Gladstone's convictions also evolved during the course of his political career, which spanned more than half a century. Furthermore, neither Cleveland nor Gladstone was an avowed disciple of Adam Smith or John Locke: Certainly, Cleveland never read *The Wealth of Nations* or *The Second Treatise;* and Gladstone explicitly expressed his low regard for the rights-oriented reasoning of Locke and John Stuart Mill. More inclined to use the word "duty" than they were to invoke the language of "rights," these liberal leaders often expressed republican values. Yet in their practice of conviction politics, Cleveland and Gladstone more closely adhered to liberal principles in economy and government than did any other conviction politicians in the liberal tradition.

William Gladstone

Gladstone entered politics with a strong sense of mission, although the content of the cause he felt destined to pursue would not become clear for many years. While the character of his convictions changed over the course of his lengthy career, his style was persistent and emphatic: He viewed politics as an eternal struggle against sin and saw dynamic leadership as his calling to convert the skeptical masses into a faithful flock. Eventually, Gladstone would tackle two demons that threatened to corrupt the soul of the state: the landed aristocracy and the Church of England. In the case of the latter, he would undergo the conversion in public life that he never experienced as an Evangelical Anglican.

To a great extent, Gladstone's public career mirrored his own personal struggle against sin. Starting in the mid-1840s and through most of his public life, Gladstone conducted "rescue work" in London, making repeated attempts to reform prostitutes. As he wandered through Soho late at night in search of souls to save, Gladstone showed the same dogged determination and moral righteousness that would characterize his public crusades. Despite his almost total lack of success, he persisted in these acts of "private charity," and when, in the process, he failed to maintain the utmost purity, he would later flagellate himself as punishment. For Gladstone, failure—private or public—meant that he had succumbed to sin.

Such charity work and punishment were unusual though not unique in the Victorian era; yet Gladstone's behavior was sufficiently odd to cause concern among his cabinet colleagues that public exposure would create a scandal. In 1886 Gladstone was finally persuaded to suspend his rescue work when he became convinced that such a scandal could jeopardize his home rule campaign.[14] Only the opportunity to combat sin in the public arena would lead Gladstone to abandon (temporarily) his personal crusade.

Gladstone's righteousness remained constant even as he developed new convictions and adjusted his positions, a fact that led many of his colleagues to accuse him of hypocrisy, but it would have been surprising if his beliefs had failed to evolve in the course of such a lengthy career. Gladstone entered Parliament in 1833, and he served in several capacities as cabinet minister and twice as chancellor of the exchequer, a position he shaped into its contemporary form and significance. In 1868 he became prime minister of the first modern British government distinguished by the sweeping range of its reforms. After his party lost power in 1874, Gladstone returned to the office of prime minister in 1880, again in 1886, and for the fourth and final time in 1892. Throughout his political career, economic, social, and political conditions changed, but certain factors help to explain why the substance and style of his leadership usually proved popular with the British public, if not always with his parliamentary colleagues.

Material prosperity, high industrial productivity, and extensive foreign trade generally characterized mid-nineteenth-century Britain. During this period, the nation acquired its reputation as the "workshop of the world." Nevertheless, an economic crisis in 1866 shattered the country's confidence and created an opportunity for Gladstone to present his economic principles as the nation's saving grace. Gladstone criticized the "spending spirit" of society in general and of the Conservative government in particular. (In fact, the economy usually took a turn for the worse when Gladstone was out of government, and consequently he could blame the Conservatives' extravagance at home and adventurism abroad for the nation's problems.) "Economy is the first and great article . . . in my financial creed," he would devoutly declare. Preaching the virtues of free trade, lower taxation, and government economy, Gladstone replaced Peel as "the sign and symbol of the triumph of the new economics."[15]

Economic and political change in Britain carried with it an emotional dimension, involving not only new types of class conflict but also animosity and rivalry among ethnic and religious groups.[16] Gladstone responded to the increasingly vocal demands of several "out groups"—especially, the Nonconformists or Dissenters, the Welsh, and the Irish.

The 1867 Reform Act opened the parliamentary system to pressure groups, and among these, Nonconformists proved to be one of the best organized and most influential. (Nonconformists included Methodists, Unitarians, Quakers, and Baptists—mainly skilled workers and lower-middle-class shopkeepers and clerks.) As early as the 1850s, Gladstone's piety had attracted Nonconformists to the Liberal fold, and when in the 1860s he promoted parliamentary reform, the abolition of compulsory church rates, and Irish disestablishment, their respect for Gladstone became outright veneration. Speaking at a conference on "Pew and Pulpit" in 1877, Gladstone thanked his Nonconformist followers for their fidelity and declared that their devotion to him had provided the "backbone of British Liberalism."[17]

Nonconformist support for Gladstone overlapped with that of other groups, including the Welsh. (Nonconformist chapels in Wales were distinguished from Anglicanism by their use of the Welsh language, and Nonconformism became closely linked to the cause of Welsh nationalism.)[18] The

Welsh supported Gladstone for several reasons: They endorsed the principles behind disestablishment and Sunday closings in Ireland and sought similar legislation for Wales; and they were attracted by Gladstone's dynamic personality and detected his "intuitive sympathy for the Welsh people."[19] Wales failed to win disestablishment until the twentieth century, but Gladstone concluded his career by promoting the cause. Welsh support for Gladstone proved critical, especially after the Reform Act of 1884, which extended the vote to miners and farmers, giving representation to the majority of the Welsh people.

By enfranchising rural laborers, the 1884 reform bill also increased the representation of the Irish, resulting in the majority Irish vote for home rule in the 1885 election. Even earlier, Gladstone had begun to win support from the Irish: From his first declaration on behalf of disestablishment in 1867 through his land reforms and concluding with his home rule bills, Gladstone identified Irish causes as critical moral issues. To Gladstone, Irish Catholics were subjected to Britain's tyrannical, demonic rule just as the Balkan Slavs were victimized by evil forces on the Continent. He increasingly came to believe that he was responsible for their rescue.

While responding to the voices of discontent expressed by the Nonconformists, the Welsh, and the Irish, Gladstone was also building support among the Radicals who pressed for reform of the franchise. Gladstone had taken part in the 1859 meeting that fused Whigs, Peelites, and Cobdenite Radicals into the Liberal party. As leader he would devote much of his political skill to bridging the gap that divided Radical and Whig factions within his political party.

Finally, Nonconformist and Radical support provided a bridge to labor during much of Gladstone's premiership. The challenge to liberalism in this period came not only from the right—persistent advocates of protectionism in the Conservative party—but increasingly from the left. Gladstone was prepared to accommodate elements of radicalism that were consistent with his liberal principles, but he adamantly opposed socialism. He tried to convince laborers that liberal economics could advance their interests, but eventually his convictions collided with the cause of a growing and independent labor movement. Socialism was one movement that Gladstone would never embrace.

In other cases, Gladstone's support often served to transform a local or factional cause into a national concern. By placing reform proposals on the national agenda and promoting them with his brilliant eloquence, he played a critical role in the formation of majority opinion on many issues. Reform movements knew Gladstone's advocacy could greatly enhance their prospects for success, but their impact on his views is difficult to assess. Gladstone never gave credit to a movement or a leader as the source of his conviction, in the way that Peel acknowledged his debt to Cobden. Instead, Gladstone always declared his principle and announced his position as if they sprang from divine wisdom or came with a flash of inspiration. As a result, he usually created the impression that he had made up his own mind, and in practice he rarely consulted cabinet colleagues or other prominent political figures. His apparent independence frequently frustrated and often infuriated the political elite, but it also provided an essential aspect of his popular appeal.

Finally, the style and the substance of Gladstone's leadership suited the culture of Victorian Britain. In the midst of dramatic transitions, the Victorian period gave rise to hero worship, and strong, confident leadership provided reassurance in an age of uncertainty. At the same time, Gladstone's core beliefs—in individual industry, equal opportunity, and moral conscience—resonated with the intellectual climate of his age, as characterized in Charles Dickens's novels and Samuel Smiles's book, *Self Help*. In the Victorian mind, individual enterprise coincided with public responsibility, and individual progress could produce general prosperity. The dominant public creed held that freedom was consistent with fairness, enterprise with morality. Those basic tenets found clear and concrete expression in the economic policies Gladstone enacted as chancellor of the exchequer.

Gladstone's budgets enhanced free trade and reorganized the nation's revenue system by shifting the government's reliance on tariffs to income tax (although Gladstone did not favor the income tax in theory). His first budget in 1853 took the tax off 130 articles of food, abolished the soap tax, and reduced the tea duty. In addition to revising the income tax, Gladstone introduced succession duty on real estate. Finally, when the House of Lords defeated his paper duties bill, Gladstone reformed the procedure for submitting finance bills to the upper chamber.[20] In general, as chancellor, Gladstone pursued Peelite principles of laissez-faire, low taxation, free trade, and gradual reform.

In contrast to his clear convictions concerning the economy, Gladstone's position on the franchise was often inconsistent and frequently equivocal, shaped by interparty competition as well as intraparty politics. On the one hand, as chancellor in 1864 Gladstone boldly announced to the House of Commons "that every man who is not presumably incapacitated by some consideration of personal unfitness or of political danger is morally entitled to come within the pale of the Constitution."[21] On another occasion when he spoke to the trades council in Newcastle, Gladstone suggested that previous parliamentary inaction extending the franchise stemmed from the indifference of the workers. To the press, members of Parliament, and his own prime minister, Gladstone's words constituted an exhortation to agitation on the part of the masses, though this was not his intent. On the other hand,

Gladstone proposed a very moderate reform bill in 1865. Following its defeat, Benjamin Disraeli passed an even more radical measure in 1866. Admittedly, the substance of Disraeli's bill owed a great deal to Gladstone's public initiative and parliamentary maneuverings,[22] but Gladstone was by no means a radical in his pursuit of franchise reform.

While Gladstone was vying with Disraeli for support among the masses, he also struggled to strike a balance within his own party. The Liberal party split on the subject of franchise reform: the Radicals against the Constitutional Liberals. To secure the leadership, Gladstone needed to steer a middle course, and he was usually prepared to compromise when it did not require a departure from his highest priorities or core principles.[23] In any event, his own moderate views on the franchise naturally placed him between the constitutionalists' resistance to change and the demands of radical reformers. The equivocal position Gladstone took on the franchise helped him to become leader, but many members of his party also distrusted him.

As leader, Gladstone could have adopted a general strategy of accommodation and tried to mediate among intraparty groups to achieve consensus on a range of issues, but such a strategy would not have built trust in the long run or rallied his troops for a higher purpose. To satisfy his private longing as well as his sense of public duty, Gladstone preferred to muster support for a moral crusade. He had shown clear conviction on the economy, but his economic principles were now firmly established as government policy. From 1867 on, Ireland became the subject that inspired and sustained Gladstone's conviction-style leadership. When he boldly declared his support for disestablishment of the church in Ireland, Gladstone focused national attention on an issue that united his party, built a popular base of support, and firmly established his reputation for strong, principled leadership.[24]

In March 1868 Gladstone, as leader of the opposition, moved several resolutions directed against the principle of maintaining an established church in Ireland. In favor of disestablishment, Gladstone argued that members of the Anglican Church formed a small minority of the Irish population: Most Irish were Roman Catholics, but a considerable number were Presbyterians. Furthermore, Gladstone pointed out, with all its special privileges and artificial advantages, the Anglican Church had never increased its following in Ireland. In his view, the privileges of a small, religious body, connected with the Church of England by the Act of Union, were just causes for national discontent. When Gladstone's resolutions carried, Disraeli dissolved Parliament, and disestablishment became the central issue in the November 1868 general election campaign.

In its coverage of the campaign, the *Times* identified aspects of the electoral environment that proved conducive to Gladstone's conviction politics, emphasizing dissatisfaction with the status quo and identifying the "tasks of reconstruction in store." The paper identified the source of discontent as the demand for more limited government but more active leadership.[25] Ultimately, public disenchantment with the existing government, the issue of disestablishment, and Gladstone's popularity produced a Liberal victory.

Gladstone's leadership strengthened his party's hold in Scotland, Wales, Ireland, and the smaller English boroughs, and the Liberals secured a majority of 110. The *Times* interpreted the electoral result as an overwhelming victory for Gladstone and his followers.[26] According to the *Times,* Gladstone secured a mandate for his liberal reform, and his new agenda would settle several significant issues: the Irish church, Irish tenancies, education, and the liberalization of universities. Voters wanted change, and they looked to a conviction-style leader as the agent of change.[27]

The nature of the election ensured Gladstone's selection as premier. The *Times* predicted, "There is, of course, no question of Lord Russell as the future premier. We believe he will recognize the verdict of public opinion, and will advise Her Majesty to summon to her councils the statesman who has been designated by all the Liberal constituencies of the Empire as the man to be entrusted with the task of directing the policy of the state. Mr. Gladstone must be called to Windsor."[28] Notification of the queen's invitation produced a dramatic scene: Gladstone read the telegram and then returned to his task of chopping wood (one of his favorite pastimes). After a few minutes, he stopped what he was doing, leaned on his axe, and declared, "My mission is to pacify Ireland."[29] This sense of mission stayed with him when, on the eve before he took office, Gladstone wrote in his diaries, "This birthday opens my 60th year. I descend the hill of life. It would be a truer figure to say I ascend a steeping path with a burden ever gathering weight. The Almighty seems to sustain and spare me for some purpose of His own deeply unworthy as I know myself to be. Glory be to His name."[30] For Gladstone, the "general will" expressed in the election was also the will of God, and he immediately took steps to fulfill his destiny.

Early in 1869, Prime Minister Gladstone introduced his bill for Irish disestablishment. He repeated his earlier arguments, describing the role of the church as one that "serves to estrange the minds of the Irish population from Imperial rule, British sympathies, and from their Protestant fellow-countrymen on both sides of the water."[31] He depicted the church as the chief source of discontent and emphasized its privileged place in Ireland. According to Gladstone, "That which was given for the whole people has come to be appropriated for the enjoyment of a mere handful of the people; and . . . at the same time the property so enjoyed, while it remains in the hands of those who now hold it, is associated with the recollection of all the grievances and bitter misfortunes that have affected that country."[32] The Church Bill of 1869 ended the establishment of the Irish church and dissolved the union of English and Irish churches, and on this issue, the Liberals remained united.

On other Irish issues, Gladstone encountered greater resistance to change. His Land Bill of 1870 became law, but the proposal divided the Liberals and failed to solve the grievances of Irish peasants. Gladstone had wanted to increase the recognition of tenant rights and achieve fixity of tenure, the principle of the second land act of 1881, but the strength of the landlord interest in Britain, Ireland, and his own cabinet thwarted his efforts. Instead, the 1870 bill legalized the customary tenant right where it already existed, included compensation for improvements and damages from disturbance in cases of eviction, and empowered ordinary courts to fix rents where they were "exorbitant." (The Land Act of 1881 would achieve a great deal more by establishing a Land Court that could completely control rents and compensation and settle all other differences between landlords and tenants.) Finally, Gladstone failed to secure approval for the Irish University Bill of 1873, an issue that almost brought down his government.

While Irish issues constituted Gladstone's central concerns, his first government also carried out several significant reforms that laid the foundations of the modern British state. In addition to civil service reform, Gladstone's war secretary, Edward Cardwell, restructured the army, which had been the preserve of the aristocracy: To avert defeat in the Lords, changes were made by royal ordinance, not by statute. Moreover, W. E. Forster achieved education reform with the 1870 Education Act, which established school boards and required compulsory education until the age of thirteen. Oxford and Cambridge universities were also opened to all religions. Furthermore, Gladstone's lord chancellor, Lord Selbourne, restructured the legal system and the courts with the Judicature Act of 1873. The Local Government Board was also established, which in 1919 would become the Ministry of Health. Gladstone's government also passed the Factory Act of 1867, the Coal Mines Act of 1872, and for the Dissenters, the Licensing Act of 1872. Finally, the Ballot Act of 1872 secured secret voting. These reforms leveled a devastating assault on aristocratic privilege and established the basis for a modern state that could respond to the demands of an increasingly diverse and complex society.

By the 1874 general election, Liberal reforms, especially the Education Act and the Licensing Act, had made many enemies of the party.[33] Other factors also played a role in the election, including the creation of an Irish party, conflict among the Liberal party elite, and Disraeli's success in establishing an efficient electoral machine.[34] The election produced a Conservative majority of at least 48 members. In 1875 Gladstone resigned as official party leader; Lord Granville led in the upper chamber and Lord Hartington in the Commons. Freed from the constraints and demands of party leadership, within a few years Gladstone would embark on his famous public crusade to promote his liberal principles.

Gladstone's Midlothian campaign in 1879 provides a striking example of the conviction politician's attempt to set the national agenda and sway popular opinion. As Gladstone spoke on taxation, land reform, Ireland, free trade, and foreign affairs, he emphasized the equality and interdependence of nations and criticized Disraeli's policies of aggression and intervention. With the notable exception of Cobden and Bright's attack on the Corn Laws, political leaders before had declined to deliver such speeches during parliamentary recess. Gladstone's declarations won wide publicity and helped to shape public sentiment in the 1880 general election campaign. For the first time, a British opposition leader went to the people in an oratorical campaign in an attempt to oust the sitting government.

Most of Gladstone's critics (including Liberal Whigs) viewed his Midlothian campaign as demagogic, but even those who disapproved of his effort had to admit that "as a succession of oratorical tours de force his performances in Scotland have never been surpassed." Gladstone impressed the nation by discussing "the whole field of politics, domestic, foreign, financial, ecclesiastical, and local." The *Times* emphasized the significance of Gladstone's initiative (even though it shocked and dismayed the paper's editors). As the paper put it, "Whatever may be the permanent value of Gladstone's criticisms, it is certain that while he thus plunged into the fray he attracted the gaze of friends and foes alike. When he retired, the strife once more languished."[35] The strife stirred by Gladstone's oratorical campaign returned in 1880 and set the tone of the general election that year.

In a "battle fought along strict party lines," the Conservatives suffered their most crushing defeat since the first election after the 1832 Reform Bill. The Liberals secured 351 seats, the Conservatives 237, and the Irish 65. Gladstone became prime minister and chancellor because, according to one contemporary account, "It could not indeed be contested that the Liberal victory was due more to the energy and eloquence of Mr. Gladstone than to the qualities, however high, of any other individual or connection. The new Liberal majority was bound, with few exceptions, by pledges of personal allegiance to Mr. Gladstone."[36] The election rendered a personal endorsement of Gladstone's leadership but not a policy mandate. In the 1880 general election, there was no single issue comparable to Irish disestablishment in 1868, and factions in the Liberal party at the elite level reflected divisions that also characterized the party in the country.[37]

Lacking clear direction and leading a factious party, Gladstone's second government accomplished much less than his first ministry achieved. He did secure passage of the Land Act of 1881, and his reform bills of 1884 and 1885 extended the vote to agricultural workers and redistributed seats, increasing the size of the Commons. In 1885 the *Times* gave Gladstone credit for accomplishing "the entire reconstruction of the representative system of the UK," but in the same report the paper lamented the "miscarriages of foreign and colonial affairs," emphasizing the "Egyptian tragedy."[38] Military intervention in Egypt presented the most substantial obstacle to reform in Gladstone's second government.

Gladstone's position on Egypt contradicted his belief in international cooperation, national autonomy, and self-determination—convictions that had always guided his foreign policy. When, in the 1850 Don Pacifico affair, Prime Minister Palmerston justified his use of force by asserting that British subjects deserved privileged treatment throughout the world, Gladstone responded by describing his nation's pride as its "besetting fault and weakness" and instructed his country to stop praising its "unapproachable greatness." During the Crimean War, Gladstone urged the warring nations to settle on the basis of a collective European guarantee of the rights of the sultan's Christian subjects in the Balkans. Warfare beyond this goal, he believed, showed only a "base lust for conquest." Confident of the righteousness of his cause, the conviction politician proved indifferent to frequent and widespread criticisms that he was a "traitor."[39] In an age of intense national pride, Gladstone's reluctance to intervene in the affairs of other nations often made him seem passive and weak, an image contrary to the strength conveyed by his conviction on domestic issues. Gladstone achieved only limited success in persuading the public of his time or his party to accept his liberal philosophy in foreign affairs. In this respect, his convictions conflicted with opportunity: the prevalent patriotism and the salient sentiments of imperialism that characterized the Victorian age. Yet when Gladstone decided to intervene in Egypt, he departed from his principles and marred his reputation as a man of lofty ideals.

Military involvement deeply wounded Gladstone's second government, and he repeatedly faltered in providing leadership during the conflict. His failures involved both his strategy and its public presentation: When Gladstone failed to rescue his commander in the field, Charles Gordon, the press reversed the initials of the prime minister's nickname—GOM (Grand Old Man)—to MOG (Murder of Gordon). The central cause of his fumbling leadership seemed to be that the "discrepancy between his own ideology on foreign policy and the realities of the situation was too great."[40] The failure of the Egyptian expedition shattered Gladstone's support at home and further fragmented his party.

At the elite level, the Egyptian expedition fractured a parliamentary majority that was already deeply divided on Irish issues. Gladstone had amended his land act to appease the Irish Nationalist leader Charles Stuart Parnell in 1881, but to secure support for the land act, the prime minister also passed a new, extremely severe, coercion bill. In June 1885, Gladstone's government was reduced to a majority of 12 when the Irish joined the Conservatives to vote against the budget. Gladstone resigned, and Lord Salisbury formed a caretaker Conservative government. Following franchise reform, the registry needed revision before an election could be held.

Gladstone maintained a low profile during the 1885 campaign: He hoped the Conservatives might reach an agreement with Parnell and devise a home rule plan that he could advise the Liberals to endorse. In this way, the pure principle of home rule would not be corrupted or compromised by a partisan struggle, or so Gladstone hoped. Parnell and the Conservatives did form an electoral pact, but the election result was inconclusive: The Liberals secured 86 more seats than did the Conservatives, but Parnell's party also won 86 seats.[41] Furthermore, Gladstone's hope that he could keep home rule out of partisan politics was dashed in December, when his son leaked the news that his father had become a firm believer in home rule. The Liberals divided, and the Conservatives continued in government until another issue reduced the Conservatives to a minority of 79. Then Salisbury resigned, and on February 1, 1886, Gladstone returned as prime minister.

By the beginning of 1886, it had became clear that home rule exercised a "fatal fascination" over Gladstone's mind,[42] but the *Times* predicted he would try to obscure his Irish policy. Mocking a phrase that Gladstone had recently uttered in the Commons, the *Times* remarked that he "is too much the 'old Parliamentary hand' to show people where he is leading them."[43] To the contrary, two months after he became prime minister again, the conviction politician introduced his first home rule bill.

Gladstone's bill would have provided for devolution to an Irish parliament and executive power except in foreign affairs, defense, and customs. His speech on behalf of the legislation stands as a clear expression of his liberal ideology put to practice. Gladstone rejected further criminal legislation and saw crime as a symptom of "deeper mischief." According to Gladstone, the law had been discredited in Ireland because "it comes to the people of that country with a foreign aspect, and in foreign garb."[44] "Stripping law of its foreign garb, and investing it with domestic character" would provide the only viable solution. The objective of legislation, Gladstone declared, should be "to restore to Ireland the first conditions of civil life—the free course of law, the liberty of every individual in the exercise of every legal right, the confidence of the people in the law, and their sympathy with the law."[45]

To protect the rights of minorities, Gladstone borrowed U.S. constitutional reasoning and remedies.[46] One chamber would prove insufficient;[47] instead, he recommended two "orders," each with a limited veto. The first order would comprise the current Irish peers and others elected for ten years; the second and larger chamber would consist of current Irish members of Parliament and 101 more.[48] The viceroyalty would be maintained as the executive, and judges would be appointed for terms of "good behavior."[49] Despite Gladstone's best effort, no amount of rigorous reasoning or brilliant eloquence could persuade the House of Commons to embrace the U.S. model and apply it to Ireland.

Gladstone concluded his speech with an appeal to noble sentiment and righteous principle. Accused of "dismemberment of the Union," he replied, "I ask that in our case we should practice, with firm and fearless hand—what we have so often preached—the doctrine which we have so often inculcated upon others—namely, that the concession of local self-government is not the way to sap or impair, but the way to strengthen and consolidate unity."[50] His appeal to conviction and consistency fell on deaf ears. The bill was defeated by a vote of 343 to 313, with 93 Liberals voting against home rule. To make matters worse, Liberals not only failed to heed Gladstone's gospel, they also portrayed him as the heretic. Objecting to both the style and the substance of Gladstone's proposal, the Liberal party made clear it would not quietly accept its prime minister's display of independent, illiberal leadership.

Following the bill's defeat, Gladstone dissolved Parliament and took the issue to the country. At the time, the active and unprecedented part Gladstone played in the campaign appalled the queen.[51] Chamberlain Radicals and the Whigs led by Hartington joined the Unionists against Gladstone's Liberals and the Parnellites. The Unionists secured a majority of 110 more than the Home Rulers had. The home rule manifesto in 1886 had won Wales, Scotland, and Ireland, but lost England. The Liberal party split left the Liberals weak and out of government for almost twenty years, with the exception of their brief government from 1892 until 1894.

In July 1892, Gladstone opened his final electoral campaign with a speech on home rule, basing his appeal on the 1886 declarations. Clearly Gladstone had "set his heart upon accomplishing an Irish revolution."[52] The Liberals secured a small majority of 40 and remained divided on a range of issues. Salisbury maintained his government until he lost a vote of confidence in August. In February 1893, Gladstone introduced his second home rule bill and secured a majority of 34 on the third reading in the Commons. The vote in the House of Lords was 419 to 41 against. Gladstone wanted to go to the country again—this time to attack the House of Lords as an institution[53]— but members of his cabinet persuaded him to avoid a direct assault on constitutional structures. Despite his firm conviction, Gladstone complied with the collective view of his cabinet colleagues and remained within nineteenth-century institutional constraints. He would not have another opportunity to take his case to the people: Six months after the Lords defeated his second home rule bill, Gladstone, at the age of eighty-five, resigned as premier for the last time.

Despite his failure to secure home rule, Gladstone had altered his nation's policies on a wide range of issues. In his first budget as chancellor and later during his great reform ministry from 1868 to 1874, Gladstone had adopted and implemented the economic policies first advanced in Peel's government, and Gladstone's success in economics seems to have settled the nineteenth-century debate about the merits of free trade.[54] The part Gladstone played in franchise reform brought new groups into the political arena and democratized parliamentary politics. The changes brought about by his first government—in the military, the universities, and the civil service—shattered the aristocratic privilege that had made these institutions the exclusive preserve of the elite. Gladstone also successfully challenged the proper place of the Anglican Church when he advocated the abolition of compulsory church rates and Irish disestablishment. In leveling an assault on the authorities of the old order, Gladstone laid the foundations for a new modern state and more democratic politics. Of course, "the mark he left on the British statute book" would have been unlikely without "his oratorical triumphs."[55]

Coinciding with the rise of mass-based politics (and facilitating it), Gladstone's oratorical campaigns introduced a style of plebiscitary leadership that would become common practice for twentieth-century conviction politicians. On at least four occasions—his budget in 1853, disestablishment in 1868, and home rule in 1886 and again in 1894—Gladstone believed he possessed "an insight into the facts of particular eras, and their relations one to another, which generates in the mind a conviction that the materials exist for forming a public opinion, and for directing it to a particular end."[56] In these cases, as Lord Bryce remarked, "It was the masses who took their view from him, not he who took a mandate from the masses."[57] After Gladstone succeeded in shaping public opinion, he would try to transform popular sentiment into political support, a strategy that sometimes worked. By 1881, the Duke of Argyll wrote, "Gladstone exercises such a sway over the constituencies that the members are afraid to call their souls their own."[58] Gladstone's strategy of "going public" marked a bold departure from the statesmanlike independence of his mentor Peel.

While the substance and style of Gladstone's conviction politics account for his legacy as a great nineteenth-century prime minister, aspects of both also limited his success. Gladstone's liberal convictions imposed some significant constraints on his constructive efforts. As indicated earlier, his commitment to self-determination, national autonomy, and international cooperation proved out of step with his times, suggesting that public sentiment sometimes resists the persuasion and rejects the principles of a conviction politician. Moreover, Gladstone promoted political reform and advocated laissez-faire economics in order to abolish privilege, but his classic liberalism prevented him from going further to assist or respond to the demands of labor.

Labor's support for Gladstone's Liberal governments fluctuated, and his record on labor legislation proved uneven. In 1868 the First Trades Union Congress met, and in 1869 the parliamentary committee of the Trades Union Congress was established. Gladstone won the support of workers for his role in reforming the franchise, and his first government passed the 1871 trade union act, which protected union funds from embezzlement. That same year, however, Gladstone's government secured approval for the Criminal Law Amendment Act, which made virtually all picketing illegal. From 1871 to 1875, labor agitation increased, and the unpopularity of Gladstone's government grew.

In 1875 Disraeli repealed Gladstone's Criminal Law Act in an effort to win union support: The 1875 Conspiracy and Protection of Property Act legalized picketing once again. But Disraeli's partisan gains proved short-lived for several reasons. Nonconformism had established a social link between labor and liberalism, and the unions returned to the Liberal fold. For many years, the British parliamentary system proved sufficiently flexible and adaptive to permit reform, and the trade unions were able to find advocates in the Liberal parliamentary party. Furthermore, the British labor movement drew on the cooperative movement, whose principle of self-help also provided the core of liberal beliefs.[59]

Despite these links, the relationship between the trade unions and the Liberal party became strained once again when a serious depression hit in the 1880s and Britain witnessed the growth of its unions and experienced an outbreak of strikes. This new unionism differed from the first wave: In the late 1880s through the early 1890s, unionism increasingly embraced socialism, and labor saw little hope of advancement through the Liberal party. Particularly after the 1886 split, Gladstone was committed to Irish home rule, not the "condition-of-England question." The labor movement came to see an independent Labour party as the only hope of direct participation in government. Gladstone was able to ride the nineteenth-century wave of liberalism, but he was ultimately swimming against the ideological tide of another, powerful movement.

Finally, aspects of the style (as well as the substance) of Gladstone's conviction politics also served to limit his success. Gladstone was not always able to translate his popularity into legislative success in part because elite and mass perceptions of his style differed. The longer Gladstone pursued his lofty principles while proudly proclaiming his independence and the righteousness of his cause, the more he annoyed and alienated his colleagues. According to one biographer, "His popular following outside the House earned him fierce hatred inside. But it was not only fear of his potentialities as a demagogue that aroused antagonism; it was the manner in which he flaunted his 'purity of purpose,' his High Anglican, Peelite priggishness that tried beyond endurance many men in a worldly, aristocratic assembly."[60] The difference between elite and mass perceptions of conviction politicians provides a persistent problem for such leaders, but the institutional erosion that takes place in the twentieth century breaks down some of the barriers. Gladstone operated in an institutional environment, however, that imposed several structural obstacles that no amount of determination or adherence to conviction could overcome.

On the issue of home rule, Gladstone faced defeat when he confronted the constraints of a strong political party, the established principle of cabinet government, and the institution of the House of Lords. Gladstone might have been "willing to risk fame and fortune in pursuing a course [his character] had once resolved upon."[61] Yet modern biographers have concluded that in the end, "he was left to consider whether the part of Peel in the crisis of 1846 had not been played, forty years later, by himself . . . and he had not Peel's consolation, the triumph of the cause for which he fought."[62] Ultimately, Gladstone's brilliant career concluded with devastating defeat on the issue he carried with the greatest conviction. His U.S. counterpart would face a similar fate, without the satisfaction Gladstone could derive from reflecting on his substantial earlier achievements.

Grover Cleveland

Cleveland's quick flight from oblivion to the pinnacle of the presidency provides a sharp contrast to Gladstone's long period of grooming to become premier. In 1881 Cleveland was elected mayor of Buffalo, where he attracted statewide attention by vetoing the legislation crafted by a corrupt city council. In 1883 he became governor of New York, where he gained national notoriety by fighting special interest legislation and tackling Tammany Hall. Cleveland's reputation as a reformer and as a man of moral principle would help him win the popular vote in three consecutive presidential elections, though his fall from grace would prove as precipitate as his initial ascendancy.

In 1884 several factors combined to create an environment conducive to Cleveland's conviction-style leadership. Although the U.S. experienced a second industrial revolution after the Civil War, not all groups in society enjoyed an equal share of the new wealth. Industrialization, urbanization, and immigration fueled a prosperous national economy but created crowded living conditions, low wages, and problems of public safety and health for ordinary workers.[63] Farmers also felt the harmful effects of economic change, and in the late 1870s they started to suffer the consequences of a price depression that would last for decades. Cleveland's remedy of tariff reform was a classic liberal solution, and the limits of his liberalism would become apparent when labor and agrarian forces organized against his leadership during the depression in his second term. In his first term, however, Cleveland attacked the selfish schemes of trusts and promised to correct the unfairness and injustice that workers and farmers were forced to endure.

Other cracks in the complacency of the Gilded Age appeared when financial panic struck in 1884, and U.S. citizens reacted in characteristic fashion, attributing signs of economic distress to political corruption. Cleveland spoke to such sentiment in the 1884 presidential campaign when he invoked Jacksonian themes that linked economic privilege to the abuse of political power. He criticized Republicans for recklessly wasting public funds, acting out of self-interest, and serving only those with privilege. Cleveland proposed a classic liberal alternative to the Republican regime: frugality in economy and government. Yet the electorate chose him more for his integrity and the strength of his character than for the specific substance of his convictions.

Cleveland's personal characteristics made him seem just the right "man for the time."[64] The son of an orthodox Presbyterian minister, Cleveland offered a rhetoric that was high-minded and righteous, with a moral content that revealed his "preacher blood."[65] To many U.S. citizens, his campaign promised to provide salvation for a country that had suffered in reputation, material prosperity, and moral character. According to William Allen White, in 1884 Cleveland was "swept onward by the tidal power that was moving in the protesting hearts of the people. . . . The revolt against Republican rule was brutal, unplanned—a barbaric yawp of disgust. . . . [The] soul of the people was sick of politics, and was nauseated at all politicians."[66] In contrast to the professional politicians, Cleveland appeared to be a hardworking, honest man—the epitome of Horatio Alger's rugged individualist. Even his personal limitations—his awkward manner of speech and his plump appearance—endeared him to the public. "Grover the Good," as he was nicknamed, had none of the vices of professional politicians, and he was virtually untainted by partisan politics.

Cleveland's good-government campaign and his lofty moral rhetoric led independent-minded Republicans to abandon their party and endorse his candidacy. Since Reconstruction, many Republicans had grown increasingly disgusted with their party's practice of spoils. In the early 1880s, they formed the National Civil Service Reform League, modeled after several state reform organizations. During the 1884 campaign, many of these reformers became known as "Mugwumps," a label applied by Charles A. Dana, editor of the New York *Sun,* and depicted by the figure of a fence-sitter with his "mug" on one side of the fence and his "wump" on the other. In general, the Mugwumps attacked partisan politics and stressed the need for a merit system, secret ballot, and independent voting. Many of them also later supported Cleveland's proposed tariff reform. Cleveland's candidacy (and his presidency) provided a national platform to promote Mugwump views. He frequently communicated with prominent figures in the movement and appointed several Mugwumps to office, including Charles S. Fairchild, a New York reformer, as assistant secretary of the treasury.[67] President Cleveland believed the Mugwumps had been critical to his victory,[68] and he would try to keep them in his coalition by responding to their demand for civil service reform. At the time of the 1884 presidential election, the support of the Mugwumps further enhanced Cleveland's reputation for integrity.

Unfortunately, the moral content of the campaign quickly diminished as allegations arose that threatened to knock Grover the Good off his pedestal. Republicans charged that Cleveland had fathered an illegitimate child, while scandal also marred their own campaign when the public learned that Republican James G. Blaine had granted congressional favors to Little Rock and Fort Smith Railroad. In a popular refrain, the Democrats declared, "Blaine, Blaine, James G. Blaine. The continental liar from the state of Maine."[69] And the Republicans responded, "Ma! Ma! Where's my pa?" (Later the victorious Democrats added, "Gone to the White House. Ha! Ha! Ha!")[70] Ultimately, Blaine's reputation suffered much more than Cleveland's did: Cleveland pledged to tell the truth and won respect for his honesty, while Blaine repeatedly and falsely denied the charges against him. Moreover, Cleveland's scandal was viewed by most as a private affair, while Blaine had betrayed the public trust. Despite the attacks on Cleveland's personal character, he emerged from the close contest with 48.5 percent of the vote, compared with Blaine's 48.3 percent. By telling the truth and maintaining the public trust, the newly elected president survived the personal scandal with his reputation for integrity intact.

In his first administration, Cleveland would have many opportunities to demonstrate his integrity and pursue his campaign pledge to fight corruption and promote fairness. Aggressively employing his veto authority, Cleveland blocked private pension bills, which were based on fraudulent claims and secured by members of Congress shamelessly courting their constituents. Furthermore, the president endorsed the Indian Emancipation Act, which he hoped would improve the economic condition and consequently enhance the moral development of Native Americans by enabling individuals to own private property within the reservation. (Despite the negative practical consequences of the legislation, Cleveland's intention was classically liberal and largely beneficent.) In the same spirit, at the conclusion of his second administration, Cleveland would veto a literacy bill that would have prohibited the immigration of illiterates. (One of his few departures from such liberal principles came as a concession to his party: Cleveland promoted and signed legislation that barred Chinese laborers who left the U.S. from returning.) Although he was reluctant to regulate business, he was willing to do so when it seemed necessary to ensure fairness: He secured legislation for a moderate version of his proposal to establish a permanent board to arbitrate labor disputes, and he signed the Interstate Commerce Act. Many of these measures stemmed from the liberal conviction that government favoritism should be abolished and individual opportunity enhanced.

The civil service provided a critical arena for Cleveland to act on his convictions and pursue the reform he promised during the campaign. Reform of the federal government had started even before Cleveland became president: Two events in the early 1880s provided the impetus for the Civil Service Act of 1883 (the Pendleton Act). On July 2, 1881, a disgruntled office seeker shot President Garfield and aroused public concern about the nature and consequences of the spoils system. Then when the Republican party suffered significant losses in the 1882 midterm election, it took steps to guard against future Democratic spoils. Republicans began to classify government positions, enabling the party to hold on to many of its offices in the event of a Democratic takeover. Modeled after British civil service reform, the Pendleton Act became law—the first serious attempt to replace spoils with a system of hiring based on merit.[71] Throughout his two presidencies, Cleveland would extend the Pendleton Act by continuing to classify government positions; and at least initially, his rhetoric implied that he would do even more by transforming this area of practical reform into a moral crusade.

In his first annual message, Cleveland promoted civil service reform "to check the progress of demoralization" and emphasized the "conviction of the correctness of the principle."[72] The president passed an early test of his commitment when he allowed a Republican to remain as New York City postmaster, a move that was applauded by the Mugwumps and abhorred by Democratic loyalists. One year later, in his second annual message, he depicted civil service reform as "an advance movement which is radical and far reaching."[73]

Nevertheless, to balance conflicting interests among his supporters, Cleveland ultimately compromised on civil service reform just as Gladstone had sought to establish a consensus on the franchise. In his first term, Cleveland found himself in a position strikingly similar to that of Gladstone in the mid-1860s. Cleveland could have adopted a conciliatory stance on other issues as well, but instead, like Gladstone, he attempted to rally his troops for a higher cause. As Gladstone focused attention on Irish disestablishment in 1868, Cleveland identified tariff revision as the single most significant issue facing the nation in 1887. Like Gladstone, Cleveland depicted his cause as a moral crusade to correct the unfairness and injustice that stemmed from the abuse of concentrated power.

Cleveland's advisors warned him that any declaration of his conviction on this controversial issue could shatter his fragile coalition. To one such cautious counselor, Cleveland replied with a rhetorical question that only a conviction politician could utter: "What is the use of being elected, unless you stand for something?"[74] After he delivered his 1887 annual message, the central purpose of Cleveland's presidency became clear. Cleveland began his message by emphasizing the moral dimension of the tariff issue. High duties and the subsequent surplus in the Treasury defy the "theory of our institutions," which according to Cleveland, "guarantees to every citizen the full enjoyment of all the fruits of his industry and enterprise, with only such deduction as may be his share toward the careful and economical maintenance of the government which protects him. It is plain that the exaction of more than this is indefensible extortion, and a culpable betrayal of American fairness and justice."[75] Tariff reduction would be necessary to safeguard the liberal principle of limited government and restore the integrity of the regime.

The president devoted a substantial part of his argument to the plight of farmers and laborers. Those who benefit from protection constitute a minority, Cleveland argued, while all farmers and laborers pay high prices for the "necessaries of life."[76] As long as imported goods were heavily taxed, domestic manufacturers would conspire to keep their prices high. Free competition should be allowed to flourish, but Cleveland explained, "It is notorious that this competition is too often strangled by combinations quite prevalent at this time, and frequently called trusts, which have for their object the regulation of the supply and price of commodities made and sold by members of the combination. The people can hardly hope for any consideration in the operation of these selfish schemes."[77] Cleveland sent his message to Congress, but he wrote it for a wider audience that included ordinary workers on the farm and in the factory.

To place tariff reduction at the center of the national agenda, Cleveland devoted his entire annual message to this one issue. He acknowledged that he was making a bold departure from nineteenth-century practice by discussing a single subject, but he explained, "I am so much impressed with the paramount importance of the subject . . . that I shall forego the addition of any other topic, and shall only urge upon your immediate consideration the 'State of the Union,' as shown in the present condition of our treasury and our general fiscal situation, upon which every element of our safety and prosperity depends."[78] Cleveland did not want to run the risk that Congress (or the press) would focus on other issues. By giving the subject his exclusive attention, Cleveland made his message clear: Tariff reform constituted his top priority, and he hoped to make it the nation's central concern.

In this respect, Cleveland seemed to succeed. The *New York Advertiser* predicted his "concise, able, and manly candid message will have a decisive weight in the future of parties and of legislation."[79] Even parts of the press that opposed tariff reduction welcomed the president's attempt to define the national agenda. The *Boston Journal* believed Cleveland should "be congratulated upon his new departure" and acknowledged, "We do not approve the President's recommendations but we may frankly say that we like the tone of his message."[80] According to the *New York Times,* the novelty of his message had "excited Congress," and the paper expressed surprise that the president had refused to "treat the tariff gingerly."[81] As Cleveland planned, the issue of tariff reform captured the public attention (and the press imagination).

Cleveland's proposed reform challenged a system of high protectionism that had been in place since Congress enacted the Morrill Tariff in 1861. Following his annual message, the president endorsed a tariff reduction bill proposed by Representative Roger Mills, even though that legislation fell short of Cleveland's objective. The Mills bill passed in the House and then died in the Senate. Cleveland had failed to secure tariff reform in his first term, but he succeeded in focusing national attention on the issue. Just as Gladstone had made Irish disestablishment the issue in the 1868 general election, Cleveland made tariff reform the focus of debate in the 1888 presidential campaign.

Cleveland's decisive leadership on the tariff issue ensured his renomination as the Democratic candidate. As Woodrow Wilson would later recall, "Mr. Cleveland was re-nominated for the Presidency by acclamation, not because the politicians wanted him, but because their constituents did"; the president was able to "force partisan leaders, for their own good, to feel his power from without."[82] Wilson's comment on Cleveland echoes Argyll's assessment of Gladstone: In 1888, Cleveland's popularity made party politicians afraid to "call their souls their own."

The Democratic party embraced Cleveland's cause and rallied behind their conviction candidate. As the *New York Times* judged Cleveland's nomination, "In a sense never so truly applicable since the renomination of Lincoln in 1864, the man is the platform. . . . His message on the protective tariff aroused the people as they were aroused by Lincoln's first call for the troops. . . . The

President's tariff message [stands] above and overshadowing everything else."[83] Even other, more negative reports in the partisan press acknowledged the significance of Cleveland's leadership, noting that the convention platform included a tariff plank and adopted Cleveland's message as its interpretation.[84]

In the general election, Cleveland's supporters in the press declared that he had introduced "a new era in national politics." According to the *New York Commercial Advertiser,* Cleveland had created a "separation of parties along lines of cleavage coinciding with those which actually divide public opinion." Before the president's tariff message, voters who chose Republican or Democratic "were voting vaguely and more or less in the dark as to the significance and effect of their vote," but Cleveland had infused partisan politics with meaning. In his message, Cleveland had pointed "out the dangers to which the country is exposed by reason of excessive taxation" and advanced "the American idea of government, which prescribes that the government shall let men alone." By contrast, the Republicans advocated "centralization and paternal government which, carried to its logical result, must end in socialism." The *Advertiser* described the voters' choice as "between an American policy of equality, light taxation and non-interference, and a localistic policy of favoritism, paternalism, and monopoly."[85] The *Washington Post* was equally generous in its assessment: As the paper put it, Cleveland was clearly "the man of destiny."[86] Whether papers endorsed or opposed Cleveland's views, all emphasized the significance of the president's tariff message in setting the agenda for the campaign.

Cleveland's proposed tariff reform determined the nature of the central campaign debate, but the impact of the issue on the election result is difficult to determine. In another close contest, Cleveland won 90,000 more votes than his Republican opponent, Benjamin Harrison, but lost in the electoral college. Republicans portrayed the threat of tariff reform as a danger to national welfare and tried to rally supporters in the Midatlantic and Northeastern states by appealing to their patriotism as well as their interest. One campaign poster depicted Harrison against the background of the U.S. flag, while Cleveland posed in front of the Union Jack. The Republicans regained control of both houses of Congress, but the number of Democrats who endorsed tariff reduction also increased. Moreover, as the *New York World* observed, "Though a Republican president was elected, the increase of the Democratic popular majority on the tariff issue gives renewed confidence to the friends of revenue reform and marks the drift of the tide."[87] The 1890 midterm elections would show additional signs that Cleveland had succeeded in swaying opinion on tariff reform.

Despite the significance of the tariff issue, several other factors influenced the outcome of the 1888 election, including the better organized and financed

Republican campaign, the treachery of Tammany Hall, and corruption in two key states: New York and Indiana.[88] Cleveland might have also been hurt by the "Murchison letter" in which the British ambassador in Washington was tricked into declaring that Cleveland's reelection would be in the best interest of Britain. In an extremely close contest, it did not take much to tip the balance between the two major parties.

Before Cleveland left office, he used his 1888 annual message to deliver the most radical rendition of his convictions. The tariff remained his central concern, but Cleveland placed the issue in a wider, more philosophical context. According to the president, through government taxation, the state had conspired with capital to the disadvantage of society as a whole. He alerted the public to the threat posed by "the communism of combined wealth and capital, the outgrowth of overweening cupidity and selfishness, which insidiously undermines the justice and integrity of free institutions," and warned that it is not less dangerous than "the communism of oppressed poverty and toil." According to the president, "He mocks the people who proposes that the government shall protect the rich and that they in turn will care for the laboring poor." Employing Jacksonian reasoning, Cleveland asserted that "any intermediary between the people and their government . . . makes the boast of free institutions a glittering delusion." Then the president concluded his message by quoting Jackson: "[I]t is not in a splendid government supported by powerful monopolies and aristocratical establishments that [the people] will find happiness, or their liberties protection, but in a plain system, void of pomp—protecting all and granting favors to none."[89] His message was written to serve as a statement of his convictions, but it also rendered a dire warning about the abuses of Republican rule.

Subsequent events appeared to confirm Cleveland's worst fears. The "Billion-Dollar Congress," as it came to be known, passed the Force Bill, the McKinley Tariff, and the Sherman Silver Purchase Act; legislative expenditures were extravagant. Although Cleveland initially avoided political controversy after he left office, his convictions could not be constrained for long, and he started to deliver speeches on the need for tariff reduction, civil service reform, ballot change, government economy, and the currency. He was heartened by the result of the 1890 midterm election, which produced a popular revolt against the Republicans and swept away their legislative majority, reducing the party to 88 members in the House. By the end of 1891, the public and the press were beginning to issue another call for conviction politics, and Cleveland was preparing to answer it.

Just as he started to enjoy renewed popularity, however, Cleveland made a move that defied all calculations of political expediency and threatened to end his political career. In a stunning display of conviction politics, Cleveland wrote a letter to E. Ellery Anderson of the Reform Club, denouncing the proposed unlimited coinage of silver. The Republicans had passed the Sherman Silver Purchase Act, and pressure was mounting among Democrats as well as Republicans to go much farther. Cleveland's declaration against silver coinage shocked Democratic party politicians and seemed to ensure that he would not be renominated in 1892. Yet Cleveland declared that he had been compelled to state his view regardless of the political consequences. He revealed to a close associate: "It seems to me that a weight has been lifted off and a cloud removed. At any rate, no one can doubt where I stand."[90] Fortunately for Cleveland, the proposed silver legislation died in the House and the issue faded in significance, but it would return to test the strength of his conviction again in his second term.

Cleveland's supporters in the press warned that his publicly declared position on silver could jeopardize his nomination. According to the *New York World,* in his declaration as in his first administration, Cleveland seemed to lack "political skill." While the absence of such skill would ruin others, the paper observed that it seemed to bolster Cleveland's reputation as a conviction politician: "Mr. Cleveland is the candidate of the anti-politicians, so to speak. He represents ideas, sentiments, aspirations, not organized purpose. Ordinarily such a candidate for a nomination would be hopeless because organization is supposed usually to count for more than ideas, sentiments, and aspirations in nominating conventions. In Mr. Cleveland's case there seems to be a widespread conviction that the rule will not hold good."[91] In the same report, the *World* attempted to explain how the "candidate of the anti-politicians" could win the nomination:

> His position to-day is not less peculiar than his career has been. With the record of a defeat at the last election against him, with all the politicians of his own state, except the little group who were office holders under his Administration, either hostile or lukewarm, and with no machine or other organization to support his candidacy, Mr. Cleveland is nevertheless the most popular man in his party in the country at large. If the nomination were to be made now and by plebiscite he would unquestionably be the Democratic candidate.

In fact Cleveland's operatives at the convention persuaded the party chieftains that the Democrats could win only by rallying behind the cause of tariff reform with the popular conviction politician as their candidate.

Early in 1892 Cleveland had attempted to set the agenda for the upcoming campaign by making tariff reform the defining issue once again. Speaking to the Business Men's Democratic Association on "Jackson Day," the anniversary of the Battle of New Orleans, Cleveland compared his struggle to secure tariff reduction with Jackson's campaign to abolish the bank. Cleveland urged his audience of partisans to carry on the Jacksonian tradition in substance and in style.

The tariff stood as the symbol of privilege just as the bank did in Jackson's day, Cleveland told his listeners. Jackson was determined to destroy the bank because it was "an institution dangerous to the liberties and prosperity of the people." Likewise, according to Cleveland, "The Democratic party of to-day, which conjures with the name of Jackson, has also attacked a monstrous evil, entrenched behind a perversion of governmental power and guarded by its selfish beneficiaries. On behalf of those among our people long neglected, we have insisted on tariff reform and an abandonment of unjust favoritism." Like the National Bank, he said, the tariff involves considerations that "lie at the foundation of the justice and fairness of popular rule."[92]

For Cleveland, Jackson's example could guide Democrats toward their proper goal and also render advice on how to achieve it. As he described Jackson's approach, Cleveland delivered a clear statement against compromise or conciliation and made the case for conviction politics. According to Cleveland, when Jackson attacked the bank, he did so "utterly regardless of any considerations of political expediency or personal advancement. . . . From the time the first blow was struck until the contest ended in his complete triumph, he allowed nothing to divert him from his purpose."[93] The lesson for Cleveland's Democrats was clear: "The least retreat bodes disaster; cowardice is often called conservatism, and an army scattered into sections invites defeat." The public, Cleveland insisted, would reject the ambiguity and equivocation that comes from pragmatic calculations. Instead, he asserted, "I believe our countrymen are prepared to act on principle, and in no mood for political maneuvering. They will not waste time in studying conundrums, guessing riddles, or trying to interpret doubtful phrases. They demand a plain and simple statement of political purpose."[94] "Inspired by the true Jacksonian spirit," Cleveland urged his partisan audience to "hold to the doctrine that party honesty is party duty and party courage is party expediency."[95]

As it had in 1888, the tariff issue dominated the campaign, but Cleveland's style of leadership attracted as much support as the substance of his convictions did. The *New York Times* declared, "The name, the character, and the principles of Grover Cleveland have been the greatest regenerating force at work in the Democratic party since its complete abasement during the war."[96] The *Washington Post* predicted, "He will go to the country with a good official record and with a personal popularity that is phenomenal . . . a man whom the people can trust to act fully up to his convictions of right."[97] The result of the 1892 election was one of the most decisive endorsements of a candidate during the Gilded Age: Although the million votes won by the Populist party prevented Cleveland from securing a majority of the popular vote, he won a clear plurality and swept the electoral college. From this high point of popularity and publicity during the 1892 election, Cleveland would soon suffer a dramatic fall. Within weeks of his second administration, a worldwide depression hit the U.S., and economic conditions transformed the conviction politician from a man admired for his principles into an apparently blind and rigid leader.

In his second administration Cleveland suffered an overwhelming combination of misfortunes: industrial and agricultural depression, financial panic, foreign embarrassments, and a fierce political revolt within his party. To avert further financial panic, Cleveland won the repeal of the Sherman Silver Purchase Act and vetoed the Bland Silver Seniorage Bill, moves that earned the endorsement of the business community but ruined his reputation as an ally of the underdog. When he sought to implement his liberal ideology (in the Gladstonian mold) in international affairs, his moves conveyed weakness and ran counter to popular expansionist sentiment. (In addition to trying to reinstate the monarchy in Hawaii, Cleveland abandoned the canal treaty with Nicaragua.) Unwilling to adapt to changing circumstances at home or abroad, Cleveland rigidly clung to his principles, even when he failed to persuade the public.

Cleveland's persistent opposition to free silver cost him the greatest amount of support. In response to the panic, Cleveland called a special session of Congress to repeal the Sherman Silver Purchase Act. He quickly secured repeal in the House, and after he refused to compromise, he also managed to win unconditional repeal in the Senate. Cleveland's bold initiative won applause from his supporters in the press, who praised "the Administration of Grover Cleveland, which has stood like a rock for unconditional repeal."[98] The president's legislative success was also hailed by bankers, brokers, and business, but as economic conditions grew worse, "terrific assaults" against Cleveland intensified.[99]

Free-silver supporters alleged that Cleveland was allied with an "Anglo-American Gold Trust."[100] The president had compared his struggle for tariff reform with Jackson's battle against the bank, but Cleveland's adherence to the gold standard made him appear to be the protector of the bank—not the U.S. Bank but the Bank of England. After attacking privilege for most of his career, Cleveland found himself identified with the interests of the aristocracy.

Cleveland's veto of the Bland Silver Seniorage Bill in 1894 delivered a final blow to his public support and party leadership. He might have sought to unify his party through compromise, but he believed any departure from the gold standard would violate his principles. Instead, Cleveland hoped to unify his party by instructing it on the merits of his principles. In 1891 he had designated the gold standard the "Ark of the Covenant" for Democrats.[101] When the party rejected Cleveland's creed, he was quick to sacrifice his party and its electoral prospects in order to preserve the integrity of the nation's finances and the government's credit.

After the veto, Cleveland tried to shore up the gold reserve by a series of bond issues that further exacerbated divisions within the Democratic party. Cleveland's actions on the currency produced two immediate consequences. His repeal of the Sherman Silver Purchase Act followed by his veto of the Bland Bill alienated agrarian politicians and their constituents, whose discontent propelled William Jennings Bryan into the party leadership. Furthermore, these moves led to the first charges that Cleveland had sold out to J. P. Morgan, a view that later appeared to be confirmed when, in early 1895, the president struck a deal with Morgan to bail out the federal government.

While Cleveland's opposition to bimetallism cost him the support of midwestern and southern farmers, in July 1894 his use of federal troops in the Pullman strike alienated labor. In the midst of the depression, George Pullman had cut the wages of his employees without reducing the rents they were forced to pay as his tenants. After Pullman fired workers who protested, 80 percent of his employees went on strike, and the American Railway Union joined them in a sympathy strike. Rail traffic through Chicago fell to 10 percent, and the strike seriously disrupted mail service. Cleveland's attorney general obtained a broad injunction that prohibited any interference with railroad traffic, and the president sent federal troops to enforce the injunction. Violence erupted as federal soldiers battled with unemployed citizens. Seven people died, and Eugene Debs was arrested with seventy other union members. It was the first time any president had ordered troops without a request from the state and contrary to the wishes of its governor. Years later Cleveland justified his action as necessary to preserve the peace and maintain order, not as a move to weaken or destroy organized labor.[102] Regardless of his motive, his decision to send the troops was widely perceived as an attempt to protect business interests at the expense of the welfare of workers.

Previously, Cleveland had made many moves on behalf of labor. In 1886 he had issued the first message to Congress in U.S. history on the subject of labor. In that message, he had proposed a permanent labor commission to arbitrate industrial disputes; and in his 1888 annual message, he had issued a violent attack on the industrial power elite as the cause of national decay. In 1893–94, however, Cleveland seemed insensitive to the plight of workers suffering in the depression. (In addition to his actions in the Pullman strike, Cleveland authorized his attorney general to take action against General Jacob Coxey, who led an army of unemployed in a march to the Capitol.)

Cleveland had advanced the interests of workers and won their support in his first term, but he permanently alienated them in his second administration.

Cleveland's unpopularity had devastating consequences for his party: In 1894 the House of Representatives went Republican, and in the critical election of 1896 the Republicans captured the White House. With the exception of Woodrow Wilson (who secured election only when the Republicans split), the Democrats did not return to the executive office until 1932.

Not only did Cleveland fail to keep his party in power, but during 1893–94, he watched the Congress mangle his proposed moderate effort at tariff reduction. After being amended more than six hundred times, the Wilson-Gorman bill was far from any reform measure, and Cleveland allowed it to become law without his signature. Like his British counterpart's, Cleveland's career concluded with a resounding rejection of his most cherished conviction.

When Cleveland left the presidency for the last time, he was widely considered a dismal failure and loathed by the very people whose cause he had tried to champion. The public's rejection and its harsh assessment of his tenure in office personally and permanently wounded the ex-president. In 1884 Cleveland had been elated to be elected to the nation's highest office, an institution he considered the product of divine inspiration. Early in his first term, Cleveland had declared, "That the office of President of the United States does represent the sovereignty of sixty millions of free people is to my mind a statement full of solemnity; for this sovereignty I conceive to be the working out or enforcement of the divine right of man to govern himself and a manifestation of God's plan concerning the human race."[103] In 1896 Cleveland could not understand why he had failed to fulfill the high purpose and divine mission of this sacred institution. Certainly, he never suspected that the source of his early success could also contribute to his ultimate failure: namely, the style and substance of his conviction politics.

Like Gladstone, Cleveland was admired by the public for his independence and righteousness, but popular admiration did not always translate into political effectiveness. Cleveland's popularity helped him secure his party's nomination because it convinced the party chieftains that he could win the election, but that popularity did not facilitate his ability to govern. Members of Congress and party officials resented the fact that Cleveland was often aloof and unwilling to consult them or negotiate a compromise. Like Gladstone, Cleveland confronted structural barriers that would limit the impact of public sentiment on elite behavior: Party organizations were at their strongest in the Gilded Age, and Congress remained the dominant institution. Cleveland did try to shift the balance of power when he used his annual message to set the national agenda, but he did not attempt to achieve major institutional reform. He thought it would be sufficient to admonish the legislature and circumvent the party without pursuing fundamental structural change.

Of course Cleveland suffered an additional disadvantage that Gladstone escaped: When the depression hit the U.S. in 1893, the public began to perceive Cleveland's central virtue as his chief vice. The conviction politician once admired for his strength and determination suddenly seemed stubborn, inflexible, and insensitive to the plight of the depression's victims. Cleveland could offer them no help without departing from his classic liberal principles, and he was not prepared to do that.

Cleveland's convictions imposed strict limits on his ability to respond to changing economic circumstances. The president remained convinced that an evil alliance between business and government constituted the root cause of all corruption in politics, and he only attempted to break up that relationship and free economic forces. Unwilling to take any additional steps, he left his potential following of farmers and laborers in search of a sympathetic and responsive presidential leader until the twentieth century.

By the end of the nineteenth century, the limits of classic liberalism had become apparent on both sides of the Atlantic. It would no longer be sufficient to purify the state of corrupt influence—aristocratic, ecclesiastical, or monopolistic. A new alliance would need to be forged between the state and "the people," and the next generation of conviction politicians would have to destroy the structures of the old order to lay the foundations for a new liberalism.

These are some of the conclusions reached by a young Welsh lawyer and a rising American academic who were waiting in the wings. As David Lloyd George and Woodrow Wilson studied the behavior of Gladstone and Cleveland, they learned valuable lessons in leadership, which they hoped would enable them to escape the fate of the aging lion and the fallen eagle.

4

THE NEW LIBERALISM:
WOODROW WILSON AND DAVID LLOYD GEORGE

Through conviction-style leadership, Woodrow Wilson and David Lloyd George promoted a new liberalism for the twentieth century. Their public philosophy redefined basic liberal principles and rendered an entirely new relationship between the state and society. Boosted by the backing of powerful reform movements and freed from late-nineteenth-century restraints, they successfully steered their countries through another common current of change.

Initially, Wilson and Lloyd George followed the lead of Grover Cleveland and William Gladstone in the liberal tradition and managed to succeed where their nineteenth-century predecessors failed. Early in his first term as president, Wilson secured tariff and currency reform. As chancellor of the exchequer, Lloyd George won support for land reform and restructured the House of Lords; later, as prime minister, he negotiated the terms for a free Irish state and oversaw the disestablishment of the church in Wales. Wilson and Lloyd George maintained the principles and supported the policies of Cleveland and Gladstone, before they decided to erect a new edifice for twentieth-century liberalism.

Eventually, Wilson and Lloyd George moved beyond the individualism of classic liberalism and advanced the notion that the state should be structured to promote the collective interests of society. Their goals included the preservation and enhancement of liberty, but they came to believe that the service of the state should be enlisted (and its authority augmented) to achieve that goal. Nineteenth-century liberals had insisted that state intervention in the economy served to protect privilege and promote the interests of an economic elite. Early-twentieth-century liberals reversed the argument: State intervention can protect society from the greed and avarice of unbridled economic forces and their accumulated, concentrated power. Wilson and Lloyd George continued the liberal campaign against entrenched, special interests, but they believed the state needed more than purification: It should also be employed to destroy the interests that comprise the core of corruption in society at large.

As they aimed to eliminate the special status and unfair advantage of the elite, Wilson and Lloyd George responded to the demands voiced by an array of reform movements. Lloyd George tried to maintain the support of traditional Liberal groups—the middle class, Nonconformists, the Irish, and the

Welsh—but newly organized forces, especially labor, called for more substantial change. At the same time, Wilson attempted to tap the reform sentiments expressed by Progressives in the United States. No direct personal contact between Lloyd George and Wilson took place until World War I, but frequent communication and improved transatlantic transportation facilitated interaction between reformers in the United Kingdom and the United States. As they discussed their shared goals and exchanged information about their strategies, early-twentieth-century reformers on both sides of the Atlantic tended to reach the same conclusion: Reform required a positive, more expansive role for the state and dynamic executive leadership.

By promoting both the expansion of executive authority and the growth of the state, Wilson and Lloyd George escaped one of the central paradoxes of conviction politics in the liberal tradition. To devolve or decentralize state power, nineteenth- and late-twentieth-century conviction-style leaders concentrated political authority in their hands. In theory and practice (and in contrast to other leaders in this study), Wilson and Lloyd George emerged as unapologetic advocates of increased centralized authority.

While they escaped the seemingly contradictory stance of expanding the executive while limiting the state, another paradox of principled leadership in the liberal tradition became more pronounced. When Wilson and Lloyd George advocated the concentration of power in both the executive and the state, they seemed to abandon the liberal tradition from which they came, even though they continued to articulate liberal goals. This aspect of their experience might account for the widely divergent assessments of the ideological character of their leadership. Lloyd George has been understood as a nineteenth-century liberal, as a radical, and as the architect of the modern welfare state.[1] Wilson has been viewed as a conservative and as a Progressive, as a "rural Tory" and as an advocate of "corporate liberalism."[2] Both leaders adopted means that were statist, while their objectives remained essentially liberal. Making simple interpretation of their leadership even more difficult, Lloyd George and Wilson started their careers as classic liberals, but their positions evolved as they became convinced that a new liberalism should be formulated for the twentieth century.

Woodrow Wilson

Wilson's Scholarship: A Vision of Conviction-Style Leadership

As a political scientist who became a political leader, Wilson provides a unique vehicle for exploring the nature of conviction-style leadership. The young academic wrote on a wide range of topics, but he was clearly preoccupied with the subject of leadership. Wilson's scholarly interest seems to have emerged from his personal frustration with the contemplative life of academe: As a university lecturer, he longed for an active political career. In 1885 he wrote to his future wife and revealed, "I do feel a very real regret that I have been shut out from my heart's first primary ambition and purpose, which was to take an active, if possible, a leading, part in public life, and strike out for myself, if I had the ability, a statesman's career. That is my heart's—or rather my mind's—deepest secret."[3] As Wilson made clear in his letter (and throughout his scholarship), he was fascinated with a particular type of leadership, one that demonstrates essential aspects of conviction politics.

The dynamic leadership that appealed to Wilson provided a sharp contrast to the passive, isolated existence he experienced as a scholar. In the same letter he continued to explain:

> I have a strong instinct of leadership, an unmistakably oratorical temperament and the keenest possible delight in affairs; and it has required very constant and stringent schooling to content me with the sober methods of the scholar and the man of letters. I have no patience for the tedious toil of what is known as "research"; I have a passion for interpreting great thoughts to the world; I should be complete if I could inspire a great movement of opinion, if I could read the experiences of the past into the practical life of the men of today and so communicate the thought to the minds of the great mass of the people as to impel them to great political achievements.[4]

Wilson's omissions reveal as much as his explicit message. He declined to declare that he possessed the requisite practical skills of a politician: the ability to mediate, to manipulate, or calculate. Instead, he referred to his strong instinct and oratorical temperament, while he revealed his passion for interpreting great thoughts. He neglected to express his hunger for power, but he identified his goals as the desire to inspire a great movement of opinion and bring about substantial political achievements. In this early letter Wilson envisioned a type of leadership that he would soon articulate fully and advocate ardently in his academic work.

Starting in 1892, Wilson planned to write a book on leadership, which would have opened with an essay entitled "Statesmanship: A Study in Political Action." Although he never completed the manuscript, his ideas for it provided the basis for a speech he delivered on several occasions in the 1890s. (Wilson gave the speech for the last time on May 24, 1898, five days after Gladstone's death.) Subsequently entitled "Leaders of Men," the speech contrasts the strengths of the scholar to the virtues of the leader.[5] It reveals a great deal about Wilson's own inner struggle between living an academic life and yearning for a political career, but more significant, it provides the single most comprehensive analysis of Wilson's concept of leadership, which he would later try to enact as president.

First and foremost, Wilson argued, a leader should "follow the commands of an unhesitating conviction." In this regard, Wilson praised Sir Robert Peel, who "saw both sides of some questions; but he never saw them both at once. He saw now one, and afterwards, by slow honest conversion, the other." According to Wilson, leaders can alter their convictions (and sometimes they should), but they must never be ambiguous or equivocal. "The consistency of unhesitating opinion," Wilson concluded, "counts as an element of success and prestige."[6] Even those who disagree with the substance of the conviction will admire the integrity and determination of firm leadership.

Conviction is also essential to achieve the ultimate goal of politics: to facilitate the progress of society. According to Wilson, society evolves and achieves higher stages of development, and leadership is necessary to move society closer to its ideal condition. In some cases, Wilson acknowledged, compromise is justified, "But it depends almost altogether upon how you conceive and define compromise whether it seem hateful or not. . . . Compromise in politics [need not] be dishonest—if only it be progressive."[7] Wilson accepted that it might be necessary to "adjust views" or "placate antagonisms," but as soon as he made this assertion, he followed it up with a discussion of leadership that does not "wear the harness of compromise." Compromise usually constrains leadership and impedes progress, whereas conviction can move society forward.

Leadership that facilitates change often requires that conviction precede calculation and that ideas be defended even when they seem unpopular. Wilson described what happens at critical junctures in political development when "one of those great Influences which we call a Cause arises in the midst of the nation":

> Men of strenuous minds and high ideals come forward with a sort of gentle majesty as champions of a political or moral principle. . . . They only speak their thought, in season and out of season. . . . They stand alone: and oftentimes are made bitter by their isolation. They are doing nothing less than defy public opinion, and shall they convert it by blows? Yes, presently the forces of the popular thought hesitate, waver, seem to doubt their power to subdue a half score stubborn minds. Again a little while and they have yielded. Masses come over to the side of reform. Resistance is left to the minority and such as will not be converted are crushed.[8]

Here Wilson described the dominant strategy of conviction politicians, leaders who speak their thought "in season and out of season." They convert "by blows," and when conversion fails, they do not seek consensus but instead crush their opponents. This approach excludes the compromise and conciliation characteristic of "the trimmer."9 It requires "men of strenuous minds and high ideas," and it is a type of leadership suited to particular circumstances.

Conditions are critical for Wilson, who insisted that "no cause is born out of its time."10 As he explained it, "Every such movement has been the awakening of a people to see a new field for old principles. These men who stood alone at the inception of the movement and whose voices then seemed as it were the voices of men crying in the wilderness, have in reality been simply the more sensitive organs of Society—the parts first awakened to consciousness of a situation. . . . They are early vehicles of the Spirit of the Age."11 Citing several examples, Wilson asked, "Were not the Corn Laws repealed because they were a belated remnant of an effete system of economy and politics?"12 (In another part of the speech, he declared, "Is Irish opinion ripe for Home Rule, as the Liberals claim? Very well then: let them have Home Rule.")13 Reform-minded leaders are able to "hear the inarticulate voices that stir in the night-watches, apprising the lonely sentinel of what the day will bring forth."14 Circumstances might be ripe for reform, but leadership is necessary to bring it to fruition.

According to Wilson, even when the public demands are inarticulate, "the ear of the leader must ring with the voices of the people."15 The leader's task is to hear the call for change, detect public sentiment, and give it the coherence it would otherwise lack; in short, the leader must identify the forces of change and then articulate and advance the general will. Wilson believed "[t]hat the general sense of the community may wait to be aroused, and the statesman must arouse it; may be inchoate and vague, and the statesman must formulate and make it explicit. . . . The forces of the public thought may be blind: he must lend them sight; they may blunder: he must set them right."16 When public opinion proves vague or fragmented, an unusual opportunity exists for strong decisive leadership. In such circumstances, Wilson alleged, "Men are as clay in the hands of the consummate leader."17 Despite his emphasis on the power of such consummate leadership, Wilson described a relationship between the leader and the public that is essentially reciprocal: The public is prepared for change (and might call for it); the leader identifies the "right" policies and then molds public opinion in specific, concrete ways.

Wilson insisted that the type of leadership he advocated is democratic. To make his point, he drew on the experience of Gladstone and addressed the allegation that this consummate leader merely followed rather than led his public:

When an Englishman declares that Mr. Gladstone is truckling to public opinion in his Irish policy, he surely cannot expect us to despise Mr.
Gladstone on that account, even if the declaration is true, inasmuch as
it is now quite indisputably the last part of the Nineteenth Century,
and the nineteenth is a century, we know, which has established the
principle that public opinion must be truckled to (if you will use a dis-
agreeable word) in the conduct of government. A man, surely, would
not fish for votes (if that be what Mr. Gladstone is doing) among the
minority. . . . He must believe, at any rate, that he is throwing his bait
among the majority. And it is a dignified proposition with us—is it
not?—that as is the majority, so ought the government to be.[18]

Wilson focused on Gladstone's efforts in the early 1890s, when majority
opinion had formed in support of home rule, but he declined to discuss
Gladstone's critical role in the formation of that opinion. (In any event, Wilson's use of the parenthetical suggests that he disagreed with the Englishman's allegation.) Perhaps Wilson feared that emphasis on Gladstone's bold
initiative and independence would make the type of leadership he advocated
seem terribly undemocratic or illiberal (especially if "men are as clay").

The reciprocal relationship between leaders and followers that Wilson endorsed catches him in a conceptual double bind. The leader he admired ad-
heres to conviction, identifies and promotes the "right" ideas, but Wilson
insisted that this type of leadership is also sensitive to public sentiment. Yet
when Wilson emphasized the leader's responsiveness to public opinion, he
needed to address the charge that "truckling to public opinion" is merely the
method of the demagogue. What distinguishes the statesman from the demagogue is the former's adherence to conviction or principle, but Wilson
could not make that distinction without engaging in circular reasoning.

Instead, Wilson attempted to establish other criteria to distinguish the
"delicate duties of the popular leader" from the not so "delicate crimes of the
demagogue."[19] For Wilson, motivation provides a clear distinction between
the demagogue and the statesman: "The one ministers to himself, the other
to the race."[20] Yet the U.S. system was designed to ensure that "interest coincide with duty." The constitutional framers understood that self-interest
could serve the public good (and, conversely, good intentions could harm
the public). Indeed, Wilson's own pursuit of a political career to satisfy his
personal longings would not keep him from rendering leadership that also
served his country. For good reason, Wilson did not rely exclusively on motivation as the distinction between demagoguery and his ideal leadership. He
articulated additional criteria based on the nature and the pace of change.

Wilson's preferred leader facilitates change that advances society's progress while keeping it within the realm of established tradition. As he explained, "Leadership, for the statesman, is interpretation. He must read the common thought: he must test and calculate very circumspectly the preparation of the nation for the next move in the progress of politics. If he fairly hit the popular thought, when we have missed it, are we to say that he is a demagogue? The nice point is to distinguish the firm and progressive popular thought from the momentary and whimsical popular mood, the transitory or mistaken popular passion."[21] Wilson added, "There is initiative here, but not novelty; there are old thoughts, but a progressive application of them."[22] The task of interpretation requires not only that leaders read the public mind; they must also understand their nation's political development and keep it on the path of progress.

In another context, Wilson encouraged "a return to old and well-recognized principles, but a return to them in such a way as will give them a new interpretation and a new meaning for the time we live in." He believed that leaders should reexamine "old principles, seeking such a reformulation of them as will adapt them to the circumstances of a new time."[23] Wilson considered the nature of proper change—the redefinition of fundamental principles—a constraint on leadership, but the leader chooses which principles to apply and delivers the definitive interpretation. In the practice of conviction politics, leaders who redefine liberal principles demonstrate that the boundaries of interpretation often provide weak constraints.

According to Wilson, as leaders redefine old principles to suit new circumstances, they should also ensure that change occurs slowly: "The evolution of [society's] institutions must take place by slow modification and nice all-round adjustment."[24] Wilson could have distinguished his ideal leader from the demagogue by declaring that leaders should preserve institutions while demagogues destroy them. But Wilson did not object to institutional evolution, so long as it takes place gradually and under the guidance of enlightened leadership.

Furthermore, Wilson expressed no concern that institutional evolution might result in institutional decay, thereby increasing the opportunity for demagoguery. He simply refused to consider institutions appropriate or desirable constraints on leadership. Instead, Wilson held "that the instructed few may not be safe leaders, except in so far as they have communicated their instruction to the many, except in so far as they have transmuted their thought into a common, a popular thought."[25] Public opinion, not political institutions, should define the limits of leadership.

Wilson's distinctions between the popular leader and the demagogue became more blurred when he identified the essential tools of leadership. Wilson emphasized the importance of style as "an instrument," something that has no "real beauty except when working the substantial effects of thought or vision."[26] Certainly, demagogues as well as many other types of leaders cultivate style as the means to realize their vision. (Indeed, demagogues are more likely than most leaders to possess "vision" or at least to appear visionary.) Wilson considered the most effective style one that is rooted in rhetoric,[27] but here again he recommended an approach characteristic of demagogues. Finally, when Wilson compared political leaders with religious ones, he highlighted the critical role of emotion in the relationship between all leaders and their followers. Wilson declared, "I do not believe that any man can lead who does not act, whether it be consciously or unconsciously, under the impulse of a profound sympathy with those whom he leads—a sympathy which is insight—an insight which is of the heart rather than of the intellect. The law unto every such leader as these whom we now have in mind is the law of love."[28] Emotion runs both ways in the relationship between leaders and followers: Leaders experience heartfelt sympathy for the people, while they are able to arouse public passion for political purpose. According to Wilson, a leader should adopt a style "to ravish the ear of the voter at the hustings."[29] Wilson rejected reliance on reason, but in doing so, he removed yet another constraint on leaders and eradicated one more distinction between liberal leadership and dangerous demagoguery.

Ultimately, Wilson failed to provide rigorous, analytic criteria for distinguishing his ideal leader from the demagogue. He alerted his audience that he would not employ traditional standards and insisted, "You must allow me to make my condemnations [of the demagogue] tally with my theory of government."[30] By the 1890s, his "theory" had changed substantially, although it would remain a vision of popular government with dynamic leadership at its core.

Throughout his academic career, Wilson altered his view of U.S. government and its capacity to produce the type of leadership he considered desirable. In 1885 he argued that the U.S. system was flawed by the dominance of Congress, an institution whose committee structure fragments authority and diffuses responsibility.[31] As a remedy, Wilson initially proposed a constitutional amendment that would change the system to a parliamentary model. After he witnessed the Cleveland presidencies, however, Wilson became convinced that strong presidential leadership could be exercised without constitutional amendment.[32] Such leadership only requires some political change—reform of the presidential nominating process[33] and innovation in executive-legislative relations[34]—but the will and talent of the president can ultimately determine the character of the government.

The changes Wilson observed between 1885 and 1908 altered both his conceptions of U.S. government and his plans for a career. When he expressed his frustration and despair in his 1885 letter (the same year he published *Congressional Government*), Wilson told his future wife, "My disappointment is in the fact that there is not room for such a career [as a statesman] in this country for anybody, rather than the fact that there is no chance for me."[35] In 1908 his published work reflected a more optimistic view of the prospects for dynamic leadership. In *Constitutional Government*, Wilson compared (and contrasted) the administrations of George Washington, Andrew Jackson, Abraham Lincoln, and Cleveland, and he concluded, "Governments are what politicians make them and it is easier to write of the President than of the presidency."[36] Wilson came to believe that even without formal constitutional change, the U.S. system could produce dynamic leadership capable of creating a new political order.

Four years later, Wilson would occupy the presidency and begin to make a new liberal government. His ears ringing with the voice of the people, by 1912 Wilson could hear the call for change and the demand for strong leadership. Circumstances had become ripe for the type of leadership Wilson envisioned, and he was prepared to become the "vehicle of the Spirit of the Age."

President Wilson and the Practice of Conviction-Style Leadership

A number of voices found expression in the age when Wilson decided to put to practice his vision of leadership. The demands of farmers and laborers—groups first organized in the nineteenth century—became more articulate at the start of the twentieth. The appeal of socialism started to resonate and register substantial support in electoral politics. Finally, a new phenomenon known as Progressivism emerged to comprise a chorus of calls for reforms. Wilson would interpret these voices and then attempt to harmonize the discordant elements by composing a new theme for the liberal tradition.

In one case, however, Wilson would deliberately and consistently halt the progress of reform: He made no attempt to advance the civil rights of African Americans. To the contrary, his racism—both social and political—was apparent in his behavior and his thought. When Wilson appealed to African Americans for their support in 1912, he promised the NAACP that he would "assist in advancing the interests of their race." Nevertheless, once he secured election, the president even refused to appoint a privately financed National Race Commission. He allowed racial segregation to be institutionalized in the federal government, and African Americans who objected were promptly dismissed. Wilson's blatant and vicious racism serves as a reminder that the term "conviction politics" is morally neutral: Its desirability ultimately depends on the nature of the convictions. Wilson's avowed convictions about race hurt African Americans, while his convictions concerning the condition of other "out-groups" enhanced their status and improved their welfare.

Wilson was willing to respond to the demands of farmers, for example, who in the early 1900s continued to issue calls for reform after achieving some success in the nineteenth century. Farmers had welcomed internal improvements, but they soon became victimized by the exorbitant rates that the railroad companies set. By the late nineteenth century, the National Grange of the Patrons of Husbandry had won control of many state legislatures in the West and South, and farmers were able to secure early legislation to regulate the railroads. At the national level, farm organizations lobbied for passage of the Interstate Commerce Act (1887) and the Sherman Anti-Trust Act (1890), although a Supreme Court decision in 1895 rendered the latter largely ineffectual.

In addition to the Grange, the Farmers Alliance—a conglomeration of state organizations with divergent concerns—campaigned to secure higher agricultural prices, lower transportation costs, and reform of the nation's financial system. The Farmers Alliance had formed the core of the Populist party in 1892 and found a champion in Democratic presidential candidate William Jennings Bryan in 1896. By the start of the twentieth century, free silver had ceased to be an issue and the Populists had disbanded, but farmers persisted in demanding new national legislation, even though regional differences kept them from speaking with a single voice. President Wilson would respond to their calls for change first by promoting tariff and currency reform and later by endorsing more radical measures.

Organized labor also continued its efforts initiated in the nineteenth century. The Knights of Labor had flourished in the 1880s: Its goals were traditional liberal ones—to enable workers to climb the economic ladder—and it opposed any militant action such as strikes. Despite its own moderate approach to reform, support for the Knights dwindled following the Haymarket riots in 1886. The American Federation of Labor (AF of L) quickly took its place and campaigned for higher wages and shorter hours. By 1901, the AF of L had more than a million members. (From 1896 to 1910 union membership tripled.) President Wilson would meet frequently with AF of L president Samuel Gompers; Wilson was the first president to address an annual convention of the AF of L; and he appointed a trade unionist as secretary of labor. More significant, by 1916, Wilson would promote a number of labor laws designed to improve workplace conditions and employee wages.

Unions in the U.S. would never provide the basis for a major political party as they would in Britain, but in the early twentieth century, socialism gained greater support from the electorate than it did at any other juncture in political development. The Pullman strike had made Eugene Debs a national hero.

While in jail for contempt, Debs read Karl Marx's *Capital,* Edward Bellamy's *Looking Backward,* and other socialist works. By 1897 he had become an avowed socialist and would run for president as the Socialist party candidate in five consecutive elections. In the 1912 elections, Debs secured close to 900,000 votes. Wilson never embraced the cause of socialism, but he and others would promote many reforms that served to blunt the appeal of socialism and undercut its support.

In the early twentieth century, many forces for change fell under the umbrella of the "progressive movement," and Progressivism quickly became the label used to characterize the spirit of the age. More accurately, the Progressive phenomenon comprised several distinct movements with a range of reform objectives.

One contingent, largely composed of journalists, campaigned against corruption and inefficiency in government. Theodore Roosevelt ridiculed the reform-minded reporters and nicknamed them "muckrakers"—after a character from John Bunyan's *Pilgrim's Progress,* the man with a muck rake so obsessed with the filth at his feet that he neglected to notice the "celestial crown" offered to him in exchange. Like the Mugwumps before them, many of whom were also journalists, muckrakers took the disparaging remark as a compliment and wore the nickname as a badge of honor.

Several other groups called themselves Progressives. A second set of Progressives picked up where the Grange and Populist movements left off and campaigned primarily for regulation and control of big business. Professional social workers comprised a third element of Progressivism: The economy was prosperous, but the gap between rich and poor continued to widen. Settlement workers took up the cause of the urban poor, and, in general, social workers lobbied for social welfare legislation, especially child labor laws. Finally, Progressive reformers tended to support the cause of woman's suffrage. Whatever their ulterior motives might have been, Progressives sought sweeping changes in politics, economy, and society, and Progressive thought reflected the various, sometimes contradictory, approaches and goals of the reformers.

Progressive political thought has often been divided into two schools: the New Nationalism, a phrase Theodore Roosevelt borrowed from Herbert Croly, and the New Freedom, the label Wilson adopted to describe his presidential campaign agenda.[37] Roosevelt's New Nationalism explicitly endorsed expansion of the size and reach of the federal government to ensure greater equality. As Croly described it, the New Nationalism advocated Hamiltonian means to secure Jeffersonian ends. Wilson's New Freedom was more traditionally liberal: It simply sought to restore free market conditions (equal opportunity rather than equality of conditions). Yet distinctions between the two schools can be overdrawn. Wilson's early scholarship reveals his belief that the state should be used to achieve broad social and economic goals; as governor, he put to practice this belief; and by 1916, he abandoned any remaining concerns he had about maintaining traditional liberal limits on the size and scope of government.

As early as 1889, Wilson envisioned an active, expanded role for the state to serve the interests of society at large. In his comparative politics textbook, *The State,* he ridiculed the "extremists who cry constantly to government, 'Hands off,' 'laissez faire,' 'laissez passer'!" and refuted the notion that government is a necessary evil.[38] According to Wilson, "modern individualism has much about it that is hateful, too hateful to last."[39] "Selfish, misguided" individualism created "the modern industrial organization [which] has so distorted competition as to put it into the power of some to tyrannize over many, as to enable the rich and the strong to combine against the poor and the weak."[40] Here Wilson employed language reminiscent of Jackson's and Cleveland's, while he laid the groundwork for a departure from their nineteenth-century notion of limited government.

As Wilson saw it, new conditions call for "adjustment" in the nature and scope of government. The goal of government should be "to bring the individual with his special interests, personal to himself, into complete harmony with society with its general interests, common to all."[41] To achieve this goal, Wilson recommended government regulation: "All combination which necessarily creates monopoly . . . must be under either the direct or the indirect control of society."[42] He preferred regulation to administration, but he did not rule out the former when regulation proves ineffectual.[43] The views Wilson first expressed in his 1889 text would later inform many of his policy initiatives, which started soon after his election as governor of New Jersey in 1910.

Wilson served only one term as governor before he became president, but his record established his credentials as a Progressive who was willing to increase the role of the state to improve social and economic conditions. Before he took office, Wilson pledged to perform as an "unconstitutional governor,"[44] one who would not allow a narrow legal interpretation to restrict his creativity and innovation. Governor Wilson created a strong public utility commission with authority to evaluate the properties of railroad, gas, electric, telephone, and express companies and to fix rates and set standards for these corporations. He also convinced the legislature to enact storage and food inspection laws and secured passage of a workers' compensation law. Furthermore, although Democratic bosses had picked Wilson as their gubernatorial candidate (believing they could easily manipulate a naive college professor), Wilson betrayed their interests and initiated reforms designed to undermine their power base. Open primaries replaced party caucuses as the nominating mechanism, electoral laws were reformed, and cities were authorized to adopt a commission form of government.[45] Like Cleveland, Wilson quickly won a national reputation as a proponent of good government, based on his record of reform and his "outsider" status.

Wilson resembled Cleveland in yet another way: As a presidential candidate, he promised to provide "strong leadership," a pledge that supplied a sharp contrast to the leadership of a deeply divided Republican party. Theodore Roosevelt had challenged incumbent president William Howard Taft by running in the primaries and then tried to translate his popular support into a convention victory. When the Republican convention renominated Taft, Roosevelt took his Progressive followers and formed a separate "Bull Moose" party. In the general election, the Republicans appeared weak and divided, whereas Wilson stood firm, able to articulate his clear convictions without the temptation to trim to win a majority.

Primary contests had taken place in 1908, but they assumed a more central role four years later. In 1912 the *New York Times,* for example, covered every primary contest on page one. Wilson's success in the Democratic primaries revealed his popular appeal[46] and enhanced his credibility within the party. Wilson clearly capitalized on the publicity the primaries can provide, but in the mixed selection system, the convention still posed an obstacle to his nomination. He secured the nomination only after forty-six roll-call votes were taken, the highest number recorded since 1860.[47]

After Wilson won his strategic victory for the nomination, he once again reaped the rewards of positive publicity during the general election campaign. Despite the critical role Bryan's support had played at the convention, the press portrayed Wilson as free of the special interests—radical and machine—that made up the Democratic party. In contrast to his predecessors (and his Republican opponent), Wilson appeared "too firm, too self-reliant, some would say too obstinate" to be captured by entrenched interests. Much of the press overlooked Wilson's own maneuvers and interpreted his nomination as "the triumph of individual convictions over the intrigues and the bargains of the bosses and the obstructive tactics of selfish rivals." "For the Democratic party," the *New York Times* concluded, Wilson's nomination "means salvation. . . . The Democratic party in the nomination of Governor Wilson is reborn."[48]

The choice of religious metaphor was apt, for Wilson resembled both Cleveland and Gladstone in the fervor of his campaign and the righteousness of his rhetoric.[49] Like Cleveland, Wilson was the son of a Presbyterian minister. He increasingly came to believe that his political career had been preordained, and like Gladstone, he would eventually find a cause that revealed his mission in life. In the 1912 election campaign, Wilson's lofty moral rhetoric resonated with Progressive elements in the public and the press.

The press praised the substance as well as the style of Wilson's conviction politics: "He is a Progressive, and so is in sympathy with the widely prevailing sentiment." Progressives "found in Woodrow Wilson their strongest man," and their choice rendered a clear distinction between the two major parties: "progressivism on one side and conservatism on the other." Consequently, the *New York Times* predicted, "political issues, rather than personalities, are likely to be discussed."[50]

Both the *New York Times* and the *Washington Post* believed that Wilson's nomination had reduced Roosevelt's "bolt to the proportions of a purely Republican quarrel,"[51] and throughout the general election campaign, the papers portrayed Wilson as building positive support for his agenda (rather than merely winning by default). Whereas Roosevelt dodged the issues of tariff and currency reform, Wilson articulated precise positions. (On the third major issue, antitrust legislation, Wilson and Roosevelt held similar views.)[52] According to much of the news analysis, Roosevelt's support was personal, President Taft had lost public confidence, and Wilson's following was distinctly issue oriented.[53] It must have warmed Wilson's heart to read the judgment of the *New York Times* after the election: Wilson won not only because the Republicans were divided, but because, the paper concluded, his victory "was predestined in our politics. It was time."[54]

The *New York Times* also drew explicit parallels between the 1912 and 1892 elections.[55] Both Cleveland and Wilson secured a vote against an incumbent president that had significant policy implications. The tide first turned against the incumbent and his party in both the 1890 and 1910 midterm elections. Furthermore, the tariff provided a central issue in both presidential elections. Finally, Cleveland and Wilson seemed to resemble each other in symbolic as well as substantive ways: Both leaders led revolts against a Republican regime when the Republican party was widely perceived as corrupt.[56]

In the 1912 election, Wilson swept the electoral college, securing 435 votes compared with Roosevelt's 88 and Taft's 8. The popular vote gave Wilson 6,286,000, Roosevelt 4,126,000, and Taft 3,484,000. If Roosevelt's and Taft's supporters had voted for a single candidate, the Republicans would have won a majority, but given the shared Progressive aims of Roosevelt and Wilson, the election can also be seen as a majority's rejection of Taft's conservatism and the status quo. When Wilson took office, he acted quickly in the two areas of public policy where the electorate had most clearly called for change and where Wilson held his firmest convictions: tariff and currency reform.

Passed in October 1913, the Underwood Tariff provided the first significant reduction of duties since before the Civil War. To facilitate competition, Wilson convinced Congress to place food, wool, iron, steel, shoes, and agricultural machinery on the free list. To compensate for lost revenue, the act provided for a graduated tax on incomes (which the Sixteenth Amendment had made constitutional in February 1913). Wilson's move to lower the rates almost shattered his political party, but he adhered to his conviction and ultimately secured the support he needed.[57]

Wilson confronted another considerable challenge when it came to banking and currency reform. The president held a firm conviction that reform was needed, but he had declined to propose a specific plan during the 1912 campaign. Wilson struggled to negotiate a compromise between the conservative chair of the House Banking Committee, Carter Glass, and radical agrarian elements within the Democratic party. Then he resolutely resisted opposition from the banking community and the eastern establishment press.

As a result of his resolution, the Federal Reserve bill passed Congress on December 23, 1913. The bill established twelve Federal Reserve Banks, which were subject to regulation and supervision by the Federal Reserve Board. All national banks and state banks that chose to participate would invest 6 percent of their capital in the Reserve Bank; the Reserve Bank would issue paper money or Federal Reserve notes in exchange for the paper that member banks took as security from commercial and agricultural borrowers. Federal Reserve notes were backed up by a gold reserve of 40 percent, and the Federal Reserve Board could veto any changes the Reserve Banks made in their discount rates. Wilson had created a stable, centralized system of banking that was effective and responsible, the nation's first since Jackson destroyed the National Bank.[58]

In 1914 Wilson continued to pursue his New Freedom agenda with legislation designed to regulate corporations. The Clayton Act identified and prohibited many unfair trade practices, made interlocking directorates illegal, and, as a concession to labor, curtailed the use of injunctions in labor disputes. (It also included language that Gompers believed would exclude farm and labor unions from antitrust legislation, although few of his contemporaries shared this interpretation, and Wilson opposed any such provision.) At the same time, Congress established the Federal Trade Commission (FTC) to take the place of the Bureau of Corporations: The FTC had the authority to review business practices and issue cease-and-desist orders to stop the illegal suppression of competition. These bills constituted only modest reform,[59] but following their passage, Wilson concluded that he had achieved the central goals of his New Freedom program.

Wilson's self-congratulatory announcement shocked and dismayed Progressives, who anticipated more sweeping change. As editor of the *New Republic*, Croly derided Wilson's progressive record as sincere but shallow. According to Croly, "Mr. Wilson's sincerity is above suspicion, but he is a dangerous and unsound thinker upon contemporary political and social problems. He has not only . . . 'a single-track mind,' but a mind which is fully convinced of the everlasting righteousness of its own performances and which surrounds this conviction with a halo of shimmering rhetoric. He deceives himself with these phrases, but he should not be allowed to deceive progressive popular opinion."[60] Wilson had fulfilled his campaign pledges to secure tariff and currency reform and antitrust legislation, but Croly was correct to criticize the president for the limited nature of his New Freedom reforms. In 1913–14, Wilson attempted to achieve only traditional liberal goals, but he was about to undergo the type of "slow honest conversion" that he had observed in the career of Peel. Once Wilson could see "the other side," he would embrace more radical reform with the same degree of conviction that he had expressed when he resisted it.

For most of his first administration Wilson advanced Progressive legislation limited to the goals of greater freedom and enhanced competition. Often the president either obstructed or failed to encourage Progressive legislation that employed more extensive state intervention in the economy and society. Wilson opposed labor legislation in the form of the Sundry Civil Bill of 1913 and provisions for rural credits provided by the Hollis Buckley Bill in 1914. In a letter to Glass, dated May 12, 1914, Wilson explained the basis for his opposition to such legislation:

> I feel that it is really my duty to tell you how deeply and sincerely I feel that the Government should not itself be drawn into the legislation for credits based on farm mortgages. . . . I have a very deep *conviction* that it is unwise and unjustifiable to extend the credit of the Government to a single class of the community.
>
> Since I have learned that my *convictions* in this matter are not shared by a considerable number of the gentlemen who have given some attention to this matter in the House and in the Senate, I have felt it my duty to consider the matter very deliberately and very carefully and you can rest assured that I would not express to you the *conviction* I have just avowed if I did not feel it my conscientious duty to do so and if I did not feel privileged to do so because of a study of the conditions and consequences of such legislation. You can see, moreover, how the very fact that this *conviction* has come to me, as it were, out of fire fixes it very clearly and permanently. (emphasis added)[61]

Nevertheless, Wilson would soon alter his "convictions" and advocate the very legislation he adamantly opposed in his letter to Glass.

Wilson's position on rural credits legislation reveals the extent of his conversion in 1916 and signals the emergence of his "new liberalism," a public philosophy that embraced the methods of Croly's New Nationalism. Rural credits remained the central objective of organized farmers, but disagreements concerning the method of supplying credit had blocked the progress of legislation in the first two years of Wilson's presidency. Senator Henry Hollis of New Hampshire and Representative A. F. Lever of South Carolina, the principal proponents of rural credits, drafted a new bill during December 1915 and January 1916. Their measure would create a Federal Farm Loan Board to supervise Federal Land Banks. The revised version of the rural credits bill incorporated elements to satisfy both Progressives and conservatives,[62] but Wilson's approval and his advocacy proved crucial to its success.

On January 28, 1916, Hollis and Lever met to discuss the farm legislation with President Wilson, and immediately the Hollis bill became an administration measure. After two weeks of debate, the Senate approved the bill by a vote of 58 to 5 on May 4, 1916. The House passed a slightly changed version by 295 to 10 on May 15, and Wilson signed the bill on July 17. When he signed the rural credits bill, Wilson explained, "The farmers, it seems to me, have occupied hitherto a singular position of disadvantage. They have not had the same freedom to get credit on their real assets that others have had who were in manufacturing and commercial enterprises, and while they sustained our life, they did not, in the same degree with some others, share the benefits of that life. . . . I sign the bill, therefore, with real emotion."[63] Wilson's "emotional" language invoked images and expressed sentiments drawn from the tradition of Jackson and Cleveland; yet the rural credits bill marked a clear departure from their nineteenth-century policies.

Principle and pragmatism combined to convince Wilson to alter his convictions concerning rural credits. On January 10, the comptroller of the currency, John Skelton Williams, sent his annual report to Congress. Williams's report showed that interest rates for farmers remained usurious in many parts of the country, and that evidence persuaded Wilson that material conditions required a new government policy. Just as the condition of farmers had convinced Peel to repeal the Corn Laws, the circumstances U.S. farmers faced led Wilson to reassess and then reverse his position. Like Peel in another respect, Wilson would cling to his new conviction just as firmly as he had maintained his old one.

In this case, Wilson's new principles also provided political advantages. Frank Odell, the secretary of the American Rural Credits Association, had warned the president, "If the Democratic party fails to give suitable legislation on the subject, it will hurt itself greatly with the farmers, especially in the Middle West. The support of farmers, which would be engaged by rural credit legislation, is necessary to the Democratic party in the Middle West to offset the pro-German vote which will be solidly Republican."[64] Rural credits legislation would provide essential relief to farmers and win their loyalty to the president's Democratic party. Nevertheless, Wilson's clear conviction supporting rural credits was part of an electoral strategy that entailed some risk and sparked substantial controversy.

The response from conservative opponents and much of the press was highly critical of Wilson's conversion. Former governor Myron T. Herrick of Ohio, a leader in the fight for a private system of rural credits, declared, "A use of government cash and government credit is contemplated for private purposes on a scale never attempted in any other country."[65] The *New York Times* leveled a scathing attack on Wilson's policy and depicted the farmer as a victim rather than a victor—"as naive as a Socialist about the impersonal, anonymous power of the State to practice unbounded benevolence."[66] When the bill passed the House, the *New York Times* declared: "[It] creates a monster agency by which the Federal Government might, if it chose to do so, gain such dominion over people's money as has never been dreamed of in any country. It is based not upon any careful study of the requirements of American agriculture, but upon the socialistic experiments of Europe in co-operative finance. . . . And to that alien pattern it adds a theory of Government paternalism in finance which lately has gained great vogue at Washington."[67] Despite critical comment, Wilson quickly implemented the measure. Ten days after he signed the bill, Wilson appointed members of the Federal Farm Loan Board, and a new rural credits system started before the election.

Wilson adopted several other measures to assist farmers. He encouraged the Department of Agriculture to shift its emphasis from scientific research to services for farmers.[68] On July 11, the president signed the Good Roads Act, which established a Bureau of Roads in the Department of Agriculture, with the money to aid states in building highways according to federal standards. A second measure, the Warehouse Act, had been recommended since 1914, and it became law in August 1916. The bill permitted bonded warehouses to issue receipts against certain agricultural commodities, which were good as collateral for loans from national banks. Together with the rural credits bill, these measures improved the welfare of farmers and enhanced Wilson's prospects for reelection.

Wilson's "new liberalism" redefined the realm of public policy in labor legislation as well as farm assistance. In March 1915 Wilson signed the seaman's bill, which strengthened safety requirements and enhanced the contractual rights of sailors. (The president delayed signing the legislation because he remained concerned about its international ramifications, but he had supported its objectives ever since it was first proposed.)[69] In August 1916 Wilson signed the Kern-McGillicuddy bill: Drafted by the American Association for Labor Legislation, the act provided workers' compensation for federal employees. In other cases, the president played an even more active role to advance the interests of labor.

Consider the case of the Keating-Owen child labor bill, a project promoted by the National Child Labor Committee. The bill was designed to prohibit interstate shipping of goods made by using child laborers under the age of fourteen. Keating-Owen passed the House on February 2 but would have died in the Senate without the president's active and enthusiastic support. The Democratic liaison with social workers told the president that the bill constituted a test of his commitment to Progressivism, and the next day, Wilson urged the Senate to allow the measure to come to a vote, insisting that the party's fortunes depended on its passage. Congress adopted the measure on August 8, and when the president signed it on September 1, once again he expressed his "real emotion."[70] Critics viewed Keating-Owen (correctly) as the beginning of new federal regulation under the commerce clause, the legislative power subsequently invoked for much of FDR's New Deal legislation.

Finally, Wilson secured passage of the Adamson Act, which established an eight-hour day for railway workers. On August 27, after negotiations between railway workers and management broke down, the workers called a strike for September 4. The next day, Wilson met with Democratic leaders, and on August 29 he outlined legislation before a joint session of Congress. By September 2, Wilson had signed the bill and averted a national strike. The Adamson Act evoked the same fierce opposition as the rural credits bill did, but when his Republican opponent Charles Evans Hughes seized the issue to revive his flagging campaign, Wilson boldly defended the legislation. The president based his defense on social justice rather than practical necessity and thereby seized the opportunity to advance the principles of his new public philosophy.[71]

Admittedly, electoral considerations figured prominently among the factors that account for Wilson's conversion.[72] From 1912 to 1916, the electoral arena had changed, and with the Republicans reunited, Wilson needed to build a majority. Yet Wilson might have attempted to win a majority by adopting Downsian strategies of ambiguity and equivocation (as his Republican opponent tried to do). Instead, to increase his popularity, Wilson defended his ideas and promoted his principles. In this case, as so often in the practice of conviction politics, the ideological proved to be the pragmatic.

Wilson's shift in 1916 was consistent with some of his early scholarly views of government as well as his concept of leadership.[73] The president might have argued that he proceeded with reform slowly, only after he had discerned the "firm and progressive thought" and distinguished it from the "momentary and whimsical popular mood." As part of his defense against charges of opportunism, Wilson might also have harked back to his own comments on Gladstone and home rule: If his policies won the majority's endorsement, he should not be condemned for "truckling to public opinion" any more than Gladstone should have been. It had been established as a "dignified position," Wilson argued in the 1890s, that "as is the majority, so ought the government to be." The reform measures Wilson adopted in 1916 brought him closer to winning a majority based on the support of Democrats, Independents, and Progressives.

Wilson's grudging support for women's suffrage completed the Progressive agenda. During the 1916 campaign, he declined to endorse a federal suffrage amendment. Nevertheless, when Wilson attended the convention of the National American Woman Suffrage Association in September, he told the delegates, "We feel the tide; we rejoice in the strength of it, and we shall not quarrel in the long run as to the method of it."[74] Wilson had initially insisted that suffrage should be granted by the states, but in his second administration he urged Congress to pass a federal amendment. At the time of the 1916 election, Wilson promoted the principle of women's suffrage.[75] In general, the Democratic platform embraced Wilson's appeal, which combined Progressive policies with the promise of peace.

The results of the 1916 race were close but decisive. Wilson won the electoral college with 277 votes to Hughes's 254; the popular vote was 9.1 million to 8.5 million. Despite his own reputation as a liberal, Hughes failed to win the support of Independents or Progressives. Wilson attracted those voters as well as labor, farmers, women, and socialists. (The Socialist party's vote fell from 900,000 in 1912 to 585,000 in 1916.) Finally, Wilson earned the endorsement of virtually all the independent newspaper editors, including the support of Croly at the *New Republic.*

Initially, the *New York Times* read the result as a personal triumph for the president, whose "force, intellect, and eloquence have broken party lines,"[76] but at the end of the year, the paper emphasized the significance of Wilson's program for Progressivism and peace. The election outcome provided "proof that he has been understood by the great unvocal masses. They were grateful for the constructive legislation enacted by his Administration." (It was as if the editors had studied Wilson's concept of leadership and found that he satisfied his own requirements by successfully interpreting the desires of the "great unvocal masses.") Among his administration's accomplishments, the end-of-year news summary listed the nomination of Louis Brandeis to the Supreme Court, the Adamson Act, the rural credits bill, and the Keating child labor bill.[77] The press and the public expressed high hopes for Wilson's second administration, but the loss of peace would soon put an end to Progressive legislation.

To many observers, Wilson's victory in 1916 had indicated that "his foreign policy was approved by the nation."[78] That policy promised to avoid U.S. entry into World War I, while it also included Wilson's efforts to replace dollar diplomacy with "missionary diplomacy." In his first administration, Wilson and Secretary of State Bryan achieved some initial success,[79] but the president quickly found himself following the policies of his predecessors, authorizing military intervention in the Dominican Republic, Haiti, and Mexico. Wilson endorsed Gladstonian liberalism, especially self-determination, but he believed the U.S. had a moral obligation to promote democracy in the Western Hemisphere, a contradiction that would become even more apparent and problematic for subsequent presidents in the twentieth century. Ultimately, Wilson's idealism found its clearest expression not in his missionary diplomacy but in World War I. Despite his electoral pledge to try to keep the U.S. out of the war, when the decision was made to enter, Wilson provided inspirational leadership. It was a war to end all wars, Wilson told his public, and the outcome would "make the world safe for democracy."

The war effort diverted Wilson's energy and attention away from his domestic agenda. At the conclusion of 1917, the annual end-of-year news summary in the *New York Times* acknowledged that "very little occurred in the closing year that has not been directly or indirectly identified with the war."[80] Again in 1918, the war dominated the news: Victory signaled "the extirpation of military autocracy and the wakening of the international conscience [which] were the great events of the year 1918."[81] Allied victory meant the triumph of democracy in Europe, and U.S. participation in the war marked the beginning of the nation's greatness as a global power. At the same time, however, the war weakened liberal democracy within the U.S.

During the war, Wilson approved legislation that severely restricted civil liberties. The Espionage Act of 1917 imposed fines of up to $10,000 and prison sentences of up to twenty years on anyone found guilty of aiding the enemy or obstructing recruitment. Even worse, the sweeping Sedition Act of 1918 made it a crime to "utter, print, write, or publish any disloyal, profane, scurrilous, or abusive language" about the government, the Constitution, or the army and navy uniforms. (Under this legislation, Debs received a sentence of ten years for delivering an antiwar speech.) The result of war fever, such legislation further fueled it. In addition, restrictions on civil liberties deeply disturbed many Progressives, providing one of many factors that weakened Wilson's 1916 coalition.

The war damaged the coalition in other ways. Wilson's administration had alienated western farmers by controlling the price of wheat, while wartime taxes had angered the business community. Labor had made significant gains during the war, but the unions grew increasingly concerned about the consequences of a return to peace. In 1919, the U.S. experienced a recession, the collapse of farm prices, a wave of industrial unrest, an outbreak of race riots, and a Red Scare. Finally, although Wilson's commitment to a postwar League of Nations did not divide the Democrats, it did serve to unify the Republicans, who had captured both houses of Congress in the 1918 elections. Wilson's subsequent battle to secure Senate ratification of the Versailles treaty, which included a provision for the creation of a League of Nations, prevented the president from pursuing any further Progressive reform or postwar reconstruction.

Wilson was determined to establish an international organization to secure world peace and ensure U.S. membership in it. He pursued his cause with zeal comparable only to Gladstone's enthusiasm for home rule. Each man viewed his political crusade as his ultimate mission in life, as a vision divinely inspired that required complete, unswerving devotion. Like Gladstone, Wilson would never have the opportunity to see his vision fully realized.

The president outlined his proposed plan for peace in the form of "Fourteen Points," which he delivered to Congress on January 8, 1918. Classic liberal principles of self-determination, freedom of the seas, and free trade constituted much of the body of Wilson's text, but the League of Nations was the heart of his proposal. To ensure support for the league at the Paris peace conference, Wilson was prepared to sacrifice many other aspects of his plan, and as a consequence, the final treaty was extremely harsh—far from the "peace without victory" that Wilson had hoped for in 1917. Instead, the Versailles treaty inflicted severe war reparations on Germany and included a humiliating war-guilt clause. Despite the treaty's substantial shortcomings, Wilson returned to the U.S. committed to securing its ratification.

Yet Wilson took no steps in preparation for the battle he would face in the Republican Senate. His personal participation in Europe meant that he was forced to neglect domestic politics. Furthermore, Wilson selected only one Republican (who was not a member of Congress) for membership in the U.S. peace commission. As a result, Republicans could not share credit for either the treaty or the league; Wilson had effectively shut them out. He offered no political advantages to senators who might otherwise have broken away from partisan ranks and voted for ratification. Moreover, members of the Senate from both parties resented the president's autocratic methods. In March, even before the peace conference concluded, thirty-seven Republicans, led by Henry Cabot Lodge, signed a statement opposing U.S. membership in the league.

Senator Lodge proposed fourteen reservations to the treaty (designed to match Wilson's fourteen points), but Wilson adamantly refused to accept any reservations or amendments, only interpretations. Rather than reach a compromise with the Senate, Wilson took his case to the people. In September he embarked on a national tour to promote the league, but on September 25 he collapsed in Colorado; shortly after he returned to Washington, he suffered a major stroke. For two months, while Wilson struggled to recover, Lodge labored to build a majority that would support his reservations. On November 19, Wilson ordered Democratic senators to vote against the treaty, and it was defeated. In early 1920 when the Senate reconsidered the treaty, Democrats defied Wilson's directions, but they failed to secure ratification. Eventually, in July 1921, Congress passed a joint resolution to formally end the war.

Throughout the battle, Wilson depicted his position as a matter of principle. When Lodge proposed to amend Article 10, the part of the treaty that described the relationship of member states to the league, Wilson stubbornly resisted any compromise, even though his behavior ensured his defeat. According to one interpretation, Lodge triggered a pattern of behavior—rooted in rigidity and resistance—that stemmed from the president's relationship to his father.[82] Another study has supplied persuasive evidence that the stroke Wilson suffered affected his mental and emotional state.[83] Yet Wilson was also acting out the role that, in his scholarship, he had envisioned for a leader.

In promoting the League of Nations, Wilson finally found an opportunity to demonstrate that he was no mere opportunist or demagogue. In his own mind, his rigid adherence to conviction might have enabled him to join the ranks of "men of strenuous minds and high ideals [who] come forward with a sort of gentle majesty as champions of a political or moral principle." He was speaking his thought "in season and out of season." He stood alone and was certainly made bitter by his isolation. Long after he lost his battle for the league, Wilson knew he appeared as a man "crying in the wilderness," but believed he was in reality simply one of the "more sensitive organs of Society— the parts first awakened to consciousness of a situation." In his last speech, delivered on the steps of his home to a crowd of veterans, Wilson declared, "I am not one of those that have the least anxiety about the triumph of the principles I have stood for. I have seen fools resist Providence before, and I have seen their destruction, as will come upon these again, utter destruction and contempt. That we shall prevail is as sure as that God reigns."[84] As Wilson attempted to realize his scholarly vision of leadership, he also unwittingly showed how personal traits could thwart a leader's ability to achieve change.

Wilson's personal shortcomings were as apparent to other world leaders as they were to his adversaries at home. World War I had provided the first opportunity for a U.S. president and a British prime minister to establish a personal rapport. When Wilson attended the Paris peace conference, he was the first president to leave U.S. territory while in office. In doing so, he defied a nineteenth-century norm that impeded the ability of presidents to develop relationships with foreign leaders through close, personal contact. (In the U.S. Wilson's critics condemned his initiative and considered it unconstitutional.) Unfortunately, Wilson's personal qualities undermined the opportunity that his daring initiative created.

President Wilson's religious zeal on behalf of the league always irritated and often exasperated his colleagues at the peace conference, including his British counterpart, Lloyd George. The British prime minister shared the sentiments expressed in the president's fourteen points and endorsed the league, but Wilson's sermonizing puzzled and amused Lloyd George. The prime minister recalled, "I really think that at first the idealistic President regarded himself as a missionary whose function it was to rescue the poor European heathen from their age-long worship of false and fiery gods. He was apt to address us in that vein, beginning with a few simple and elementary truths about right being more eternal than force." According to Lloyd George, leaders of the Allied nations were "impatient at having little sermonettes delivered to them."[85] Frances Stevenson, who accompanied Lloyd George to Paris, also observed Wilson's fanatical devotion to his league. "By the way it is a pity that history has been deprived of Wilson's first speech on this subject," Stevenson wrote and then mocked, "He explained in his speech how Christianity had failed in its purpose after 2,000 years. But the League of Nations was going to go one better than Christianity and would supply all defects."[86] Lloyd George's view of Wilson was only slightly more tolerant than that of Clemenceau. (The French president compared talking to Wilson with the experience of talking to Jesus Christ and wryly observed that since mankind had been unable to keep God's Ten Commandments, it was unlikely to do better with Wilson's fourteen points.) At Paris, Wilson's self-righteous preaching won few converts to his cause and threatened to alienate some of those who were already members of his flock.

Wilson made matters worse by implying that he understood European public opinion better than the European leaders did. As Wilson saw it, he had a world "mandate" for his fourteen points, including the League of Nations, a perspective that struck the others as strange given Lloyd George's overwhelming landslide reelection and Clemenceau's recent victory (in the same year that Wilson's party lost control of Congress). Wilson behaved as if he considered the electoral process—liberalism's mechanism to register public sentiment—less significant than his own ability to read the public mind. He expressed this view long before the peace conference, in his "Peace Without Victory" address to the U.S. Senate, when he declared:

Perhaps I am the only person in high authority amongst all the peoples of the world who is at liberty to speak and hold nothing back. I am speaking as an individual, and yet I am speaking also, of course, as the responsible head of a great government, and I feel confident that I have said what the people of the United States would wish me to say. *May I not add that I hope and believe that I am in effect speaking for liberals and friends of humanity in every nation and of every programme of liberty? I would fain believe that I am speaking for the silent mass of mankind everywhere who have as yet had no place or opportunity to speak their real hearts out.* (emphasis added)[87]

Wilson thought he could discern the "general will" on a global scale, and he believed he was better equipped to do so than anyone else.

David Lloyd George

As Lloyd George saw it, personal traits, not political convictions, had clipped Wilson's wings. Lloyd George praised Wilson as a "noble visionary" and an "exalted idealist," but he also considered the president stubborn and arrogant and "a man of rather petty personal rancours."[88] "This extraordinary mixture of real greatness," Lloyd George concluded, was "thwarted by much littleness."[89] Lloyd George shared Wilson's lofty vision and high ideals, but the president's rigid personal qualities provided a stark contrast to the flexible character of his British counterpart.[90]

If Wilson provided a caricature of the conviction politician, then Lloyd George's behavior at the Paris peace conference must have supplied a sharp contrast. In this case, the British prime minister succumbed to pure expediency. Lloyd George's behavior was certainly less lofty than Wilson's, but perhaps more easily explained: Lloyd George proved constrained by his electoral pledges, limited by Conservatives in his coalition government, and frequently forced to travel back to London to address Parliament. In general, Lloyd George seemed sensitive to institutional constraints (and political reality) in ways that Wilson was not. Rather than sympathize with Lloyd George's constraints, Wilson was disgusted by the prime minister's pragmatism and apparent lack of principle. Only a couple of years earlier, the roles had been reversed. In 1916 Wilson tried to mediate by asking the two sides to state their terms for peace. At the time, Lloyd George told an American journalist, "The fight must be to the finish—to a knockout."[91] Neither personalities nor timing was right for a "special relationship" between Wilson and Lloyd George.

To a great extent, interpersonal conflict kept the two leaders from pursuing their common goals. At the peace conference, the aims of the U.S. and

Britain dovetailed: Wilson wanted his fourteen points, and Lloyd George hoped to keep Germany strong enough to preserve the balance of power. In other words, both wanted to check French demands, but Wilson and Lloyd George made separate and largely unsuccessful assaults on the French position.[92] When Lloyd George proposed to soften the terms of the treaty (rather late in the game), Wilson sulked and remained silent. In the end, Wilson's extreme adherence to conviction and Lloyd George's political maneuvers clashed, creating dire consequences for the future of international liberalism after the war.

Despite their personal conflicts during the peace conference, years later Lloyd George would applaud several aspects of Wilson's leadership style. In his memoirs, Lloyd George assessed Wilson's strengths and weaknesses in a manner that reveals a great deal about the British prime minister's personal qualities and political style. He found Wilson's "stern and dauntless Radicalism" appealing and considered it admirable to provoke the disdain of certain enemies. Lloyd George observed that President Wilson "was disliked by Wall Street and feared by millionaires," and he added, "I had not myself been a particular pet of financiers or of the ultra-rich."[93] The prime minister also "admired [Wilson's] oratory—his phrases which were like diamonds, clear cut, brilliant, if hard."[94] Essentially, he endorsed those aspects of Wilson's style that he believed characterized his own leadership: Dauntless radicalism and brilliant oratory constituted critical components of conviction politics for Lloyd George.[95]

Lloyd George developed a distinctive oratorical style, in which he adopted (and adapted) traditional practices of the Welsh preacher. In fact, Lloyd George was raised by his uncle, a Baptist preacher famous throughout North Wales for his rousing sermons. Uncle Lloyd would start his sermon in a soft, slow voice and then intensify his speech until he entered a trancelike state known as the "hwyl," which induced a dazed or excited condition in members of his congregation.[96] Lloyd George found he needed to adapt this approach to English listeners because he believed it was essential to capture their attention at the start, but his speech would also create a crescendo and culminate in a peroration that enraptured his audience. According to one observer, "[W]hen he spoke, the wonderful voice, every note of it under absolute control, would cause thrills to pass through those who listened, making them laugh and cry alternately, and always ending by rousing them in a frenzy of enthusiasm."[97] Even more so than Wilson, Lloyd George relied on his oratory to arouse popular passions and cultivate a personal following.

Lloyd George's oratorical style was more emphatic and pronounced than his ideological zeal. Indeed, among conviction-style leaders, Lloyd George emerges as the least dogmatic. Ideas usually provided a powerful motivating force and defined his broad objectives, but Lloyd George never proved doctrinaire.[98] He launched his career by espousing nineteenth-century radical and liberal ideas.[99] During World War I and its aftermath, he was forced to maneuver to a much greater extent than other conviction politicians were. (He certainly faced a more complex and demanding political environment than the other leaders in this study.) Nevertheless, throughout his career, he seized critical opportunities to promote radical and liberal causes, and ultimately he used both as the basis for building a new public philosophy.

The issue that split the Liberal party in the nineteenth century, home rule for Ireland, provided an early opportunity for Lloyd George to define his own liberalism and begin to develop a political identity. Lloyd George supported Gladstone's home rule campaign, while he was also attracted to Joseph Chamberlain's radical "unauthorized programme" for domestic social reform. Ultimately, serendipity determined his choice: Lloyd George missed a critical meeting of the Chamberlain radicals and ended up staying with the Gladstonian Liberals. He wholeheartedly endorsed home rule for Ireland—as prime minister, he would sign the treaty that made Ireland a free state—but he was disappointed when Gladstone made home rule the single, defining issue for Liberals, thereby neglecting other reforms. In Lloyd George's view, Liberals could not afford to neglect the dire need for social change, and he was dismayed by Gladstone's tendency to equivocate on some radical issues. In the 1885 campaign, Lloyd George criticized Gladstone's party leadership and declared, "Humdrum Liberalism won't win elections."[100] He determined there would be nothing humdrum about the liberalism he would espouse.

Among the issues Lloyd George believed Gladstone neglected, none were closer to his heart than those that pertained to the condition of Wales. Lloyd George had hoped that reforms in Ireland would provide a model for subsequent change in Wales, but he doubted the sincerity of Gladstone's commitments to Welsh disestablishment and other Nonconformist issues such as temperance and education reform. The interests of Wales provided the basis for Lloyd George's earliest and clearest convictions.

In 1886 Lloyd George was a founding member of the nationalist movement Cymru Fydd—"Young Wales"[101]—and a branch secretary of the Anti-Tithe League, which sought to reduce rents and establish land courts in Wales as in Ireland. When he became a parliamentary candidate in 1890, he immediately advocated home rule for Wales and made disestablishment the cornerstone of his campaign. (In his first election address, he revealed his priorities by focusing on Welsh disestablishment, home rule for Ireland and Wales, and land reform.) After narrowly defeating his conservative opponent—a country squire—Lloyd George quickly established his parliamentary reputation by successfully amending the Conservative government's tithe bill and elementary education bill (albeit unsuccessfully speaking on behalf of Nonconformist schools). At the conclusion of Parliament, the young Welsh MP clashed with Gladstone over the clergy discipline (immorality) bill, thereby creating an intraparty division for which he was attacked in the subsequent election campaign.[102]

In 1894 Lloyd George's frustration with his own government's failure to pass Welsh disestablishment led to another revolt, in which he and three other Welsh MPs refused the Liberal party whip. Lloyd George opposed the Liberal government's established church (Wales) bill on the first reading, arguing for disendowment as well as disestablishment. Following the example of the Irish Nationalists, Lloyd George attempted to create a separate Welsh national party at Westminster. Yet when Prime Minister Rosebery renewed the party's pledge to secure disestablishment, all the Welsh MPs (except the four insurgents) expressed their confidence in the government. Lloyd George and the other three rebels then returned to the Liberal fold.

Then Lloyd George turned his attention to promoting the movement back in Wales, where he traveled extensively to encourage the formation of branches of the Cymru Fydd League. In 1895 the Liberal government once again submitted a disestablishment bill, and again Lloyd George opposed it. (This time the government resigned before the second reading.) Back in Wales, Lloyd George failed to unite the North and South Wales Liberal Federations, and only the North joined the Cymru Fydd League. Ultimately, the "Welsh Parnell" abandoned his hope of forming a separate Welsh party in Westminster or in Wales.

During the period of Liberal opposition from 1896 until the end of 1905, Lloyd George shifted the focus of his attention from Wales to other radical causes, and he seized every opportunity to speak about education, trade, land and franchise reform, as well as the war in South Africa. Land reform always constituted one of his central convictions. As a young lawyer, he battled landlords on behalf of tenants, and as an activist and a candidate, he sought land reform modeled after change achieved in Ireland. As chancellor of the exchequer, he would level the first taxes on the land, and as prime minister, he would struggle to secure further reform of the land for public use. Throughout Lloyd George's career, land reform persisted as his preoccupation, and the landed aristocracy—liberalism's traditional enemy—remained the central target of his radical assaults.[103]

In addition to land reform, the franchise provided another radical issue on which Lloyd George expressed firm and consistent conviction. Throughout his career, he endorsed universal male suffrage and women's suffrage. Despite his sympathy and his support, however, suffragettes considered him a hypocrite because he was willing to serve in Liberal governments that refused to pursue franchise reform. The suffragettes were brutal in their attacks on Lloyd George, consistently demonstrating at his scheduled speaking engagements (and frequently preventing him from delivering his speeches), and in one instance burning his home. Lloyd George came to speak out against the methods suffragettes employed, but he never wavered in his support for their cause.[104] In 1917 Lloyd George's government would secure passage of the Representation of Peoples Act, and women (more than thirty years of age) finally secured the vote.

In contrast to most of these issues, the war in South Africa provided a case when Lloyd George did not tap the aspirations of any particular movement but instead acted on his own, out of pure conviction and in opposition to popular sentiment. True to the Gladstonian intellectual tradition of anti-imperialism, Lloyd George opposed the war on several grounds. He argued that imperialist aggression always impedes progress and the universal fight for freedom and that it detracts from reform at home. He depicted South Africa as a small, weak nation suffering at the hands of an imperialist bully. Finally, he pointed out the hypocrisy of the government's action, based ostensibly on the desire to protect the rights of an oppressed minority abroad when franchise reform was needed in Britain.[105] Later Lloyd George shifted his criticism to the conduct of the war, but in every argument he expressed convictions that ran against public opinion and the prevailing war fever.

Finally, on one nineteenth-century liberal issue—free trade—Lloyd George took a purely pragmatic view. He opposed Chamberlain's campaign for tariff reform (protectionism) in the early 1900s, but he later supported such legislation as the 1917 Corn Production Act and the 1921 Safeguarding of Industries Act. Lloyd George never attempted to justify these departures as constituting a conversion in his convictions. Instead, he insisted that he preferred free trade but that practical considerations determined his position on this issue.[106] In any event, protectionism was consistent with Lloyd George's belief in state intervention to promote the general welfare. At the time he approved of protectionist measures, he was advocating state intervention on an unprecedented scale to pursue war aims and achieve domestic reform. By then he had moved far beyond classic liberalism to the creation of a new liberal philosophy and the construction of a modern liberal regime.

Lloyd George never repudiated the principles of nineteenth-century liberalism—on home rule for Ireland, Welsh disestablishment, and women's suffrage, he ensured the final realization of those principles—but he did seize the opportunity to construct a new political order for the twentieth century. According to Winston Churchill, Lloyd George understood the potential for transformation inherent in the historical moment of the Liberal landslide in 1906:

[T]his moment of political triumph occurred in a period when the aspirations of 19th century Liberalism had been largely achieved. Most of the great movements and principles of Liberalism had become the common property of enlightened men all over the civilized world. . . . Thus at the moment when the Liberal Party became supreme, the great and beneficent impulses which had urged them forward were largely assuaged by success. *Some new and potent conception had to be found by those who were called into power.*

It was Lloyd George who launched the Liberal and Radical forces of this country effectively into the broad stream of social betterment and social security along which all modern parties now steer. (emphasis added)[107]

Churchill's assessment overstates the success of traditional Liberalism—some of its goals remained to be attained—but he was correct to identify 1906 both as the pinnacle of the party's success and as the beginning of its demise.

Almost immediately after the 1906 Liberal victory, the government started to lose the support of the middle class, Nonconformists, the Irish, and labor—the voting bloc responsible for the Liberal landslide. Under Herbert Asquith's leadership starting in 1908, the Liberal government encountered the defiance of Protestant Ireland, the army, suffragettes, and workers. Most significant, trade unions were gaining substantial strength and working-class consciousness was rapidly rising, resources that would be tapped and mobilized by the Independent Labour party.

Initially, Lloyd George's radicalism and Nonconformism as well as his natural sympathy for ordinary laborers enhanced his ability to appeal to the working class. As president of the Board of Trade, his first government position, he successfully negotiated critical industrial disputes. In one case, he secured concessions from the railway directors that were sufficient to avert a national strike. After the war, Lloyd George would lose the support of labor, but for much of his career his leadership was preferred by the unions and popular with the working class.

As early as 1906, Lloyd George correctly read the signs of social and economic change when he declared, "I believe there is a new order coming for the people of this country. It is a quiet but certain revolution."[108] In 1908 on the floor of the House of Commons, Lloyd George boldly announced, "These problems of the sick, of the infirm, of the men who cannot find means of earning a livelihood . . . are problems with which it is the business of the State to deal; they are problems which the State has neglected too long."[109] To some extent, Lloyd George's commitment to using the state for social goals stemmed from his affinity with nineteenth-century Radicals, who promoted state action of behalf of the elderly, sick, poor, and unemployed.

Lloyd George has been viewed as the last in the British Radical tradition,[110] but he also advanced and implemented his ideas with his contemporaries at the forefront of his mind. In his first bold move as chancellor of the exchequer, Lloyd George seized the opportunity to attack an old liberal enemy and, at the same time, lay the groundwork for a new liberal state.

From the moment Lloyd George became chancellor in 1908, he demonstrated his determination to transform the relationship between the state and society and reconstruct the political order. To a great extent, he achieved more in this position than he would as prime minister. Like Gladstone in the nineteenth century, Lloyd George used the budget as a vehicle to advance his political philosophy, but his efforts at reconstruction also broke through the constraints of Gladstone's classical liberalism.[111]

As soon as he moved from the Board of Trade to the Treasury, Lloyd George discovered a critical need to raise new revenues. He secured quick passage of the old age pensions bill primarily drafted by Asquith[112] and immediately began to worry about the cost. At the same time, the government needed to find a way to finance its dreadnought program, designed in response to the German naval initiative in the fall of 1908. Moreover, several economic indicators suggested that unemployment would continue to rise. Within Parliament, protectionists were calling for tariff reform as the solution to the deficit, but Lloyd George preferred to preserve free trade. As he assessed the situation, the chancellor declared in dismay, "I have no nest eggs. I am looking for someone's hen-roost to rob next year."[113] Eventually, he found a source of funding by robbing the landlords' hen-roosts.

Lloyd George's 1909 budget became known as the "People's Budget." It increased income tax and death duties, charged earned incomes at a lower rate than unearned, imposed a supertax on incomes above 5,000 pounds, and placed higher taxes on spirits and tobacco and new taxes on cars and gasoline. Yet the most controversial aspect of his budget proved to be the land taxes. They placed a development tax on the added value of land sold where the new value stemmed from the effort and expenditure of the community. They also imposed a tax on increment value and a reversion duty on enhanced value when property reverted to the landlord at the end of a lease. Essentially, Lloyd George had invented a way to achieve social reform through budgetary reform.

His budget accomplished several political objectives as well as his economic goal. It leveled a devastating assault on the traditional enemy of liberalism, the landlords, and it appealed to a traditional constituency within the party, free traders. At the same time, the budget attracted the support of labor and the working class. Lloyd George's innovation proved popular with his party and the people in the country, but it immediately aroused opposition from the press and in Parliament, where the House of Lords vetoed the People's Budget.

To win support for the budget, Lloyd George campaigned for institutional reform of the House of Lords. (See chapter 8.) The result, the Parliament Act of 1911, deprived the House of Lords of their absolute veto,[114] although its immediate impact on legislation produced mixed results for the Liberals. On the one hand, the Lords used their new suspensory veto to delay Irish home rule and Welsh disestablishment; on the other hand, the act removed the Lords as a permanent obstacle to home rule. Lloyd George finally realized Gladstone's ideological objective only by achieving the structural reform Gladstone had been prevented from pursuing. Just as significant, the Parliament Act permitted the passage of the National Insurance Act, which soon followed. Indeed, the People's Budget had a ripple effect and created a wave of reform: The budget led to the battle with the Lords, which produced the Parliament Act, which in turn allowed Lloyd George to institutionalize another innovative idea—a system of national insurance.[115]

In his 1910 budget statement, Lloyd George announced that in the following year he would produce a national insurance bill, which he considered a logical extension of the old-age pensions plan. The cabinet considered his proposal on April 5, 1911, and the bill was introduced on May 4. The bill provided a plan of state insurance to be administered by any private, non-profit agency that applied for official approval ("approved societies"). All working people between the ages of sixteen and sixty-five (who earned less than the lower limit of income tax) would be required to join. At first the proposal met serious opposition from the public and the press, but once again, Lloyd George embarked on a national tour to promote his reform. He also expected the legislation to undergo change during parliamentary consideration, but the Conservative leader Arthur Balfour firmly opposed the measure and declined to reach any compromise.[116] With the new Parliament Act in place, the legislation soared through both houses of Parliament and on December 16 received royal assent. The National Insurance Act created a system of national health insurance that paved the way for the National Health Service established in 1948.

The chancellor's economic innovations and social reforms had made him a popular crusader, but in 1912 a scandal threatened to destroy his reputation as a man of the people. Lloyd George had bought shares in the U.S. Marconi Company, while the English Marconi Company—though a separate organization—secured a government contract. It was not only the appearance of impropriety that created controversy: Lloyd George had bought his shares based on information unavailable to the general public. As a result of the chancellor's skillful maneuvering and the support of his prime minister, a parliamentary select committee exonerated him. Nevertheless, the Marconi affair was the first in a series of scandals concerning Lloyd George's finances. He escaped serious damage in 1912, but this and other scandals would raise questions about Lloyd George's character and contribute to his downfall ten years later.

In the 1913–14 parliamentary sessions, the Liberal government continued to pursue its traditional liberal causes. Home rule and Welsh Church bills became statutes that would go into effect after World War I. To Lloyd George, these causes had started to seem anachronistic, but he maintained his zeal for land reform. In 1912 he had established a commission to study land reform, and in October 1913 he launched a national land campaign. By the summer of 1914, however, World War I made it clear reform would have to be postponed, although some of the commission's recommendations would be included in the wartime Corn Production Act.

Social and economic conditions proved conducive to Lloyd George's success as chancellor of the exchequer, but the war and the weakness of Prime Minister Asquith's leadership put him in the premiership. In 1915 Asquith formed a coalition government, in which Lloyd George served first as minister of munitions and later (for only five months) as war secretary. Lloyd George persistently tried to convince the government to wage a more vigorous war effort, but Liberals were deeply divided over the need for conscription and armaments. Disagreements concerning the conduct of the war culminated in a leadership crisis: Lloyd George appeared to be the only leader able to provide the strong leadership and clear conviction needed to win the war.

Lloyd George insisted that public support could sustain his independent leadership, and he refused to succumb to intraparty pressures. His courage and conviction enhanced his public prestige, but his zeal for the war had alienated the radical wing of his party and evoked the scathing condemnation of the Liberal press. In a letter to his friend and confidant, Sir George Riddell, Lloyd George assessed the situation and explained, "The Radical Party do not control public opinion; the people form their own view. If they are of the opinion that in a crisis like this I am useful—I won't say indispensable—to the nation, as a man who thinks things out and points the way, they will stand by me, and no threats by the Radical Party and no intrigues against me in the Cabinet can injure me."[117] Lord Northcliffe and Geoffrey Dawson (owner and editor, respectively, of the *Times*) greatly assisted Lloyd George in his public relations campaign. While the Liberal press attacked him—convinced that he was simply maneuvering to replace Asquith— Northcliffe portrayed the war secretary as the nation's savior. To a great extent, as Lloyd George predicted, public opinion—molded by the *Times* and other sympathetic newspapers—led to Asquith's fall.[118]

The *Times* as well as much of the popular press urged "reconstruction of the government"[119] and favored Lloyd George's plan for "reform": a newly organized war council without Prime Minister Asquith. When the prime minister at first seemed to accept and then later rejected the proposal, the newspapers described Asquith's change of mind as characteristic of his weak, indecisive leadership. Lloyd George's subsequent resignation was hailed as a "point of principle." The *Times* refused to acknowledge Lloyd George's personal ambitions and instead insisted that for him, "Personal questions, though important, always came second."[120] In this case, it does seem that Lloyd George was more eager to control the conduct of the war than to attain the highest political office.[121] On December 7, after much maneuvering and some confusion,[122] Lloyd George became prime minister.

Lloyd George managed to constitute a new government of ministers from all the major parties. Despite rumors to the contrary, Liberals were willing to serve in his government, and 126 Liberal MPs supported his leadership (while the rest sided with Asquith). Lloyd George also secured the support of the Labour party and included the Labour leadership in his coalition. Members of the Conservative and Unionist party held many of the most significant posts, and Lloyd George formed a partnership with their leader, Andrew Bonar Law, who took responsibility for managing parliamentary affairs. The balance of parties fostered the appearance of national unity, but the coalition also created constraints that the prime minister would try to circumvent.

To enhance his autonomy and augment his authority, Lloyd George adopted many innovations in both administrative strategy and press relations. He immediately constructed a new, streamlined war cabinet and devised his own system of securing advice. During the war, he routinely bypassed the foreign office and relied instead on private advisors. In doing so, Lloyd George made the first move away from reliance on the civil service and toward a system of advising based at Number 10 Downing Street. At the same time, to win over critics in the press, Lloyd George employed two central strategies: He made several press magnates ministers in his government and awarded honors to owners, editors, and principal shareholders of the major newspapers. Lloyd George's distribution of honors also enabled him to build the Lloyd George Political Fund, an independent campaign chest intended to compensate for his lack of party organization. These strategies enhanced prime ministerial authority, but Maurice Hankey was correct in October 1918 when he declared "that the P.M. is assuming too much the role of a dictator and that he is heading for very serious trouble."[123] Extraordinary measures that were tolerated during the war would become subjects of controversy in its aftermath.

World War I not only provided a justification for the expansion of executive authority but also rendered a rationale for rapidly accelerating the government's control of the economy. Among other things, the Defense of Realm Acts gave the government extensive authority to commandeer factories and workshops for the production of war materials. The government managed shipbuilding, regulated the supply of wool and cotton, and controlled food production and distribution. The Corn Production Act of 1917 directed farmers to meet specific targets set by the County Agricultural Committees and backed by the threat to take over the land of those who failed to cooperate. (Its primary objective was to increase production, but the act also guaranteed minimum corn prices and minimum wages for farmworkers.) Essentially, the demands of the war fueled Lloyd George's efforts to engineer new state-society relations.

As in the U.S., the war and the expanded scope of the state carried some significant costs. To his credit, Lloyd George refused to endorse any statutes that would have led to the prosecution of antiwar protesters. On the other hand, in the name of national security, he did condone other practices that infringed on civil liberties. Before the war, the security services routinely conducted internal surveillance of anarchists and Irish nationalists. Those practices were vastly extended during the war. In the spring of 1917, MI5 had compiled 250,000 cards and 27,000 personal files on suspected enemy aliens, even though only 70,000 such adults had been officially identified. During the war and its aftermath, several ministries, sections of the armed services, and MI5 made reports on members of the labor movement. In 1920 the government stopped its surveillance of industrial workers, but it continued its investigation of others on the left. What was deemed necessary for the sake of national security could be redefined and expanded along with the scope of the state itself.

In this atmosphere of rapidly expanding state intervention, Lloyd George also seized the opportunity to design a positive program of social reconstruction. He created a number of committees to explore plans for reconstruction and appointed a wide range of reformers to them.[124] He established a Ministry for Reconstruction under Christopher Addison, which would become responsible for housing policy. He endorsed H. A. L. Fisher's education reform: The 1918 act extended compulsory education to fourteen years and took steps toward the creation of a complete system from nursery school to adult education classes, to be financed by a grant from the government to local authorities. Finally, Lloyd George encouraged the formation of "Whitley Councils," joint committees of employers and unions. Under the Ministry of Labour, twenty industries set up such committees by 1918. These measures constituted a significant program of social and economic reform, although the costs of the programs and the constraints imposed by Conservatives in the coalition would limit their development and their impact after the war.

In addition, Lloyd George secured passage of the Representation of People Act. The product of an all-party conference, the bill transformed the prewar electorate of less than 8 million to one of 21 million, including 8.4 million women voters. The bill conferred manhood suffrage and votes for women at the age of thirty if they were householders or the wives of householders. Plural voting was abolished except for businesses or universities, and the franchise became universal in elections for local government. With this legislation, Lloyd George simultaneously achieved an ideological objective, franchise reform, and a political goal: Men in the armed forces would have an effective vote in the next general election. As a consequence, the Representation of People Act fulfilled one of Lloyd George's radical goals, while it also greatly enhanced his political power.

The new electorate provided a good reason to call a general election immediately after the war, and Lloyd George was eager to capitalize on his reputation as the man responsible for victory. The Liberal prime minister negotiated an agreement with his coalition partners to campaign together (and against most of Asquith's Independent Liberals). He and Bonar Law agreed to send letters to the constituencies, assessing the candidates as pro- or antigovernment. Asquith mocked this process as the distribution of "coupons," and the 1918 contest came to be known as the "coupon election." To justify his campaign against many Liberals, Lloyd George came up with a rationale that greatly increased the likelihood that the Liberal split would prove permanent.

Lloyd George insisted that many Liberals had been unreliable supporters of the government during the war, and in particular he identified as traitors those who voted against him in the "Maurice affair." On May 7, 1918, Major-General Sir Frederick Maurice, director of military operations until April 20, had accused Lloyd George of giving incorrect statements to Parliament. Lloyd George managed to defend himself brilliantly, even though some of Maurice's allegations were valid. As in the Marconi affair, Lloyd George escaped serious damage at the time (although Maurice would go public with his charges again in 1922, when Lloyd George was much more vulnerable). In the 1918 election, however, Maurice had given Lloyd George a pretense for campaigning against many of his former colleagues in the Liberal party. Hence, a Machiavellian maneuver was at least partially concealed by a cloak of patriotic conviction.

The 1918 contest was a classic khaki election, with Lloyd George campaigning as the man who won the war. Initially, he pledged his commitment to "a just peace," but as the campaign wore on, his rhetoric became increasingly vengeful. Succumbing to popular pressure, Lloyd George concluded his campaign by promising a "stern peace." Later, that pledge would constrain him at the peace conference when he would try to secure a more equitable settlement. During the campaign, however, harsh rhetoric about the nature of the settlement bolstered the appearance of strong leadership, an image Lloyd George cultivated at the expense of his liberal, internationalist principles.

Despite the centrality of the war to the campaign, Lloyd George also used the election as an opportunity to promote his program for reconstruction. He promised minimum wages, reduced hours of labor, a housing scheme, and agricultural reform. The *Times* praised his program for reconstruction, which paved a new path for the public to follow, and predicted voters would show "they have no intention of going backward to what may be called without offense an Asquith regime." According to the *Times*, "It would have been so easy to be conventional," but Lloyd George chose instead to advance "progressive social policy."[125] To do so required not only a new public philosophy but also a creative leadership style—free of traditional partisan politics.

In the 1918 election, the coalition won a landslide: Conservative-Unionists secured 478 of the 525 coalition seats; Asquith's Liberals held onto only 30 (Asquith himself lost his seat); and Labour became the official opposition with 60 members of Parliament. The election results delivered a fatal blow to the Liberal party: The handful of Asquith Liberals blamed Lloyd George for the party's demise, and his own coalition Liberals had won their seats only because no Conservative candidates had opposed them. (In some sense, their political fortunes depended on the goodwill of the Conservatives as much as did those of Lloyd George.) The Liberals would never again be fully united and govern on their own, and Lloyd George's repeated attempts to form a new center party had failed. It was clear that he would have to govern as prime minister without the assistance of any party machinery.

Lloyd George actually preferred to govern as he campaigned—as a leader without a party—but he was attempting to do so in an extremely volatile political environment. Moreover, his ability to mold his own following was severely restricted by the need to rely on the Conservatives, the party with whom he had the least in common ideologically and culturally. Not surprisingly, the domestic record of Lloyd George and his coalition government after the war was mixed, although the prime minister did manage to realize some of his goals.

Following the election, Lloyd George immediately returned to the pursuit of land reform, and in this area the constraints imposed by his cost-conscious Conservative colleagues became clear. Three of Lloyd George's reforms became law—the land settlement facilities bill, the Acquisition of Land Act, and the act establishing a Forestry Commission—but the scope of these measures fell short of the prime minister's objectives. In particular, the land settlement facilities bill, which enabled local authorities to purchase land for small holdings, applied only to ex-servicemen, whereas Lloyd George had wanted to extend it to the nation. Moreover, an early draft of the Acquisition of Land Act shocked the radical sensibilities of the prime minister. After reading it, Lloyd George declared, "The Bill was supposed to be one to facilitate acquisition of land for most urgent public purposes, speedily and at a fair price. It has been transformed into a Bill which will be represented as making sure that the landlord gets a good price, that the lawyers get their pickings, and that there should be no undue hurry in the completion of the transaction. . . . The country is in no mood to tolerate reactionaries, high or low."[126] Lloyd George managed to secure some changes (especially diminishing the rewards to be reaped by the lawyers), but he remained dissatisfied with the results of the reforms. Despite their limitations, the land bills moved the state in the direction of progressive reform, and it is doubtful any such change would have taken place at the time without Lloyd George at the helm.

In another effort to alter the state's responsibility for the public welfare, Lloyd George secured approval for the housing and town planning bill, which made local authorities responsible for building houses and required them to submit plans to the Ministry of Health. The government promised to make up the difference between rent and capital costs. In total, the government intended to subsidize the building of one hundred thousand houses within the first year. The actual number fell far short of this target, and Addison's failure led to calls for his resignation. Despite the political controversy that ensued and the limited immediate impact of the legislation, the housing bill was significant for its long-term implications: Housing became a social service of the state.

Lloyd George promoted other significant reforms, although in each case he wanted more than he was able to secure. The Unemployment Insurance Acts in 1920 and 1922 extended Lloyd George's 1911 plan to virtually all workers; the special out-of-work donation for the unemployed, due to end in mid-1919, was extended to March 1920; and old-age pensions were raised. Led by Lloyd George, the coalition government also created Health and Transport Ministries. Finally, Fisher began to put into effect the central proposals of the 1918 education act by establishing a program of school building and instituting evening classes.[127] In all these areas—social security, health, and education—Lloyd George continued to lay the foundations for a new relationship between the state and society.

Lloyd George's program of reconstruction was based on his belief that the state should play an active role in promoting the public welfare, and postwar conditions called for substantial intervention. In former munitions centers, the influx of workers had created housing shortages and unstable industrial relations. Returning servicemen swelled the ranks of the unemployed. Food shortages and high prices hit consumers hard, while profiteering created a public call for greater fairness. To make matters worse, Lloyd George himself had fueled high expectations with his promise to provide a "fit land for heroes to live in," a lofty vision that clashed with the grim reality of postwar Britain. Such conditions were not only conducive to unrest; they were ripe for the rise of socialism.

Lloyd George sincerely believed that the best way to fight socialism was to remove the causes conducive to its success. In 1919, he wrote to Riddell, "It may be that they [the Bolsheviks] are sent by Providence to keep the rich in check. It may be just as well that they should have something to fear. Now that Lenin is here, I hope that he may last for another six weeks, so as to give us an opportunity to carry out reforms which are necessary for the safety of society."[128] To Lloyd George, traditional liberalism needed to be transformed to preserve the liberal tradition in the face of the socialist challenge. To his Conservative coalition partners, this was a powerful and persuasive argument: Most of them did not like Lloyd George and did not share his core convictions, but his reforms were safer than the revolutionary alternative.

Conservatives genuinely feared revolution both in Ireland and at home—whether instigated by Bolshevism or ignited by the "Triple Alliance" of trade unions (the miners and the transport and railway workers). In 1920 St. Loe Strachey summed up the dominant view of the prime minister's Conservative colleagues when he confessed to Sir Edward Carson, "I distrust LG probably more than you do, but at the same time I am terribly afraid of anything like splitting the forces opposed to revolution whether in Ireland or here."[129] Lloyd George's leadership was seen as the bulwark against revolution. When the threats would dissipate, so too would the perceived need for his premiership.

While Lloyd George struggled to secure social reform at home, the subject of Ireland continued to trouble his government. To quell the unrest, the prime minister resorted to repression, a move that bolstered his standing with his Unionist colleagues but aroused the ire of Liberals in Britain and inflamed Republican passions in Ireland. Eventually, Lloyd George negotiated a settlement: The fourth home rule bill, which partitioned the country of Ireland, passed in 1920; in 1921, the Irish Free State was officially declared. The partition of Ireland removed the Irish controversy from domestic British politics (albeit temporarily), but the Unionists never forgave Lloyd George, and the political repercussions of the settlement clearly constituted a contributing factor to Lloyd George's eventual fall.

In addition to Ireland, labor disputes threatened the survival of the coalition government. As in the U.S., a wave of labor unrest followed the armistice, and from 1919 until 1922, Lloyd George spent more and more of his time attempting to avert strikes. Here again, Lloyd George's leadership was viewed as indispensable to the coalition government. Conservatives feared a general strike—in 1920 the Emergency Powers Act restored wartime emergency authority to meet that threat—and the power of the Triple Alliance. To some extent, Lloyd George was a victim of his own success: He had adopted a strategy of divide and conquer to weaken the Alliance and routinely negotiated privately with union leaders. When, during the coal strike in 1921, the Triple Alliance proved weak and fragile, Lloyd George's leadership was no longer vital in the view of the Conservatives.

Furthermore, Lloyd George lost much of his working-class support when he sided with the managers and defeated the miners in the coal strike. He had also refused to implement the recommendations of the Sankey Commission, including nationalization of the mines. In the public mind, Lloyd George was starting to resemble his Conservative colleagues—just as the Conservatives were preparing to dethrone their Liberal premier.

While his leadership was becoming less necessary and less popular, two incidents combined to create the immediate catalyst for his fall. Lloyd George had adopted unusual methods to cultivate public support and to circumvent the bureaucracy; both had enhanced his autonomy and authority during the war. In peacetime, however, those strategies stimulated skepticism and aroused criticism about his leadership style. The two crises that led to calls for his resignation seemed to highlight the dangers inherent in his innovative and independent leadership.

The first focused on one of Lloyd George's methods of building a personal following. In June 1922, the "honours scandal" erupted when Lord Harris asked why Sir Joseph Robinson from South Africa had been nominated for a peerage when he had recently been convicted of fraud. Others quickly joined in the attack: The Duke of Northumberland pointed out that since 1918, forty-nine privy councilorships, peerages, baronetcies, and knighthoods had gone to proprietors, editors, and managing directors of major newspapers. It had been common knowledge that Lloyd George had recommended honors in exchange for funds, and the major parties had followed a similar practice. What was unusual about Lloyd George's distribution of honors was that the money was going to his personal fund and not to a political party. Furthermore, the rate at which Lloyd George had "sold" honors was unprecedented, but he needed to build his funds fast in order to compensate for the absence of party organization. Lloyd George responded to the charges by recommending the formation of a Royal Commission to consider the procedure in the future. As in the past, he narrowly escaped any concrete reprisal, but this time severe damage was done to his reputation. Instead of looking like a popular crusader, Lloyd George appeared preoccupied with his personal fortunes—financial and political.

Immediately following the honors scandal, the "Chanak crisis" raised new questions about Lloyd George's independent and impetuous leadership style. To stop any Turkish advance, Allied troops were stationed in Chanak, a small town on the Asian side of the Straits. All the war-weary Allied leaders—except perhaps Lloyd George—wanted to avoid further military engagement. At a meeting in Paris, the British foreign secretary, George Nathaniel Curzon, persuaded the French and Italians to join him in sending a telegram to Mustapha Kemal, proposing an international conference to resolve the conflict. The telegram was sent on September 23, but on September 29, Lloyd George and Churchill sent a telegram to Lieutenant-General Sir Charles Harington, the commander in the field. They advised him to deliver an ultimatum to the commander of the Turkish troops, threatening to open fire if he failed to comply with their demands. Acting on his own and contrary to the plans or knowledge of his foreign secretary, Lloyd George almost precipitated the start of World War II. Fortunately, Harington ignored the prime minister's telegram. A conference was held, and an agreement was signed in October.

That same month, backbench Conservatives led a revolt that put an end to the coalition government and resulted in Lloyd George's resignation. Immediately, Bonar Law called an election for November 1922. In the general election Conservatives won 344 seats; Labour, 142; Asquith, 60; and Lloyd George's National Liberals, 55. Lloyd George would remain in Parliament but never return to Downing Street.

Yet even after Lloyd George lost hold of the reins of power, Riddell's remark about him would continue to ring true: "He always seems sure that he has taken, or is about to take, the right course."[130] Like other conviction politicians, Lloyd George possessed a sense of mission. He once told Riddell about a letter he had received from a fortuneteller, who wrote that he was destined for a great mission and that guiding spirits would protect him. "That is a remarkable statement," observed Lloyd George, "because I am myself convinced that nothing will be allowed to happen to me until I have accomplished some great work for which I have been singled out. I feel that I shall be quite secure until then." When Riddell asked, "But what is to happen afterwards?" Lloyd George quickly replied, "Ah, afterwards! Well, afterwards I suppose I shall share the fate of all other men who have been selected to perform great works. I shall be left to my fate. I shall be deserted."[131] (As an example, he named Gladstone.) Lloyd George agreed with the soothsayer's prophecy, while he could also foresee his inevitable demise and his immediate subsequent isolation.

As Lloyd George had concluded about Wilson, personal qualities contributed to his own demise. Numerous scandals had raised serious questions about his character—in particular, his trustworthiness. The lack of trust seems to have stemmed from many sources: the frequent scandals concerning his finances, the less-than-forthright responses he delivered to Parliament, and his unconventional private life. In addition to carrying on countless extramarital affairs, starting in January 1913 Lloyd George had a steady mistress (also his secretary), whom he eventually married after his wife died. That relationship was widely known but never the source of public scandal, perhaps because there were no divorce proceedings and his wife protected him. (In contemporary parlance, she "stood by her man.") Nevertheless, Lloyd George's marital infidelity revealed a character flaw that was consistent with the way he conducted his finances, and many people simply believed he could no longer be trusted. A damaging reputation for any political leader, untrustworthiness can be especially devastating for one who tries to govern through extra-institutional means.

Another factor—related to the issue of trust—helps to account for Lloyd George's downfall: While he was never doctrinaire, he became increasingly willing to compromise his convictions as he struggled to cling to power. Especially after the war, he needed to appease the Conservatives in his coalition government; his premiership depended entirely on their continued support. If Wilson's rigidity helps to explain his demise, then Lloyd George suffered from the opposite shortcoming—extreme flexibility. At the end of his premiership, Lloyd George seems to have lost sight of the source of his early success.

To make matters worse, while the coalition forced him into an alliance with his natural enemies, his natural constituency was being rapidly usurped by the Labour party. He struggled to appeal to workers at the same time he decried the dangers of socialism and attacked Labour as a threat to British democracy. During the 1922 campaign, for example, he criticized Independent Liberals for "treating the Labour Party as if it were still merely the left wing of the Liberal Party." Instead, Lloyd George alleged, "It preaches doctrines that would make all the great Liberal leaders of the past shudder. What would Gladstone, Cobden, Bright, Lord John Russell say to the programme of common ownership, state protection and elimination of individual effort which is presented by Labour?"[132] Yet his attack on Labour was disingenuous. By 1922, it had become clear that the British Labour party posed no danger to parliamentary democracy. (In contrast to many of its Continental counterparts, the British Labour party was more social democratic than socialist; it accepted the parliamentary system and embraced much of the British liberal tradition.) Furthermore, Lloyd George endorsed most of Labour's proposed reforms. Indeed, his new liberalism had laid the groundwork for the modern welfare state that Labour governments would eventually construct.

Freed from the need to maneuver and compromise within his coalition government, Lloyd George seemed to rediscover his radicalism in purer form from 1922 to 1945. As Charles Masterman remarked on Lloyd George's return to the backbenches, "I have to confess, when Lloyd George came back to the party, ideas came back to the party."[133] (In reality, he never fully reunited with his former Liberal colleagues; instead, he was content to remain a "genius without a party.")[134] On his own, he wrote numerous policy recommendations, including a "yellow book" entitled "We Can Conquer Unemployment," in which he proposed a British version of the New Deal. In doing so, Lloyd George returned to his radical roots and, at the same time, continued to advocate the growth of the modern welfare state.

After he left Downing Street, he did experience one more triumph, when he toured the United States. Rejected by the political elite and the mass public in Britain, Lloyd George remained a popular hero on the other side of the Atlantic. Warm, enthusiastic crowds greeted him everywhere he went, and the press celebrated his heroic accomplishments as the man who won the war. According to one U.S. correspondent, "At every stage of his American visit he has enjoyed a welcome, genuine to its very core. . . . Lord Robert Cecil touched the American intelligence and conscience. Clemenceau made an appeal for sympathy, but Lloyd George will carry away with him a kind of affection which people of one country rarely, if ever, bestow upon the citizen of another."[135] It was the first time—but not the last—that U.S. citizens would demonstrate their tremendous affection for a British prime minister who had been recently rejected by the British public. More than once, the U.S. public would wonder at the sudden downfall of someone whom they considered a great leader.

Yet circumstances common to the U.S. and the U.K. help to explain the demise of Lloyd George as well as of his U.S. counterpart. The success of conviction-style leadership depends on conditions, and those conditions are subject to change. In both countries, by the 1920s the public and the political elite had grown weary of constant controversy and continuous change. At the start of 1921, the *New York Times* acknowledged that the tide had turned and noted that some "despairers are gloomily speaking of 1920 as the year for America of lost leadership, of lowered aims, of abandoned ideals."[136] On the other side of the Atlantic, according to the *Times's* annual review, "Domestic politics in 1922 were less concerned with the legislation and parliamentary business of the year than with the revival of party politics."[137] During the general election, Conservative party leader Stanley Baldwin and Labour leader Arthur Henderson promised their parties would govern without the supervision of "supermen" such as Lloyd George or Churchill. Just as the Republican win in the 1920 presidential election signaled a return to "normalcy," the Conservative victory in 1922 indicated the public preferred "a policy of tranquility and stability."[138] The moment conducive to conviction-style leadership had clearly come to an end.

Both Lloyd George and Wilson were essentially discredited at the end of their terms in office, and yet both leaders had a major impact on political developments in the twentieth century. When they promoted state action on behalf of the public welfare, they transformed nineteenth-century liberalism and established the foundations for a new edifice. Franklin Delano Roosevelt and Clement Attlee's Labour government often receive credit for the construction of the modern welfare state, but they were building on ground that had been broken by Wilson and Lloyd George. As the architect of the New Deal, FDR considered himself a Wilsonian Democrat and a Progressive reformer. Britain's first Labour government instituted a massive program of reconstruction, but it drew on the blueprint for social security drafted by a Liberal, Sir William Beveridge. Although Labour added its own substantial innovations to the Beveridge report, the 1945 government could tap (as well as shape) an emerging consensus in support of an active state with expansive responsibility for the public welfare. By midcentury, the principles of the new liberalism had won wide acceptance from the public and the political elite in both nations.

After World War II, the British Labour party and the U.S. Democrats continued to take the lead in promoting the growth of the welfare state, while their Conservative and Republican opponents came to accept the assumptions and endorse the goals of the new political order. In the U.K. fundamental agreement on these principles and objectives became known as "Butskellism," a phrase that combines the names of Conservative chancellor R. A. Butler and Labour leader Hugh Gaitskell in the 1950s. In the U.S. the designation of "Me-Too Republicans" captures the same phenomenon: When Democrats recommended reform, Republicans tended to say, "Me too." On both sides of the Atlantic, the major parties and their official leaders shared a vision of the legitimate authority of the state.

Central aspects of the postwar consensus were common to both countries. The teachings of British economist John Maynard Keynes generally guided economic policy. According to Keynes, governments need not balance their budgets; instead, they should stimulate the economy through public spending and strive to combat unemployment. In addition to Keynesian economics, the postwar consensus put responsibility for health and education on the shoulders of the state rather than let it rest with the initiative or ability of the individual. The development of the welfare state continued to shift and erode the nineteenth-century liberal distinction between private and public realms.

In fact Lloyd George and Wilson gave new meaning to the word "liberal." After their leadership, liberalism came to signify state action on behalf of the public welfare, and major political forces on the left embraced the new liberalism. Any attempt to revive classic liberalism—with its assault on concentrated power and its tendency to exalt individual enterprise above collective interest—would have to come from the right.

5

NEOLIBERALISM: MARGARET THATCHER
AND RONALD REAGAN

When Margaret Thatcher and Ronald Reagan promised to practice convic-tion politics, once again conditions proved ripe for the rise of resolute lead-ership and receptive to the construction of a new regime. In the 1970s the British and U.S. economies experienced high inflation accompanied by slow growth—what the British called "slumpflation" and U.S. citizens labeled "stagflation." Constrained by global interdependence and hit by worldwide recession, neither government possessed the autonomy or resources neces-sary to manage its economy in a Keynesian fashion. Furthermore, economic decline followed dramatic failures in foreign policy at Suez and in Vietnam that diminished the international prestige of the United Kingdom and the United States. Finally, social and cultural change in the 1960s started to al-ter traditional gender and race relationships, improving opportunities for political minorities but inducing anxiety among those who had previously occupied dominant positions in the home and the workplace as well as the political arena. By the 1970s, powerful forces of change at home and abroad had dealt a serious blow to the political order and shattered its governing consensus. Thatcher and Reagan promised to fill the void by supplying strong, decisive leadership and promoting a new public philosophy.[1]

In place of the welfare state, Thatcher and Reagan recommended a return to nineteenth-century liberalism, with some late-twentieth-century adapta-tions. At the core of their neoliberalism lay a firm belief in free enterprise and the market economy. To give citizens greater choice and to stimulate the economy through private spending and investment, they recommended tax reduction. To free business from the burdens of government control, they promoted privatization and deregulation. At the same time, they sought to weaken the unions, which they believed served to obstruct free choice and free enterprise. In general, they attempted to cut the bureaucracy, which they argued distorts both the conduct of markets and the character of individuals.

In addition to these laissez-faire prescriptions, Reagan and Thatcher ap-plied a more recently developed economic remedy of monetarism. Mone-tarists insist that governments can halt inflation by controlling the money supply and recommend that they should do so even if tight control fuels high unemployment. (Eventually, economic growth will create jobs, according to the monetarist model.) By resurrecting nineteenth-century free-market principles and injecting them with a late-twentieth-century economic cure, Reagan and Thatcher hoped to resuscitate their domestic economies.

To boost the health and vitality of their economies, Reagan and Thatcher sought to shrink the size and scope of the state; but to pursue other goals, they also needed to augment state authority. Both leaders increased defense spending and adopted more aggressive postures in international affairs as ways of reversing their nations' declining prestige in the world and promoting their neoliberal principles abroad. They also advocated stern law-and-order measures, in Britain initially to stifle the domestic unrest that accompanied the radical restructuring of society. Most relevant to this study, at home and abroad, Reagan and Thatcher pledged to provide strong leadership of their newly strengthened states.

Enhanced, centralized authority was not a central feature of their public philosophies, but it did supply a formula for the leaders to achieve their ideological goals. The promise of strong leadership combined with concrete measures adopted to strengthen the state has called into question the leaders' commitment to their neoliberal principles. Their combination of "the free economy and the strong state" appeared to reveal an inherent contradiction in their beliefs.[2] Yet strong leadership and a strong state provided useful means that the leaders employed to achieve their liberal ends. Even more often than earlier conviction politicians, Reagan and Thatcher practiced illiberal leadership in the name of liberalism.

When they promised to provide strong leadership and proposed an alternative public philosophy, Thatcher and Reagan proved able to tap several political, economic, and intellectual movements. Two other prominent political figures, Enoch Powell and Barry Goldwater, had already leveled scathing attacks on the welfare state and proposed laissez-faire alternatives. Powell and Goldwater failed to attract a majority following, but the substantial support they did garner in the 1960s provided an early indication that the postwar consensus was vulnerable to a neoliberal critique. In the 1970s, neoliberal views that emphasized the need for tax reform and cuts in government spending gained wider acceptance within the Conservative party in Britain and outside the party system in the U.S., as evidenced by Proposition 13, the popular tax revolt in California. Furthermore, within intellectual circles, the monetarist ideas of Milton Friedman and the free-market philosophy of Fredrick Hayek became fashionable alternatives to Keynesian reasoning. To promote these ideas and develop them into specific policy recommendations, a spate of neoliberal think tanks appeared on both sides of the Atlantic. In the 1960s and 1970s, political insurgents, grassroots activists, and intellectuals planted the seeds of revolt against the welfare state, although it would take conviction politicians to bring their vision to fruition.

Connections between reformers in Britain and in the U.S. were more direct and pronounced than during any previous period, and they existed at all levels where the reform impulse was felt. Hayek and Friedman joined forces and established a network of neoliberal economists who met regularly as members of the Mont Pelerin Society, an organization founded by Hayek in 1947. That network expanded to include experts at think tanks and universities. In Britain, the Institute of Economic Affairs, the Adam Smith Institute, and the Centre for Policy Studies established close links with the Heritage Foundation, the American Enterprise Institute, and the Hoover Institution in the U.S. At the level of party politics, National Republican Committee chairman William Brock studied Thatcher's 1979 campaign and then hired consultants from Saatchi and Saatchi, the firm employed by the Conservative party. In the 1970s economic theorists, policy analysts, and political strategists traveled back and forth across the Atlantic, creating an ideological wave that would help sweep Reagan and Thatcher into office.[3]

Of course the clearest connection established a link between the leaders themselves. From their first meeting in 1975, Reagan and Thatcher forged an alliance much closer than any previous connection between a U.S. president and a British prime minister. In her memoirs, Thatcher recalled that when she met Reagan she "was immediately won over by his charm, sense of humour and directness."[4] Many officials in the Reagan administration (interviewed for this study) described Thatcher as "the only 'other woman' in his life." On the other hand, the leaders' "special relationship" was not always as harmonious as it seemed: In this pair, the eagle frequently flaunted its majesty as it soared along an independent course, while the lion often behaved more like a fox. (See chapter 9.) Yet their personalities, their interests, and their ideology tended to bring the two leaders together, and their political partnership with its central common cause created a truly transatlantic transformation.

Margaret Thatcher

Margaret Thatcher's path to power provides one of the most remarkable and surprising stories in this study. The speed at which she moved from obscurity to occupy the highest political office in Britain is matched only by the meteoric rise of Grover Cleveland in the U.S. Furthermore, her qualifications as an "outsider" exceed those of other conviction politicians: In addition to her lower-middle-class background and limited political experience,

her place as a woman in a man's world made her stand out. Indeed, her gender kept her out of the inner circle of Tory party elite against whom she
would rebel. Her background, experience, and gender made her an unlikely
candidate for Conservative party leader or British prime minister. Before
1975, few could have predicted that she would lead her nation or lend her
name to a distinct public philosophy, "Thatcherism," a phrase that has come
to characterize her age.

In contrast to most British politicians, Thatcher had a modest class background, which she insists helped to shape her beliefs and values. By her own
account, while living above her father's grocery store in the small town of
Grantham, Lincolnshire, she learned the virtue of hard work, thrift, and responsibility. A self-made man who owned and operated his own shop,
Thatcher's father became her role model. (A lifelong Liberal, he also served
as the town's alderman and as a lay preacher at the local Methodist chapel.)
"I owe almost everything to my father," Thatcher declared after her victory
in the 1979 general election.[5] And long after she left office, she recalled his
profound impact on her style: His "upright qualities, which entailed a refusal
to alter your convictions just because others disagreed or because you became unpopular, were instilled into me from the earliest days."[6] Throughout
Thatcher's career, tributes to her father peppered her public statements, and
everyone interviewed for this study identified him as the single most significant influence on her life. The story of Thatcher's childhood reveals a central source of her convictions, but the tale would also provide a useful
allegory to promote the Victorian values of Thatcherism.[7]

Few events or accomplishments distinguished Thatcher's career until she
won the party leadership contest in 1975. She earned an undergraduate degree in chemistry from Oxford University and worked as a researcher in industry for only three years. She became active in Conservative party politics
and in 1949 secured selection as a parliamentary candidate but lost in the
general election. In 1953 she was admitted to the bar and practiced law for
five years. Finally, the Conservative association in Finchley, a suburb of London, chose her as its parliamentary candidate, and following the Conservative landslide in 1959, Thatcher entered parliament at the age of thirty-two.

Nine years later, in a speech she delivered at the Conservative party conference, Thatcher gave an early indication of the conviction politics she
would practice as premier. Party leader Edward Heath chose Thatcher to
speak because he expected her to address a subject of interest to women, but
in her own words, she "decided on something more topical which might appeal to thinking people of both sexes."[8] In her speech, she seized the opportunity to attack the bureaucracy, emphasize the need to restore free
enterprise, and recommend control of the money supply as the means to halt

inflation. More revealing, she presented her proposals in the context of a fundamental critique of consensus politics.

"What's Wrong with Politics?" Thatcher asked in the title of her speech and then quickly delivered a decisive answer: Politicians who make false promises and compromise principles are the primary culprits. Almost thirty years later, she emphasized the significance of that address (along with two newspaper articles she published at the time). In her memoirs, Thatcher recalled, "In particular, I argued the case for the ideological clash of opposing political parties as essential to the effective functioning of democracy. The pursuit of 'consensus,' therefore, was fundamentally subversive of popular choice. . . . The fraudulent appeal of consensus was a theme to which I would return again and again, both as leader of the Opposition and as Prime Minister."[9] Notwithstanding her daring declarations in 1968 and her radical recollections in retirement, Thatcher did briefly participate in the prevailing consensus during her only government experience before she became prime minister.

From 1970 until 1974, Thatcher served as secretary of state for education and science in Heath's cabinet. When the government decided that older elementary school children should no longer receive free milk, "Thatcher the Milk Snatcher" was vilified in the popular press. (The fact that it was a woman who deprived the children of their milk no doubt made the story especially newsworthy.) Despite the mean and miserly image portrayed by the press, Thatcher generally sought to defend her department and its programs in the face of budget cuts. Her performance as education secretary provides few hints of the radical assault she would soon level against the welfare state.

To a great extent, the failure of Heath's 1970–74 government determined the nature and timing of Thatcher's rise to the leadership. Contrary to contemporary perceptions of the two leaders, in 1970 Heath and Thatcher were very much alike. Prime Minister Heath not only shared her class background, he also espoused ideas (with the exception of his pro-Europe stance) that would later be called Thatcherite. The 1970 Conservative manifesto promised lower taxes, trade union reform, law and order, minimal state interference in industry, and reduced social services. In contrast to Thatcher, however, Heath would execute a dramatic U-turn, a fateful move that would trigger an ideological revolt within his party and against his leadership.

Several factors led Prime Minister Heath to retreat from his party's manifesto commitments. The government secured sweeping trade union reform with its 1971 industrial relations bill but then proved unable to enforce it.[10] When unemployment reached 1 million in 1972, the government decided to cut taxes and increase public spending to stimulate the economy, creating what would be "the last Keynesian 'fling' by the Treasury."[11] Then the prime minister adopted the incomes policy that he had earlier opposed. Finally, when Heath faced the threat of a miners' strike (for the second time), he caved in to the union's demands. By the time the prime minister called a general election in February 1974, he had totally reversed his positions on key issues in the 1970 manifesto.

The Conservatives lost both elections in 1974, and within the party a move gained momentum to replace Heath and the collectivist consensus he came to reflect. Circumstances beyond his control (largely created by the worldwide recession) had convinced Heath that the 1970 manifesto commitments were impractical, but his critics within the party attributed his failure to the weakness of his will and the absence of a well-developed philosophy. Those who became disillusioned with his leadership and his policies set out in search of someone who would demonstrate determined leadership and provide an alternative public philosophy.

Before 1974 only Enoch Powell had rendered a clear voice that revealed an alternative vision. In 1958 he resigned as a junior minister at the Treasury because Prime Minister Harold Macmillan refused to pursue the spending cuts recommended by the department. Powell served as minister of health in 1961 but left the cabinet two years later because he refused to work under Sir Alec Douglas Home. After 1964 Powell consistently advocated laissez-faire doctrines, speaking against incomes policy and in favor of controlling the money supply. In the late 1960s his ideas influenced the party in opposition, and some of the key commitments in the 1970 manifesto reflect his impact. By 1970, however, Powell had personally ceased to be a powerful party-political force.

In 1968 Heath dismissed him from his post as shadow defense minister, after Powell delivered a shocking speech in which he warned that "rivers of blood" would flow if immigration by people of color remained unrestricted. Although his racist views got him dismissed from the shadow cabinet, they attracted substantial support from portions of the public. Powell received 110,000 letters (most of which endorsed his views), and 5,000 dockers went on strike to express their support.[12] During Heath's 1970–74 government, Powell remained a persistent critic, condemning the government's statutory prices and incomes policy as well as British membership in the European Economic Community (EEC). In 1974 he left the Conservative party and returned to Parliament as an Ulster Unionist. Ironically, Powell departed just as his ideas were gaining prominence in the Conservative party.

Powell would have no further impact on the party, but in her memoirs Thatcher paid tribute to his influence on her intellectual and political development. (He never thought a great deal of her potential as a leader, however. "That dreadful voice, and those dreadful hats," he once exclaimed.)[13] She described Powell as "the only member of the Shadow Cabinet who was opposed in principle to all kinds of incomes policy—voluntary or involuntary," and then declared that "Enoch was right." Furthermore, when Powell traced the source of inflation to the money supply (and not to incomes policy), Thatcher admitted that he made "intellectual leaps in economic policy which Keith Joseph and I would only make some years later."[14]

"Some years later" arrived in 1974, with the end of Heath's government and the ideological conversion of Keith Joseph, the man who became Thatcher's mentor. Joseph had served as secretary of state for social services from 1970 to 1974, but he alleged he only became a genuine "conservative," a right-wing critic of the collectivist consensus, after the defeat of the Heath government. According to Joseph, "Between the February 1974 general election and those Shadow Cabinets I had been persuaded by Alfred Sherman, Alan Walters and Peter Bauer, three very disenchanted old friends, very disenchanted by the errors of our policies."[15] Two of the people Joseph identified would also prove critical to Thatcher's philosophy and policies. Walters became her private economic advisor at Number 10 from 1981 until 1984 and returned in 1989. Among other activities, Sherman organized a group called "the Argonauts," who helped to shape industrial policy during the first Thatcher government. Together Sherman and Joseph also established the Centre for Policy Studies (CPS), a radical resource of economic policies. Joseph never claimed credit for the development of Thatcher's ideas—instead, he insisted that she "had seen the light herself"[16]—but he and others helped Thatcher to transform her early preferences into the principles of a public philosophy.

When they promoted her candidacy for the leadership, however, Thatcher's views reflected only her convictions, not a well-developed ideology. As Sherman recalled, Thatcher "got into power because the Conservative party was in disarray and people were despairing of ever being able to get Britain out of its nosedive. And she really had no idea—she was a woman of beliefs rather than ideas."[17] Thatcher herself admitted that her convictions came before the development of her ideology: "It would take many years before I came to understand the philosophical background to what I believed," and yet she added, "I always knew my mind."[18] At the time she contested the leadership, her ideas remained underdeveloped, but Thatcher and her supporters understood the need to seize the opportunity created by dissatisfaction with Heath's leadership and subsequent disarray within the party. Fortunately for Thatcher, discontent with the party's policies and its leader fueled the institutional change in leadership selection that enhanced her chance to become the new Conservative leader.

As soon as she secured the leadership, Thatcher showed that she fully grasped the meaning of Machiavelli's message. Sly as a fox, she understood how skillful manipulation of appearance could shape political reality. Just as significant, she knew a leader must also learn to be a lion. Immediately after her selection, she declared to a group of young radicals, "We must have an ideology."[19] Inside and outside the party, the right wing rallied to help their leader develop a message that would render a roar.

The Centre for Policy Studies provided the most significant source of ideas. Shortly after Joseph and Sherman established the think tank in 1974, they named Thatcher as vice chairman. According to Joseph, they designed CPS "to research, and then to market, social market philosophy."[20] In her memoirs, Thatcher endorsed Sherman's description of CPS as an "animator, agent of change, and political enzyme."[21] Economists and policy analysts did conduct research at CPS as Joseph intended, but he and Sherman quickly discovered that Thatcher's leadership could provide the most effective agent of change and the most efficient vehicle for selling market theory. Using the resources of CPS and conducting informal sessions, Sherman and Joseph essentially tutored the future prime minister. As Sherman recalled, "The early Thatcher whom I discovered had great intellectual curiosity and thirst for knowledge. . . . We had great classes for her—reading, arguing, listening—and Mrs. Thatcher at the end of it was a totally different person."[22] The different person who emerged from these tutorials held radical views that were totally at odds with the mainstream Tory tradition.

Traditional Tories continued to support the postwar collectivist consensus, often invoking Benjamin Disraeli's notion of "one nation."[23] After serving as secretary of state for employment and later secretary of state for Northern Ireland, James Prior emphasized the difference between Thatcherism and genuine conservatism. As he reflected on his own experience, Prior insisted, Thatcher's "government is not conservative. It is a laissez-faire liberal government in some respects, in economic policy. And in other respects, it's a very radical government. But it's not a conservative government. I used to say I was the only conservative left."[24] Like many other conventional conservatives, Prior expressed a sense of noblesse oblige and continued to endorse the use of state power to promote the public welfare.

In particular, Thatcher's neoliberal ideology made a dramatic break with conservative paternalism. Even an ex-minister who initially endorsed Thatcher's economic policies came to condemn the excesses of her ideology (as well as her style). John Biffen derided the prime minister's approach and expressed a newfound appreciation for traditional conservatism when he explained, "Tories are paternalists. They have always been more understanding of the forces of socialism. . . . She is not a Tory, never would be, never could be. As far as she's concerned, it's a whole lot of housekeeping."[25] According to Biffen, "She remains firmly committed to a few lower-middle-class issues,

which she got from her father—a Gladstonian liberal of the meanest kind."
Another intraparty critic who remained faithful to the Tory tradition described Thatcher's "strength" in a disparaging way that revealed his distaste
for her radical departure. According to Timothy Raison, Thatcher demonstrated "her ability to attract the upper working class—the rather macho end
of the working class. The man with the tattooed arm who used to be Labour
is now Conservative. They liked her rough-and-ready style."[26] For traditional
Tories, responsibility requires taking care of the lower classes, not appealing
to them as "one of us." Their distaste for Thatcher seemed to stem from several sources: the fact that she was a woman, her "classless" style, and her neoliberal convictions.

Thatcher's radical ideology and her "rough-and-ready" style repelled her
enemies within the Conservative party, but the combination won accolades
from her opponents on the far left. (Indeed, as Thatcher pulled her party to
the right, conviction politicians within Labour struggled to shift their party
to the left.) In the 1970s and 1980s, two significant conviction politicians
emerged on the left—Ken Livingstone, leader of the majority Labour party
on the General London Council (GLC), and Tony Benn, who campaigned
unsuccessfully for Labour's deputy leadership. (Despite his defeat, Benn did
manage to rally an array of radical left factions to achieve constitutional reform and policy change.) Both were quick to pay tribute to Thatcher's success as a leader. Livingstone emphasized the importance of strong, decisive
leadership as a catalyst for change: "Change requires leadership," he declared, and "Thatcher realized that you have to educate all the time." Describing his own style as "the mirror image of hers," he added, "People didn't
like us but they thought we could take tough decisions."[27] In contrast, Benn
stressed the significance of Thatcher's ideas when he explained, "What is
more important [than the personalities of the leaders] is the current of
ideas—Keynes, then Friedman. There was a much greater injection of intel-
lectualism into the Conservative party than into Labour. There has been no
uniquely socialist analysis since 1945 and, when we won in 1945, they said
'Don't rock the boat.' It blanked out and marginalized serious analysis of
what we were doing."[28] According to Benn, the postwar Labour party failed
to articulate a distinct public philosophy. Instead, "the New Deal and the
Labour governments ran into the ground of over-bureaucracy. They never
addressed the central question of power." As a consequence, "democracy was
deprived of its content and it became mere form." Dynamic, conviction-
style leadership was needed on the left, Benn concluded, but only to facilitate the infusion of new ideas.

Just as Thatcher carried out an internal coup in the Conservative party,
Benn marshaled forces on the far left in a revolt against Labour's own

centrist, consensus-style leaders. Dissatisfied with the performance of Labour governments in the 1960s, the Labour left gained strength in the period of opposition from 1970 through 1974. As chairman of the National Executive Committee's Home Policy Committee, Benn incorporated extensive nationalization and renationalization provisions into "Labour's Programme for Britain." Harold Wilson, the party's leader and former prime minister, rejected the program, refusing to implement one of its major proposals, the nationalization of twenty-five major industries. His refusal led to the formation of the Campaign for Labour Party Democracy (CLPD), the left-wing faction responsible for major reforms of the party constitution in the late 1970s. The party as a whole blamed Wilson for its loss in the 1970 election, while the left wing condemned him primarily for failing to pursue radical change. Radical reformers wanted to replace the postwar social democratic consensus with a purer form of socialism. The measure of success they achieved would enable Thatcher to attack the Labour party as a dangerous group of socialists, an allegation that would have lacked any credibility before 1980.

In the 1970s, however, several steps brought the left closer to its goals. First, reformers convinced Labour to abandon its "proscribed list," which banned radical groups from party membership. Then, in the two 1974 elections, the Tribune group of left-wing MPs increased from 46 to 68 members and from 68 to 88 members, reflecting the growing militancy of constituency activists. Finally, the left gained strength in the industrial wing of the party, and new union leaders signaled the new radical direction of trade union politics. Victory in 1974 only temporarily unified the party: When Wilson resigned in 1976, his successor, James Callaghan, managed to antagonize both the party activists and the trade union leadership.[29]

Prime Minister Callaghan quickly confronted the limits of funding and sustaining the modern welfare state in an interdependent global economy.[30] In 1976 the sterling crisis and balance-of-payments deficit sent Callaghan to seek assistance from the International Monetary Fund (IMF). The IMF in turn assigned limits on public sector borrowing, set specific dates for debt repayment, and established targets for output and inflation. As Benn recalled, the IMF "simply said to the 1976 Labour Cabinet, 'We are not allowing you to do that any more. Whatever you choose to do, we are not having this high level of public expenditure because we regard it as undesirable.' . . . In 1976, I had hoped, when the IMF forced the choice between a socialist solution and a social-democratic defeat, that a Cabinet majority might be created for a more radical response. But that is not what happened."[31] After conforming to the constraints set by the IMF, in 1978 Callaghan attempted to enact phase four of his incomes policy, which called for a 5 percent pay norm.

Adding insult to injury, Callaghan then misled union leaders to expect a fall election. The combination created a clash between the Labour prime minister and the labor movement, triggering the series of strikes in the notorious "winter of discontent." As in Heath's 1970–74 government, once again Britain seemed ungovernable, and a Labour prime minister—himself a former trade unionist—proved unable to curb the might of the unions.

At the end of 1978, one conservative columnist depicted the dire state of Britain's domestic scene. As he described it, "The most constant theme of public life continued to be the steady, relentless, drizzle of industrial unrest—closing hospitals, causing bread queues, blacking out television screens, making the life of commuters an almost daily frustration, bringing Ford and large parts of British Leyland to a standstill."[32] Failure at home and abroad made many members of the public receptive to the advice he offered in the title of his column, "After 1978: Put Not Your Trust in Politics." "For those who see the hopes of mankind as lying through politicians, 1978 must have been one of the gloomiest years in history," he concluded. Britain was "drifting without vision" and "at the tail-end of a Parliament, Britain's political leaders seemed more than usually impotent and on the defensive." The columnist depicted a desperate state of affairs, apparently unaware that he was also describing an environment ripe for the rise of resolute leadership.

The following year, Thatcher offered the electorate a vision of a brighter future and seized the offensive. As she initiated her crusade to convert the British public to a new public philosophy, she instructed the voters: "*In politics, I've learned something . . . . : If you've got a message, preach it. I am a conviction politician. The Old Testament prophets did not merely say: 'Brothers I want a consensus.' They said: 'This is my faith and my vision. This is what I passionately believe. If you believe it too, then come with me.'* Tonight I say to you just that. Away with the recent bleak and dismal past. Away with defeatism. Under the twin banners, choice and freedom, a new and exciting future beckons the British people" (emphasis added).[33] Slow to embrace the new faith, the British electorate nonetheless proved quick to question the orthodoxy of the postwar consensus.

Without producing a positive endorsement of Thatcher and the Conservatives, the general election of 1979 did render a negative referendum on Callaghan and his Labour party.[34] The Conservative party won support for its policies on taxation, trade unions, and law and order, but on the two principal economic issues, inflation and unemployment, voters preferred Labour as often as or more often than they favored the Conservatives. Moreover, a disproportionate number of voters who switched from Labour to the Conservative party offered as their reason: "I had reservations about the party I usually vote for."[35] With only 44 percent of the vote, the Conservative victory did not appear to mark a watershed in British politics. Conviction-style leader Thatcher captured office with a clear voice and a new vision but without converting the masses to her cause.

Nevertheless, the 1979 election results did signal change more substantial than the rejection of an incumbent administration, a frequent phenomenon in both Britain and the U.S. The Conservative manifesto made clear the party's intention to break with the past consensus, lending some credence to Thatcher's assertion that she had secured a mandate for change. Moreover, the election produced a 5.6 percent national swing from Labour to the Conservatives, and the Conservatives' 7 percent lead over Labour represented the largest since 1945. Most significant, the election results confirmed long-term trends pointing to the erosion of the Labour party's base of support.

Class voting had been steadily declining since the 1960s,[36] and in 1979 the Conservative party substantially increased its support among the working class.[37] Election studies reveal that more manual workers favored reducing the highest rate of income tax than supported the introduction of a wealth tax, one of the central proposals in the Labour manifesto. Only one-third of Labour supporters favored further nationalization, and two-thirds thought the trade unions had become too powerful. Eighty-five percent of the electorate and 86 percent of the working class endorsed the sale of council houses, a policy Labour officially opposed.[38] Furthermore, party identification had diminished throughout the 1970s, a trend that proved more damaging to Labour as the majority party.[39] The breakdown of traditional class allegiance and party identification rendered conditions ripe for the reconstitution of British politics when Thatcher became prime minister in 1979.

In her first government, Prime Minister Thatcher took immediate steps to tap public disenchantment and shape the forces of discontent into solid support for her new regime. Almost immediately, council estate tenants became eligible to buy their homes at substantial discount and with the possibility of securing 100 percent mortgages. Her government also quickly adopted measures to curb immigration.[40] Using language reminiscent of Powell's "rivers of blood," Thatcher had warned in 1978 that Britain would be "swamped" if the country failed to stem the rising tide of immigration. As prime minister, she hoped new restrictions placed on immigration would restore the "purity" of British identity and alleviate anxiety among those who feared displacement. Both housing and immigration policies targeted the working class, and the support she secured from C1s and C2s, unskilled and skilled workers, would prove critical to keeping Thatcher in power for more than a decade.

In fact, core features of her ideology produced pragmatic results. The sale of council estates transformed tenants of public housing into private homeowners, and later privatization would yield a crop of citizen shareholders in the middle class. Thatcherism clearly created new constituencies for her Conservative party and her neoliberal regime.

Success of the Thatcher revolution required not only the reconstitution of British society but also a restructuring of the economy and the state. Privatization needed substantial preparation, and, with few exceptions, Thatcher postponed privatization plans until her second government. In her first government, however, she focused on two central goals: designing budgets that would establish new priorities and achieving trade union reform, a fundamental step in dismantling the corporatist state.

In the 1979 campaign Thatcher had pledged to cut taxes and reduce the Public Sector Borrowing Requirement (PSBR) without explaining how she would achieve these two seemingly contradictory goals. To make matters worse, the Conservative party and its leader also succumbed to the pressure of the campaign and agreed to honor the Clegg Commission awards to public sector employees.[41] Thatcher's first chancellor of the exchequer, Geoffrey Howe, had opposed the campaign pledge and later admitted the Clegg awards "contributed to sharp growth in public spending in the years immediately following the election." "Against our will," the chancellor insisted, "we were forced to validate all the outstanding claims."[42] Despite this costly campaign commitment, the first budget lowered the standard rate on income tax from 33 to 30 percent and cut the top rate from 83 to 60 percent, while it reduced the PSBR to 8 billion pounds. (In Thatcher's third government, the top rate would be further reduced to 40 percent.) To make up the difference between revenue and expenditure, the government doubled the value-added tax (VAT) to 15 percent. In doing so, Thatcher shifted the burden of taxation from income to consumption, a regressive form of taxation but one that reflected her Victorian values of self-help, industry, and thrift.

In 1980 Thatcher's government continued the trend set in 1979. The 1980 budget maintained stringent money supply targets and kept the PSBR at the same level as 1979. The chancellor also introduced enterprise zones, providing major tax breaks for businesses in designated, depressed areas. (In doing so, Howe established a model for the U.S.)[43] As cost-cutting measures, the budget included new prescription charges and declined to increase social security benefits with inflation. To raise additional revenue, the government placed higher duties on alcohol, tobacco, and gasoline. As in 1979, Thatcher concocted a mix of monetarism and fiscal responsibility that she considered "good housekeeping."

Most significant and controversial, Thatcher's government announced its Medium Term Financial Strategy (MTFS), which set specific monetary targets for the next several years. Although the targets were never actually met, the MTFS did signal the government's commitment to monetarist principles.

(Thatcher would later allege that the MTFS figures were meant to be "illustrative rather than firm targets," but they were viewed as specific objectives at the time.)[44] This bold monetarist move won the admiration and respect of financial interests in the City but perplexed many members of the public and observers in the press. At the conclusion of 1980, the conservative *Times* compared Thatcher's government with Reagan's administration and observed that in both countries, "There was often a sense of unreality as politics moved far into uncharted areas."[45]

Of course previous governments had been forced to chart and follow a monetarist course. As Howe recalled, "The key to monetary management—the key thinking—had been in place by the IMF in relation to Denis Healey's budget from 1976 onwards. [At the Treasury], they had been setting broad targets. . . . We took that and were able to build on the foundations."[46] In fact as early as 1969, the IMF forced another Labour chancellor, Roy Jenkins, to comply with "tight targets" for growth in the money supply.[47] What distinguished the monetarism of previous governments from Thatcher's policy was the rationale: Earlier governments had acted out of necessity, but Thatcher adopted monetarist measures because she wanted to do so. No longer a matter of expediency, monetarism became part of the new public philosophy.

For Thatcher, economic policies that constitute philosophical principles should not be compromised regardless of the costs. At the Conservative party conference in the fall of 1980, she defiantly declared her determination to stay on course and instructed her audience: "To those waiting with bated breath for that favorite media catchphrase, the 'U-turn,' I have only one thing to say, 'You turn if you want to. The lady's not for turning.' I say that not only to you, but to our friends overseas," and then she added in typical Thatcherite fashion, "and also to those who are not our friends."[48] By the start of 1981, inflation had doubled and unemployment exceeded 2 million (increased from 1.2 million in 1979). Rather than retreat, the Thatcher government introduced a budget for 1981 that Walters, its chief architect, called "the biggest fiscal squeeze in peacetime."[49]

A deflationary budget in the midst of recession delivered a frontal assault to Keynesian conventional wisdom. The Treasury predicted that unemployment would reach 3 million in the following year, which it did. (Yet devaluation of the pound was expected to revive manufacturing.) In contrast to the first two budgets, the government actually relaxed its money policy after the monetarists convinced Thatcher that control had been excessive,[50] but the "fiscal squeeze" that Walters designed was extremely tight. The budget raised 4.3 billion pounds in new taxes—not by raising income taxes directly but by declining to increase the tax thresholds. And once again, taxes were raised on roads, alcohol, tobacco, and gasoline, while benefits and allowances were not increased with inflation. The budget also raised the cost of insurance contributions, prescriptions, and dental and eye care. As the prime minister entered the Commons to hear the chancellor's statement, she told Walters, "You know, Alan, they may get rid of me for this. But at least I shall have gone knowing I did the right thing."[51] Whatever the political costs, Thatcher remained determined to demonstrate the courage of her convictions.

Her stubborn determination conquered the initial opposition of her chancellor and the permanent undersecretary to the Treasury, Douglas Wass. Both had argued that public spending was under control and there was no need to cut the PSBR any further. Yet Thatcher insisted, and the chancellor eventually came up with additional cuts. Throughout these years, the Treasury failed to obstruct the government's agenda in any significant way. Howe insisted he always received "strong support from the Treasury" but noted, "the party was reacting with understandable dismay at the constraints involved in budgeting at the time of the 1981 budget."[52] Thatcher usually preferred to attack the civil service rather than admit that the most serious opposition came from within her own party.

Many critics in the Conservative party simply objected to Thatcher's departure from Keynesian conventional wisdom. Ian Gilmour, the principal spokesman on foreign affairs in the Commons from 1979 to 1981, recalled, "She increased the VAT and doubled inflation. Instead of cutting public expenditure, she should have expanded the economy." According to Gilmour, "In 1982 and 1983, the improvement was the result of the American boom and the relaxation of money," not the effect of the prime minister's policies.[53] Thatcher's detractors tended to attribute the subsequent economic improvement to some combination of the revival of world trade, revenues from the North Sea oil, and U.S. deficit spending, while her supporters insisted that the government's policies created a British renaissance.[54] Nevertheless, all agreed that Thatcher's bold initiatives in the early years signaled a new direction and set new priorities. At the end of 1981, the *Times* observed, "Whether or not Mrs. Thatcher was right in her policies, as unemployment rose from 2.2 million to almost 3 million, and public spending cuts fell hardest on the poor; she was not persuasive. Wetness thrived among her own backbenchers."[55] At the time of the 1981 budget, her detractors outnumbered her supporters within the Conservative parliamentary party; yet Thatcher did not need to persuade as long as she controlled the agenda.

Her control of the agenda provided another, perhaps more serious, source of criticism. Thatcher had managed to keep the 1981 budget secret from cabinet members until shortly before its formal announcement. As a result, when they heard the news, critics within the cabinet condemned not only the substance of the budget but also the prime minister's style of independent leadership. The 1981 budget was the first of many controversial cases when the prime minister preferred to rely on private advisors and circumvent cabinet colleagues. According to Gilmour, with that budget Thatcher demonstrated "the enormous power of the prime minister." As he explained:

> She controlled the agenda by excluding the cabinet from economic policy making. The senior members—Willie Whitelaw and the others—went along with her when we should have said, "Up with her we will not put."
>
> I do regret that I did not resign. It would have been the right thing to do, [but] it wouldn't have made any difference to her. Jim Prior and I were at the same official dinner the night before [the budget was announced], and that was the first we heard of it. It was a fait accompli. Normally you resign to stop something, [but] our resignations would not have made a difference.[56]

For Thatcher's enemies in the cabinet, pragmatic considerations often overrode "the right thing to do," a habit that repeatedly placed them at a disadvantage in their struggle against a conviction-style premier.

Despite Gilmour's insistence that they could not make a difference, the resignations of prominent cabinet ministers such as Prior, then secretary of state for employment, or Whitelaw, the home secretary, might have put an early end to Thatcherism. Throughout the spring and summer of 1981, urban race riots erupted in London and Liverpool, leading many critics (inside and outside the party) to conclude that Thatcher's economic policies had ripped apart the social fabric of "one nation." Moreover, Thatcher's approval ratings were steadily sinking and would plunge to the lowest level of any prime minister in the history of Gallup polls by the fall of 1981. Nevertheless, the rage of her cabinet ministers failed to produce an open revolt. At the time of the 1981 budget, the reluctant rebels missed a rare opportunity to stage a palace coup: In September 1981, Thatcher sacked Gilmour and exiled Prior to Northern Ireland.

To a great extent, the radical 1981 budget was presented when the prime minister could afford to continue her controversial course despite dire economic conditions and historically low approval ratings: In January 1981, after years of internal wrangling, the Labour party formally split. Four prominent Labour party politicians—Roy Jenkins, Shirley Williams, William Rodgers, and David Owen—launched the new Social Democratic party (SDP) in March, and the SDP soon formed an alliance with the Liberals. Support for the new party skyrocketed during its first year: By December 1981, the SDP alone attracted 29 percent and, with the Liberals, the "Alliance" earned 41 percent of the public support (compared with 20 percent for Labour and 19 percent for the Conservatives).[57] From that peak of popularity, support for the Alliance began a steady descent—at first, triggered by disputes within the SDP and also between Social Democrats and Liberals within the Alliance. (Later, the revival of the Conservative government's popularity during the Falklands war fueled further friction within and between the Alliance parties.) Eventually, the "new" SDP simply reproduced the pattern of internal conflict that characterized the old Labour party.[58] Throughout the 1980s warring factions continued to feud on the left in Labour and in the center within the SDP and the Alliance, creating a leadership void that only Thatcher continued to fill. At the same time, the style and substance of Thatcherism created additional conflict among her divided opposition, and nowhere was this more apparent than in the area of industrial relations and trade union reform.

Thatcher faced her first challenge from the unions in 1980 when steelworkers declared a national strike. As secretary of state for industry, Keith Joseph was the minister in charge of steel. Despite the fact that steel was a nationalized industry, he and the prime minister took the unprecedented position that the government should not intervene in the dispute. Instead, they insisted that responsibility rested solely with the management of the British Steel Corporation (BSC). The steel strike continued for thirteen weeks, and, even though the steelworkers secured a 16 percent pay increase, the duration of the strike sent a new, hard-line message to the trade union movement. Thatcher was able to maintain her position in part because the strike caused no major disruption or shortages, while her government's firm stand against the unions was also bolstered by the efforts of the "Argonauts," a group founded by Alfred Sherman at the start of the strike.

To convince them to resist union pressure, Sherman organized a meeting of British trade associations. (He acted with several others—Tom Boardman, the president of the Association of British Chambers of Commerce, Michael Ivens from Aims of Industry, John Hoskyns from the Number 10 policy unit, and David Wolfson, Thatcher's chief of staff.) According to Sherman, "We feared that the [steel] unions would get other unions to support them and that British industry would press the government to give in." As he recalled, "We tried to convince them that their interest lay with the government and cheap steel, not with the steel unions. And that's why I called it the Argonauts. You may remember that Jason, faced with the armed men who were going to attack him, threw a stone and got them fighting amongst themselves."[59] To defeat the unions required breaking the corporate bond that linked them to their industries. Like their namesake, the modern-day Argonauts believed a strategy of divide and conquer would place the Golden Fleece within their grasp.

The Argonauts continued to meet after the steel strike, attempting to exert pressure on representatives from industry and cabinet ministers during other industrial disputes. When the group briefly attracted some negative publicity in 1983, it changed its name to the more benign "Luncheon Club." By then Sherman had been removed from the directorship at CPS, and he handed over management of the club to Ivens. From that point on its influence appears to have waned, but it had an important impact on Thatcher's first government.[60]

In general, Thatcher's early treatment of the unions engaged in industrial disputes indicated that she would yield little to their demands. After the steel strike, in 1981 civil servants went on strike for twenty-one weeks and the government refused to comply with their demands. In 1982, the government also refused to surrender to railway workers on strike or succumb to the pressure of hospital workers in their disruptive action. After workers at the Government Communications Headquarters declared a strike in 1982, in her second government, Thatcher outlawed the union. In only one case did she clearly concede union demands: Faced with massive pit closures, the miners threatened to strike in January 1981. The National Coal Board (NCB) immediately withdrew the closure proposals and agreed to reexamine them in consultation with the miners. According to Thatcher, "It became very clear that all we could do was to cut our losses and live to fight another day, when—with adequate preparation—we might be in a position to win."[61] She immediately took steps to ensure victory on "another day."

Industrial disputes forced Thatcher's government to respond to circumstances beyond its control, but it could seize the initiative in the legislative arena, and in 1980 Thatcher won approval for moderate trade union reform. The 1980 Employment Act placed some restrictions on the closed shop, outlawed secondary picketing, and curtailed union immunities during secondary action. The legislation's chief architect was Prior, then secretary of state for employment and the only traditional Tory appointed to an economic post in Thatcher's cabinet.

According to Prior, he and the prime minister differed on the pace and nature of reform. As he explained their differences, the employment secretary also drew familiar contrasts between consensus and conviction politics. "She wanted to push on a lot quicker than I was prepared to push on," Prior recalled. As a consensus politician, he believed change should proceed incrementally, whereas his conviction-style leader appeared to demand quick, decisive action. Furthermore, Prior wanted to initiate trade union reform, but he did not see the issue in ideological terms as Thatcher did. As he explained, "Ideologically, on things like the closed shop, she was much more opposed to a closed shop and the implications of a closed shop, where people didn't have the freedom to decide whether they wanted to belong to a union or not. She was much more stuck on that than I was."[62] Even in the period of opposition, Prior opposed a right-wing document on trade union reform, primarily because it emphasized the need "to win the argument" before actively pursuing change. During the 1979 campaign and later, Prior and other moderates hoped to avoid the ideological clash that the right wanted to invite.[63]

Finally, the employment secretary and the prime minister saw the relationship between change and public opinion in different ways that highlight another contrast between consensus and conviction politics. The conviction-style leader always wanted to "lead from the front," but Prior declared, "My strategy was to keep behind public opinion and also right-wing opinion as expressed by a number of backbenchers, really as expressed by Margaret Thatcher." In retrospect, Prior believed his efforts proved successful: He achieved reform while he also kept Thatcher's radical instincts and impulses in check.[64]

Yet there are many reasons to believe that Prior's "step-by-step" approach was part of Thatcher's plan to ensure the success of trade union reform. During the period of opposition, right-wing reformers—including Hoskyns, Sherman, and Joseph—endorsed a proposal entitled "Stepping Stones," which mapped out the stages of reform. Their ultimate goals might have differed, but both the moderates and the right wing wanted to avoid a repeat of the calamity that followed Heath's Industrial Relations Act. Heath's inability to enforce that legislation indicated that a cautious, incremental approach would prove more successful. Furthermore, because Labour perceived Prior's efforts as the best hope of checking Thatcher, he secured the cooperation that a more radical reformer might not have gotten. Prior himself admitted, "[My approach] always made it very hard for the trades unions to get up a campaign against the legislation because I was always portrayed as the reasonable man, having to fight for what was reasonable against the rather outlandish demands of a combination of the right wing of the Conservative party, Mrs. Thatcher on occasion, and the right wing press—the 'pops' were thirsting for blood."[65] In addition, the apparent tug-of-war between Prior and Thatcher shifted the debate to the right: Conflict occurred between the moderate and the right wings of the Conservative party, not between Labour and the Conservatives.[66] Perhaps most significant, it served Thatcher's purpose to have a minister whose moderate, consensus-building approach would highlight the distinctive qualities of her own leadership style. Throughout the passage of the 1980 act, Thatcher appeared to adhere to her convictions, while Prior's moderation and compromise moved policy in the direction she wanted. Certainly these considerations played a role in her decision to make Prior the minister responsible for trade union reform.

By making trade union reform credible, Prior's achievement laid the groundwork for more radical reform to follow. With more irony than gratitude in his voice, the next employment secretary, Norman Tebbit, acknowledged his debt to Prior: "Before Thatcher, it was assumed that nobody could do anything about the unions. And so there was a credibility gap that had to be overcome. . . . Jim's work ahead of me made reform credible."[67] Shortly after Prior finished his work on the first employment bill, Thatcher promptly removed him, and Tebbit, a much more radical reformer, took his place.

In contrast to Prior, Tebbit demonstrated Thatcherite zeal in his approach to union reform. The Employment Act of 1982 substantially weakened the closed shop, greatly increased the rights of individuals to bring suits against their unions, outlawed political strikes, and exposed union funds to liability for unlawful industrial action. Tebbit assessed its impact as profound and irreversible:

> I think that before the [1982] act and during the passage of the act the trades unions were seen as a major cause of British problems. Indeed, in the wake of the miners' strike which brought down Mr. Heath and the so-called winter of discontent which really brought down Mr. Callaghan, they were seen by a large number of people as a constitutional problem, as a threat to the democratic structure. And you'll recollect that there was a great deal of talk in both British and foreign newspapers around the theme of "Is Britain governable?" and that always went back to the role of the trades unions. *That discussion no longer happens. It's something which nobody talks about anymore.* And so the public I think sees the unions as no longer relevant to the structure of government. They no longer see the union as being one of the powerful parts of the establishment. (emphasis added)[68]

Thatcher's government fundamentally (and skillfully) altered not only the structure of the unions but also their place in the political order and the public mind.

Trade union reform also produced short-term political advantages. It placed the Labour party in the untenable and unpopular position of defending the unions. Just as significant, the second employment bill triggered the first of many identity crises for the new SDP. With only one exception, the Social Democratic MPs came directly from the Labour party, and several had been sponsored by trade unions. Yet the SDP leadership was acutely aware of public sentiment against the unions and decided to vote with the government. Five SDP MPs defied the party whip and one abstained, creating the first of many cleavages in the parliamentary party. Even more damaging to the SDP's reputation as a new party with lofty ideals was the demonstrated lack of principle the vote seemed to reveal. The undersecretary of state for employment reminded the SDP of Winston Churchill's advice: "It is all very well having one's ear to the ground, but it often leads to a very undignified posture."[69] The SDP's preoccupation with opinion polls provided yet another contrast to Thatcher's conviction-style leadership.

The virtues of the prime minister's leadership became more vividly apparent in April 1982 when the Argentineans invaded the Falkland Islands, which Britain considered its sovereign territory, and the prime minister rendered a swift, decisive response. Before the war, the SDP-Liberal Alliance led in the polls with 30 percent, while Labour secured 22 percent and the Conservatives 25. Labour's support remained relatively constant through the 1983 general election, but "floating voters," especially skilled workers, who had moved to the Alliance returned in droves to the Conservative party. By May 1982, Alliance support fell to 23 percent, and in May 1983 at the start of the general election campaign it sank to 14 percent. In contrast, the Conservatives began a steady recovery and started the campaign with 44 percent.[70] The actual impact of the Falklands war has been disputed and probably overestimated—several factors account for the shift in support— but the war provided a dramatic event that transformed the prime minister with a preference for Victorian values into the heroine of the Victorian era, the ancient Queen Boadicea.[71]

Thatcher's wartime leadership served to highlight her strength and determination, a critical source of her public support even when her approval ratings were low. Opinion polls indicate the public admired Thatcher for her strength as prime minister, and some evidence suggests the role conviction politics played in building and maintaining her support.

Consider the public's perception of Margaret Thatcher's leadership qualities. From November 1980 through January 1990, Thatcher consistently ranked above opposition leaders as "a capable leader" and "good in a crisis."[72] When Gallup asked voters to choose statements that described particular leaders, Thatcher led the list of strong leadership qualities, including "you know where he/she stands on issues" and "says what he/she believes."[73] From 1985 through 1989, voters described their prime minister as "determined," "tough," "decisive," and someone who "sticks to principles" far more frequently than they attributed these qualities to any of her opponents.[74] Throughout this period, voters also viewed Thatcher as "most likely to get things done" and "most likely to improve Britain's standing abroad."[75]

Furthermore, some additional evidence suggests the role her conviction-style leadership might have played in building her early support. A little more than a year after her first election, Gallup questioned voters who altered their opinion of Thatcher. Among those who viewed her more favorably ("If your impression of Mrs. Thatcher has gone up, why do you say that?"), 51 percent said she "sticks to policies" and 33 percent stated she was "a good strong leader." For those who viewed Thatcher less favorably, 25 percent cited "not kept promises."[76] In other words, the public's perception of Thatcher's degree of conviction created shifts in her support.

By the spring of 1983, the British public saw a sharp contrast between Thatcher's strong leadership and the weakness of her opponents. Hoping to take advantage of that perception and the "Falklands factor," Thatcher called a general election for June 9. Boosted by high approval ratings, the Conservatives faced rival parties riddled with internal conflict.

Throughout the campaign, Labour's internal disputes primarily focused on its defense policy. Three prominent Labour party politicians—Roy Hattersley, Denis Healey, and James Callaghan—spoke out against the party's official policy of unilateral nuclear disarmament. (The party's unilateralism combined with its plans for further nationalization led commentators to quip that the Labour manifesto provided the longest suicide note in history.) Moreover, it was Labour that foolishly focused attention on the Falklands war. To intensify attacks on the Conservative government, Healey criticized Thatcher for "glorying in slaughter."[77] Following Healey's remark, Neil Kinnock accused the prime minister of spilling "guts on Goose Green" to prove the strength and conviction of her government.[78] These desperate attacks only served to remind the electorate of victory in the Falklands and thereby solidify support for Thatcher. In contrast to the prime minister, who seemed strong and courageous, Labour leaders appeared weak and unpatriotic. The press portrayed Labour's official leader, Michael Foot, as a dottering old professor unable to instruct or discipline his pupils. In the last week of May, fewer than 20 percent of those surveyed were satisfied with Foot's performance.[79] The "Foot factor" as well as the "Falklands factor" ensured Labour would pose no threat to the Iron Lady.

The Alliance campaign also showed signs of confusion and weakness. Among Alliance leaders, disagreements on the future of nuclear deterrence attracted some negative publicity, although policy differences in the Alliance were minor compared with disputes in Labour. More important, "Prime Minister Designate" Roy Jenkins proved almost as unpopular as Labour leader Foot. One week before the election, only 27 percent of those surveyed were satisfied with Jenkins's leadership.[80] His unpopularity led to an unsuccessful coup by Liberal leader David Steel to replace Jenkins at midcampaign. Like Labour, the Alliance failed to offer clear policies and certain leadership.

As in 1979, the outcome of the election registered the voters' rejection of Labour, not their enthusiastic endorsement of the Conservative party or its leader. The Conservatives secured a majority of 144 seats, but Thatcher's party won only 42.4 percent of the vote, less than in 1979. On the other hand, Labour won only 27.5 percent of the vote, while the Alliance attracted 25.4 percent.[81] Based on its average share of the constituency vote, Labour suffered its worst defeat since its founding in 1900.[82]

The 1983 results provided additional evidence of Labour's long-term demise. Labour's party identifiers fell by 24 percent, and, for the first time, there were more Conservative than Labour identifiers. Several factors explain Labour's diminished support: Many Labour identifiers defected to the Alliance; more Labourites switched to the Conservatives (7 percent) than the other way around (4 percent); and, for the first time, young voters split evenly between Labour and the Conservatives.[83] Furthermore, the Labour vote remained mostly working class, but most working-class voters failed to support Labour—a remarkable result in a year when unemployment had reached 3 million.

Thatcher's reconstituted electorate continued to erode Labour's base. Among skilled workers, the Conservatives led Labour by 12 percent. During the first Thatcher government, owner-occupied households increased from 55 to 60 percent, and the Conservatives won 47 percent of those votes. Labour secured 49 percent of the votes from residents in council estates, but by 1983, they constituted only 29 percent of the electorate. Finally, in the south of England, Labour won only 3 of the 186 seats outside London. The *Sunday Times* concluded that "Labour is now the party of declining Britain, Thursday's poll results show. Overall, Labour did badly, losing a fifth of the votes which it won in 1979. But in relatively prosperous Britain—southern, home-owning, white Britain outside the cities—it performed catastrophically. . . . [I]ts prospects of forming another majority government in Britain are now remote."[84] As Thatcher read the results, the 1983 electorate rendered a decisive vote against the Labour party and the postwar order it had constructed.

At the start of her second government, the prime minister determined to deliver a final blow to the Labour party's core constituency, the trade unions. In doing so, she intended to remove any vestiges of the corporatist state, which she believed also provided the driving force behind socialism. When she formed her government, she asked another traditional Tory, Peter Walker, to become the secretary of state for energy and immediately alerted him, "Sometime in the life of this Parliament we're going to have a dispute with [Arthur] Scargill,"[85] the militant leader of the National Union of Mineworkers (NUM). When the Yorkshire Coal Board announced the closure of the Cortonwood pit because it was deemed "uneconomic," Scargill replied with what became his refrain: There is no such thing as an uneconomic pit. Conviction clashed with conviction, and in March 1984 Scargill led his miners out on strike.

Ever since circumstances had forced Thatcher to comply with the miners' demands in 1981, she had been preparing for a battle she knew she could win. Starting in 1981, she directed the National Coal Board to produce much more coal than the nation could possibly consume; likewise, she instructed the Central Electricity Board to begin extensive stockpiling. Just as significant to the outcome of the 1984–85 strike, she prepared the police, although initially those efforts had been taken in response to the urban race riots of 1981.

After the riots, Thatcher's government financed new police vehicles, weapons, communications, and protective gear. By 1984, 140,000 police had received military training in "tactical operations" and the use of riot-control equipment. The Police National Reporting Centre became permanent and acquired the character of a national police force. Long after the miners' strike, Thatcher would assert that her government had learned "the lessons of the 1981 inner-city riots," and they also applied to the miners: "Mob violence can only be defeated if the police have the complete moral and practical support of the government."[86] In the yearlong conflict that ensued, the police greatly outnumbered the pickets, and they were well equipped to tackle the "mob." Thatcher had essentially reversed the reform of her nineteenth-century predecessor: Peel established the Metropolitan police as a liberal alternative to the army, but Thatcher's initiatives made the police more closely resemble the military.

The nightly news captured scenes of violent clashes between police and pickets that shocked the nation. (In one of the worst confrontations, viewers watched mounted police charge ten thousand pickets at a coking plant outside Sheffield.) Most of the public sided with the government in the dispute, but many others—especially members of the mining communities in the depressed North—were disheartened by the state's violent action against the miners. British miners had occupied a special place in the nation's history: In the nineteenth century, their labor essentially made Britain the industrial workshop of the world; in the twentieth century, they helped to win two world wars.[87] Of course the miners had also occupied a special spot in the heart of the Labour party and the labor movement. This fact combined with the militancy of the miners' leader enabled Thatcher to depict them as dangerous socialists—the "enemy within"—comparing the miners' threat to liberty at home with the Argentine threat to liberty abroad.[88] When the Scargill factor took the place of the Falklands factor, once again the ideological proved to be the pragmatic.

The impact of the miners' struggle and their eventual defeat rippled throughout the Labour party, the movement, and the NUM itself. Labour leader Neil Kinnock tried to distance himself and his party from Scargill, but at the 1984 party conference, members rebuffed their leader and voted to support the miners. The Labour movement split: The Trades Union Congress (TUC) officially endorsed the NUM, but the largest union, the Transport and General Workers Union (TGWU), failed to offer active support, and as a result, coal moved easily around the country and through its ports. (By 1984, many trade union leaders openly embraced a "new realism" that acknowledged the impact of the 1980 and 1982 legislation and declining union membership.) Finally, in October 1985, the Nottinghamshire miners voted to break away from the NUM and form the Union of Democratic Mineworkers. Thatcher's decisive leadership on the right exacerbated divisions on the left, and the center of gravity started to shift.

Thatcher's victory in the miners' strike vindicated her leadership style and brought her closer to her goal: the amelioration of the corporatist state structure. As one of her cabinet ministers recalled, "She wanted to smash the National Union of Mineworkers. Anybody [else] would have always left something for the other guy . . . because you didn't want to smash, *you didn't want to destroy the power structure,* but she found these things exhilarating" (emphasis added).[89] With the miners' defeat, much of the power structure had been smashed, but one piece remained. Municipal and local governments survived as the last bastion of socialism.

Thatcher wanted to reform local government for several reasons. She hoped to abolish the local rates, which local governments could set without restraint. Furthermore, the spending of local authorities consistently exceeded the government's PSBR targets. Finally, and most significant to the prime minister, the left had established a power base at the level of local government. To achieve her goals, Thatcher proposed two initiatives: capping the rates to force cuts in local spending and abolishing the General London Council (GLC), led by Livingstone, and six other metropolitan councils. Both proposals met substantial resistance, but as in the miners' strike, the struggles that ensued wounded the Labour party more than they harmed the Iron Lady.

The Rates Act of 1984 created a clash between the government and local authorities, especially in Liverpool, where the Trotskyite faction known as the Militant Tendency controlled the city council. The "Merseyside Militants" refused to cut spending and ran up an illegal budget deficit, bringing their city to the brink of bankruptcy. Labour leader Kinnock eventually managed to get the militant councillors expelled from his party, but for more than a year, Labour endured substantial intraparty strife.

Thatcher's second initiative also succeeded in harming Labour: When she moved to abolish the GLC and six other councils, Thatcher shifted attention from the Merseyside Militants to the "Looney Left" in London. As leader of the GLC, Livingstone used the council's budget to deliver grants to radical groups and to promote socialist causes. The GLC and its leader presented a persistent obstacle to a Labour party struggling to revamp its image and appeal to moderate voters. Nevertheless, for a brief while it looked as if Thatcher's plans might backfire: When she proposed to substitute an appointed Conservative council for the elected Labour one, the GLC waged a brilliant campaign "to save London democracy." In a reversal of its nineteenth-century role, this time the House of Lords defended democracy: The Lords vetoed the legislation, and abolition was postponed for a year. By the time abolition went into effect, Thatcher's zealous assault on democratic governance had faded from public memory, but Labour's identification with the Looney Left remained a fixed part of the party's image.

Throughout Thatcher's second government, internal disputes continued to preoccupy and divide her opponents on the left and in the center, but Thatcher's own party also suffered splits. First a backbench revolt thwarted the prime minister's attempt to introduce university tuition fees. Then Francis Pym formed "Centre Forward," a group opposed to the government's social and economic policies. Finally, 1985 concluded with a controversy concerning the sale of Britain's last helicopter company, Westland, which almost brought down the government. In the parlance of the day's press, Thatcher's government kept slipping on "banana skins." In 1986 it would slide even further, as backbenchers opposed the sale of British Leyland to General Motors and Ford, voted against the government's shops bill, and rebelled against Thatcher's decision to support the U.S. bombing raid on Libya. Despite warnings from within her own party, Thatcher persisted in the pursuit of her convictions, alienating an already deeply dissatisfied public.

Conservative party fortunes continued to dwindle as Thatcher's approval ratings continued to fall throughout 1986. In the summer, the prime minister refused to impose sanctions against South Africa, a decision that threatened the survival of the Commonwealth and produced a confrontation with the monarchy. By the end of 1986, the Thatcher government had clashed with just about every major British institution, including the universities, the Crown, and the Anglican Church.[90]

Fortunately for the prime minister and her party, gains accrued by the Alliance or Labour never lasted long. Intraparty divisions deepened as disputes concerning defense preoccupied the opposition parties. As in domestic policy, Thatcher's firm convictions concerning defense fueled splits in Labour and the Alliance. By the start of 1987, the Conservatives recovered the top spot in the polls and prepared for another general election.

Despite a divided opposition, Thatcher's second government accomplished much less than her first. Perhaps the parliamentary majority of 144 proved too large to cohere. Just as significant, the 1983 manifesto had failed to establish specific plans or clear priorities. In general, Thatcher seemed to lose her radical zeal, though she would recover it after 1987.

Even in the budget process, the pace of radical reform slowed significantly in the second government. Admittedly, the new chancellor, Nigel Lawson, secured additional tax reform in 1984. His first budget reduced capital allowances in the corporation tax, abolished the investment income surcharge, created a higher threshold for development land tax, widened the base for VAT, allowed more generous tax treatment for stock options, and abolished life insurance premium relief.[91] Yet as Lawson has acknowledged, despite substantial change in taxation, the government never reduced the overall burden as a proportion of the gross domestic product. In economic policy, the major accomplishment of Thatcher's second government concerned privatization, not taxation.

In contrast to trade union reform, plans to privatize Britain's nationalized industries required bold initiative and active leadership of public opinion. As Tebbit recalled, "Public opinion was a major factor, very much the major factor in the trades union legislation. . . . There was a demand there and it was an urgent demand." By contrast, privatization "didn't come so high up on [the public's] agenda of concern." Tebbit explained why:

> I don't think there was any love of nationalized industries. They were generally seen to be failures, but they were regarded as something which governments couldn't deal with. It was like the weather—out of the hands of man and something the British just had to live with. . . . There was a great deal of mockery at the time [of the Civil Aviation Act of 1980] on the part of the Labour party—you know, "You're not going to be able to denationalize British Airways. Nobody would buy it." . . . At first people didn't think it could be done.[92]

In the case of privatization, Thatcher clearly set the agenda for the public, but to persuade them she needed to make possible what seemed impossible.

Substantial structural and technical obstacles stood in the way of privatization—another contrast to trade union reform—and the challenges varied from one industry to another. According to Tebbit:

> British Telecom had no accounting. So we had to create an accounting system. We had to create a competitor, and we had to create a licensing system and regulatory authority—none of which existed. So there were a whole lot of steps along the path before we could denationalize it. British Airways was easier because it was already in a competitive

arena. . . . British Steel in the same way. We had to persuade people it was a viable business, but we didn't have to create a new structure for it. . . . With water we needed to create not only a competitive arrangement but also the regulatory authority.

Privatization required extensive planning and careful preparation as well as dogged determination.

The case of electricity (privatized in the third government) illustrates many of the challenges Thatcher faced and demonstrates that industry could cling to the corporatist state even more firmly than the trade unions had. Cecil Parkinson, secretary of state for energy,[93] recalled one of many confrontations with industrial interests as Thatcher's government prepared to privatize electricity. According to Parkinson, "The vested interests obstructed us every step of the way, and she took a lot of them on. . . . At one point, Walter Marshall [chairman of the Central Electricity Generating Board] threatened me. He said the entire board would resign. I went to her and we put together a shadow board. She would not stand for blackmail. As she said at the time, 'We didn't defeat the miners so we could be beaten by the barons.'"[94] Thatcher has provided an account of the conflicts that occurred that is more benign than Parkinson's recollections, although she admits that electricity was "the most technically and politically difficult privatization."[95] Regardless of its accuracy, Parkinson's account reveals the perception of many of Thatcher's ministers that she was determined to bust the trusts, whether formed by the unions or by the barons of industry.

Despite the difficulties, Thatcher's governments managed to produce a long list of privatized industries throughout the 1980s. In her first government, the privatization of British Telecom (1981) provided her primary achievement. The 1980 Aviation Act also paved the way for later privatization of British Airways, and in 1981 the government sold British rail subsidiaries. After 1983, the pace of reform quickened. During the second government, Thatcher focused on energy and transportation: Britoil had been privatized in 1982; shares in Enterprise Oil were sold from 1984 to 1988; the last share of British Petroleum was sold in 1987; and British Gas was privatized in 1986. Both British Aerospace (1985) and Rolls Royce (1987) were also privatized. Her third government proved even more radical, privatizing British Steel (1988) and creating the controversial Water and Sewerage Companies (1989). When she left office, legislation had also been enacted to permit privatization of electricity, and long-term plans had been made for British rail and British coal. By 1991, only one-third of the 1979 publicly owned commercial sector remained. Even before the 1987 general election, psephologists had concluded that Thatcher made many "converts to the free enterprise philosophy" by swinging public opinion in favor of pri-vatization.[96] The conviction politician had defied the naysayers and made possible that which seemed impossible.

By the spring of 1987, Thatcher prepared to achieve another unlikely goal, her third electoral victory, which would make her the prime minister with the longest consecutive years in office during the twentieth century. En-couraged by local election results in May and hoping to capitalize on an im-proving economy, Thatcher called a general election for June 11. Despite growing concern about the prime minister's style—fear that her greatest virtue had become her central vice—the electorate remained unconvinced that the opposition parties could provide a viable alternative to Thatcherism.

At the start of the campaign, Thatcher and the Conservative party at-tacked what they considered the central threat: the new opposition in the form of the Alliance. Yet when Thatcher questioned the center parties about their defense policy, she easily triggered new conflict within the divided Al-liance. Internal disputes sent the Alliance on a downward reciprocal spiral. Decline in the polls fueled additional feuds: at first the result of rivalry be-tween Social Democratic and Liberal leaders who campaigned as a dual lead-ership team; later the consequence of conflicting views on how and with whom to negotiate in the event of a hung Parliament. In defense as in eco-nomic policy, SDP leader David Owen was moving rapidly to the right in an attempt to appeal to the new Thatcherite electorate, but this Downsian calculation fueled conflict within his own party and between the SDP and the Liberals.

Labour also made an attempt to move to the right. The party abandoned its old cloth-cap image and offered the electorate a glossy new product. Not only did the red rose replace the red flag, but also the leader, Neil Kinnock, took the place of the party. Indeed, Kinnock delivered a dazzling perfor-mance, modeled after the style and approach of the recently successful U.S. presidential candidate. His first party election broadcast imitated a Reagan television commercial in 1984: Kinnock starred, and his wife played the role of leading lady.[97] To make the message clear, the broadcast provided a voting cue for the public: The word flashed across the screen was "Kinnock," not "Labour." Yet even the new modern campaign could not conceal Labour's continuing conflict, and when the leader attempted to clarify his party's de-fense policy, he fudged the issue in a way that indicated Labour might ren-der Britain defenseless.[98]

Despite the Conservatives' steady lead in the polls, at times their campaign also floundered. Instead of another spectacular show orchestrated by Saatchi and Saatchi, the Conservatives rendered a lackluster performance. To a great extent, conflict between the Conservative Central Office, led by Tebbit as chairman, and the prime minister determined the character of the party's campaign. By 1987, the two ideological soul mates had become political rivals: Tebbit grew convinced that Thatcher had become a liability, and the party's official advertising agency, Saatchi and Saatchi, tried to minimize her role in the campaign. Thatcher distrusted Tebbit and the Saatchis and relied on the advice of her own team of consultants—Gordon Reece, Tim Bell, and (unofficially) a separate advertising firm, Young and Rubicam. In the final week of the campaign, when a rogue poll showed a narrow lead between the Conservatives and Labour, conflict erupted into chaos, a "fiasco" as John Banks from Young and Rubicam described it. At Number 10 Downing Street, "Bell would be in one room, the Saatchis in another, and I'd be in another." He described a situation where the advertising experts had "all become power mad."[99] As they each maneuvered to secure control of the campaign, the substance of their disputes centered on whether Thatcher's conviction-style leadership remained an asset or had become a liability. After the election, Thatcher's own image-makers became increasingly preoccupied with improving her image, for during the campaign the dark side of conviction politics had started to come to light.

As its central campaign tactic, Labour attacked the prime minister's stubborn independence and insensitivity, and Thatcher's remarks often seemed to confirm Labour's allegations. When asked if 1987 would be her last general election campaign, Thatcher replied that she intended to go "on and on," sounding more like a monarch than a prime minister.[100] Questioned about her own private health treatment, Thatcher defended her right to seek care "on the day, at the time, with the doctor I choose," seemingly indifferent to the plight of those who depended on and waited for care from the National Health Service.[101] Forced to respond to critics who charged that she was insensitive, Thatcher proved their point by mocking those who "drool and drivel about caring."[102] Labour successfully focused attention on the shortcomings of Thatcher's leadership style, but the party nonetheless proved unable to convince voters to choose "caring" and reject "conviction."

Notwithstanding the public's growing concern about the prime minister's leadership style, Thatcher achieved her historic victory in the 1987 general election. With 43 percent of the vote, the Conservatives secured 376 seats, a majority of 101. Labour earned 32 percent and 229 seats, and the Alliance won 23 percent of the vote, yielding a meager 22 seats, only 5 of which belonged to the SDP.

The pattern of Thatcher's previous elections persisted in 1987. Labour remained strong primarily in the declining industrial North, while the Conservatives swept the prosperous South. With 3 million still unemployed, the Conservatives nonetheless won 36 percent of the working-class votes, the highest ever. Council house sales and privatization continued to restructure class voting to the benefit of the Conservatives.[103] The percentage of homeowners had increased from 52 percent in 1979 to 66 percent in 1987, and council house residents fell from 35 to 27 percent. Among working-class homeowners, 44 percent voted Conservative, while only 31 percent voted Labour. The percentage of shareholders increased from 7 percent in 1979 to 19 percent in 1987: Of those who bought shares in the 1980s, 56 percent voted Conservative, only 16 percent Labour.[104]

Despite its shift to the right, Labour suffered from its image as "extremist." According to public opinion polls, references to extremism increased from 19 percent in 1983 to 27 percent in 1987. (The percentage rose from 25 to 42 among Labour defectors.) According to one election analyst, "The party's campaign organizers managed to keep its 'looney' left out of sight but not, apparently, out of mind."[105] Labour learned that old images die hard and are not easily replaced, even by a Labour leader who expounds the virtues of "supply-side socialism," as Kinnock tried to do in 1987.

By the 1987 general election, the myth of a mandate came closer to reality: Thatcher did win a clearer, more positive endorsement for her policies than she had secured in earlier elections. As in the past, the Conservatives led Labour on law and order, defense, and taxes, and this time they also won on inflation. Substantial portions of the general voting public believed the economy had improved (45 percent), living standards had risen (38 percent), and "opportunities to get ahead" had increased (46 percent). Furthermore, among the 35 percent that considered defense important, Labour trailed the Conservatives by 63 percent. To sum it up, in 1987 Thatcher and her party won credit for "prosperity at home and peace abroad."[106] The electorate appeared to endorse the view expressed in the Conservative campaign slogan: "It's great to be great again."

Yet Thatcher should have detected warning signs that appeared in the course of the campaign. Public concern that the prime minister was "uncaring" might constitute more than a public relations problem. Public opinion shifted in favor of many conservative policies, but the majority of British voters continued to believe that the state should "care" for its citizens in at least two significant areas of public policy: health and education. Furthermore, Thatcher had tried to tap new nationalist fervor by highlighting her firm resistance to the European Union. Nevertheless, the response to a Conservative campaign poster depicting a British bulldog with a French poodle and a German shepherd was largely ridicule and disgust, expressed by commentators in the elite press across the ideological spectrum.[107] On the reform of domestic social policy and in the context of European affairs, Thatcher should have proceeded with caution. Instead, she saw the election result as a signal to embark on new, radical reform in uncharted territory.

With the renewed confidence that came with her third consecutive victory, Thatcher moved into the area of education reform, a political minefield she had previously avoided. Pressure to reform education had constituted a critical part of the breakdown of postwar consensus.[108] Voters and politicians agreed that Britain needed to bridge its gap between academic study and practical training in order to modernize its economy and create greater equality of opportunity. Ironically, a 1983 report issued in the U.S. by the National Commission for Excellence in Education, *A Nation at Risk: The Imperative for Educational Reform*, stimulated the reform impulse in Britain. (The same report inspired Reagan to wage one of his most successful public relations campaigns, but he declined to take any concrete initiatives. See chapter 7.) The U.S. report attacked mediocrity in education and depicted the dire state of education as a threat to national security and prosperity. Reformers on both sides of the Atlantic started to ask, "How could education provide a source of renewed national greatness?" In her third government, Thatcher would provide a neoliberal answer with her 1988 education reform bill.

The 1988 act had two objectives: to provide a national curriculum and to allow schools to opt out of the control of the local education authorities (LEAs). Ultimately, Thatcher was dissatisfied with the way the national curriculum developed, and she blamed her education secretary, Kenneth Baker, for the overly bureaucratic and administratively awkward system he created. Nevertheless, the national curriculum accomplished some of her central goals: It diminished the influence of both the LEAs and the teachers' unions, who also lost their ability to negotiate pay, and it ensured that all students would have the opportunity to acquire certain core skills.[109] More important to Thatcher, by allowing schools to opt out of the control of the LEAs, she increased the "choice" of parents and hoped to make the system more efficient and cost-effective. Both Thatcher and Joseph, education secretary from 1981 to 1986, wanted an education voucher scheme, and the 1988 act brought them closer to that goal.[110] In addition to opting out, the act provided for open enrollment and per capita funding. Grant-maintained schools took the place of local authority schools. At the same time, the legislation changed the way education policy would be made, ending negotiation between the government and pressure groups, including the unions. Management replaced consensus, and education became a matter of economic, not social, policy.[111] The 1988 reform met opposition from the Department of Education and Science, local authorities, teachers, and churches. Yet after a bruising battle Thatcher secured victory.

In 1988 the prime minister weathered the political storm stirred by the education act, and her government recovered in the polls as Britain experienced continued economic improvement: Unemployment fell, incomes rose, taxes were cut, and the budget balanced.[112] Thatcher took advantage of her government's public support and escalated plans for privatization as well as other economic and political reforms. Environment Secretary Nicholas Ridley announced plans to sell ten water authorities in 1989, and Parkinson unveiled the government's plan to privatize electricity in 1990. In contrast to most of the other privatized industries, water and electricity were viewed by the public as necessities of life and therefore were considered the responsibility of the state. Plans to privatize water and electricity were eventually carried out, but they encountered greater opposition than earlier privatization initiatives did. As with education and health care reforms, privatization of water and electricity renewed doubts about Thatcher's compassion and concern for the less fortunate members of society. Undaunted by such criticism, in June 1988 she took the first step toward restructuring the health service when she announced that the Department of Health and Social Security (DHSS) would be divided, thereby removing the DHSS as an institutional obstacle to reform.

For political reasons, Thatcher proceeded more cautiously with health care reform than she had with other policies, and she stopped short of proposing a scheme of private insurance to replace the National Health Service (NHS).[113] Earlier, a radical report from the Central Policy Review Staff (CPRS), the government's own think tank, was leaked to the *Economist,* and Thatcher responded to public outrage with the assurance that the NHS is "safe with us," a pledge she repeated in the 1987 election. In fact, throughout the 1980s, real spending on health increased substantially, but the costs of health care were rising even more rapidly, as they were in most postindustrial democracies. Until 1988, failure to pursue health care reform frustrated Thatcher's right-wing supporters, and floods of policy papers had poured out of the neoliberal think tanks on both sides of the Atlantic.[114] Only after Thatcher secured her third electoral victory was she prepared to reform Britain's most popular institution.

In January 1988 Thatcher established (and chaired) a small group of ministers to conduct a fundamental review of the NHS. One year later, they published a government white paper, "Working for Patients," which identified the basic structure of reform that the government would pursue. Immediately, the Conservative party fell in the polls, and the controversy that ensued has been blamed for at least two subsequent by-election losses. The proposals sparked immediate condemnation from the British Medical Association, the Royal Colleges, health trade unions, and the other parties in Parliament. In the midst of overwhelming opposition, in 1989 Health Secretary Kenneth Clarke unveiled the government's plan.

Thatcher's reform separated the provision and the financing of health care. The NHS would continue to be funded through general taxation, but "money would follow the patient." Hospitals could choose to opt out of the control of local health authorities, although they would remain within the NHS as self-governing "trusts." (Now they could determine pay and conditions of staff and contract out services in the public and private sectors.) General practitioners with large practices could manage their own NHS budgets. The reform also provided tax breaks for private health insurance premiums paid for by those over age sixty. Essentially, the state would continue to provide funding, while market forces would determine the level of support.[115] Thatcher had proceeded cautiously with health reform, but her health service and community care bill eventually brought about substantial change. It also immediately turned the tide of public opinion against her, and a flood of political difficulties soon followed as her government struggled to survive a recession, the implementation of the "community charge," or poll tax, ministerial resignations, and intraparty conflict concerning the European Union.

Thatcher promoted the poll tax as the most effective way to replace property taxes or rates, but it also appealed to her because it would deliver a final blow to the authority of local government. As early as 1974, Thatcher pledged that her government would abolish the rates, and her party renewed its commitment in the 1983 manifesto. She and other critics of the rates argued persuasively that the system needed reform for several reasons. Local governments spent one-quarter of all public expenditures, and the central government provided half the funding but exercised no control over spending. (Whenever the government cut funds, local authorities simply raised the rates and continued to overspend.) Although the tax took only 2 to 3 percent of income, taxpayers resented it because they had to pay the tax in a single lump sum. Moreover, only 18 million (out of an electorate of 35 million) paid the rates; therefore, business carried much of the burden. To replace the rates, Thatcher proposed the poll tax, essentially a flat tax on all adult residents (with partial rebates for low-income residents). According to Thatcher's plan, the poll tax ensured "that everyone should contribute something, and therefore have something to lose from electing a spendthrift council." As she explained, "The principle of accountability underlay the whole reform."[116] Yet Thatcher wrongly assumed that taxpayers would hold their local government accountable and not hers.

Thatcher chose to ignore all the warning shots that came as rapid fire from her backbenches, her party conference, and her own cabinet. Critics within the Conservative party attacked the reform as regressive, unjust, administratively awkward, hard to collect, and a menace to civil liberty. As early as May 1985, Chancellor Lawson adamantly opposed the proposed new tax. In a memo he circulated to committee members responsible for the reform, Lawson warned, "[L]ocal authorities would seize the opportunity to bump up their spending and revenue and blame it all on the imposition by the Government of an alien system of taxation. . . . The proposal for a poll tax would be completely unworkable and politically catastrophic."[117] Shortly after Thatcher secured approval for her local government finance bill (to be implemented in England and Wales in April 1990), the unworkable and politically catastrophic nature of the reform became apparent.

At the time of its implementation, the public rendered swift and dramatic opposition. On the day before the poll tax took effect, a demonstration erupted into a riot in Trafalgar Square. Mounted police stormed the protesters, creating scenes reminiscent of the 1985 miners' strike, but this time the police attacked ordinary taxpayers, who could hardly be depicted as "the enemy within." Throughout England and Wales, citizens simply refused to pay. Following the furor that accompanied the poll tax, Thatcher's approval ratings sunk below the nadirs she had hit in 1981 and again in 1985–86. Six months after its implementation, when she was challenged in the leadership contest, all the contestants declared their commitment to review the tax, and in 1991 a reformed rating system (and increased VAT) replaced the poll tax. Convinced that the problems concerned its implementation and not its design, conviction politician Thatcher might well have maintained the tax.

Between passage of the local finance bill and its implementation, another issue increasingly threatened the survival of Thatcher's third government. Whereas the poll tax alienated the public, Thatcher's position concerning Europe split her cabinet, creating a rift that would culminate in the resignations of Chancellor Lawson and Howe, the ex-chancellor and ex–foreign secretary. (See chapters 8 and 9.)

The day after Howe delivered his resignation speech to Parliament, Michael Heseltine, the cabinet rebel during the Westland affair, announced his candidacy for the leadership. On the first ballot on November 20, Thatcher secured 204 votes, Heseltine won 152, and 16 MPs abstained. Thatcher's vote fell 4 short of the supermajority she needed to win on the first ballot. The same selection mechanism that helped propel Thatcher to power facilitated her downfall eleven years later. Like Heath, Thatcher withdrew from the leadership contest before the second ballot, and on November 27, John Major became leader of the Conservative party and the new prime minister.

The strength of the leadership challenge in 1990 appeared to catch Thatcher by surprise, but she should have seen it coming. A year earlier she had confronted another challenge: The insurgent then, Anthony Meyer, was not a prominent MP or a viable alternative, but precisely because Meyer was not a serious contender, the votes he secured clearly rendered a negative referendum on her premiership. A "one nation, unrepentant Heathite," Meyer based his appeal almost entirely on his critique of the prime minister's style, attacking her "divisive approach" and her tendency to "rejoice in conflict." "She knows exactly what she wants and [thinks] nobody else does, but so did Hitler," Meyer declared. Even after his local association deselected him as a parliamentary candidate (by a 2-to-1 vote), he did not regret his bold move: "I let fresh air in, encouraged people to think the unthinkable: She is not invincible."[118] Meyer exposed the disillusionment within the parliamentary party, but at the time Thatcher's public support shielded her from any serious coup. One year later, without her fortress of public approval, she proved unable to withstand the assault from her intraparty enemies.

In a section from his memoirs entitled "Why Margaret Had to Go," Lawson attributed her downfall to the poll tax and European policy but also emphasized her style. Both the public and the parliamentary party agreed that

> where a change of leader clearly would make a difference, was Margaret Thatcher herself and her "style." Margaret had always been a leader who polarized opinion. Most people either admired, respected and even loved her, or they saw her as at best intolerable and at worst evil. Very few were indifferent to her. In the early years the votes gained by her strong personality clearly outweighed the votes lost by it. In her third term the balance began to switch. Conservative Members found that increasing numbers of their erstwhile supporters, let alone congenital floating voters, saw her as disagreeably strident, excessively authoritarian, and unbearably bossy.[119]

Others agreed with Lawson's assessment. As Prior put it in the summer of 1990, "There's a lot of call for a 'kinder and gentler' prime minister, but they won't get it from her. That's not her style. It may well be that she has now outlived her usefulness."[120] Another ex-minister mused, "I always entertained the hope that Boadicea would become Florence Nightingale. That's what we need now—Florence Nightingale."[121] Once admired for her resolution, at the end of her reign Thatcher incurred wrath for her rigidity.

Thatcher's style remained fixed, even though conditions and expectations changed. By 1990, economic conditions raised new doubts about the long-term viability of the prime minister's policies. In 1989 the U.K. accumulated record-high trade deficits, and mortgage rates rose as inflation soared. When pay offers fell below the inflation rate, a series of strikes followed and continued throughout the summer. Despite the economic downturn, the conviction-style prime minister declined to initiate a U-turn. Yet Thatcher had survived fluctuations in the economy before, most notably the recession in 1981. Economic downturns and upswings always affected her approval ratings, but public dissatisfaction had never before destroyed her political viability. Indeed, while the British blamed their prime minister for short-term economic hardships, they also gave her credit for reviving long-term economic prosperity.[122] The changing conditions that account for the end of Thatcher's premiership are more fundamental than month-to-month fluctuations in the public opinion polls.

To a great extent, Thatcher misread the message in her "mandate" of 1987. Substantial portions of the public endorsed key aspects of her economic policy and approved of the structural changes she had brought about, but public support for Thatcherism also had its limits.[123] In particular, the public was growing increasingly concerned about some of the social implications of the government's harsh policies and its radical leadership. Indeed, Thatcher's zeal for reform seemed to intensify just as the public issued a call for greater compassion and caring, not firm conviction. In short, the conviction politician continued to pursue radical change even after her historic window of opportunity slammed shut.

Thatcher's premiership concluded in 1990, but her legacy became more apparent in the decade that followed. Within the Conservative party, Thatcher's convictions became the basis for a new consensus: According to the party chairman at the time Thatcher left office, she had firmly established a "consensus within the party on the market economy" and removed all remnants of traditional Tory paternalism.[124] Thatcher tapped growing neoliberal sentiment within her party and transformed it into the party's dominant creed.

At the same time, she undermined those movements that promoted a left-wing alternative to the postwar regime, including many of the trade unions, the Campaign for Nuclear Disarmament (CND), and an array of militant groups operating inside and outside the Labour party. Indeed, change within the Labour party provides some of the most convincing evidence of her ideological impact. Largely in response to Thatcher and her perceived success, the Labour party eventually reformed its own constitution in ways that shattered the political foundation of trade union influence and demolished the ideological framework of socialism.[125] In the 1990s, Labour's leader Tony Blair struggled to build a new base for his party by endorsing individual responsibility, promising law and order, and promoting family values. The 1997 government was formed by "New Labour"—even the word "party" was dropped—and the New Labour government clearly accepted the basic social, political, and economic convictions of the neoliberal consensus.

One of her most prominent adversaries was quick to concede that Thatcher had won the ideological struggle to replace the postwar order. Emphasizing the extensive structural change and what he perceived as a shift in public philosophy, Benn declared, "I've often thought we should have a 'Mrs. Thatcher global repeal bill.' But if every act were repealed it would not achieve much. She persuaded so many people. She's had a long-term intellectual impact."[126] The new edifice of the British state stands as the greatest testament to Thatcher's success, and the longer it stands unchallenged, the more firmly planted in public consciousness its principles become.

Finally, when Thatcherism took root, it made Britain more closely resemble the U.S. At home, many British observers have concluded that their nation became "Americanized": Thatcher's supporters applauded the new entrepreneurial spirit and enterprise culture, while her detractors lamented the increased homelessness, the rise in violent crime, and the growing prevalence of "bad manners." Not surprisingly, on the other side of the Atlantic, Thatcher and her policies earned more widespread praise. U.S. citizens warmly embraced Thatcher and applauded her accomplishments. Like Lloyd George, Lady Thatcher could command large, enthusiastic U.S. audiences long after she left office. (The U.S. public never understood how the British could reject such a great leader, echoing their earlier view of Lloyd George's fate.) They tended to see Thatcher as a heroic figure, indeed, the twentieth-century model of success.[127] Her popularity in the U.S. remained greater than at home in Britain, and it even surpassed and outlasted the admiration U.S. citizens expressed for their own conviction-style leader, Ronald Reagan.

Ronald Reagan

Like other conviction politicians in this study, Reagan was an outsider, known to his nation as a film star and television personality long before he took the oath of office as president. Yet his early experiences in acting prepared him for his later political roles, and he easily transferred his professional skills from the Hollywood studio to the Washington scene. President Reagan quickly acquired a reputation as the "Great Communicator": To advance his agenda, he would deliver stirring speeches designed to evoke great emotion and thunderous applause from his audiences (and subsequently secure the support of their representatives in Congress). Moreover, in the late 1930s and 1940s, film producers tended to typecast Reagan as the "good guy"—honest, straightforward, an ordinary man of simple virtue and firmly held beliefs who could also achieve heroic feats. Reagan felt comfortable with the type and believed it reflected his values and his aspirations—American ideals and the ideal American. By the time he entered electoral politics, he had carefully crafted his public persona and rehearsed the role of a man of conviction. (To play a consensus politician—a wheeler and dealer—would have forced Reagan to break out of character.) The style and substance of his acting career made Reagan ready to respond to the casting call for a conviction-style leader in 1980.

Reagan and his advisors wrote a script that depicts his life as a classic Horatio Alger, rags-to-riches tale, and their depiction comes closer to reality than do most mythic accounts about the humble origins of U.S. presidents. Born in Tampico, Illinois, Reagan first lived on Main Street above the general store where his father worked. (Thatcher's family also lived above the store where her father worked, but he owned and operated his own shop.) Reagan spent most of his early life in the small town of Dixon, Illinois, although his father's alcoholism and frequent unemployment often forced the family to move. He greatly admired his mother, a devout member of the Disciples of Christ Church, who instilled in Reagan Christian values and beliefs that would influence his political rhetoric and shape his strong sense of destiny. When Reagan left home, he did so to attend Eureka College, located twenty miles east of Peoria. The college's name and location portend key aspects of Reagan's popularity as a politician: He appeared to have found simple answers to problems that perplexed more sophisticated politicians, and his solutions usually proved to be ones that played well in Peoria. Reagan came from the "heartland" of America, and rarely would he lift his finger off the pulse of public sentiment.

In surprising ways, Reagan's college experiences presage sources of his appeal as president. To attend college, he secured an athletic scholarship, and in the summers he worked as a lifeguard. In addition, he became president of the Booster Club and cheerleader for the basketball team. President Reagan would be admired (and ridiculed) for his ability to convey an American can-do spirit and make people feel good. As president, Reagan would also respond to charges that he failed to grasp economic theory by pointing out that he had majored in economics at Eureka. Of course, Reagan studied pre-Keynesian, essentially nineteenth-century economics, and consequently, the neoliberal economics of Friedman must have seemed familiar. (Reagan's assertion that his college studies prepared him to manage the late-twentieth-century economy proves no more absurd than Thatcher's frequent insistence that she understood the Strategic Defense Initiative because she had majored in chemistry.) Finally, in his college years Reagan also experienced the Depression, and like most Americans, he considered Franklin Delano Roosevelt his hero. Long after he rejected the substance of FDR's New Deal, Reagan continued to emulate aspects of his style. Among other things, Reagan would frequently quote FDR: Not surprisingly, his favorite phrase reminded the American public to consider their "rendezvous with destiny."[128]

For more than thirty years after college, Reagan remained outside the arena of electoral politics, but several aspects of his career provide clues to the character of his presidency and might well have trained him for it. One oft-told story recalls that in his first job as a radio sports announcer, Reagan continued to describe a baseball game after the wire went dead, by fabricating the details in a remarkably convincing way. As president, Reagan's storytelling could captivate an audience even when more fiction than fact informed the tale.[129] During Reagan's Hollywood acting career, he generally secured roles in low-budget films, but some of them proved to be successful at the box office, and at least one might be considered a classic. In *Knute Rockne, All American* Reagan played George Gipp, a Notre Dame football player who suffers an early, tragic death. At practice, when Coach Rockne asks Gipp whether he can carry the ball, he quickly responds, "How far?" President Reagan's rhetoric would often exude a similar optimistic attitude, implying that human effort and achievement confront no natural limits. Gipp's dying words in the film—"Win one for the Gipper"—would also become an amusing slogan for Reagan as candidate and president.[130] Finally, in 1947 the Screen Actors Guild elected Reagan to serve as president of the union, which he did for five years, returning to the post once again in 1959. Politicians interviewed for this study believed that Reagan acquired his impressive negotiating skills as president of the guild. As president of the United States, Reagan would demonstrate that he could strike a bargain as successfully as the most adept professional politician could, although he took care to keep such negotiations privately concealed behind the public face of his conviction-style leadership.

After making films for the government during World War II, Reagan struggled to return to the silver screen, but when he achieved only limited success he moved to the medium of television. General Electric (GE) first hired Reagan to introduce its series *General Electric Theatre* and later host and occasionally act in the GE-sponsored *Death Valley Days*. In addition to television performances, the GE job required that Reagan travel throughout the country promoting the company's products and meeting its employees. GE's former executive, Edward Langley, recalled, "Year after year, in smokey factories . . . he tried to woo [the workers] with Hollywood jokes. But they weren't buying. They wanted, and in time forced him, to hear and respond to their concerns, their growls against the government. . . . No other politician I can think of has been so steeped in the native conservatism of working America."[131] If Hollywood brought Reagan a long way from Dixon, GE sent him back to the heartland. While working for GE in the 1950s, Reagan came into frequent contact with big business as well as the "little guy," and he grew to admire corporate as well as middle America. He also learned how to campaign face-to-face at the grassroots level in addition to using the electronic media to deliver his message. In a number of ways, GE helped to shape Reagan's ideology, mold his style, and move him into the political arena.

Reagan traced the source of his political convictions to an even earlier period in his acting career. He insisted that he experienced firsthand how progressive taxation could place artificial limits on creativity by forcing actors to limit the number of movies they made each year. In his autobiography, he explained that his views stemmed from his exposure to civil-service bureaucrats during the war, the "attempted Communist take-over" of the movie industry,[132] and his experience filming *The Hasty Heart* in Britain in 1949, when Labour governed the country.[133] Reagan alleged that the Democratic party betrayed the principles of Thomas Jefferson—"the definitions and the axioms of a free society"—and, like Andrew Jackson, Reagan presented himself as the genuine heir to the Jeffersonian legacy.[134] Despite his insistence that he remained consistent while the Democrats changed, Reagan's ideology did shift from the worldview of a New Deal Democrat to the philosophy of a neoliberal Republican.

The last on the list of influences might well have been one of the most significant. When divorced Reagan married his second wife, Nancy Davis, her ultraconservative stepfather took Reagan under his wing. In a fateful move, Dr. Loyal Davis introduced Reagan to Barry Goldwater. Reagan officially became a Republican in 1962, shortly after meeting Goldwater at the home of his wife's parents and after reading Goldwater's book *The Conscience of a Conservative*. Reflecting on his initial encounter with Goldwater, Reagan recalled that he "admired him greatly" and found in his book many of the same themes Reagan had developed in his speeches while working for GE.[135]

Like Powell in Britain, Goldwater rendered a radical critique of the postwar political order at the peak of its popularity. On the eve of Lyndon Johnson's "Great Society," Goldwater promoted a clear alternative based on the principles of free enterprise, limited government, and strong national defense. Goldwater's campaign theme, "A Choice, Not an Echo," could serve as the motto for all conviction politicians who reject middle-of-the-road, consensus politics. In his acceptance speech at the Republican convention, Goldwater shocked the nation when he rejected the style as well as the substance of the postwar consensus: "Extremism in the defense of liberty is no vice," Goldwater declared and then added, "moderation in the pursuit of justice is no virtue."[136] In a landslide election, the electorate of the 1960s rejected Goldwater's message, but his campaign paved the way for Reagan's agenda in the 1980s.[137] In the short term, the Goldwater campaign also put the spotlight on Reagan.

As cochairman of Goldwater's presidential campaign in California, Reagan traveled around the state giving speeches on behalf of the Republican nominee. When a group of wealthy Republican contributors asked Reagan to deliver a nationally televised speech, Reagan revised the text he had been delivering for years at GE. In his speech entitled "A Time for Choosing," Reagan issued dire warnings about the dangers of communism, big government, and excessive taxation. Despite Goldwater's own inflammatory rhetoric, his campaign advisors considered Reagan's speech too radical, especially his attack on social security. Nevertheless, after Goldwater viewed an advance tape of the speech, he overruled his advisors and endorsed Reagan's bold broadcast, which proceeded to air one week before the election. The speech failed to influence Goldwater's electoral fortunes, but it did make Reagan a rising political star.

The subsequent relationship between Reagan and Goldwater would follow a rocky road. Goldwater declined to endorse Reagan's presidential candidacies in 1968 and 1976. In fact, while working for Ford during the 1976 campaign, Goldwater delivered an anti-Reagan radio spot.[138] A decade later, while serving on the Senate Intelligence Committee, Goldwater also attacked the Reagan administration for its covert policy in Central America. Lyn Nofziger, Reagan's press secretary during the 1976 campaign, attributed the conflict to political and personal factors. "Goldwater became part of the establishment," according to Nofziger, "and he was and is jealous of Ronald Reagan superseding him as the conservative leader."[139] Whether Goldwater's opposition to Reagan was personal or principled, tension between the two suggests that the senator came to regret the unintended role he played in paving the way for the Reagan presidency.[140]

Shortly after he delivered his televised speech for Goldwater, a small group of millionaire businessmen urged Reagan to run for governor of California. Additional encouragement came quickly from the political consulting firm of Spencer and Roberts. Then and throughout his political career, Reagan failed to rely on his party or consult party officials. Indeed, his outsider status bolstered his image as a man who could unify and heal the intraparty divisions that lingered in the wake of the divisive 1964 contest between Goldwater and liberal Republican Nelson Rockefeller. (Stuart Spencer and William Roberts had managed Rockefeller's 1964 campaign.) At the same time, as a former New Deal Democrat, Reagan offered an appeal that extended beyond partisan Republicans. These factors, combined with Reagan's star qualities, convinced his supporters that he had a promising political career. To launch it, they formed the "Friends of Ronald Reagan" in 1965.

Several aspects of the political environment proved conducive to Reagan's election as governor in 1966. California has a strong Progressive tradition and a weak party system that make it relatively easy for an outsider to enter electoral politics. Moreover, the social unrest that accompanied the race riots in Watts and the free speech movement at the University of California sparked support for Reagan's conservative pledge to restore law and order.

Perhaps most significant, Reagan promised to provide an alternative to the failed leadership of incumbent Democrat Edmund G. (Pat) Brown, and his campaign attributed public policy failures—especially concerning taxation and welfare—to the incumbent's lack of leadership. In response to the charge that Reagan himself lacked the experience necessary to offer strong leadership, he and his advisors invoked the image of Cincinnatus, the Roman general who left his plowshare to defend his republic, an ancient figure who stands today as the model of simple virtue. No matter that the modern Cincinnatus had grown from a small-town boy into a millionaire by 1966: Myth overshadowed reality and helped to shape it.

Reagan's record as a two-term governor proved mixed in style and substance. He managed to cultivate the image of a strong leader with clear convictions, while he also proved quite adept at negotiating with the Democratic leadership of the state assembly.[141] (In fact Reagan's least productive years were 1969–70, when he had Republican majorities in both the state senate and assembly.) Nor did he prove to be a rigid ideologue on all the social issues: Governor Reagan signed the Therapeutic Abortion Act of 1967, although he later alleged that he had failed to anticipate that it would make abortion more frequent and accessible. Furthermore, scandal marred the righteous image of his administration when the public learned that a group of homosexuals had been working in the governor's office. (Providing an early indication of President Reagan's administrative style, the governor's advisors were slow to inform him of the scandal, and Reagan's subsequent public comments on the subject were designed to deceive the press and the public.)[142] Perhaps most surprising, to balance the budget (as California's constitution requires), Governor Reagan raised taxes.

On the other hand, when tax increases produced a budget surplus, Reagan returned the money to the taxpayers rather than use it to fund new government programs. Furthermore, in a dramatic display of his determination to restore law and order, Reagan sent the National Guard onto the University of California campus at Berkeley. (Governor Reagan repeatedly clashed with the universities concerning subjects that ranged from academic tuition to political protest.) He also won approval for the California Welfare Reform Act of 1971, which tightened eligibility requirements and included workfare provisions. Finally, in spite of his tax increases, Reagan did manage to slow the growth of government just as he had pledged in his 1966 gubernatorial campaign.

In 1968 Reagan mounted a very limited effort to secure the Republican nomination for president. For the most part, he allowed others to act on his behalf and insisted that he was not a candidate. Only at the convention did Reagan formally declare his candidacy, but by then Richard Nixon had the nomination wrapped up. Although Reagan and his supporters did not know it at the time, the Nixon administration and its demise would serve to facilitate Reagan's rise to the presidency.

The Watergate scandal sparked anti-Washington sentiment throughout the nation, creating an environment conducive to the success of outsiders. Reagan never explicitly criticized Nixon—he failed to grasp the seriousness of Watergate, especially the constitutional issues—but he was the direct beneficiary of public dissatisfaction with the traditional Republican party and the Washington establishment. To a great extent, in 1976 the same public sentiment that served to boost prospects for Democrat Jimmy Carter also advanced the insurgent candidacy of Reagan.

Along with growing public concern about corruption in Washington, dissatisfaction with the major political parties increased. Watergate had so severely discredited the Republican party that Reagan briefly considered forming a third party.[143] At the same time, the Democrats suffered the lingering effects of the deeply divisive 1968 convention and the 1972 presidential candidacy of George McGovern. Like the British Labour party, U.S. Democrats were perceived as unable to provide decisive leadership and out of touch with mainstream public opinion. As a governor of Georgia and conservative Southern Democrat, Carter initially offered hope to his party by providing an alternative: leadership untainted by Washington politics and independent of interest groups. When the press asked, "Jimmy who?" throughout the 1976 campaign, they bolstered Carter's appeal by putting the spotlight on his status as an outsider. Both Carter and Reagan stood outside the Washington establishment and outside the political parties.

When Reagan challenged President Ford for the Republican nomination in 1976, he believed that public dissatisfaction ran deeper than the temporary disenchantment that followed Watergate. To Reagan, members of the public were beginning to reject the postwar order that traditional Republicans, such as Ford, endorsed. Indeed, Reagan attracted the support of many neoliberal Republicans who shared his view: They considered Ford just as likely to uphold the old order as Nixon was. (Many disenchanted Republicans believed Nixon, like Heath, executed a dramatic retreat from principle when the president introduced wage and price controls.) After Ford chose Rockefeller as his vice president and then supported amnesty for those who refused to serve in Vietnam, Reagan concluded that Ford was a hopelessly weak leader who lacked any genuine convictions. One week after Ford announced that he would seek reelection, Reagan formed his own political action committee—"Citizens for the Republic"—to assess (and, unofficially, start to build) support for his candidacy. He and his supporters became convinced that once again the electorate needed a clear choice, not a faint echo.

Reagan failed to win the nomination, but the substantial success he did achieve made him the front-runner four years later.

In 1980 Reagan easily dominated a primary field filled with traditional Republican candidates.[144] The keenest competition took place between Reagan and George Bush. Bush's assertion that Reagan preached "voodoo economics" would come back to haunt him when he became Reagan's running mate in 1980 and later in 1988 when he campaigned as Reagan's successor. Yet the Reagan-Bush ticket that emerged from the convention provided a unified team and a sharp contrast to their Democratic opponents.

While Reagan scored successive victories and solidified his support, President Jimmy Carter faced a bruising battle with his intraparty opponent Edward Kennedy in the Democratic primaries. Kennedy's challenge not only weakened Carter but also exposed divisions and discontent within the Democratic party. Like the British Labour party, Democrats were closely identified with the postwar order. The breakdown of consensus fueled public disenchantment with the party and also sparked internal conflict as rivals disputed whether to chart a new course or cling to the old order. As the *New York Times* described the situation in 1980, "Liberals and Democrats finally ran out of gas, and many ruefully acknowledged that the programs and philosophy that had sustained them for a quarter of a century had ceased to work."[145] To a great extent, confusion in the Democratic party only mirrored uncertainty in the wider public.

At the end of 1979, the *New York Times* determined that "Americans seem to be 'Between Idea Systems.'" The paper recalled, "In 1976, those who had turned away from the old order elected a President, Jimmy Carter, who voiced their concerns and spurned the old party alliances." In 1979, however, "many officials and political scientists deplore the fragmentation of authority. . . . Those Members [of Congress] who brought it about, the post-Watergate Independents, have grown weary of chaos and have called for a return to stronger, centralized leadership."[146] After four years in office, Carter appeared to be held captive by the special interests that the public held responsible for corrupting Washington and creating stalemate in the national government. The "confidence gap" that started in the late 1960s only widened during Carter's presidency.[147] By contrast, Reagan's neoliberal ideology promised to elevate discourse and policy above the interplay of entrenched interests. Offering strong, determined leadership, Reagan pledged to restore confidence in government and make it more responsive and efficient. The Reagan campaign successfully presented the virtues of its conviction-style leader in ways that served to highlight Carter's shortcomings on election day.

Gallup described the 1980 election as "one of the most unusual," but its negative, anti-incumbent vote made it similar to many others, including

1828, 1884, and 1912. When asked, "What was the main reason why you voted for Reagan?" voters most often responded by expressing anti-Carter sentiment—either "dissatisfaction with Carter" (22 percent) or "time for a change" (21 percent). Only 14 supported Reagan's policies in general (although 17 percent endorsed his economic policies). Like Thatcher, Reagan seized the opportunity presented by an unpopular incumbent, and like Jackson, Cleveland, and Wilson, Reagan appeared as a "strong man" in contrast to his feeble opponent.[148] During the 1980 campaign, 62 percent of those polled considered Reagan a "strong leader," while only 32 percent held a similar view of Jimmy Carter.[149] The rock group Genesis would soon capture the significance of Reagan's image as a strong leader when, in a popular music video, they cast Reagan in the role of Superman, who tries to save the day in a "Land of Confusion."

Although negative voting largely explained the outcome, other factors lend credence to Reagan's assertion that he had secured a mandate. Reagan scored a decisive victory in the popular vote, winning almost 51 percent, compared with Carter's 41 percent and independent candidate John Anderson's less than 7 percent. Moreover, the electoral college made the result appear to be a landslide: Reagan won 489 votes, while Carter secured only 44. In addition, Reagan had clearly articulated the agenda he would pursue as president. In staking out his positions, Reagan expressed the sentiments of several "reform" movements that had surfaced or gained strength in the late 1970s. As a result, Reagan appeared to be riding a rising ideological tide when he swept into office.

In 1978 the U.S. witnessed the success of a grassroots tax reform movement in Reagan's home state. By a two-to-one margin, California voters approved a radical tax measure known as Proposition 13. The initiative limited local property tax to 1 percent of a property's value; included no provision to overturn that limit by popular vote; and provided tax breaks for business and industry, while requiring severe cuts in public spending for education. Magnified by the media, Proposition 13 came to symbolize "an attack against inflation, large and arrogant government, and taxes of all kinds."[150] According to Reagan, "people were rebelling, trying to get government off their back and out of their pocketbooks. That prairie fire . . . was really spreading across the land, and it shouldn't have surprised anyone."[151] It certainly failed to surprise Reagan, who had advocated a similar, albeit less radical, reform as governor in 1973.[152]

California's grassroots tax revolt took place in the context of professional economists' growing support for tax cuts. Arthur Laffer from the University of Southern California and Jude Wanniski, columnist for the *Wall Street Journal*, advocated "supply-side economics"—the simple notion that tax cuts stimulate business activity and that therefore taxes should be cut even during periods of inflation. Supply-side reasoning informed the Kemp-Roth tax cuts in 1978, which Reagan endorsed, but it was only one of several schools of economic thought that Reagan would tap. Perhaps more significant, Governor Reagan met Milton Friedman for the first time in 1970, when Friedman visited the University of California at Los Angeles for a semester. Reagan was immediately impressed, and Friedman's subsequent influence on Reagan would be clearly demonstrated in the president's 1981 economic program (alongside supply-side reasoning). In fact, in all respects but one (a balanced budget), President Reagan would follow Friedman's prescription for economic recovery: cut domestic spending, cut taxes, cut regulations, and control the money supply by working with the Federal Reserve.[153] Friedman had also played a critical role in the Proposition 13 campaign, endorsing the measure in an influential television commercial. The ideas of Friedman and the experience of Proposition 13 seem to have had more significant impact on Reagan than did any curve supposedly drawn on a cocktail napkin.[154] In any event, unlike Thatcher, Reagan never developed a coherent economic outlook; instead, he chose the components of different theories that proved consistent with his convictions.

In addition to mounting criticism of the economy, popular and intellectual discontent with foreign policy provided yet another source of support for Reagan. While President Carter struggled to secure Senate approval for the Strategic Arms Limitation Treaty (SALT II), the Soviets invaded Afghanistan, a move that exposed the vulnerability of the U.S. and its leadership. Carter's response—a grain embargo and U.S. boycott of the Olympics in Moscow—seemed to impose greater costs on the U.S. public than on the Soviets, or so Reagan argued during the 1980 campaign. Most significant, Carter proved unable to secure the release of fifty-two U.S. citizens held hostage in Iran for 444 days. Foreign policy failures in the Carter years intensified the growing sentiment after Vietnam that U.S. influence in the world was steadily declining.

Carter's foreign policy provided a steady target for attacks from the right and revived an intellectual trend that emerged after Vietnam, "neoconservatism,"[155] another movement that Reagan would tap for ideas and talent. In general, neoconservatives argued that the U.S. had lost its will to lead the West after Vietnam and that consequently the Soviets had achieved strategic superiority. As a remedy, they recommended increased defense spending and advocated military intervention whenever communist expansion threatened U.S. interests. Reagan clearly endorsed their ideological objective: to promote liberal values throughout the world.

Reagan actively recruited neoconservatives for his campaign and his administration.[156] Richard Allen, a former member of the Committee on the

Present Danger (a group that documented U.S. strategic weakness compared with the Soviets), advised candidate Reagan and became the president's first national security advisor. After Allen gave Reagan an article written by Jeane Kirkpatrick in 1979,[157] the candidate immediately wrote her a personal note. According to Kirkpatrick, Reagan clearly acted on his own initiative then and later when they met.[158] Kirkpatrick recalled, "He was very interested in the issues," and she added, "It really is a puzzle: He is genuinely interested in issues, but he doesn't talk easily and comfortably about them. [As a result] he gives the impression that he's not very bright." Impressions can be misleading: Kirkpatrick remembers that when they spoke about security policy in Central America, Reagan proved to be better informed than she expected and "more interested in Latin America than most American presidents," something she attributed to his experience as governor of California. At their first meeting, Reagan found an ideological soul mate, and the neoconservative professor of political science at Georgetown University would become his U.S. permanent representative (ambassador) at the United Nations. In general, the neoconservatives supplied intellectual arguments and empirical evidence to support Reagan's political convictions.

Neoconservatives had their greatest influence in international affairs, but on domestic policy they also tended to share Reagan's views. According to one of the most prominent neoconservatives, Irving Kristol, "[T]he political tradition . . . which neoconservatives wish to renew and revive . . . is the political tradition associated with the birth of modern liberal society—a society distinguished from all others by representative government and a predominantly free-market economy."[159] The neoliberal ideology of neoconservatives provides a sharp contrast to the views of yet another right-wing group, the Religious Right. Like other trends, the Religious Right has had its intellectual advocates,[160] but Reagan attempted to tap the more popular expression of these views.

Throughout the 1960s and 1970s, portions of the public had grown increasingly concerned about the moral decline of the U.S. and the diminished role of religious values in public life. A series of Supreme Court decisions—in particular, those that banned school prayer and protected abortion as a constitutional right—increasingly angered and alienated conservative Christians, but once again dissatisfaction with the Carter administration provided the catalyst for protest. In 1975 the Internal Revenue Service (IRS) revoked the tax-exempt status of Bob Jones University, a Christian school in Greenville, South Carolina, because it discriminated against minority students and therefore was not a "charitable institution" eligible for tax exemption. Although Nixon initiated the policy and Ford continued it, Carter incurred the wrath of the right when in 1978 the IRS announced its plans to revoke the tax exemption of all private schools that did not meet certain standards of racial integration. Such schools alleged that integration conflicted with their religious beliefs, and for the Reverend Jerry Falwell, Carter's IRS created the need for organized opposition. In response, in 1979 Falwell founded a national organization called the Moral Majority.[161]

Reagan actively courted the support of the Moral Majority and included its leaders in his 1980 campaign planning sessions.[162] Conservative Christians initially considered John Connally an "attractive alternative" to Reagan, but Reagan won them over by speaking their language, often recalling biblical passages he had learned from his mother.[163] Their subsequent efforts on his behalf were extensive: Falwell and other conservative Christian leaders, such as Bob Billings of the National Christian Action Coalition, worked on outreach programs for Reagan during the general election campaign. With Pat Robertson, Falwell also founded the Religious Roundtable in 1980 to organize preachers to support Reagan's candidacy.[164] As president, Reagan in his rhetoric would put conservative Christian causes on the national political agenda, but economic issues and foreign policies would remain his top priorities. As if it were his calling, Reagan was determined to reverse his nation's apparent economic and global decline.

To fulfill his mission, President Reagan knew he would need to embrace and pursue the psychological dimension of political leadership. During the 1980 campaign, one of his chief policy advisors, Martin Anderson, warned Reagan that his credibility on economic issues would depend on psychological factors. "Compounding the problem for any presidential candidate is the public's pessimism," Anderson wrote in a memo. "They believe that there is little that the President, any President, can do about [the economy]."[165] Several years after the Reagan presidency, Edwin Meese, Reagan's White House "counselor" and later his attorney general, considered the psychological effect of Reagan's leadership even more significant than the ideological impact, somewhat surprising given the value Meese would otherwise accord to ideology. As Meese revealed his perception of the conditions in 1980, he recalled, "The economy was weak, and we were weak in not having military strength, but we were also weak in terms of leadership. People believed the wave of democracy was over, and it seemed socialism was rampant. Everyone had the feeling we were in bad shape." In this context, Reagan needed to convince the public that "the best days were ahead," and for this reason, "his sense of optimism" proved critical to his success, according to Meese.[166] Like FDR, Reagan would try to dispel fear and urge immediate, bold action—ironically, in order to undermine the policies and legacy of FDR's New Deal.[167]

Reagan's first inaugural address provides a striking example of how he employed a psychological approach as he promoted his public philosophy. As

Reagan described it, commitment to freedom not only constitutes a core conviction in the national creed; it can also provide the source of renewed strength for the individual and the nation. At the start of the speech, Reagan assured citizens that "we as Americans have the capacity now, as we've had in the past, to do whatever needs to be done to preserve this last and greatest bastion of freedom."[168] He identified the culprit responsible for national decline when he delivered his familiar refrain: "[G]overnment is not the solution to our problem; government is the problem."[169] Then Reagan described his solution in terms of the liberal principle of "self-rule" and limited "government for, by, and of the people."[170] In place of pluralism, Reagan wryly recommended greater concern "for a special interest group that has been too long neglected . . . in short, 'We the people,' this breed called Americans."[171] Finally, Reagan returned to his thesis: Greatness in the past stemmed from the fact that "freedom and the dignity of the individual have been more available and assured here than in any other place on Earth," and greater freedom could provide the basis for renewed domestic prosperity and international preeminence.[172] In his inaugural address, Reagan tried to deliver a statement of his convictions that would inspire new public confidence.

At the same time, Reagan urged ordinary citizens to invent bold dreams and pursue courageous action. As he instructed his audience, "It is time for us to realize that we're too great a nation to limit ourselves to small dreams. We're not, as some would have us believe, doomed to an inevitable decline. I do not believe in a fate that will fall on us no matter what we do. I do believe in a fate that will fall on us if we do nothing. So, with all the creative energy at our command, let us begin an era of national renewal."[173] Reagan's call for imagination and action offered a subtle reminder of his own virtues as a conviction-style leader, while he also managed to maintain his connection with the mass public. "We have every right to dream heroic dreams," the president explained. "Those who say that we're in a time when there are not heroes, they just don't know where to look."[174] Reagan proceeded to direct the public's attention to heroic figures found in factories, in shops, on farms, in businesses, and in churches across America.

Reagan reconciled his call for extraordinary creativity and courage with the egalitarian assumptions of liberal democracy by asserting that all citizens are capable of heroism. As he reminded his audience, "The crisis we are facing today . . . [requires] our best effort and our willingness to believe in ourselves and to believe in our capacity to perform great deeds, to believe that together with God's help we can and will resolve the problems which now confront us." "And after all, why shouldn't we believe that?" Reagan asked and then answered, "We are Americans."[175] Vision and heroism constituted critical components of Reagan's solution, and although they were not aspects of his neoliberalism, for Reagan they proved compatible with it if the vision focused on greater freedom and the nation relied on the efforts of "ordinary heroes."[176]

Reagan's rhetoric in his first inaugural address was more than a mere psychological ploy to lift the spirits of the nation or a subliminal way to highlight his own perceived virtues as a conviction-style leader: Reagan believed what he said. As president, he would frequently focus national attention on the heroic achievements of ordinary citizens. (This became a trademark of his state of the union addresses and a technique adopted by his successors). Just as significant, Reagan continued to see himself as an ordinary hero, an oxymoron that enabled him to embrace what many critics among the elite perceived as a contradiction: President Reagan appeared to be both king and commoner; superman and everyman.

Ultimately, Reagan would concentrate power in the executive as much as—indeed more than—most conviction-style leaders, but he rarely distinguished himself from ordinary citizens or directly and explicitly encouraged their reliance on his strong leadership.[177] Nor did he purport to possess special knowledge or unique wisdom. (He would never have compared himself with Old Testament prophets as Thatcher did!) In his ability to maintain the common touch even as he evoked hero worship, Reagan closely resembled Jackson. Reagan's image as a common man capable of heroic deeds unveils a significant secret of his success: It enabled the members of the public to overlook his human frailties and facilitated their willingness to embrace Reagan's core convictions as their own.

Those convictions determined Reagan's agenda and established his priorities. Reagan intended to revive the economy with an economic program that would cut taxes, control domestic spending, cut regulations, and control inflation.[178] In the first term, foreign policy ranked second to domestic affairs, but Reagan immediately proposed massive increases in defense spending. Finally, Reagan publicly promised to balance the budget by eliminating "waste, fraud, and abuse," although he proved willing to postpone the pursuit of that goal in order to achieve the others.

Reagan knew he needed to act quickly (as FDR had) to take advantage of the honeymoon period newly elected presidents enjoy, to act before the economy grew worse, and to reinforce his image as a strong leader. Immediately after the election, David Stockman, who would become director of the Office of Management and Budget (OMB), provided a blueprint for Reagan's economic program that urged immediate action to avoid "a GOP economic Dunkirk" in 1982.[179] Richard Wirthlin, Reagan's pollster, also urged the president to move quickly in order to give concrete expression to what the public perceived as his greatest asset, his strong, firm leadership.

According to Wirthlin, Reagan's convictions enabled him to act quickly and decisively. The president's pollster recalled that "[o]ur political information system in 1980 was not designed to set an agenda. His agenda was already set. . . . If you have an agenda, you don't need to ask the question, 'Now what do we do?' That's the payoff in having the consistency that comes from conviction. He didn't waste days or even hours deciding what position was most beneficial. Our talents could be used in a different way: Given that position [of Reagan], how can we best leverage it?"[180] Public opinion polls provided little policy guidance, but they did help the president craft the public presentation of his economic program.

Reagan first presented his plan to the public on February 5, 1981, in a televised speech to the nation. Before he outlined his economic program, he made clear his intention to break with the past by declaring, "It's time to recognize that we've come to a turning point. We're threatened with an economic calamity of tremendous proportions, and the old business-as-usual treatment can't save us. Together, we must chart a different course."[181] Reagan then revealed his top priority when he promoted a 10 percent across-the-board tax cut for three years (a version of the Kemp-Roth proposal) and, employing supply-side reasoning, predicted that tax cuts would actually increase tax revenues by expanding the economic base. His additional proposals tapped other economic theories: Reagan emphasized the need for deregulation to encourage enterprise and shrink the scope of government, spending cuts to balance the budget, and "sound monetary policy" achieved by working with the Federal Reserve Board. Although his specific measures did not conform to a coherent theory, they did reflect his core convictions.

Reagan concluded his televised speech by repeating many of the themes in his inaugural address. After noting the enormous growth in government spending, he asked, "How much better off are we for all that? Well, we all know we're very much worse off. When we measure how harshly these years of inflation, lower productivity, and uncontrolled government growth have affected our lives, we know we must act and act now. We must not be timid. We will restore the freedom of all men and women to excel and to create. We will unleash the energy and genius of the American people, traits which have never failed us."[182] Finally, Reagan assured the public that "[t]he only special interest that we will serve is the interest of all the people."[183] Less than two weeks later—approximately one month after his inauguration—the president formally submitted his package of budget cuts and tax reform to a joint session of Congress.

While the White House aides labored to lobby Congress, the president's personal involvement in negotiations also helped win legislative approval for his program. Senator Paul Laxalt, Reagan's closest ally on Capitol Hill, emphasized "the importance of personal relations on the Hill" and recalled,

"Most members of the House and Senate didn't know him personally. I arranged meetings with members from both sides of the aisle—Weicker and Javits and Rostenkowski—the people who thought he had horns on. I wanted them to get to know him."[184] During the first one hundred days, Reagan held sixty-nine meetings with 467 members of Congress. The president's gracious manner dispelled preconceived notions of his demonic demeanor, and his considerable charm disarmed many of his adversaries in both parties.

Although Reagan skillfully employed traditional techniques to influence legislators, he relied much more on his ideas and his popularity to win congressional support for his measures. Southern Democrats endorsed Reagan's proposals because they shared his political philosophy, while Republicans (even liberal ones) proved reluctant to rebel against their popular president. In February 1981, Reagan's approval rating was 55 percent; by March that figure rose to 60; and in April and May, it jumped to 67 and 68.[185] The steady increase tracks public approval of Reagan's leadership and support for his economic package, while it also reflects public sympathy for the president in the wake of a dramatic event. On March 30, after Reagan delivered a speech to trade union representatives at the Washington Hilton Hotel, a deranged assassin, John Hinckley Jr., shot him.

The public would have rallied around any president in such an event, but Reagan's behavior contributed to the outpouring of public affection. Under extreme duress and in substantial pain, Reagan delivered a string of one-liners when he arrived at the hospital: Borrowing a line from the boxer Jack Dempsey, he declared to his wife, "Honey, I forgot to duck." And to the doctors, Reagan joked, "Please tell me you're Republicans."[186] In this case, Reagan displayed extraordinary heroism, as FDR had in a similar crisis. Surviving the assassination attempt with confidence and courage made Reagan seem invincible.

The mythic dimension of the event also contributed to Reagan's own sense of invincibility and special destiny. While the president was still recuperating, Terence Cardinal Cooke paid a visit to the White House. When the cardinal declared, "The hand of God was upon you," Reagan replied, "I know. And whatever time He's left for me is His."[187] Reagan always possessed a strong sense of destiny, and his brush with death intensified this belief.

With newfound fervor, Reagan returned to the mission of rescuing the economy. At the end of April, he delivered another stirring speech to Congress, and from April through July, Reagan and his White House staff lobbied Congress to secure support for the budget and tax reform. In April the Senate endorsed the administration's budget priorities, and in May the House voted (253-176) for Gramm-Latta I, the budget resolution that supported most of Reagan's proposed cuts in social programs and defense increases. (Every Republican and sixty-three Democrats supported Gramm-Latta I.) In

July the House voted on a second budget resolution that continued to endorse the administration's budget priorities (although it passed by only 6 votes with thirty-one Democrats). With Gramm-Latta II, the House proposed to cut $16 billion in spending, substantially less than Reagan's request and far short of the $250 billion that was needed to reach a balanced budget by 1984 as the administration had promised. Throughout July, members of the House and the Senate met in conference committee to reconcile the differences in their budget resolutions.

In the budget process, Reagan had an advantage most of his predecessors lacked. To facilitate the passage of his budget, he seized the opportunities provided by the Congressional Budget Act of 1974. Part of the post-Watergate reforms, that bill was designed to restore the spending authority of Congress: It centralized the budget process by forcing tax and spending decisions into a single annual budget resolution. Paradoxically, the reform gave the president a better opportunity to monitor and influence the budget. In 1981 Reagan's use of OMB as a clearinghouse further centralized the budget process by shifting authority from departments and agencies to OMB and the White House. The combination of this innovation within the executive branch and congressional reform greatly enhanced Reagan's ability to advance his budget through the legislature.[188]

At the end of July, Reagan delivered a final pitch for his economic package in another televised address to the nation. He reiterated the themes of his earlier messages and portrayed his administration's progress as the source of new optimism and the triumph of the people over the special interests. As Reagan concluded, he placed his economic proposals in the context of national principles—"what America is all about." According to Reagan, "Our struggle for nationhood, our relenting fight for freedom, our very existence—these have all rested on the assurance that you must be free to shape your life as you are best able to, that no one can stop you from reaching higher or take from you the creativity that has made America the envy of mankind."[189] By embarking on a "bold and hopeful" path, the president promised, "we will make America great again." Once again, Reagan rendered an emotional appeal that rallied the public and solidified support in Congress.

When Congress passed the Economic Recovery Tax Act (ERTA), it approved most of Reagan's original proposal. ERTA reduced the federal income tax by 25 percent: 5 percent on October 1, 1981; 10 percent on July 1, 1982; and another 10 percent on July 1, 1983. The legislation reduced the highest marginal rate from 70 to 50 percent and cut capital gains from 28 to 20 percent. Furthermore, to stop "bracket creep," tax brackets were indexed to the rate of inflation. Finally, the legislation provided major tax breaks to business and industry.

While Congress approved the largest tax cut in U.S. history, it also added $7 billion to the defense budget and cut more than $35 billion in nondefense spending in the Omnibus Reconciliation Act. To the OMB director, congressional failure to cut spending further signaled "the triumph of politics" over ideology, but even Stockman acknowledged, "For the first time in modern American politics, we had put the spending constituencies on the defensive. That was no mean feat."[190] The shift in budget priorities altered the terms of public debate: After 1981, advocates of government programs needed to make the case for spending and against cuts.

Despite this change and regardless of Reagan's rhetorical assault on special interests, some groups continued to fare better than others did. Budget cuts focused on energy, environment, transportation, housing, health education, employment training, and aid to state and local government. The overall share of the budget for these programs in 1980 was 24 percent; by 1988, that figure would fall to 15 percent. Cuts in Aid to Families with Dependent Children (AFDC), housing subsidies, and school lunch programs meant that spending reductions hit children and urban communities the hardest. On the other hand, the budget included no major cuts in programs for well-organized, highly financed groups such as farmers and the elderly.[191]

Flexed by the American Association of Retired People (AARP), the political muscle of the elderly blocked one of Reagan's lifelong goals: to reform social security. Early in the 1981 budget process, Reagan failed to support a measure proposed by Senator Pete Domenici, chair of the Senate Budget Committee, and Senator Fritz Hollings that would have frozen social security cost-of-living adjustments (COLAs). Reagan refused to risk his tax reform by engaging in a damaging political controversy. (At the time political strategists in the White House appeared to orchestrate Reagan's retreat without his full involvement.) Later in the year, Reagan endorsed Stockman's more radical proposals that would have raised the retirement age for social security and dropped the minimum benefit. To test the public's reaction, Secretary Schweiker announced the proposals at the Department of Health and Human Services. Widespread condemnation—including fierce opposition from congressional Republicans—led Reagan to support a bipartisan commission whose compromise would eventually provide only a short-term solution. In this area, Reagan proceeded with caution as Thatcher did initially, but unlike Thatcher, Reagan never again attempted to restructure social security.

Another dramatic event quickly reinforced Reagan's image as a strong leader and overshadowed his retreat from social security reform. Following his legislative victories in July, the president took decisive action against striking members of the Professional Air Traffic Controllers Organization

(PATCO). When thirteen thousand union members walked out on August 3, Reagan immediately held a press conference to announce that they would lose their jobs if they did not return to work within forty-eight hours. In his statement, Reagan reminded the public of his role as president of the Screen Actors Guild, stating that he was "the first one to ever hold this office who is a lifetime member of an AFL-CIO union." Nevertheless, he insisted he must uphold the law that prohibits strikes by government employees responsible for public safety.[192]

White House staff and cabinet members present at an emergency meeting held at the White House recalled that Reagan drew up his own statement. According to Deaver, "Everyone was arguing about what to do. Reagan wrote his own statement in fifteen minutes and later read it [to the public]. It made good copy—the president standing up to the unions. The last time that happened was with Harry Truman. Reporters like strong leaders and courage in politicians, especially if they stick with it."[193] In his memoirs, Reagan revealed that he fully grasped the significance of this event: The strike was "an important juncture for our new administration. I think it convinced people who might have thought otherwise that I meant what I said."[194]

During the PATCO strike, Reagan demonstrated his determination to adhere to his convictions even when they conflicted with public opinion. As Wirthlin recalled, "During the air traffic controllers strike, our polls showed 65 percent said public employees had the right to strike. Reagan believed it was wrong that the country should be held hostage, and he went on television and said so. There's one case where the president's position changed the public position."[195] In this case, public opinion shifted in favor of Reagan's action, and he maintained his 60 percent approval rating through September.

Reagan's popular support started to diminish in the fall of 1981, but at the end of the year, his presidential popularity still seemed to be soaring high. In its annual news summary, the *New York Times* declared, "The first session of the 97th Congress ended Wednesday amid acknowledgement that it bore the conservative imprint of President Reagan and had reversed a half-century of growth in social programs. The President's popularity, political skills and firmness were cited as qualities that enabled him to persuade Congress that his election was a mandate for fundamental change." According to the report, "Congressional leaders acknowledge that the ideology of the Administration took root in a normally pragmatic Congress."[196] The article focused specifically on the tax reduction, the largest peacetime military spending increase, cuts in domestic programs, and the omnibus spending resolution.

The *Washington Post* proved even more effusive in giving credit to the president for his legislative success. In an article entitled "Dominated by Reagan, Session Makes Much History in a Hurry," the newspaper concluded, "The first session of the 97th Congress ended yesterday as it began: dominated by President Reagan and his crusade to cut taxes, strengthen the military and reverse a half century of growth in social welfare programs. The Republican Senate and Democratic House, although split along party lines, came together under the Reagan spell to make more history in a few months than most Congresses have made in two full years."[197] The *Post* did acknowledge "Reagan's biggest budget failure" as Congress's "refusal even to consider major cuts in Social Security," which forced Reagan to make an "about face." But the report depicted this retreat as the exception to Reagan's rule. An article on page one quoted Speaker of the House Thomas P. (Tip) O'Neill: "We gave the president of the United States everything he wanted." O'Neill's remark rendered "an only somewhat exaggerated summary of President Reagan's impact," according to the *Post* reporter.

In their annual retrospective reports, the press applauded Reagan's accomplishments, but the president's public support had already begun to diminish, and his approval ratings would follow a steady descent throughout 1982. One precipitating factor occurred in November: News organizations announced the shocking contents of an article written by William Greider in the December issue of the *Atlantic*. Entitled "The Education of David Stockman,"[198] the article drew on a series of conversations with the OMB director, during which Stockman revealed his growing doubts about the viability and credibility of "Reaganomics." The revelations embarrassed the administration at the time, but the allegations might well have been forgotten had Stockman's worst fears failed to materialize.

Instead, by the end of 1981 the national debt exceeded a trillion dollars, and the adminstration's own budget projections anticipated a deficit of $162 billion by 1984, the year Reagan had promised to achieve a balanced budget. The rapid pace of reform bolstered Reagan's image as a strong leader, but the policy advantages of incrementalism were lost: There was no time for inconsistencies to be resolved or for testing propositions along the way. The theoretical contradictions produced concrete consequences: Supply-siders based their calculations on continued inflation, but ERTA indexed income taxes to the rate of inflation, and the Federal Reserve's monetary policy brought inflation down. The Federal Reserve's policies—tight money and high interest rates—were designed to brake economic expansion, while the tax cuts were intended to spark an economic boom. Supply-siders tend to advocate a return to the gold standard rather than monetarism; by endorsing aspects of both supply-side economics and monetarism, Reagan came up with an economic plan that placed fiscal and monetary policy on a collision course.

In any event, as Stockman revealed to Greider, the numbers simply did not add up to a balanced budget. Reagan had failed to cut major entitlements such as social security, while he secured the most substantial tax reduction in history and the largest defense buildup in peacetime. (Defense Secretary Caspar Weinberger insisted that "building defense is not bad for the economy because it creates jobs,"[199] but Reagan did not promote defense spending as a jobs creation scheme.) Even Thatcher had grasped the need to raise the VAT in order to offset the loss of revenues from income tax cuts and the consequences of tight monetary policy.

In the summer of 1982, Reagan reluctantly followed a similar course when he endorsed the Tax Equity and Fiscal Responsibility Act (TEFRA), which raised taxes (although not on personal income) and restored some of the budget cuts secured the previous year. Reagan tried to reconcile the tax increase with his neoliberal convictions by concluding that TEFRA constituted tax "reform," but conditions had forced the president to compromise his principles. Reagan was not about to suffer the fate of Cleveland, who failed to be flexible when faced with dire economic conditions.

On the other hand, Reagan refused to bend his position on monetary policy. As early as 1979, the Federal Reserve had shifted its policy from controlling interest rates to regulating the money supply. During the 1982 recession, supply-siders joined the Democrats in attacking Federal Reserve chairman Paul Volcker, alleging that too little money and high interest rates had caused the economy to contract. Even political strategists in the White House tried to use Volcker as a scapegoat, but Reagan declined to exert any pressure on the Federal Reserve or its chairman to loosen its monetary restraints during the recession. In fact, the only time Reagan did criticize the Federal Reserve was when it had failed to tighten the money supply enough in the period of November 1981 through January 1982. By October 1982, world economic conditions would convince Volcker to shift from monetarism back to the traditional approach of managing interest rates, but as a result of the Federal Reserve's policies—and Reagan's resolution—inflation fell from more than 12 percent in 1980 to 5 percent in 1982.

In the same period unemployment rose from 7.4 percent to 10 percent, hitting its highest level since 1941 and paving the way for the GOP economic Dunkirk Stockman had feared. In the November midterm elections, the Democrats gained 26 House seats and Reagan lost his working majority. The president's own approval rating was about to sink to its lowest level, at 35 percent in January 1983.

Despite the recession and midterm congressional losses for the Republicans, the *New York Times* concluded at the end of 1982, "the President nevertheless set the tone and the agenda."[200] The report acknowledged Reagan's concessions: He was forced to sign a gas tax/highways/jobs bill and approve a three-year tax increase and the extension of unemployment benefits, while

Congress rejected the administration's request for the MX missile. On the other hand, Reagan won approval for further increases in defense spending and secured additional cuts in AFDC and food stamps. As in 1981, the *Washington Post* gave Reagan even more credit. It assessed that the year in Congress was "a historic session, which, under prodding from Reagan, escalated the nation's military buildup, reversed the trend toward ever-larger domestic welfare programs and aimed for economic revival through lower taxes on those who can afford to invest in growth producing endeavors." "Even in the lame-duck session—with increasing restiveness even in the GOP ranks," the *Post* concluded, "Reagan was calling the tune."[201] It would become increasingly difficult for Reagan to "call the tune" in the legislature after he lost his working majority in the House, and the president would never again match the level of legislative success he scored in his first year.

On the other hand, congressional Democrats remained on the defensive, unable to promote new social programs or reverse the Reagan agenda in the direction of the old order. Furthermore, Reagan could continue to advance his convictions by other means—through executive orders, innovative administrative strategies, judicial appointments, and the conduct of foreign affairs. In every respect, Reagan's success depended on his public support, and starting in February 1983, the president's approval ratings—along with the economy—began to improve.

In the meantime, deregulation provided an area where the president could bypass Congress, and in contrast to the obstacles Thatcher encountered when she initiated privatization, Reagan entered a regulatory environment in which his predecessors had paved the way for his reform. Deregulation started with Nixon, continued under Ford and Carter, and then proceeded at a slow but steady pace during the Reagan administration. Reagan did break new ground by adopting a different approach and mapping out new territory, but he also cultivated the appearance of taking bold action even when he followed the path of previous presidents.

To pursue deregulation, Reagan started his presidency with symbolic gestures before he took any concrete steps. On his first day in office, he ordered a federal hiring freeze (which continued the policy under Carter), and he quickly moved to abolish the Council on Wage and Price Stability. To signal his commitment to deregulation, Reagan chose Murray Weidenbaum, a prominent advocate of regulatory reform, as chair of the Council of Economic Advisors (CEA). Immediately, the administration suspended almost two hundred regulations, while it began a process of rigorous review.

Nixon, Ford, and Carter had restricted their efforts to economic regulation, but Reagan also attempted to change regulation that affected health, safety, and the environment. Throughout the 1970s, public opinion favored

economic deregulation, but little public support existed for the social deregulation that Reagan pursued in the 1980s. As a consequence, Congress generally resisted the administration's efforts to change the law. Rather than
relax the regulatory restraints in the Clean Air Act, for example, Reagan had
to resort to reducing personnel and enforcement at the Environmental Protection Agency (EPA). Ironically, when Reagan did seek statutory change, he
received more support from House Democrats who represented northern industrial cities than he secured from Republicans. Most members of Congress
remained sensitive to public opinion opposed to deregulation in the areas of
health, safety, and the environment.[202]

By taking independent executive action, Reagan managed to achieve
many of his objectives, though his administration left a controversial legacy.
Lax regulatory enforcement at EPA made the nation's hazardous waste problem worse, for example, and deregulation of oil wasted energy. Certainly, the
major failure in deregulation occurred with the relaxation of regulatory restraints on thrift institutions. Yet Congress shared responsibility with the
president for the subsequent savings and loan debacle, which cost taxpayers
an estimated $500 billion.

In the global arena, Reagan also acted independently. He sent troops to
Lebanon in 1982 without reporting to Congress as the war powers resolution requires. Then on October 23, 1983, a terrorist attacked the U.S. Marine barracks in Beirut, Lebanon, and killed 241 U.S. soldiers. Two days
after the terrorist attack in Beirut, Reagan ordered troops to invade Grenada,
following a coup on the island and in response to a request by the Organization of Eastern Caribbean States. That time Reagan did report to Congress
in a manner consistent with the war powers resolution, although he insisted
his independent action constituted legitimate exercise of his power as commander in chief. In foreign affairs, members of Congress often objected to
Reagan's independent initiatives, but the public generally applauded his actions as demonstrations of the nation's renewed military strength.

Reagan quickly acted in Grenada before Congress or the public could
hold him accountable for the massacre of U.S. Marines in Beirut, and as a
result, his approval ratings jumped rather than fell from October to November (from 45 to 53 percent). Throughout the following year, Reagan's ratings
remained above 50 percent, topping 60 percent during the month of his reelection. Economic recovery largely accounts for the high ratings, but the appearance of strong, decisive leadership in the case of Grenada gave the
president an additional boost.

Faced with a popular president, the new Democratic House of Representatives struggled to rein in the Reagan revolution. Toward the end of 1983,
the *Washington Post* splashed its assessment across page one: "Congress

Slows, Doesn't Halt Reagan Changes."[203] In another edition, the paper quoted Reagan's judgment: "Perhaps the greatest contribution of the Congress was not what it did for us but what it didn't do to us."[204] Reagan proved unable to win approval for significant new initiatives, but Congress failed to force him to consider proposals that were not already on his agenda.

The following year produced more partisan bickering and greater rancor between the president and Congress—mostly political posturing in anticipation of the election. In only one case did Congress take the lead—when it established the Martin Luther King Jr. national holiday; this Democratic proposal won the support of congressional Republicans concerned about Reagan's low popularity among African-American voters. In the days leading up to the election, the *New York Times* rendered an assessment strikingly similar to the analysis the *Washington Post* had provided one year earlier. According to the *New York Times,* Congress "did just what [the president] wanted—that is, not much of anything." The report concluded, "Despite the Democrats' gains in the 1982 midterm election, which again gave them firm control of the House, the 98th Congress generally approved only what Mr. Reagan proposed. It failed to press for what he opposed."[205] In 1984 Reagan encountered little opposition from Democrats in the House of Representatives and no serious challenge from the Democratic nominee for president.

Democrats chose as their candidate Walter Mondale, former U.S. senator and vice president under Carter. Mondale had endured a bruising battle during the primary season, and to a great extent his intraparty opponents set the agenda for the general election: They attacked the front-runner as a candidate beholden to special interests, a lapdog of the unions, and a weak, ineffectual leader. At the national convention, Mondale suffered a self-inflicted wound when he confessed that he would raise taxes (as he asserted any responsible president should do). Finally, Mondale attempted to be daring and innovative when he put the first woman vice presidential candidate on a major party ticket, but his plan backfired: Immediately after her selection, Geraldine Ferraro became embroiled in a controversy concerning her husband's taxes. The Democratic ticket never gained sufficient strength or momentum to threaten Reagan's reelection.

Capitalizing on the nation's revived economy and renewed patriotism, the Reagan campaign summed up public sentiment in one of its commercials, which declared, "It's Morning Again in America." As U.S. athletes scored successive victories at the summer Olympics in Los Angeles (during the Soviet boycott), Reagan read the results as evidence of the country's restored vitality. His campaign adopted a slogan designed to draw attention to his greatest virtue: "Leadership That's Working." Even Reagan's poor performance in the first presidential debate failed to foil his reelection bid. (After he rambled aimlessly in the Louisville debate, the press briefly focused on the president's age as an issue, but Reagan recovered during the second debate when he delivered one of his famous one-liners: "I am not going to exploit, for political purposes, my opponent's youth and inexperience.") In fact, the campaign had little effect on the outcome: Almost half the voters had decided early in the year, and only a quarter waited for the debates. Throughout the campaign, the polls showed few fluctuations. Whether the election took place in January or November, Reagan would have won.[206]

The 1984 presidential election produced the largest electoral college vote landslide in history. Reagan won forty-nine states (525 electoral votes to Mondale's 10) and more than 59 percent of the popular vote. Furthermore, he won the majority of every ethnic group except Jews, African Americans, and Latinos and also won a majority of women, youth, every income group except the poorest citizens (those earning less than $10,000), and every region except the largest cities. Mondale won two-thirds of the Jewish vote, nine-tenths of the African-American vote, and the majority of the poorest voters, the unemployed, and members of union households. The distribution of the vote reveals the diminished base of the Democratic coalition and the reconstitutive dimension of Reagan's presidency.

Reagan's policies and public philosophy reconfigured the U.S. electorate. His Religious Right rhetoric (with its emphasis on pro-life) attracted Southern Democrats who were evangelicals and urban ethnic voters who were Roman Catholic. Tax reform transformed the primary identity of many voters from beneficiaries of government programs into taxpayers. Cuts in domestic programs divided the New Deal coalition by pitting interest groups against each other as they competed for diminishing resources. Furthermore, deregulation broke the bond of common interest between unions and employers.[207] Finally, the new patriotism created an "America-can-be-great-again" coalition that joined otherwise disparate groups.[208]

Among those left out of the new governing coalition, African Americans registered the strongest protest, expressing discontent that stemmed from several sources. Budget cuts had disproportionately hurt urban communities with large African-American populations. Moreover, Reagan's rhetoric extolling the virtues of individualism and attacking affirmative action as preferential treatment threatened to erase some of the gains of the civil rights movement. Just as significant, Reagan's political positions revealed his reluctance to enforce established legal protections against discrimination. In 1982, for example, Reagan initially sided with Bob Jones University and the Goldsboro (North Carolina) Christian Schools in their attempt to reinstate their tax-exempt status even though the schools practiced racial discrimination.[209] Later in Reagan's second term, Congress would pass the Civil Rights

Restoration Act (1988), but it would have to override the president's veto.[210] Few critics accused Reagan of being racist, but they did attack his policies for exacerbating racial tensions and dividing the country along racial lines. In the 1984 presidential election, African Americans made clear their opposition to Reagan's policies, and the fact that the president acted out of conviction only made matters worse.

By contrast, the majority of those who were polled admired Reagan for his conviction-style leadership. In 1984, 61 percent believed Reagan "has stronger leadership" than his opponent, while only 25 percent considered Mondale the stronger of the two.[211] Three out of five voters cited "strong leadership" and "experience" as major reasons for their choice, and four of five voters who mentioned strong leadership were Reagan supporters.[212]

The president's policies also influenced the voters' choice. In its election analysis, Gallup concluded "the character of Reagan's support [was] markedly different than in '80." According to Gallup, "Reagan's vote in 1984 was a decidedly pro-Reagan rather than an anti-Mondale vote, with the voters naming Reagan's economic policies and leadership as the reasons for their choice. By a 6-1 ratio, Reagan supporters said their vote was more *for* Reagan than *against* Mondale, while Mondale voters were about equally divided." In 1984, Gallup's polls show 24 percent supported Reagan because they "liked his economic policies," while another 11 percent liked his policies in general.[213] According to a different study, by 1984 Reagan drew support from new national conservative trends that endorsed central aspects of his agenda, especially in the areas of criminal law and tax reform.[214]

Voters' positive assessments of the economy provided the chief source of support for Reagan. Reagan had repeatedly asked the electorate to consider the question Are you better off now?—the question first posed by FDR—but voters' perceptions of the national economy proved even more significant than individuals' assessments of their pocketbooks.[215] Of course, presidents can influence perceptions of the national economy more easily than they can affect the calculation of personal finances, and Reagan's rhetoric about "Morning Again in America" might well have inflated the public's impression of economic recovery. In any event, the president's optimism proved to be contagious.

Opinion polls indicate substantial shifts in public sentiment about the health of the economy. When Gallup asked respondents to express their satisfaction "with the way things are going in the United States at this time," in 1984 more respondents were satisfied than dissatisfied, whereas in 1979 only 10 percent had said they were satisfied.[216] On the day of the 1984 election, 57 percent of the voters said they thought the economy was better than it had been four years earlier. In a different poll, a plurality believed the economy was beginning a long-term recovery, while another quarter expected at least temporary improvement.[217] Without knowing what specific steps Reagan would take in his second term, voters seemed to believe the president when he repeatedly assured them, "You ain't seen nothing yet."

Like Thatcher in 1983, Reagan provided few clues to the policies that he would pursue in his next administration. The lack of specific issue content to the campaign had concrete consequences for Reagan's second term, which lacked the clear direction of the first (again, like Thatcher's second government). Moreover, the group of White House advisors that served the president well in his first term departed in his second. On the other hand, Reagan's record and his rhetoric gave voters good reason to expect that he would continue the course he had set in 1981, at least on tax reform, which remained his top priority.

Reagan announced his administration's new tax reform plan in a nationwide televised speech on May 28, 1985. As he pledged to pursue change that would give new meaning to the word "freedom," Reagan explained, "The first American Revolution was sparked by an unshakable conviction—taxation without representation is tyranny. Two centuries later, a second American revolution for hope and opportunity is gathering force again—a peaceful revolution, but born of popular resentment against a tax system that is unwise, unwanted, and unfair." In his familiar fashion, the president concluded by urging the public to "not let the special interest raids of the few rob us of all our dreams."[218] Instead, he promised to provide a bill that would benefit all the people by simplifying the tax structure and further reducing personal income tax.

As early as his 1984 state of the union address, Reagan had revealed his intention to secure additional tax reform. He had instructed Treasury Secretary Donald Regan to design a plan, which he would consider after the election. During the campaign, the president's critics mocked his decision to postpone tax reform and offered wild speculations about the contents of his "secret plan," but James Baker later defended the decision and explained, "If we had proposed the tax reform earlier, we might have lost the election. Instead, we got it and we didn't have to run on it. Reagan had a mandate to continue his policies. That was enough. Campaigns are run on principle, not policy."[219] Failure to discuss the specific contents of tax reform enabled Reagan to avoid controversy during the campaign, but it also kept him from being able to allege that he had secured the public's backing for the specific measures he proposed.

Change in personnel also made the task of tax reform in Reagan's second administration more difficult than it had been in his first. Regan and Baker swapped jobs: As secretary of the treasury, Regan designed the initial tax bill known as "Treasury I," but Chief of Staff Baker took his place before the administration submitted its proposals to Congress. Regan was more familiar with the substance of tax reform and might have promoted the new legislation with greater conviction. He recalled that initially, "Baker opposed it all the way. He did everything he could to block it. Nineteen eighty-four was an election year, and he didn't want to take any risks. Then, when we switched jobs, it became Baker's baby!"[220] At the very least, Baker needed time to become acquainted with his new responsibility. On the other hand, Baker was the consummate political strategist, and he labored in an environment that cried out for conciliation.

After the 1981 tax legislation, interest groups mobilized in anticipation of further reform. According to Jeffrey Birnbaum, a reporter who covered the process for the *Wall Street Journal,* "The first economic package led to increased lobbying activity. After that, every interest came to town to protect itself. Every time government changes, there's a new influx of interest groups. An activist president always brings an influx of new interests."[221] Indeed, Birnbaum's study of the 1986 tax reform extensively documents the wide array of interests that lobbied to secure concessions from the administration and sway legislators.

Regan agreed that "everybody was being hurt [by the 1986 tax reform]. So the special interests took over Congress,"[222] and this reform was especially difficult because it leveled new taxes on corporations, thereby delivering blows to traditional Republican allies. According to Baker, "The 1986 tax reform was really tough. We were trying to close the loopholes and that meant taking on our own constituencies. There was a lot of opposition within the party—from Trent Lott, Dick Cheney. . . . But we managed to get rid of a lot of loopholes with Democratic support—the Bill Bradley Democrats."[223] As in 1981, the president engaged in private negotiations and public promotion, but the 1986 legislation truly tested the talents of the Great Communicator and stretched the skills of his strategists.

While the administration struggled to win support for tax legislation at home, Reagan also attempted to score some success abroad by initiating discussions with the new Soviet leader, Mikhail Gorbachev. Months before he became general secretary, Gorbachev had impressed Thatcher as a man she "could do business with," and she urged Reagan to schedule a summit between the superpowers. At their first meeting in Geneva in November 1985, Reagan and Gorbachev reached no new agreements, but they did promise to hold future summits. In the absence of any negotiations during Reagan's first term, the leaders' pledge to continue discussions seemed a significant accomplishment.

As in 1983 and 1984, congressional Democrats tried to impede the progress of the president's policies. According to the *New York Times,* "Thomas P.

O'Neill, Jr., the Speaker of the House, said Democrats in that body had had an 'excellent year,' but he defined their success mainly on how they had checked or altered the initiatives of Senate Republicans and Mr. Reagan." In an editorial in the same issue, a prominent columnist declared, "Next year should be the sternest test yet of Mr. Reagan's powers of persuasion."[224] The reporter-pundit observed that the president's influence continued to diminish, but he neglected to notice that Reagan still firmly controlled the agenda.

Even the one significant initiative taken by Congress was consistent with Reagan's convictions (though not with his politics). Congress passed the Gramm-Rudman-Hollings law, a bill that would automatically reduce deficits by increasing amounts in the course of five years. According to the legislation, when the deficit exceeds a specified amount, automatic cuts occur as calculated by the General Accounting Office (GAO). In 1986 the Supreme Court declared the GAO provision unconstitutional, and Congress subsequently passed a weaker version of the measure in 1987. Reagan did not invite this radical budget-balancing measure, but, constrained by his avowed convictions, he was forced to endorse it.

In October 1986, Reagan finally secured passage of his tax reform. Birnbaum described the president's role as critical, despite the dominant influence of organized interests, because "[h]e communicated the goals and the principles. His determination was extremely important. He drew a line in the sand and wouldn't budge. He would have allowed it to fail if it didn't lower the rates, and if it didn't simplify the tax system. He had an entire worldview into which this reform fit."[225] Although Treasury I underwent substantial revision in the legislative process, the final product generally remained true to Reagan's principles.

Tax reform reflected Reagan's core conviction that personal tax rates should be reduced, the only principle that informed both the 1981 and the 1986 tax bills. When the president signed the 1986 law, he gave credit to "the many thinkers who have struggled to return economics to its classical roots,"[226] and several aspects of the legislation did reflect nineteenth-century free-market theory. The bill eliminated most tax shelters and corporate loopholes, and it lowered the marginal tax rate to 33 percent. At the same time, however, it shifted the tax burden from individuals to corporations and removed many low-income households from the tax rolls by nearly doubling the personal deduction. In these respects, the legislation reflected neither laissez-faire nor supply-side theories but came out of concession and compromise. To achieve his central goal, Reagan proved flexible once again, and to a great extent, the combination of pragmatism and principle accounts for the legislation's success. As he signed the bill, the president was pleased to quote the judgment of the press: With the 1986 tax reform, "The Impossible Became the Inevitable."[227]

At the end of the legislative session, the *Washington Post* declared, "'Productive' Congress Goes Home: Wide-Ranging Record of Major Changes." The report highlighted the tax reform but also took note of changes in immigration law and the budget process. Even though Congress "was selectively pumping money back into social welfare programs," the paper concluded, "Reagan's vision of a scaled-back welfare state had become a reality."[228] Despite substantial change at home, 1986 was also a year when dramatic events in foreign affairs often overshadowed domestic politics and reinforced Reagan's image as a strong, determined leader.

On April 14, 1986, Reagan ordered the bombing of Libya, ostensibly in retaliation for the terrorist attack that killed one U.S. soldier and injured fifty other U.S. citizens at a West Berlin disco. Once again, the president failed to fulfill the reporting requirement of the war powers resolution, and in this case he consulted no members of Congress before he launched the attack. The bombing of Libya ignited some opposition in the legislature and sparked critical comment from around the globe, but the public generally applauded Reagan's display of decisive leadership.

Another critical event followed in the fall: In October 1986, Reagan and Gorbachev held a second summit in Reykjavik, Iceland. When the Soviet leader insisted that the U.S. limit its research on the Strategic Defense Initiative (SDI), Reagan walked out of the negotiations. For a president who had made no progress on arms control, his move threatened to produce a public relations disaster, but in fact Reagan's rigidity enhanced his image as a strong leader. Failure to achieve results at Reykjavik did no damage to Reagan's approval rating, which remained at 63 percent.

The president's extraordinarily high approval ratings took a hard hit in November when the public first learned about the Iran-Contra affair from a report in a Beirut newspaper. According to the report, the Reagan administration had sold arms to Iran (contrary to the administration's official policy) and sent weapons to the Nicaraguan Contras (in violation of the Boland Amendment). Furthermore, in a complicated covert operation, officials of the Reagan administration also diverted profits from the sale of arms to Iran to fund the Contras. The scandal had an immediate impact on Reagan's ratings, which plummeted to 47 percent in December and generally remained below 50 percent throughout the following year.

The Democrats regained control of the Senate in the 1986 midterm elections, and in doing so, they also recaptured some control of national agenda. In 1987 Congress revised the deficit reduction legislation, cut military spending, and created a major housing bill and a homeless aid bill. Moreover, clean-water and highway bills passed over presidential vetoes. Congress also extended the authority of the independent council investigating the

Iran-Contra affair. On the other hand, Congress continued to carry out aspects of Reagan's agenda when it voted to cut Medicare and agricultural programs.[229] Nevertheless, 1987 proved to be a bad year for the president, with one notable exception.

In February 1987, Gorbachev relented and agreed to separate the issue of SDI from the negotiations to cut intermediate-range nuclear force (INF) missiles. Reagan and Gorbachev signed the INF treaty in Washington in December. For the first time, existing weapons would be destroyed and on-site monitoring of the destruction would take place. Although the two leaders would meet again—in New York and in Moscow—the INF treaty constitutes their major joint achievement.

By the end of the Reagan presidency, the *New York Times* boldly announced, "Congress Regains Its Voice on Policy in 1987–88 Sessions."[230] Democratic control of the Senate led the legislature to become more assertive, but "outside factors"—Iran-Contra, improved U.S.-Soviet relations, and the October 1987 stock market crash—also diminished presidential influence. Congress changed civil rights law, strengthened fair housing law, saved the farm credit system, expanded Medicare to cover catastrophic illness, and ended Contra aid. Yet, as in 1987, Congress also continued to endorse elements of Reagan's program, starting to overhaul the welfare system and approving the Canada free trade agreement and trade bill.

While the *New York Times* emphasized the importance of Democratic victories, the *Washington Post* also took note of their concessions. In the course of the Reagan presidency, the center had clearly shifted, according to a report in the *Post*, which continued:

> Accommodation became easier as Democrats trimmed their sails, constrained by deficits and election-year qualms about being portrayed as big spenders. They accepted work-related provisions in the welfare bill that would once have been anathema; and shelved an expensive long term health-care bill. Moreover, costs of some of their new programs, which previously would have been tacked onto the deficit, will be borne by recipients, private industry and other levels of government. Some issues, such as trade and drugs, became political imperatives in what amounted to a bidding war between the parties as the elections approached.[231]

The enduring impact of the Reagan presidency would be reflected in the new national agenda and the emerging consensus that both major parties endorsed.

After Reagan, the social issues of religious conservatives became mainstream matters of public discourse. In his speeches, Reagan had devoted limited but significant attention to social issues, emphasizing the need for traditional values, articulating a pro-life position, and promoting school prayer.[232] Although the Moral Majority officially disbanded in 1987, Pat Robertson's presidential candidacy in 1988 revived the movement and led to the formation of the Christian Coalition, a powerful presence in the politics of the 1990s. Reagan's use of his bully pulpit elevated the concerns of social conservatives to the national agenda, while they also gained some new ground as a result of his judicial appointments.

Reagan's impact on the courts constitutes one of the most significant and enduring aspects of his legacy. He appointed almost half of the federal judiciary: 78 judges to the appellate courts and 290 to the district courts. To the Supreme Court, Reagan appointed Sandra Day O'Connor, the first woman justice, in 1981; Antonin Scalia in 1986; and Anthony Kennedy in 1988 (after a controversial and ultimately unsuccessful attempt to persuade the Democratic Senate to confirm Judge Robert Bork). Reagan also promoted William Rehnquist to chief justice in 1986. It was not only the number but the nature of his judicial appointments that accounts for Reagan's impact: He established the President's Committee on Federal Judicial Selection, staffed by the White House and Justice Department, which carefully screened potential nominees to ensure that they shared the president's views.[233]

To pursue his law-and-order agenda, Reagan relied on his judicial appointments and introduced several legislative initiatives. The Rehnquist Court would bring about the most significant change in the area of criminal law where it retreated from the Warren Court's expansive interpretation of the rights of the accused by substantially weakening the *Miranda* protections and allowing exceptions to the exclusionary rule. Reagan achieved less success in the legislative arena: On drug policy, he managed to shift budget priorities from treatment and education to law enforcement, but he proved unable to revise the federal criminal code in significant ways. Nevertheless, Reagan shifted the national debate on crime from a focus on procedural guarantees to the goal of achieving public safety, and crime legislation in the 1990s would ultimately achieve many of the objectives he sought in the 1980s.[234]

Public support for tougher criminal laws continued to increase throughout the Reagan years and beyond, but other trends in public opinion that initially endorsed Reagan's ideology appeared to change direction during his presidency. In the 1980s resistance to cuts in social programs increased,[235] demand for greater defense spending diminished, and desire to shrink the size of the federal government declined.[236] Rather than indicate a leftward shift in public opinion, however, such polling data might provide signs of Reagan's success. After Reagan cut social spending, increased defense, and scaled back the role (if not the overall size) of the government, the public altered its views of what needed to be changed. (Polls ask respondents to assess the status quo, but Reagan transformed the environment.) Perhaps most significant, opinion polls in the 1980s and 1990s provide no indication that the public wished to reverse Reagan's economic policies.

When he left office, Reagan received credit for the remarkable economic recovery that took place in the 1980s. The boom that started in 1983 continued through most of the 1990s, creating the longest peacetime expansion in U.S. history. Unemployment dropped from 7.1 percent in 1980 to 5.5 percent in 1988, and 18 million new jobs were created. Inflation fell from 12.5 percent in 1980 to 4.4 percent in 1988, and the prime interest rate went from 15 percent to 9.3 percent. Every income group did better, although the gap widened between rich and poor. At the same time, Reaganomics inflicted long-term damage: The national debt tripled, while the trade deficit quadrupled. In the eight years of his presidency, Reagan submitted eight unbalanced budgets.

The budget deficit was the inevitable result of Reagan's convictions that called for tax cuts, increased defense, and a strong dollar, but some critics of the administration charged that Reagan deliberately increased the deficit in order to force budget cuts later. In fact, in his first television address to the nation, the president seemed to indicate that he would pursue just such a strategy. At that time Reagan revealed, "Over the past decades we've talked of curtailing government spending so that we can then lower the tax burden. Sometimes we've even taken a run at doing that. But there were always those who told us that taxes couldn't be cut until spending was reduced. Well, you know, we can lecture our children about extravagance until we run out of voice and breath. Or we can cure their extravagance by simply reducing their allowance."[237] Whether or not the budget deficit constituted part of the president's strategy, Reaganomics did reduce revenue in a way that ensured budget balancing would become a priority in the nineties.

Reagan disappointed many traditional Republicans in another area. The president failed to pursue the New Federalism that Nixon first proposed. Instead, the Reagan administration cut federal aid but left the states to raise their own revenues. Congress generally refused the administration's request for block grants and maintained most federal restraints, but Reagan never lobbied hard for change. Indeed, Reagan rarely revealed any serious interest in restoring federalism. Like Thatcher, he seemed more committed to eliminating government at all levels than to devolving power.[238]

In other areas, the issues that Reagan refused to promote led to changes in the national agenda. During the Reagan presidency, at least three policies either declined in importance or fell off the agenda: national health care, environmental protection, and civil rights. Reagan also proved slow to act when the AIDS epidemic hit the country: He declined to use his bully pulpit to educate the public or win support for research funding, although his surgeon general, C. Everett Koop, eventually took the lead in 1986. Finally, Reagan failed to monitor the behavior of his subordinates or maintain standards of integrity in his administration. During the Reagan years, the good-government aura of the post-Watergate era vanished into thin air.[239]

Yet even when most of the Iran-Contra scandal became public knowledge, Reagan escaped the blame and suffered only short-term injury to his popularity. Iran-Contra did stop the steady increase from 1983 to 1986 of public confidence in government, and the majority of the public believed the president lied when he alleged he knew little about the scheme.[240] Nevertheless, the public continued to perceive the president as a strong leader and proved less disturbed than they should have been when the strength of his convictions proved weightier than the safeguards of the Constitution. Few public calls for greater executive accountability followed the Iran-Contra investigation. Reagan concluded his presidency with higher approval ratings than any president before him since FDR, and his vice president, who was also implicated in the scandal, secured election with the promise to continue the course of the Reagan regime, albeit in a kinder, gentler fashion.

Immediately after the 1992 presidential election, it appeared that the nation might experience change that would reverse the neoliberal trend established by Reagan. The campaign of President William Clinton had declared, "It's Time for a Change," and the Democratic president seemed eager to breathe new life into the issues of national health care, environmental protection, and civil rights. Subsequently, a Democratic Congress defeated the president's proposed health care reform; the Clinton administration produced a weak record on the environment; and at the conclusion of his first term, the president signed a welfare reform bill that disproportionately harmed children, immigrants, and African Americans. In the 1994 midterm elections, Republicans won control of the House of Representatives after they campaigned on a platform called the "Contract with America," based on planks from the Reagan agenda. Finally, the Democratic president rendered the highest tribute to Reagan's achievement when he declared in his 1996 state of the union address: "The era of big government is over."[241] Conviction politics in the 1980s created a neoliberal consensus in the 1990s, and even change in party control of the presidency would fail to alter the new relationship between the state and society.

The leadership of Reagan and Thatcher constitutes part of a pattern in political development that reveals the recurrent role of conviction politicians as agents of change. To establish a new national agenda, conviction politicians practice strong, principled leadership, and, at least initially, their style supplies the central source of their popular support. Dissatisfaction with the status quo, the breakdown of consensus, and calls for change always characterize the context conducive to conviction politics.

Other aspects of the environment vary over time, especially the nature of parties, the role of the media, the structures of government and the state, and the global arena. Conviction-style leaders try to alter their ideological and institutional environment, but when they attempt to do so, they encounter distinct opportunities and constraints at different stages of political development. While differences exist across time, developments in the two countries become more closely linked, and the similarities that surface prove much more significant than many distinctions commonly drawn between the U.S. presidential system and the British Westminster model.

PART II
THE CHANGING CONTEXT OF CONVICTION POLITICS

6

THE PURSUIT OF PRINCIPLE
AND PARTY CONSTRAINTS

Political parties can obstruct the ideological change that conviction-style leaders strive to secure. Historical analysis reveals that late-nineteenth-century parties proved incompatible with conviction-style leadership, while at other junctures in political development parties more easily succumbed to the direction of determined leaders. Moreover, cross-national comparisons indicate that parties in the United States and the United Kingdom have been more similar than generally acknowledged.

Since the late nineteenth century, dissatisfaction with their own party system has led U.S. political scientists to look across the Atlantic for "responsible parties," cohesive teams with leaders who articulate and promote distinctive programs for public policy. Yet political scientists in the U.S. have been misguided when they have searched for a different, superior set of parties in the U.K.[1] British parties have never possessed the internal cohesion characteristic of the responsible-parties model. Nor have they empowered their leaders to pursue change. When parties prove significant, influence operates in the British environment much as it does in the U.S. context—as a commodity bargained for among groups within the two major parties.[2]

In pluralist societies with two-party systems such as Great Britain and the U.S., each political party comprises multiple interests. To satisfy diverse interests, party leaders are often forced to compromise and follow strategies based on ambiguity and equivocation, not on principle or conviction. Political parties (and the multiple interests they comprise) vary over time in terms of how well organized or entrenched they are, but in Britain as in the U.S. executive initiative succeeds only when parties are not well positioned to resist their leaders' independence or when leaders manage to circumvent their parties.[3] The character of political parties and interest groups can also vary within party systems, and the opportunities or limits on party leadership will be determined by several factors: the number and diversity of interests, the nature of interests—factions or tendencies,[4] ideological or instrumental—the strength of groups, and their place in the party. In general, strong "parties" support strong, principled leadership only when parties themselves are defined (and behave) as flexible groups that form around particular candidates.

189

Woodrow Wilson envisioned such candidate-oriented organizations when he promoted parties as a way to empower presidential leadership, but this aspect of his political thought has been frequently overlooked or misunderstood. Responsible-party theorists attribute their ideas to Wilson when they criticize the candidate-oriented nature of modern presidential campaigns and call for party renewal, but Wilson actually promoted candidate orientation to strengthen presidential leadership.[5]

On the other hand, responsible-party theorists remain true to their intellectual progenitor when they distinguish between parties in the U.S. and the U.K.: In this regard, however, Wilson's original analysis proves flawed. He correctly assessed late-nineteenth-century parties in the U.S. as constraints on strong leadership, but he failed to find a parallel in British parties of the same period. Instead, Wilson looked only at the leadership and adopted William Gladstone as the prototype of the successful British party leader.[6] Of course, Gladstone's pursuit of principle actually split his political party, and without his party he failed to achieve his primary goal.

Wilson not only misrepresented the nature of British parties; he also altered his views during the course of his scholarly and political careers, providing another source of confusion for later responsible-parties theorists. His original position endorsed cabinet government as a cure for the ills of U.S. politics, but he became convinced that the executive could provide the coherence and direction that the U.S. "leaderless" system lacked.[7] By the time Wilson became president, he had abandoned his original reform proposals based on his understanding of the British model in favor of candidate-oriented organizations and a presidency-centered system.

Nevertheless, as president and party leader, Wilson could hardly advocate independent executive initiative as a replacement for party "responsibility" without alienating his own party. As a consequence, he continued to pay homage to his party's authority even as he designed and promoted his own policies. In other words, Wilson's presidential rhetoric sounds as if he continued to advocate party responsibility, although he actually exercised executive discretion and independent judgment.

At least one of Wilson's contemporaries saw through his guise: Herbert Croly alleged that Wilson's conciliatory and deferential manner deceived the people. Rather than "speak for his party," the president actually "spoke to them at a time when they were going astray and told them what to do." According to Croly:

> [President Wilson] can, of course, hide behind the fiction of partisan responsibility, whenever he wants to avoid speaking to his party about a legislative proposal upon which he is likely to encounter serious resis-

tance; but no suavity of manner and no amount of wise self-restraint in the employment of his power can obscure the real facts of the situation. At the final test the responsibility is his rather than that of his party. The party which submits to such a dictatorship, however benevolent, cannot play its own proper part in a system of partisan government.[8]

Croly accused Wilson of failing to practice what he preached. Indeed, Croly understood that only strong presidential leadership could yield unified party action, but that type of leadership ultimately would weaken the party. Both Croly and Wilson knew that decisive leadership could be practiced only at the expense of party responsibility. Wilson came to believe that this was desirable, while Croly saw the dangers inherent in such a "benevolent dictatorship." Croly suspected that Wilson's rhetoric deliberately deceived his partisans and his public, but the next generation of responsible-party theorists took President Wilson at his word.[9]

Wilson's experience, along with that of other conviction politicians, shows that the relationship between the strength of political parties and the strength of executive leadership is considerably more complex than responsible-party theorists have recognized. Throughout political development, parties have not been consistently "strong" in Britain while they have been "weak" in the U.S. The state of parties and their effect on leadership are subject to change. In both countries, however, conviction-style leaders succeed in securing fundamental change in the absence of any responsible parties and only when they manage to circumvent what constraints their parties do try to impose. In the late nineteenth century in both the U.S. and the U.K., parties proved too strong to permit conviction-style leadership. At other junctures in political development, the weakness of parties generally facilitated presidents' and prime ministers' ability to promote new ideas and public policies.

Democratization and Party Formation:
Andrew Jackson and Sir Robert Peel

Andrew Jackson and Sir Robert Peel practiced conviction politics before the formation of a competitive two-party system and viable national organizations in the U.S. and the U.K. Jackson succeeded because he faced an opposition as fragmented as his own following and maintained the personal allegiance of his followers, including many who objected to the substance of his policies. Peel ultimately built a policy coalition based on support from members of the elite that cut across party lines. When Jackson destroyed the National Bank and Peel abolished the Corn Laws, they adhered to their convictions and fundamentally altered the relationship between state and society, but they succeeded in pursuing their principles only by escaping party constraints.

When Jackson made the National Bank the central issue of his reelection campaign in 1832, he ran the risk that opposition forces would rally against what they considered his act of executive tyranny. After all, Jackson had made a bold departure from the practice of his predecessors when he vetoed the bank legislation on policy grounds as well as constitutional considerations. Throughout the campaign, the *National Intelligencer*—the administration newspaper until 1828—attacked Jackson's use of the veto as an attempt to establish the "dominion of one man"[10] and urged opposition groups to unite against him. During the bank controversy, the Whig charge of executive despotism might well have unified the opposition and splintered Jackson's support.

Instead, the president's fortress of popularity withstood the vicious assaults launched by his opponents. Jackson tried to forge an ideological consensus among workers and farmers and various sections of the country, but in this regard he achieved only limited success. Radicalism in the West, for example, was always inconsistent and unreliable, but Jackson sustained the region's support because of his personal popularity in that part of the country.[11] At the state level, where parties were stronger, the bank controversy did create some splits: In 1835, Conservative Bank Democrats left the Locofocos and endorsed the Whig candidate for governor of New York. At the national level, however, Jackson's personal appeal held together the same coalition his principles and policies placed in jeopardy.

Jackson succeeded because he maintained an extensive personal following, not because he constructed a strong political party. Although he engaged in some grassroots "party building" during the 1834 campaign,[12] in this case party building primarily consisted of the president making a personal appeal to supporters throughout the country. Jackson might have attempted to fortify the Democratic organization or appease some of his intraparty opponents by altering his principles. Instead, he limited his effort to strengthening the personal allegiance of his followers. The president and his deputies successfully campaigned on behalf of Democratic candidates in the midterm election, and the result rendered "a personal triumph for Jackson."[13]

From the start, the Democratic party was an organization structured around Jackson. The party first formed in opposition to the Adams-Clay coalition that had "stolen" the presidency from Jackson in 1824. To promote his views and his future candidacy, Jackson formed a central committee after the election. When Martin Van Buren returned to the Senate in 1827, he organized conferences among Jackson's supporters in Congress and established a network for communication with Jackson's central committee in Nashville. Van Buren also formed a central committee, composed of Jacksonian members of Congress in Washington, D.C. Then "Jackson committees" were established in counties, cities, and towns throughout the country. State parties held their conventions on January 8, 1828, the anniversary of Jackson's New Orleans victory. For the first time, a majority of states endorsed a single candidate for president, but the fact that no national convention took place provides a sign of the party's organizational weakness.

To enhance his popular support and ensure that Van Buren would become his vice presidential nominee, Jackson supported his party's first national convention in 1832. No discussion of principles or issues occurred at the meeting; delegates left that task to the candidate.[14] Nevertheless, the nature of the convention did ignite attacks in the opposition press: "In what will our republic differ from a monarchy, if the people relinquish to the President the power of nominating his successor?" the *Telegraph* asked the public.[15] As the newspaper observed, Van Buren's nomination also sparked conflict among groups at the convention, providing a hint of the party problems that would later plague Van Buren's presidency. (The *Telegraph* concluded its account with sarcastic commentary, gleefully noting "how delightful it is for friends to dwell together in harmony!") Initially, Van Buren used Jackson to build the Democratic party by linking Jackson's presidential popularity to organizational development. Later, without the popular President Jackson, Van Buren inherited a different, stronger party and faced the constraints of party leadership that Jackson had escaped.

Despite his support for the first Democratic national convention, President Jackson essentially opposed the formation of national party organizations. In his first annual message, Jackson proposed a constitutional amendment to "remove all intermediate agency in the election of President and Vice President."[16] According to Jackson, "To the People belongs the right of electing their Chief Magistrate; it was never designed that their choice should, in any case, be defeated either by the intervention of electoral colleges, or by the agency confided, under certain contingencies, to the House of Representatives."[17] Instead, Jackson proposed direct election of the president, although he hoped a system could be designed to preserve the relative weight of each state in the selection process. If no candidate secured a majority on the first vote, a second runoff election would be held between the top two contenders. In that case, the initial contest would essentially provide a national primary.[18]

Jackson's proposed reform indicates that he did not want to shift power from Congress to the national party organization as Van Buren did. Instead, Jackson explained, "In [presidential selection] as in all other matters of public concern policy requires that as few impediments as possible should exist to the free operation of the public will. Let us, then, endeavor so to amend our system that the office of Chief Magistrate may not be conferred upon any citizen but in pursuance of a fair expression of the will of the majority."[19] Jackson wanted majoritarian, popular support that would empower the president and permit executive initiative.

To the limited extent that he engaged in party building, Jackson faced restrictions, and equivocation rather than conviction facilitated his party-building efforts. On the tariff issue, for example, the East generally wanted protectionism, while the South demanded free trade. To satisfy both sides, in 1832 Jackson lowered the tariffs but left them protective. Lacking firm convictions concerning free trade, Jackson allowed concrete interests to outweigh presidential preference. In other areas, including the bank, the general weakness of parties—the division of his opponents and the candidate orientation of his own followers—enabled him to practice strong leadership in pursuit of his principles.

On the other side of the Atlantic, the weakness of parties also permitted the independent leadership of Peel. In Britain, political alliances of any kind consisted of loose configurations until the great reform bill of 1832. Previously, both government and opposition groups favored policies that would foster economic competition, preserve the Corn Laws, secure aristocratic interests, and prevent land reform. The reform bill rendered the first significant basis for cleavage, and the Tories' failure to support that electoral reform led to their devastating loss in 1832.

As an unanticipated consequence of the reform bill, the clause that provided for registration of voters encouraged the formation of local groups, which provided the basis for party organizations. In these conditions, Peel saw a unique opportunity to win broad-based support for a new public philosophy, but before he could do so he needed to build an electoral majority.

Peel's task of party building presented a problem that was threefold. First, he needed to distinguish his party from the Whigs while he also endorsed their reform. Second, he had to attract Whigs to his party without drawing fundamental distinctions between the two groups. Third, Peel had to avoid splitting his own party. (Economic and social issues failed to divide the Whig-Liberal-Radical coalition, but they did create cleavages within the Conservative party.)[20] This classic Downsian dilemma yielded a classic Downsian solution: Peel designed a strategy that combined his personal appeal with ambiguous declarations on policy. He then issued the first publicized party manifesto based on vague principles of moderate reform.

In the "Tamworth Manifesto," Peel as leader of the Conservative party accepted the reform bill he and his party had previously opposed. As he described it, the reform bill settled a great constitutional question, and he would accept the task of interpreting the "spirit of the bill." Peel acknowledged the need to articulate principles to win public confidence but confessed that "such declarations of general principle are, I am aware, necessarily vague." When the party leader attempted to apply his principles to specific issues, he continued in an equivocal tone. (The text is peppered with frequent use of the word "but.")[21] As an electoral ploy, Peel shunned a clear statement of his principles and adopted a broad-based appeal. He then sent his Tamworth Manifesto to the three major newspapers—the *Times,* the *Morning Herald,* and the *Morning Post*—and won wide publicity for his initiative.[22]

In the 1835 general election, Peel greatly increased the number of Conservative seats but failed to secure a majority. Throughout the 1830s, he repeatedly articulated the broad principles of moderate reform, which he first stated in the Tamworth Manifesto. By 1836, Sir John Benn Walsh observed that the Conservative party "includes all shades and degrees of public opinion" and a "vast proportion of the population."[23] For the first time in British politics, in 1841 the electorate turned out a majority in government and transformed a minority into a governing majority. Peel succeeded as a party builder, but to do so, he needed to adopt a strategy of evasion and equivocation.

The *Times* predicted that Peel's majority would prove sufficiently large to enable him to resist compromise and adhere to principle.[24] The newspaper failed to understand, however, that a large party could impose great constraints on leadership (and increase the likelihood of cleavage). Furthermore, during the 1841 campaign, Peel had declined to address the fundamental issue of the Corn Laws, although he did hint that he might recommend repeal.[25] After the election, when Lord John Russell predicted that the composition of the Conservative party would prevent Peel from following his enlightened economic views, the prime minister defiantly replied, "I will not hold office by servile tenure," only with the "approval of my own conscience."[26] Following his conscience once his conviction grew firm, Peel would pursue enlightened economic principles—but only at the price of party unity.

In 1845, Peel temporarily suspended the Corn Laws, a move he alleged he made "without reference to mere party considerations."[27] His cabinet divided, and he resigned but returned when the Whigs refused to form a government. Following suspension, protectionist landlords in Peel's own party joined forces under the leadership of Lord George Bentinck and Benjamin Disraeli to attack their premier's "treason." Despite fierce intraparty opposition, Peel decided to call Parliament into session to secure repeal. His chancellor of the exchequer warned him that the decision would lead to the party being "broken in pieces by a destruction of confidence in its leaders."[28] Nevertheless,

Peel shunned party loyalty and defied party constraints because he was "impressed with the conviction that the policy we advise is correct."[29]

Peel's repeal passed the House of Commons with the support of the Whigs, the Irish, and the free traders of the Tory party. On the night of passage, his intraparty enemies joined the Whigs and the Irish to defeat their own prime minister on the Irish coercion bill and force his resignation. Peel knew he would "leave a name, severely censured by many who, on public grounds, deeply regret the severance of party ties."[30] In fact, his move did split the Tory party into two factions and led to two decades of Whig-Liberal rule. Peel's party lost power, but his principles became government policy.

Even before repeal of the Corn Laws, Peel's conviction on another reconstitutive issue in Britain, church and state, came into conflict with his party's preference. When Peel proposed to increase the grant to Maynooth College, a Catholic seminary in Ireland, he won large majorities in both houses but needed Whig support on the third reading in the Commons. The Maynooth grant vote foreshadowed the cleavage on Corn Law repeal: Conservatives divided 159 (for) to 147 (against) on the second reading, and 149 to 148 on the third reading of the Maynooth bill. Of the 159 Conservatives who voted for the Maynooth grant on the second reading, 82 voted for repeal of the Corn Laws and 59 voted against. Of the 147 opponents of Maynooth, 111 voted against the government and only 19 voted for repeal of the Corn Laws.[31] Peel's principles split his party on not one but two fundamental issues; yet in both cases, Peel secured support for his policies.

For Jackson and Peel, the pursuit of principle endangered the unity of their parties. Forced to choose between personal determination and party obligation, both opted to adhere to an independent course. Jackson's opposition remained divided, and the various groups within his own party remained loyal to their leader. Peel did split his party, but he won the policy argument. The two leaders suffered different personal consequences—Jackson remained president, while Peel was forced to resign—but this difference stems from the contrast between governing structures in the U.S. and the U.K. Despite the different constitutions, the character of political parties in the two nations proved similar. Jackson and Peel succeeded in pursuing their principles because their political parties were weak by any standard—characterized by weak (newly formed) party loyalty in the electorate, uneven and undeveloped organization in the country, and loose configurations at the elite level. Both leaders engaged in party building only to a limited extent (to enhance their electoral prospects). Peel at first faced a united opposition and therefore labored to build an electoral majority. He achieved substantial success in constructing the Conservative party, and then he destroyed his own creation.

The "Golden Age" of Parties: Grover Cleveland and William Gladstone

Political parties in the U.S. and the U.K. grew to their greatest strength in the second half of the nineteenth century. During that period, extensive organizations developed throughout the two countries, party loyalty spread and intensified among voters, and the positions of the two major parties grew more distinct on some critical issues. Nevertheless, the parties did not conform to the responsible-parties model in at least one crucial respect: Parties in the late nineteenth century served to obstruct rather than facilitate programmatic change. When politicians in the executive office chose to pursue their own policies rather than preserve party unity, they split their political parties and also failed in the policy arena. Throughout this period, parties in Britain proved no more "responsible" than they did in the U.S.

When Cleveland secured the Democratic nomination in 1884, many people in his own party knew his approach would differ from traditional party leadership. At the 1884 Democratic convention, delegates from Tammany Hall, the New York City political machine, delivered Cleveland's two seconding speeches and used the time to denounce him personally. In fact, the Democratic party chose Cleveland because the public viewed him as operating outside the realm of partisan politics.

Despite the strength of party organizations and the high degree of party identification in the Gilded Age, the public was growing increasingly dissatisfied with the two major parties. Both parties were plagued by special interests and dominated by the professional politicians who courted them. Wheeling and dealing within the parties produced candidates who shamelessly sought to maximize their votes at the expense of their principles. As expressed by the press, the Republican party in 1884 resembled the Democrats in 1860: in need of "purification" and an "awakening of conscience." The Republicans were guilty of "the pursuit of office for the sake of office."[32] The Democratic party in New York was also corrupt, but with Cleveland as its candidate, the *New York Times* concluded, it "appeals with unmistakable directness to the moral sense of the people of the United States."[33] Most newspapers emphasized the opposition of Tammany Hall to Cleveland's selection. As the *Commercial Advertiser* put it, "In making Grover Cleveland their candidate his party has been deaf to the mandates of the self-seeking politicians in whose path the Governor has stood 'like a stone wall' and has made an effective appeal for the Independent vote of the country."[34] Tammany's opposition to Cleveland enhanced his reputation for integrity and conviction. With "A Public Office Is a Public Trust"[35] as his campaign slogan, Cleveland appeared "independent of partisan tyranny," and his leadership promised to provide "the instrument for the task at hand"[36]—namely, reform.

As an outsider, Cleveland's leadership also appeared to offer an instrument of party unity. Democrats divided along several lines of cleavage: regional, ethnic, and economic. The party chose Cleveland because he was unidentified with any particular group and not indebted to any entrenched interest. Soaring above the fray of factional disputes, Cleveland cast a broad appeal to diverse Democrats as well as independent voters.

In his first administration, Cleveland chose the issue of tariff reform to show just how independent he could be. During the 1884 campaign, the Democratic party platform had been ambiguous and equivocal on the issue.[37] Nevertheless, Cleveland grew increasingly frustrated with stalemate in the national legislature, and in 1887 he delivered a clear attack on the tariff in his annual message. Unable to persuade members of his party in Congress who had defeated tariff reform the previous year, the president used this occasion to call for a "spirit higher than partisanship." Cleveland sent the message to Congress, but his language—attacking the "selfish schemes" of trusts—indicates he hoped to attract the attention of a broader public audience, including ordinary farmers and laborers.[38]

As the first time a U.S. president devoted his entire text to a single policy, Cleveland's tariff message constituted a bold initiative, and the press and the public approved of his innovation. When the press did render critical judgment, they focused on Congress, reporting divisions in the Democratic ranks and condemning members of Congress for their failure to show conviction.[39] According to the *New York Times,* Democratic senators and representatives believed their party could win only if it promoted tariff reform in some states and protection in others.[40] Despite opposition from his congressional party, Cleveland's tariff message did start to cultivate public support for his policy.

After the president's message, the Democratic party adopted Cleveland's position and used it to garner votes in the next two presidential elections. The 1888 campaign focused on the tariff issue, and Cleveland won the popular vote, although other factors led to his loss in the electoral college. When Cleveland secured the nomination again four years later, a united Democratic party continued to endorse his policy on the tariff. The *New York Times* described Cleveland's electoral victory that year as "the sweeping revolution known as a 'tidal wave.'" According to the *Times,* "Never before since 1860 was there such a host of significant changes from one party to the other. These changes are not individual. They are of groups and of classes."[41] The press listed farmers, workers, independent manufacturers "outside of trusts and combinations," and the "moral revolt" that included clergy, lawyers, and college professors. By pursuing the principle of tariff reform, Cleveland expanded the appeal of his party, but he also increased the opportunity for cleavage. Tariff reform attracted various groups to the Democratic party, but Cleveland's conviction on the issue of currency would soon divide them.

In his first administration, Cleveland had attempted to suspend silver coinage, but his own party in Congress defeated him. Deadlock characterized the last two years of his first term: Cleveland proved unable to repeal silver coinage, and Western silver supporters were unable to obtain free and unlimited coinage. In his second administration, Cleveland remained conscious of his "hungry party" but declared, "I am trying to do what is right."[42] In response to the 1893 panic, Cleveland called a special session of Congress and secured repeal of the Sherman Silver Purchase Act. According to the *New York Times,* "At that moment, as often before, between the lasting interests of the nation and the cowardice of some, the craft of others, in his own party, the sole barrier was the enlightened conscience and iron firmness of Mr. Cleveland."[43] The press then attacked the Democratic party as a constraint on its principled president because party leadership required that Cleveland harmonize various interests. But "to harmonize," the *Times* advised, "would be a criminal blunder."

Cleveland made no attempt to harmonize the various elements in his party. Instead, the following year, he proceeded to veto the Bland silver seniorage bill, a step that ensured an intraparty split. The House passed the Bland bill by a vote of 168 to 129. Nineteen Republicans voted with the Democrats for the bill, and only 49 Democrats opposed it. ("House Democrats voted for it who were afraid of the silver vote in their own districts," according to the *New York Times,* which contrasted their "political motives" to Cleveland's conviction.)[44] In the Senate, three Populists and eleven Republicans joined the Democrats to secure its passage. Asked to comment on the motives of congressional Democrats, Cleveland replied that the subject required "consideration from a higher standpoint than that of political expediency."[45] When the president delivered his veto and the House failed to override it, his move "demonstrated consistency, [but] it also accentuated party divisions."[46]

Cleveland chose to pursue his principles rather than preserve party unity, and both his presidency and his party suffered as a result. Democrats lost control of the Congress in 1894 and surrendered the presidency to the Republicans in the election of 1896. Cleveland's rigid adherence to his principles sparked the intraparty revolt that gave rise to the rule of William Jennings Bryan, and fear of Bryan and his followers helped to keep the Democrats out of the White House for the next sixteen years. Of course, the nature of the party system provided only one of the obstacles to Cleveland's success, but failure to practice skillful (and conciliatory) party leadership in this period would have ensured the ruin of any president's regime-building efforts.[47] Furthermore, Cleveland would have fared no better as a leader in the British party system during the same period. His British counterpart faced similar party constraints and ultimately suffered the same dismal fate.

For two decades after repeal of the Corn Laws, parties in Britain once again resembled loose configurations, and like Peel, William Gladstone labored to construct a party that would enable him to form a majority government. At the elite level, Gladstone took part in the meeting that fused Liberals, Radicals, and Whigs in 1859, and following franchise reform in 1867, the growth of local organizations enhanced his efforts to build a party in the country. To expand his party's base even further, Gladstone initially adopted an approach similar to Cleveland's strategy on the tariff: Gladstone found a single issue—in this case, disestablishment of the church in Ireland—that united his party, extended its electoral appeal, and enhanced his reputation for strong, principled leadership.

Gladstone's decisive declarations in favor of disestablishment made it the central issue in the November 1868 general election campaign. According to the *Times,* parties often obstruct "the sense of the country" because people vote according to party identification and not the issues, but the number of independent voters made the 1868 electorate different.[48] To appeal to the newly enfranchised voters, across the nation Gladstone's Liberals distributed leaflets highlighting the cause of disestablishment. The issue rallied Nonconformists, Roman Catholics, the Welsh, and the Scots to support the Liberals, who won the election with a majority of 110.

After the election, the new prime minister faced a formidable leadership task: According to the *Times,* Gladstone needed "to reconcile conflicting pretensions, and to provide for the public service without weakening the coherency of his party."[49] To meet that challenge, Gladstone immediately acted to secure disestablishment, but he also responded to mounting public pressure for extensive egalitarian reform. Gladstone's famous reform ministry of 1868 to 1874 brought about substantial change in legislation and further expanded the base of the Liberal party.

When Gladstone returned to face the electorate in 1880, the nature of electoral politics differed dramatically from the 1868 campaign: This time it was a "fierce party struggle"—the "hottest political struggle ever."[50] Several factors determined the outcome of the campaign: dissatisfaction with Disraeli's government, Gladstone's popularity, and the strength of the Liberal party organization. Certainly, Gladstone's Midlothian campaign in 1879 stirred up sentiment against the government and enhanced his own popularity, but no single issue rallied the vast array of Liberal supporters as disestablishment had done in 1868. Instead, the Liberals owed much of their electoral success to the efforts of Joseph Chamberlain's Radical machine—the National Liberal Federation. The result was a large majority party that comprised numerous, diverse factions. As the *Times* correctly predicted, the dangers of the Liberal majority "will be in its superabundance of strength. Great majorities, at least on the Liberal side, always present so to speak, 'lines of cleavage,' and careless manipulation may too easily break them up."[51] Personal allegiance to Gladstone would prove insufficient to achieve and maintain party unity, and when he did attempt to manipulate, he was forced to abandon his principles.

Gladstone betrayed his commitment to liberalism abroad, for example, when he chose to intervene in Egypt, and intraparty pressures largely determined that decision. Within the Liberal party, older radicals such as John Bright opposed intervention (and the government's decision led to his resignation). At the same time, many from the younger generation of radicals pressured Gladstone to intervene. In particular, Chamberlain emerged as "almost the greatest Jingo," according to the 2nd Earl Granville. Many of the Whigs, including Lord Hartington, also emerged as advocates of intervention. In the end, the majority of Gladstone's ministers thought intervention was necessary.[52] To maintain party unity, Gladstone abandoned his principles and complied with party constraints.

Initially, Gladstone's preoccupation with preserving party unity also led him to conceal his growing conviction that Ireland should secure home rule,[53] but in 1886 he decided to risk a party split by clearly articulating his position. According to the *Times,* Gladstone's independent initiative showed that he labored under the fatal "misapprehension" that "the Liberal party would follow him, with blind and unreasoning devotion, in any policy he might choose to declare for."[54] Yet as Gladstone made clear in another context, he saw party triumph as "not the end, but the essential beginning" of the pursuit of his principles.[55] By the time Gladstone declared his campaign for home rule, members of his parliamentary party—both Whigs and Radicals—had taken quite enough of his self-righteous moralism and excessive independence. Gladstone knew he was losing their support but hoped he could continue to govern with the support of the followers of the Irish nationalist Charles Parnell. When Gladstone became prime minister for the third time in February 1886, he shunned his party's preferences and quickly acted on his conviction that Ireland should secure home rule.

The style as well as the substance of Gladstone's proposal met immediate criticism from Liberals and their supporters in the press. The *Times* attacked Gladstone's "attempt to elevate his personal views upon the Irish question into the authorized programme of the Liberal party."[56] By propagating "the Home Rule doctrine out of doors," and then presenting it to cabinet, Gladstone marked a "new departure . . . so violently wrenched away from the principles and traditions of Liberalism."[57] Not only editorial comments but also letters to the editors attest to the discontent among Liberals. In one such letter, signed "A Fighting Liberal," the author declared, "I unhesitatingly assert that Mr. Gladstone is alienating a large body of Liberals from their allegiance." Speaking for the rank and file, the activist insisted, "What we want are reforms for the mechanic, the labourer, and the tenant farmer. . . . Why cannot Mr. Gladstone ascertain, through the usual channels, what Liberals of all shades are saying?"[58] Gladstone sealed off the usual party channels and charted an independent course, preferring "to part with his colleagues rather than to modify his views."[59] The historical significance of Gladstone's initiative was clear, according to the *Times:* "Its gravity lies in the fact that an English prime minister has chosen to shatter the Liberal party."[60] Parliament rejected Gladstone's home rule bill by a vote of 343 to 313, with ninety-three Liberals voting against their government.

Gladstone immediately dissolved Parliament and took the issue to the country. In the 1886 campaign, home rule split the Liberal party. Chamberlain Radicals and the Whigs led by Hartington joined the Unionists to defeat Gladstone's Liberals and the Parnellites. The split left the Liberal party weak and out of power until 1906, with the exception of Gladstone's brief government from August 1892 until March 1894. In February 1893, Gladstone introduced his second home rule bill, which passed the House of Commons but met defeat in the Lords. Gladstone wanted to go to the country again—and this time challenge the authority of the Lords—but cabinet colleagues prevented him from doing so. Consequently, Gladstone's career concluded with defeat on the issue he carried with the greatest conviction. Just as important, from that point on the Liberal party had "to fear a malady of disintegration."[61]

In the late nineteenth century in the U.S. and the U.K., conviction politicians could not hold their parties together by force of personality alone (as Jackson had done) or win on policy without party unity (as Peel had managed). By any standard—at the elite level, in the electorate, and as organizations—parties proved too strong to permit independent, principled leadership. When Cleveland and Gladstone did play the role of party leader, they betrayed their principles. Cleveland relaxed his civil service rules although he had advocated civil service reform with great enthusiasm, and Gladstone intervened in Egypt despite his belief in self-determination. When they stubbornly adhered to the substance of their convictions, they eventually split their political parties. In the golden age of parties, both leaders proved unable to promote their public philosophies without party machines. Their successors (in the tradition of conviction politics) achieved what Cleveland and Gladstone could not, but Woodrow Wilson and David Lloyd George operated in a dramatically different parties environment.

From Party Organization to Candidate Orientation: Woodrow Wilson and David Lloyd George

By the early part of the twentieth century, the nature of political parties had started to shift: The extensive organizations of the late nineteenth century were beginning to give way to organizations aligned with the personality-driven and issue-oriented nature of modern campaigns. As a scholar and as a politician, Woodrow Wilson actively promoted this institutional transformation, at least in part because he was inspired by the example of Cleveland. Wilson admired Cleveland's bold exercise of executive power and praised his notion of party as candidate and issue oriented. Describing Cleveland as a "man without a party," Wilson acknowledged that "partisans will fail to assess Cleveland's fame in the future," but predicted "his greatness will be authenticated" by those "who love candor, courage, honesty, strength, unshaken capacity, and high purpose such as his."[62] Cleveland had failed in his own century but provided a model better suited for the next. It was not a model of "responsible parties," but one of independent, determined leadership freed from party constraints.

In the 1912 presidential election Wilson campaigned as "a strong man" of principle whose leadership supplied a sharp contrast to the split in Republican ranks and the weakness of his opponents.[63] Just as significant, during the campaign, the public perceived Republicans "not as a party of the people, but as an instrument of business interests, of interests seeking special favors."[64] Democrats had also succumbed to the influence of special interests, but with Wilson's guidance the Democratic party would be "regenerated and renewed," the press predicted. The *New York Times* drew explicit parallels between 1912 and 1892: Wilson's leadership would resemble Cleveland's because "his principles will be [his party's] principles," but Wilson would succeed with "a firm, strong, true hand" where Cleveland had failed.[65]

Tariff reform gave Wilson his first opportunity to demonstrate decisive leadership. Before he became president, Wilson concluded that Cleveland had failed to reform the protective tariff because he refused to cooperate with Congress. According to Wilson, "No doubt a good deal of the dislike which the houses early conceived for Mr. Cleveland was due to the feeling that he was an 'outsider,' a man without congressional sympathies and points of view."[66] An outsider himself, Wilson was nonetheless determined to avoid making the same mistake. Yet Wilson failed to detect any contradiction in the lessons he derived from the Cleveland presidencies: He admired Cleveland's independent, principled leadership but also criticized him for his failure to consider other points of view represented in Congress. Wilson's comments on Cleveland's experience provide few clues to the strategy he would develop to escape his predecessor's dilemma and his fate.

At first, Wilson adopted an approach that combined traditional party leadership with skillful "parliamentary" maneuvering, although from the start he also made it clear he was prepared to innovate. To submit his initial proposal, Wilson called Congress into a special session and shattered precedent by appearing in person to deliver his message on April 8, 1913. He quickly abandoned his previous plan to work only with progressives and adopted a more partisan approach, attempting to reconcile conflicting views among the congressional Democrats.[67] Wilson employed the mechanism of the caucus to secure commitments from House Democrats, but as he did so, he hinted at the way he ultimately planned to escape party constraints in order to pursue his principles. Wilson won the support of reluctant representatives only by assuring them that he would "go to the people" if necessary.[68]

When his attempt to use the party caucus in the Senate failed, Wilson did appeal to the public. In a letter released to the press (and published in *Collier's Weekly*), Wilson attacked special interest groups and exposed their influence in Congress. The president alerted the public: "It is of serious interest to the country that the people at large should have no lobby and be voiceless in these matters, while great bodies of astute men seek to create an artificial opinion and to overcome the interests of the public for their private profit. . . . Only public opinion can check and destroy it."[69] Wilson's message ignited public controversy about the role of lobbyists in Washington (what he called the "invisible government") and sparked a congressional investigation. The investigation found ample evidence of special influence by a powerful sugar lobby; just as significant, for the first time in U.S. history, the financial interests of senators became public information. Wilson's move "persuaded" several senators to switch their vote and support his tariff bill, while he also demonstrated the strong leadership he had promised to provide.

Even the partisan press who opposed tariff reform praised the president for his bold, independent leadership. According to the *New York Press,* "President Wilson by driving through his tariff measure—*and it is his*—may cause loss to the American people; but they must respect him for having the same principles after he was elected as he said he had before he was elected, and *for fighting for those principles in the White House, when members of his party seek to confound them* and to repudiate their campaign pledges" (emphasis added).[70] To succeed where Cleveland had failed, Wilson chose to expose the special interests within his own party and subject them to public scrutiny—hardly an indication that the president shared "congressional sympathies and points of view"! Instead, Wilson made a direct public appeal that emphasized the principle of popular rule and rejected the role of organized interests.

In general Wilson wanted to construct a party that would rally around basic principles rather than patch together a coalition of interests. When he needed to transform his 1912 minority into a 1916 majority, he developed a strategy that would appeal to a wide range of progressives. In 1916 he struggled to secure passage of a revised farm credit bill and three crucial labor bills. Then at the convention he endorsed a Democratic platform that included social reform and favored women's suffrage. When he accepted the nomination, he could honestly announce, "We have in four years come very near to carrying out the platform of the Progressive party as well as our own; for we also are progressives."[71]

The parties environment permitted Wilson to promote his policies and build his party from the top down. After 1908, the nominating process consisted of a mixed system based on primaries and a national convention. Although the results failed to bind delegates, the primaries provided a vehicle to win wide publicity for candidates and their causes. During the 1912 and 1916 campaign seasons, the press quickly grew preoccupied with candidate performance and popularity as measured in the primary votes.

At no time in the preconvention period did any Democrat seriously challenge Wilson's candidacy for renomination (although his military preparedness program briefly threatened to spark an intraparty revolt). Wilson officially entered the preconvention race on February 14, when he gave formal permission to the Ohio Democrats to put his name on the ballot in the presidential primary, and he went on to win 99 percent of the primary vote.[72] At the 1916 Democratic convention, the delegates offered almost unanimous support for Wilson. (By a vote of 1,092 to 1, delegates renominated him.) In fact, for the first time in history, the Democrats renominated the entire ticket: Wilson and his vice president, Thomas Marshall. (And for the first time in two decades, Bryan was not a major force at the convention.) In its accounts of the convention proceedings, the *New York Times* acknowledged that "Mr. Wilson is visibly stronger than his party."[73] Yet Wilson was able to revive his party's fortunes by rallying Democrats around his strong leadership and progressive principles.

In this respect, Wilson had a distinct advantage over his opponent, Republican candidate Charles Evans Hughes. Although the Republican party had officially reunited, bitter internal factionalism continued to flourish, forcing Hughes to equivocate and remain ambiguous on critical issues, including peace. Wilson even expressed sympathy for his opponent, who struggled to strike a balance between conservatives and the progressives who remained in Republican ranks. "He dare not have opinions," Wilson remarked; "he would be sure to offend some important section of his following."[74] According to the *New York Times,* "ambiguities and petty criticisms" characterized the Republican campaign, whereas the Democrats under Wilson's leadership clearly promised the "social justice which the Progressives cried for."[75] In theory and practice, Wilson showed how electoral majorities can form around candidates when voters are attracted to the principles leaders promote. In 1916, Wilson won the support of labor, former Progressives, women, the South, and the West, but the coalition lasted only one election. (In 1920, the Republicans reunited and held the White House until 1932.) Wilson's personal "force, intellect, and eloquence had broken party lines,"[76] but the new party configuration proved temporary and depended on Wilson's candidacy and the strength of his leadership.

Wilson wanted presidential candidates to create political parties in their own image; he did not want parties to produce candidates and then constrain them. His own presidency demonstrated that candidate-oriented parties could provide and support independent and determined leadership, but the leader, not the party, would initiate policy and promote programmatic change.

At the same time on the other side of the Atlantic, Wilson's British counterpart provided another vivid illustration of the pursuit of a personal policy agenda without party constraints. When David Lloyd George replaced Herbert Asquith as prime minister in 1916, antiparty sentiment in Britain ran strong. The Liberal party had already lost much of its support among the middle class, labor, Nonconformists, and the Irish—the voting bloc responsible for the Liberal victory in 1906. The government increasingly encountered the defiance of Protestant Ireland, the army, suffragettes, and workers. Liberals split at the elite level on issues such as conscription and the need for more arms. Perhaps most significant, the war created an atmosphere in which partisan loyalty and activity seemed tantamount to treason.

The *Times* summed up the prevailing sentiment when it described Asquith's coalition government in an article entitled "Weak Methods and Weak Men": Members of the cabinet were "frankly incapable of facing new conditions" because they were "encrusted in the old party habit."[77] The newspaper proved quick to contrast Asquith's equivocal and uncertain leadership with Lloyd George's decisive and independent style. According to the paper, the British "regime of patchwork and compromise" had stemmed from "the development of the party system."[78] The *Times* predicted Lloyd George would supply fresh talent "hitherto stifled by the narrow conditions of the traditional party game." In a country that "loathes party politics,"

Lloyd George represented "the embodiment of the public desire to close ranks and get on with the war."[79]

Even in this antipartisan environment, Lloyd George described his "first tasks" as prime minister in terms of coping with party constraints. He recalled that if his hands had been free, he could have chosen the best talent for his government; instead, he was "working under a parliamentary system." If his party had been united, he would have been freer, but the Liberals "divided into two parts." Confronted with these constraints, Lloyd George was not alone among party leaders. The Conservative party also restricted Bonar Law: To avoid a split, he needed to bring Conservative ex-ministers into the new coalition government. Even the young Labour party presented obstacles to decisive leadership: The trade unions wanted to support the government, but pacifist Socialists did not.[80] Lloyd George did secure the backing of Labour by delivering a speech that reassured the party of his commitment to workers, and in that speech he expressed his sincere wish "there were no parties during the war."[81]

Lloyd George's party allegiance had always been relatively weak. He considered joining the Labour party when it formed, and he proved quick to predict his own party's demise (in which he played an essential role). On November 24, 1917, Lloyd George wrote to George Riddell, "The Liberals will have to choose whether to follow me or not. There will be cleavage." On January 27, 1918, he acknowledged the Liberal party was "a thing of the past." At the time, Riddell observed, "He thinks that it may come to a fight between him and [the Labour party leader] Henderson and that all parties will be split and reconstituted."[82] For the 1918 election, Lloyd George established an independent fund-raising drive for "the Lloyd George fund" and prevented the money from going to the Liberal party. After the war, Lloyd George spoke to Winston Churchill about forming a center party. He promoted the center party as a fusion of coalition partners, but coalition Liberals opposed it, and his idea for a new party died. Lloyd George's old Liberal party officially ceased to be a significant political force after the 1918 "coupon election," in which the prime minister and his coalition partners agreed to endorse each other. Asquith and his followers were devastated, and Labour became the official opposition.

The war settlement provided the central issue of the 1918 campaign, but the nature of the election placed the desirability and legitimacy of political parties at the center of debate. To many in the public and the press, Lloyd George's "one man appeal" marked the "disappearance of the old party divisions." According to the *Times:*

> The claim of the "underdog"—in the shape of the displaced munitions worker and the returning soldier—is assuredly not going to wait

for any politicians' bargain. It is loud and insistent already. *No mere party machine can satisfy it any longer.*

[Lloyd George] knows, far better than any other man, how often the pressure of party interests, the claims of this or that influential politician, the grotesque necessity to preserve a "balance of power" in his appointments, has thwarted or delayed some vital piece of work. (emphasis added)[83]

Instead of practicing partisan politics, Lloyd George promised to take on "the task of reshaping the life of his country"[84] by "articulat[ing] and pursu[ing] the main ideas of thinking men and women on a progressive social policy."[85] During the campaign, he successfully promoted a progressive program that promised minimum wages, reduced hours of labor, a housing scheme, and agricultural reform. In the 1918 government, Lloyd George struggled to return to his radical agenda for reform, which he started when he served as chancellor of the exchequer before the war.

As prime minister of a coalition government, Lloyd George managed to achieve some of his goals, but in 1922 the Conservatives voted to campaign as a separate party, and Lloyd George's premiership came to an end. While explaining the "decline and fall of Lloyd George," the Tory magnate Lord Beaverbrook observed, "Few people stopped to think on the amazing and unprecedented position of Lloyd George. Certainly his own colleagues, Bonar Law, Chamberlain, Birkenhead, even Churchill, showed no sign of consciousness of the extraordinary political situation. Lloyd George was a prime minister without a party."[86] In 1918 he campaigned and secured victory as "the man who won the war," and he cultivated a tremendous personal following. In these respects, Lloyd George's situation was unusual, but his example demonstrates how strong leaders could emerge in twentieth-century Britain and govern without the aid of "responsible" political parties.

In other regards, Lloyd George's experience was not unique. Contrary to popular perceptions of British party government (especially in the U.S.), seven governments in the twentieth century have been coalition or national governments. Furthermore, in no general election in the twentieth century has the prime minister's party secured a majority of the popular vote (although Harold Macmillan won 49.4 percent compared with Labour's 43.7 percent in 1959). The closest Britain has come to having strong party government is the Labour government from 1945 to 1950, but many of its characteristics fail to conform to the responsible-parties model.[87] In any event, the 1945 Labour government provides the exception to the rule: On both sides of the Atlantic, strong parties tend to obstruct programmatic change and constrain the leaders who attempt to pursue it. The next case of strong, principled leadership in

Britain would occur only in the context of party decline. In the 1980s independent executive leadership managed to facilitate substantial change, but few signs of "responsible parties" could be found on either side of the Atlantic.

Weak Parties and Strong Leadership: Ronald Reagan and Margaret Thatcher

By the time Ronald Reagan took office, the primaries had replaced the mixed system of selection as the presidential nominating process. The reforms of the 1970s facilitated the process of party decomposition already under way, and public politics in a media environment increasingly came to take the place of party politics.

According to John Sears, Reagan's campaign manager in 1976 and again at the start of 1980, the new nominating system was the single most important factor in Reagan's decision to enter the race, because "Now you could run against the president."[88] Under the old system, an incumbent president could easily secure the support of the party elite who controlled the convention. In the new open system of primaries, a challenger could reach outside the inner circle of professional politicians and muster popular support for an insurgent revolt.

Reagan proved well equipped to score substantial success in the new system. He "had all the qualities one needed in the new structure," Sears emphasized. "He was trained to be before the public. He knew how to handle crowds."[89] Whether Reagan was speaking directly to a large audience or communicating through the mass media, his acting experience and star qualities enhanced his ability to wage a modern primary campaign.

The primaries also allowed Reagan to articulate precise positions on controversial issues, whereas the old system of conventions had encouraged candidates to compromise and build consensus. Early in the 1976 campaign, for example, Reagan seized the initiative (and sparked controversy) when he proposed a massive project to transfer federal programs and revenue to the states. The issue orientation of primary campaigns generally highlights the strength of conviction politicians, although in Reagan's case it also exposed the candidate's personal weakness by revealing his limited knowledge. On one occasion during the New Hampshire campaign, his ignorance proved especially costly: While attacking the federal government for preempting so much of the tax dollar, Reagan declared that the states should raise revenue, apparently unaware that residents of New Hampshire pay no state income tax. After a close loss in the New Hampshire primary, Reagan recovered by focusing on the Panama Canal as an issue. As Reagan criticized the U.S. plan to return the canal to Panama, he described the decision as a symptom of weak leadership and a sign of the nation's declining global status. The positions he took during the 1976 primary campaign repeatedly revived his flagging campaign, and they would also help set the agenda in the general election four years later.

Reagan carried his 1976 campaign all the way to the Republican convention. In fact, he made one of his boldest moves when he selected Richard Schweiker as his running mate before he secured the nomination (and when it seemed unlikely he could do so). Presidential candidates often have a decisive say in the selection of their running mates, but no candidate had ever attempted to bypass the party convention so entirely and blatantly by usurping its role in shaping the ticket. As Sears recalled, the media, not the party, determined the nature and timing of Reagan's decision: "CBS was planning to announce Ford's nomination, and we stopped the announcement. [Reporters] weren't sure what was going on."[90] Schweiker's place on the ticket might have given it balance, and his home state of Pennsylvania was one of the "loose delegations" according to Sears, but these were secondary considerations. Although the campaign held little hope that he could win the nomination when he chose Schweiker, the announcement kept the media spotlight focused on Reagan at center stage. By the time the convention took place, the candidate had shifted his own focus to 1980—a performance enhanced by the script he followed in 1976.

In the 1976 campaign Reagan mobilized the right wing of the Republican party, including many who had been searching for a principled politician since Goldwater's defeat and Nixon's betrayal. But once he sealed the support of the right, Reagan could soften his image in a way that appealed to the broader public. Sears recalled:

We came into 1980 with a much more moderate image. To change image, you don't change positions. A lot of people don't understand that [as Sears said this, he glanced over at the Bush White House]. If you change positions, you lose credibility. There are other things you can do to change image. We could get Reagan to move from telling stories about the welfare queen to talking about the plight of the poor—the need to raise people up from poverty and create jobs. No one ever tampered with his positions.[91]

Articulating the issues in 1976 made it possible for Reagan to concentrate on enhancing his image in 1980, and the media environment made the manipulation of his image much easier than it would have been within a traditional political party.

Reagan's performance in 1976 made him the front-runner in 1980, and just as significant, Reagan established a personal following on a national scale that could provide the organizational basis for his campaign four years later. After the 1976 race, Lyn Nofziger quickly moved to form a political action committee (PAC) called "Citizens for the Republic" (CFR), whose initials also intentionally stood for "Citizens for Reagan." As Nofziger explained, "At first, I didn't think Reagan was going to run, but I wanted to promote his ideas. It was mainly to help people who think like Ronald Reagan. When it became clear he was going to run, our objective changed. . . . We wanted them [the candidates] to owe us, to feel friendly toward us."[92] CFR would languish once Reagan became president. He simply "walked away from it," according to Nofziger, but the PAC took the place of the party as an electoral vehicle designed to carry candidate Reagan to the White House.

Reagan never developed a close relationship with the Republican National Committee (RNC) or its chairman, William Brock. As Nofziger continued to explain:

> Ronald Reagan is not an organization politician. He was willing to give lip service to the party, but he didn't understand its uses. The Reagan White House underutilized the national committee as a support organization. . . . Reagan was just not interested in organization. The party was never strong out there in California—mainly because of the laws out there. And we fought the party in '76. And in the years in between [1976 and 1980] we fought Brock. Brock was not a Ronald Reagan person. Reagan wanted people who shared his beliefs. He was campaign oriented—I mean candidate oriented—rather than party oriented.[93]

In the 1980 campaign, "Republican organizations helped out a little at the state level," but according to Nofziger, "mainly we relied on our own organization. We had a vitriolic feud with Brock over the Panama Canal," when Reagan raised the issue again in 1980. Brock tried to copy the British Conservatives' campaign in 1979 by attacking the incumbent and the failed policies pursued by the left, but the party chair shunned any attempt to stake out new and controversial positions. Of course, the Reagan campaign derived benefits from the RNC's efforts to mobilize Republican voters, but Nofziger concluded that lack of coordination between the presidential campaign and the national committee "didn't make any difference."[94] Indeed, the candidate's independence might well have been an asset: Armed with his own personal organizational and financial resources, Reagan escaped many traditional party constraints.

Even after he became president, Reagan refused to use the Republican National Committee. Asked how the national party helped Reagan to achieve his goals, RNC chairman Frank Fahrenkopf was caught by surprise. "That's a good question and a hard question. I've never been asked that," Fahrenkopf replied. After some thought he concluded, "The party didn't really help Reagan, but he helped the party."[95] According to Fahrenkopf, Reagan's popularity gave the party a boost in fund-raising and recruitment.

Reagan's appeal—personal and ideological—did reconstitute the electorate, broaden the base of the Republican party, and mobilize at least one new group, the Religious Right. But with the exception of his court appointments, Reagan satisfied religious conservatives by pursuing few concrete initiatives on their behalf. The open parties environment of the 1980s facilitated Reagan's ability to satisfy interests at the level of rhetoric and symbolic gestures. (The multiplicity of interests within traditional parties tended to employ tangible measures and methods to assess presidential performance and ensure accountability.) After Reagan, the Religious Right became a more significant force within the party, as demonstrated by the specific planks they secured in the 1992 and 1996 platforms. In those elections, they did constrain the Republican candidates, while their role also exposed the growing cleavage within the party between "moralizers" and "economizers."[96] Reagan's successors faced party constraints that he escaped and, paradoxically, that he helped to create.

To some extent, Reagan also benefited from a parties environment in government that was weaker than what he bequeathed to his heirs. In the early years of the Reagan revolution, members of Congress were sufficiently independent to be swayed by Reagan's ideology or moved by the public pressure that a popular president can exert.

After the 1980 election, Reagan had a Republican Senate and a working majority in the House based on a coalition of Republicans and conservative Southern Democrats known as Boll Weevils.[97] The Republican party in Congress included many members who endorsed central aspects of Reagan's program but also some factions who opposed it, especially liberal Republicans, or Gypsy Moths,[98] in the House and traditional budget-balancers in the Senate. To hold this fragile coalition together, Reagan employed traditional techniques of bargaining and bartering, but his public support and political ideology proved to be even more significant factors.

Responsible-party theorists might expect ideology to link the president and his party in Congress and predict that presidents will use public pressure to win support from the other side, but Reagan did just the opposite. The president's popularity rallied factions within his own party. Senator Laxalt explained what unified the Republicans "was initially fear. He had a mandate. They knew he would go over their heads. . . . His philosophy mattered more to the Democrats. Phil Gramm and the Boll Weevils agreed with it, and they were willing to go with Reagan. The conservative philosophy was very important to them."[99] Essentially, the public approach threatened Republicans, while Reagan's ideas won the support of Southern Democrats.

In the first year, popularity and ideology combined to maintain Reagan's coalition for both tax reform and his budget. Recalling the passage of the 1981 tax reform, James Baker (then chief of staff) rendered an assessment similar to Laxalt's view. Baker remembered, "It was easy [to win over the Boll Weevils]. They were on the same wavelength as the president. . . . It was more difficult to keep the Republicans together. In politics, it's your friends who do you in. But most of them found it politically impossible to oppose."[100] Support for the president's budget came from the same surprising source, according to Kenneth Duberstein, in 1981 an LSG staffer who lobbied for the first House budget resolution. Duberstein recalled, "Reagan got sixty-three Democratic votes. That's what the press focused on. What is little remembered is that every single Republican in the House voted with the president. After the vote, I went to [Speaker of the House] O'Neill's office to shake hands with his chief of staff. He said, 'You guys are real professionals. I salute you—not on getting sixty-three Democrats, but on a substantive vote getting every House Republican.'"[101] The chief of staff to the speaker of the House knew how difficult it could be to maintain party unity on a nonprocedural vote. On that first budget resolution, Reagan achieved perfect party unity, but it would not have been possible without the political clout that came from substantial presidential popularity.

Reagan mastered the art of "going public" to win legislative approval for his proposals,[102] and like other conviction politicians, he campaigned for the triumph of the people over the special interests that plague the parties in Congress. In his final televised appeal to the nation on behalf of the 1981 tax reform, Reagan urged viewers to contact their representatives in Congress and reminded them that "[Members of Congress] get plenty of input from the special interest groups. They'd like to hear from their home folks."[103] Reagan's populist appeal enhanced his personal stature and advanced his political principles, while enabling him to circumvent party constraints.

Like the RNC, the congressional party generally failed to impose limits on its popular president. As Fahrenkopf recalled, "If Reagan wanted to go a certain way, the party fell in line, but the congressional party can limit the president. Newt Gingrich and his crowd have certainly given Bush a hard time. But they didn't stop Reagan. He was too popular."[104] Congressional parties did become stronger and more ideological during the 1980s and the 1990s. Several factors account for this development, and Reagan's leadership was one critical variable: His conviction politics produced a polarizing effect on the congressional parties.[105] Of course, whether such ideological parties enhance or constrain presidential leadership depends on the ideological compatibility between the party in Congress and its president.[106]

In the case of the Reagan presidency, divided party control of government provided few obstacles to his pursuit of principle, and his own party usually rallied around its popular president.[107] The remarkable success Reagan achieved in his first term did not come from the strength he derived from his party, but it did represent the "triumph of ideas" and reflect his "good salesmanship."[108] To a great extent, the rhetorical presidency that Woodrow Wilson envisioned—where followers are attracted to the leaders and their messages—found realization in the Reagan regime.[109]

Margaret Thatcher ultimately proved even more successful than Reagan did, and like Reagan, she did not derive strength from a "responsible" political party. On the contrary, Thatcher reversed the direction of the transatlantic search for a model of effective government. She preferred the U.S. system to the British and tried to adopt a model of independent executive leadership. The condition of British parties enhanced Thatcher's ability to capture her party's leadership even though she was an outsider, win three consecutive elections without an electoral majority, and pursue radical change on her own.

Like her U.S. counterpart, Thatcher took advantage of the reform of her party's leadership selection process. The Conservative party adopted its first formal procedure for electing a leader in 1965. Previously, leaders "emerged" from a consensus among the party elite within a "magic circle."[110] The 1965 procedure made members of Parliament the selectors: To win on the first ballot, a candidate needed to secure a majority of 15 percent among those voting. If no one achieved this, a simple majority on the second ballot proved sufficient to win. That selection mechanism facilitated the rise of Edward Heath (also an outsider) to the leadership, but the next change would make it more difficult for him to maintain his position.

One month before Thatcher's selection, the party adopted new rules that maintained members of the parliamentary party as selectors but called for annual elections. Under the new rules, the winner required a majority of 15 percent of *eligible voters*. If no candidate succeeded, then on the second ballot, the victor only needed to secure a simple majority over the combined votes of her opponents.[111] The new rules made it more difficult for an incumbent to hold on to the leadership (a majority of 15 percent of eligible voters rather than actual voters presented a higher hurdle to overcome) and opened the opportunity for an insurgent revolt, if anyone was bold enough to deliver it.

Initially, the right wing hoped Thatcher's mentor, Keith Joseph, would challenge former prime minister Heath, but when Joseph withdrew his name, his disciple quickly took his place. Thatcher was not very well known in the country at large, and when she defeated Heath on the first ballot, she stunned both the public and the press. Following Heath's resignation, four other candidates entered the second ballot, but many selectors saw them as pure opportunists in contrast to the bold conviction politician. Thatcher defeated her primary rival, William Whitelaw (a Heath loyalist), and secured a slim majority of 16 votes.[112] During the selection process, first a vote against Heath and then a second ballot against his followers put Thatcher in the leadership. Yet she was not content to win by default and then rest on her laurels.

Thatcher immediately took steps to improve the prospects for further success, but rather than engage in party building, she set out to enhance her own personal image.[113] In 1974 Thatcher met a former television producer, Gordon Reece, and four months after the leadership contest, Reece joined her staff full-time. Although he briefly served as director of publicity at Conservative Central Office, he performed primarily as her private consultant. In the pursuit of the perfect public persona, Thatcher also enlisted the assistance of Tim Bell, whom she met (through Reece) while he worked for Saatchi and Saatchi and who also became her private consultant. As soon as Thatcher assumed the leadership, she surrounded herself with personal consultants, avoiding the need to rely on the party or its advertising experts.

In addition to image building, Thatcher cultivated a personal following based on the principles she espoused (and the decisive way she advanced them), and once again the parties environment facilitated her independent efforts. When Thatcher won the party leadership in 1975, the electoral base of the Conservative party had shrunk, and the loyalty of activists waned.[114] The *Times,* by now a conservative newspaper, was forced to acknowledge that "Mrs. Thatcher has not inherited a position of Conservative strength. . . . [Her selection] is a gamble, and strong parties do not have to gamble; it is a true blue choice, designed to reassure the faithful rather than win the doubtful; it is a choice made against the predominant wishes of the old Shadow Cabinet, and quite largely inspired by hostility to the Conservative establishment. She inherits, therefore, a badly bruised minority party."[115] To attract new followers, Thatcher believed she needed to articulate and promote specific policies that would reflect her public philosophy.

For the source of new ideas, Thatcher turned to Joseph's think tank, the Centre for Policy Studies (CPS), and not to the Conservative party's research department. In theory, CPS focused on changing public opinion, while the research department continued to produce policy briefs.[116] In retrospect,

James Prior recalled that in reality Thatcher's intraparty opponents "under-estimated enormously the change in the whole philosophy of the right and the changes in the Conservative Party which were taking place. . . . The Conservative Research Department was reduced to a nonentity . . . [and] the Centre for Policy Studies was built up to rival and usurp it."[117] Thatcher shunned the use of the party apparatus and preferred to rely instead on a mechanism guaranteed to produce policies that were distinctly Thatcherite.

If the Conservatives had faced a single, unified opponent, they might have forced their leader to extend her electoral appeal by moderating her views and softening her style, but when the Labour party split in 1981, fragmentation on the left freed Thatcher from the need to build an electoral majority. Moreover, the decline in party identification throughout the 1970s and 1980s eroded Labour's electoral majority and facilitated Thatcher's ability to reconstitute the voting blocs traditionally aligned with her opposition.[118] In the electorate and as organizations, British parties had weakened substantially by the time Thatcher became prime minister.

Only rarely did the party organization limit Thatcher's independent, decisive leadership. When the Conservative party faced a single major-party opponent in 1979, intraparty pressures forced Thatcher to endorse the Clegg Commission's recommended pay increases for public sector employees. In the 1987 election, the party exercised considerably less influence than it had in 1979: Party chairman Norman Tebbit struggled to direct his party's campaign, but Thatcher pursued a different strategy, acting on her own and following the advice of her private consultants, Reece and Bell. Her independence created friction with the Central Office, but the party failed to restrict her efforts. Finally, in only one major policy area—reform of the legal profession—did a powerful group within the Conservative party thwart Thatcher's ability to pursue change. With these exceptions, the party organization otherwise proved a weak restraint on its leader's radical zeal.

In theory, the party's role in government most clearly distinguishes the British and U.S. systems, yet a significant factor in Thatcher's escape from party constraints proved to be her ability to "presidentialize" the prime minister's role by circumventing her cabinet. During her eleven years as prime minister, Thatcher strengthened the means of support for her independent leadership at Number 10 Downing Street. Only months before she was dethroned, Prior remained skeptical about rumors of her imminent demise, and he insisted, "Although there's been lots of chuntering about palace coups and one thing or another, nothing has happened. And this I think is a reflection of how difficult it is—how the whole machine goes into operation—especially the Number 10 press machine . . . to support the prime minister and to quash any opposition."[119] As in the U.S., the media grew in significance as the party declined, and Thatcher's successful media management made party management less essential. In this media-oriented atmosphere, ministers found it difficult to compete with their premier's "press machine," but in the new open environment public opinion started to rival the traditional party as a constraint on executive independence and initiative.

In many cases, the public registered its preferences through individual members of Parliament, reflecting yet another change in British parties: MPs have grown more constituent oriented,[120] and consequently are more susceptible to the pressure of public opinion. For much of her premiership, Thatcher's approval ratings ensured the support of her parliamentary party and shielded her from backbench revolts. At times, however, according to Norman Tebbit, "The radical agenda did throw quite a lot of strain on the parliamentary party here. Members of Parliament can get quite windy when they get masses and masses of word-processed letters saying the government's doing this and that, and it's upsetting. They begin to say we're upsetting too many people."[121] Backbenchers declined to rebel against their prime minister when Thatcher's approval ratings ran high, and they did not always rebel when her public approval was low. But they dared to rebel only when she or her policies clearly lacked public support.

The most vivid examples can be drawn from Thatcher's second government when fluctuations in her public support fueled frequent backbench revolts. In 1984, when Joseph—then secretary of state for education— proposed to introduce university tuition fees, 180 Tory backbenchers signed motions of protest and forced Thatcher's government to retreat. In 1985, in the midst of a sterling crisis and renewed urban race riots, Francis Pym formed "Centre Forward," a group of thirty-two Conservative MPs who opposed the government's social and economic policies. (In a television interview during the 1983 campaign, Pym had warned against a landslide, a comment for which the foreign secretary was sacked immediately after Thatcher secured her parliamentary landslide.) That same year concluded with a major controversy concerning the sale of Britain's last helicopter company, Westland: What started as a rare conflict in cabinet (between Thatcher and her secretary of state for environment, Michael Heseltine) evolved into a Downing Street cover-up, resulting in ministerial resignations and almost bringing down the government. Thatcher found herself (and her government) on a downward reciprocal spiral, where dips in the polls diminished support in Parliament, and backbench revolts further damaged her credibility.

From January through August 1986, the Conservative party ranked third in the opinion polls,[122] and the unpopularity of Thatcher's government stirred even more unrest among Conservative backbenchers. In February 1986 a backbench revolt opposed the sale of British Leyland to General Motors and

Ford. According to Market and Opinion Research International (MORI), only 19 percent of the public favored the sale.[123] Then in April, sixty-eight Conservative MPs voted against the government's shops bill, which would have liberalized Sunday trading laws. That same month (and within a week of losing a critical by-election in Fulham), the Conservatives suffered another blow to their popularity: Thatcher supported the U.S. bombing raid on Libya and permitted the U.S. to use its British-based F111s for the attack. On April 17, ten Conservative MPs, including former prime minister Heath, rebelled against Thatcher's decision. A MORI poll showed 71 percent of the public thought Thatcher was wrong to permit the use of British bases, and 66 percent opposed the bombing.[124] Thatcher's approval ratings rebounded after 1986 (and backbenchers settled down), but she would not recover as easily the next time she lost public confidence.

Of all Thatcher's radical reforms, none "upset the people" more than the poll tax, and ultimately public opposition to the tax determined the timing of the revolt that removed her from office. Ministerial resignations based on opposition to Thatcher's style and her policy concerning Europe were among the immediate catalysts for the coup, but public reaction to the poll tax explains why she was seriously challenged then (and not earlier). Moreover, the growing importance of public opinion was reflected in the nature of the 1990 leadership contest.

In the House of Commons, Thatcher's primary challenger, Heseltine, lobbied members for their support, but the central campaign was conducted in the public, not in the party or Parliament. One of Thatcher's loyal lieutenants recalled, "I was under enormous stress—doing television, radio, round the clock. People in the country were putting pressure on members here, so it was very important."[125] A journalist explained how "the press created a feverish atmosphere by publishing the polls. . . . [They] all said the Tories would lose under Thatcher and win under Heseltine."[126] According to one of Thatcher's long-term critics in the Conservative party, "What is remarkable is that we did get rid of her. She always regarded herself as a presidential figure. She is an enormously tiresome woman. She created lots of enemies. But that wasn't enough to get rid of her. After the poll tax, there was a growing conviction that the party wouldn't win with her. Then the worm that is the Conservative party did at last turn."[127] In the fall of 1990, Thatcher learned a painful lesson: If a prime minister can build and maintain public support, she can generally ensure that members of Parliament will go along with her policies. But the opposite also holds true: When a prime minister loses public support, she will find it more difficult to remain leader of her parliamentary party. As U.S. presidents well know, the public approach carries risks, and public opinion can impose its own limits. Yet

Thatcher's presidential style enabled her to promote her principles much longer than the constraints of "party government" would have allowed.

Conclusion

If political parties provided efficient, effective vehicles of change, conviction-style leaders might well endorse them and seek to strengthen them. Instead, conviction politicians repeatedly attempt to circumvent party constraints and openly express their disdain for the requirements of party leadership. Peel admitted he lacked "essential qualifications which are requisite in party leaders" and listed "patience to listen to the sentiments of individuals whom it is equally imprudent to neglect and an intolerable bore to consult."[128] Cleveland struggled to free himself from the grasp of his "hungry party." Lloyd George expressed relief that he had been released "from the irksome and peculiarly thankless duty of leadership in a political party."[129] Conviction-style leaders agree that political parties constitute, in Wilson's words, "unmitigated nuisances" that "must be roughly shaken out of their insolence and made to realize that they are only servants."[130]

Of course, political parties can also impose legitimate limits on leadership and help to ensure accountability. Indeed, this was one of the goals of early responsible-party theorists. The 1950 APSA report, *Toward a More Responsible Two Party System,* expressed the hope that responsible parties would prevent "the danger of overextending the presidency."[131] Its authors believed that such parties would provide presidents with sufficient strength so that "with greater responsibility, the President's position as party leader would correspond in strength to the greater strength of his party, and he would be in less need of going his own way."[132] Unfortunately, the responsible-parties school of thought proved flawed in theory and practice: If parties comprise multiple interests and abide by a degree of intraparty democracy, they will produce proposals based on compromise and equivocation, not proposals based on coherent programmatic change. Furthermore, their leaders will be prevented from pursuing change on their own, unless they can circumvent their parties. For this reason, conviction-style leaders on both sides of the Atlantic prefer to "go their own way" when they can.

Traditional parties might suit more pragmatic political animals, but they cage in leaders from the family of the lion and the tribe of the eagle who prefer to roam free of restraint and soar above the mundane concerns that arise in the interplay of interests. Conviction-style leaders seek an environment that will magnify their majestic displays of courage, and they find the modern media supply a much more congenial habitat than the context of partisan politics.

7

THE DEPICTION OF CONVICTION:
PRESIDENTS, PRIME MINISTERS, AND THE PRESS

While political parties often restrict executive initiative, the media tend to assist the conviction-style leader who independently seeks to establish a new national agenda. Journalists usually welcome the prospect of fundamental change and applaud the leader who crusades against special interests that preserve the status quo and thwart the "public good." As a consequence, conviction politicians generally find media management easier than party management, even though media relations can present more considerable challenges than presidents and prime ministers originally anticipate.

Admittedly, their efforts to manage the news can entrap these leaders in one paradox after another. Conviction-style leaders in the liberal tradition accept the principle of free press, but once in office they seek to manipulate (and sometimes weaken) it. Furthermore, they enlist the assistance of the press to bypass traditional institutions, but then they often attempt to circumvent the press. Finally, the professionalization and institutionalization of the national press corps might have enhanced the independence and credibility of journalists, but in fact these developments have only made it easier for willful (and skillful) executives to manage or manipulate the news.

Situated between the president or prime minister and the public, the place of the press in the political order provides a crucial key to understanding the media's depiction of conviction-style leaders. Historical developments have brought the media closer to the executive and created structures conducive to news management. At the same time, journalists increasingly have seen themselves as "representatives" or guardians of the public interest, and their values reflect that perception. An adversarial relationship between leaders and the press has existed from time to time throughout these developments, but in the late twentieth century the structure of interaction and the nature of news values finally combined to enhance the success of conviction-style leaders on both sides of the Atlantic.

Presidents, Prime Ministers, and the Press in Political Development

The United States

Andrew Jackson fully appreciated the potential of the press to provide an essential link between the president and the public, but he inherited only the limited resources of a nascent national press. The congressional press gallery was established in the mid-1820s, but reporters simply recorded congressional debates. From 1800 until 1825, local newspapers derived their news of the national government from a single source, the *National Intelligencer:* Thomas Jefferson had brought the paper with him to Washington and made it the authoritative "spokes vehicle" for the executive branch, but the paper went Whiggish when Jackson became president. To make matters worse, Jackson could not rely on the steady support of a partisan press as Jefferson had been able to do; both the parties and the press fragmented following Jefferson's presidency. Newspapers became tied to individual candidates rather than to political parties, and candidates needed to court editors and cultivate personal relationships with them. (To buy the support of newspaper editors, in the absence of well-developed party organizations, candidates often struggled to raise money on their own.) While few resources existed to manage the news on a national scale, the influence of the press had grown. From 1801 until 1833, the number of newspapers increased from 200 to 1,200, and the press in the United States acquired a larger aggregate circulation than in any other nation.[1] These conditions and Jackson's aspirations to popularize the presidency encouraged him to innovate.

Jackson started to create his own machinery for news management even before he became president. After his 1824 defeat, he mobilized the newspapers in his home state of Tennessee to condemn the corruption in John Quincy Adams's administration and call for reform. As Jackson advised his campaign manager, "The papers of Nashville and the whole State should speak out with moderate but firm disapprobation of this corruption, to give a proper tone to the people, and to draw their attention to the subject."[2] Jackson extended his efforts beyond Tennessee and created a national network of local papers, which worked in unison to secure his election.[3] When he won substantial press support for his crusade against corruption, Jackson also demonstrated that a candidate's skillful news management could help to set the tone and the agenda for the campaign.

Corruption did constitute the dominant theme of the 1828 contest, although the virulence of attacks printed in the press exceeded the "moderate but firm disapprobation" Jackson had recommended. And, as it turned out, both sides focused as much on personal impropriety as they did on public misconduct. Adams's supporters revealed that Jackson's wife had failed to secure a divorce from her first husband and labeled her a bigamist. The Jacksonians alleged that Adams had lived with his wife before marriage and, as ambassador to Russia, supplied a virgin to the czar. Sensational press coverage of these and other sordid allegations reveals that the press enjoyed an early "feeding frenzy" during the 1828 campaign.[4] Jackson would find it much easier to manage the news once he left the campaign trail and entered the White House.

While the press emphasized the candidates' personal shortcomings, Jackson's campaign also attracted newspaper reporters to his cause of governmental reform. He quickly secured the support of James Gordon Bennett Sr., the first Washington correspondent (a reporter for the *New York Enquirer* and later the founder and editor of the *New York Herald*). Bennett's colorful depictions of Washington politics served to enhance Jackson's image and damage the credibility of his adversaries. In a report on the politics of the tariff, for example, Bennett informed his readers: "The Adams party are afraid of losing the advantage of riding the Tariff hobby. The animal is sliding from beneath them. They try to catch his tail, as the witch did that of Tam O'Shanter's mare, but their vociferations, etc., will not avail them. It will be found that the Jackson party are the truest friends of the country, and that they will encourage every interest, but favor none."[5] Bennett consistently communicated to the public the message Jackson wanted to convey: The "Adams party" remained tied to special interests, whereas the "Jackson party" promised to pursue only the public good.

Even more significant support came from the three newspaper reporters who formed the core of Jackson's circle of advisors known as his "kitchen cabinet." Amos Kendall, editor of the *Kentucky Argus,* turned against his former friend Henry Clay and then approached Jackson with information he thought might assist the president in discrediting his adversary. According to one member of Congress, Kendall's influence grew until he became "the president's thinking machine, his writing machine—aye, and his lying machine."[6] Kendall brought with him an associate from the *Argus,* Francis Blair, while the editor of the *Telegraph,* Duff Green, recommended that Jackson enlist the assistance of a third reporter, John Rives. Initially, Kendall served as Jackson's chief advisor on matters of policy, and Blair focused more on public relations. When Jackson established his own newspaper, the *Globe,* Blair became the editor and Rives assumed the role of business manager. These three journalists provided two-way communication between the president and the public: As members of the kitchen cabinet, they advised Jackson on how to craft popular policies, and then they used the *Globe* to cultivate popular support.

Journalists drawn to Jackson, including his trio of advisors, came to pursue their personal goals as well as the cause of political reform, and the president knew how to satisfy them. Jackson rewarded loyalty from newspaper editors the same way he acknowledged the support of others who helped him—by obtaining positions for them in his new administration. (Kendall secured appointment as the fourth auditor at the Treasury and later became postmaster general.) Predictably, Adams denounced Jackson's appointments, which "almost without exception, are conferred upon the vilest purveyors of slander during the late electioneering campaign," and Senator Daniel Webster expressed his determination to stop "the typographical corps" from seizing the spoils.[7] Jackson's critics exaggerated the extent of his rewards, but the president did initiate a new practice: Previously, politicians—including presidents—had repaid loyal newspaper editors by helping them secure government contracts, but Jackson was the first to give them government jobs.

Some of Jackson's supporters also voiced concern about the nature and consequences of his appointments, but they were more worried about the implications for journalism. Thomas Ritchie of the Richmond *Enquirer* wrote, "[W]e lament to see so many of the Editorial Corps favored with the patronage of the Administration." Although many of them had "fought manfully to put out a corrupt coalition," Ritchie feared that journalists themselves would become corrupt if they held public office. "Under the profession of Reform changes will be made to the public inquiry. . . . The contest will be for office and not for principle," Ritchie warned.[8] This astute observer was one of the first to criticize what contemporary commentators decry as the "revolving door" through which journalists pass in and out of politics. Then and now, the practice creates a common bond between the press and public officials, which can compromise the integrity and cloud the judgment of journalists.

Jackson employed other heavy-handed techniques for managing the news and even endorsed forms of press censorship. He recommended legal penalties for the circulation of any press that advocated abolition of slavery, a position that increased his popularity in the South. As postmaster general, Kendall allowed the local postmaster in Charleston, South Carolina, to stop the delivery of abolitionist newspapers. Later he proposed legislation that would have enabled his department to prevent the circulation of all "obnoxious papers in the southern states," but Congress refused to pass it.[9] When a free press obstructed Jackson's goals, he tried to restrict it.

In general, the candidate-oriented nature of the press during Jackson's tenure both limited and enhanced his opportunities. His own press praised Jackson for the courage of his convictions, but his opponents attacked those same convictions with equal force. Jackson probably never won the support of the majority of newspapers (and he certainly failed to do so during the bank war). On the other hand, the administration's own paper, the *Globe,* provided several advantages: Jackson used it to free himself from Vice President John C. Calhoun, and the *Globe* provided the independent means for Jackson to announce that he would seek a second term.[10] More significant, the *Globe* gave Jackson the propaganda machine he needed to disseminate information to the public (and attack his enemies). Read at home and abroad as the definitive account of Jackson's preferences and policies, the *Globe* had a capacity to set the agenda that other newspapers lacked.

While Jackson tried to manage the news to cultivate his own following, his supporters often used the news to mobilize grassroots support for the emerging Democratic party. In particular, editors and publishers used their newspapers to build political machines at the state level. Isaac Hill, editor of the *New Hampshire Patriot,* constructed a machine for the Jacksonian Democratic party in his state. A prominent Democratic leader in Massachusetts, David Henshaw, was also the publisher of the *Boston Statesman.* While employed by the *Argus,* Kendall and Blair organized Jacksonian Democrats in their home state of Kentucky. Apparently, the press facilitated the early development of parties,[11] but changes in the news business would put an end to the period when parties could rely on press loyalty.

By 1880 one-fourth of the press had become independent, and by 1890 the proportion rose to one-third.[12] Mass production, mass distribution, and mass marketing generally explain the move away from partisanship.[13] Technological advances and low postal rates diminished the cost of producing and distributing the news and help to account for the rise in readership. Advertising revenues freed publishers from their financial dependence on parties. Finally, the rise of big-city daily papers popularized the news—and drove local and state partisan papers out of business. In 1841 Bennett, as founder and editor of the *New York Herald,* established the first Washington bureau, and his competitors—Benjamin Day of the *New York Sun* and Horace Greeley of the *Tribune*—soon followed his lead. The distance between Washington correspondents and their home papers fueled reporters' independence from parochial, partisan perspectives.

The shift from partisan local papers to independent big-city dailies also nurtured the development of the "professional idea" in journalism: News, not editorial opinion, became the chief function of reporting.[14] Washington correspondents could witness national political events firsthand, and accuracy replaced loyalty as the standard by which the public assessed the press. (With the rise in literacy, the public became increasingly skeptical of accounts in the partisan press and demanded more objective reporting.) Freed from formal partisan ties, the press engaged in greater freedom of criticism. (Major newspapers such as the *New York Tribune,* the *New York Herald,* and the *Chicago Tribune* remained nominally identified with a party, but these papers frequently found fault with both of the major parties and their leaders.) As the press became more independent, journalism attracted better-educated reporters, which in turn enhanced the credibility and prestige of the profession[15]—and created even greater distance between the press and the parties.

An increasingly independent press initially served the interests of the fiercely independent candidate, Grover Cleveland. When Republican papers bolted from Blaine in 1884, they established a precedent that made it easier for newspapers to abandon their partisan allegiance in the future.[16] Cleveland welcomed endorsements from the Mugwump press, especially the support he secured from E. L. Godkin, editor of the *Nation* and the *Evening Post*. Other major news outlets—the *New York Times,* the *Herald, Harper's Weekly,* and the *World*—also rallied behind Cleveland's independent leadership. No longer formally tied to parties or candidates, many newspapers asserted their own independence when they endorsed Cleveland's candidacy and the cause of good government he promised to pursue.

At the same time, much of the press qualified their support with a warning that President Cleveland would be held to high standards, ones that reflected the changing place of journalism in the political order. After the election, Joseph Pulitzer put it bluntly: "The *World* is chained to no conqueror's chariot. It will gladly and zealously support all that is good in President Cleveland's administration, but it will oppose anything clearly wrong or mistaken. The *World* is as great a public trust as the Presidency."[17] By 1884 journalists had started to see themselves as the unelected representatives of the people and guardians of the public interest. Nevertheless, not all aspects of the new, professional journalism were as lofty as the sentiment expressed in Pulitzer's pledge that the press would monitor the behavior of public officials. Indeed, the self-proclaimed watchdog function also provided a self-serving rationale for pursuing commercial objectives.

An independent press now needed the public just as earlier papers relied on candidates or parties: The size of a newspaper's readership largely determined its advertising revenues. To attract a wider audience, the big-city dailies published human-interest stories, including reports that placed greater emphasis on political personalities. Ironically, at the same time the emerging profession of journalism elevated the stature of reporters and enhanced their reputation for integrity, journalists slid back down into the mud of sensationalism and scandal, which had characterized the partisan press.

The costs of this development quickly became apparent to Cleveland. In 1884 the press focused on the charge that Cleveland had an illegitimate son. Two years into his presidency, the press also covered Cleveland's wedding and haunted him during his honeymoon, despite the president's best efforts to shroud the event in secrecy and guard his privacy. Reporters remained stationed outside the honeymoon cottage and reported on every visible detail of the couple's appearance and activity. In the development of professional journalism, the event marked the start of personal coverage of president.[18] At the time, the nature of news on the president's honeymoon sparked a debate among journalists about the propriety of the press prying into the president's personal life.

The Mugwump press tried to maintain its lofty mission and keep the news focused on public affairs. Coining the phrase "keyhole journalism," the *New York Evening Post* condemned the big-city editors. According to the *Evening Post*, "They have not only hired and directed reporters to dog the President's steps and poke their noses into the sanctity of his private life, but they have published the results to the world every day, and have spared no effort to outdo one another in the vulgar profuseness and minuteness of the narrative." The same report urged the public to "think of the spectacle which these accounts present. Here are five great metropolitan newspapers hiring men to sit out in the shrubbery around a private house to watch and report for publication every motion made by the inmates who are a man and his wife on their wedding journey. To be sure the man is President of the United States and a public character, but has a public man no private rights, and are they not as sacred as those of any other man?" Finally, the *Evening Post* predicted, "We do not believe that newspaper enterprises of this kind [are] desired by the American people or will be long tolerated by them."[19] To the contrary, the public relished every detail and hungered for more.

No one understood popular tastes better than Pulitzer did, and his newspaper took the lead in defending the new "investigative" methods of journalism. At first, the *World* offered the simple justification that "newspapers naturally wish to supply their readers with interesting news." Then the paper explained the nature of its reporters' activity as follows:

> Newspaper correspondents are remarkable for their fidelity and devotion. They stop at neither danger nor fatigue in performing their duties. To throw obstacles in their way is to spur them to greater efforts to insure success. They decline to be circumvented. Yet . . . [t]hey will meet those who favor them with their confidence in a spirit of fairness and candor. But their pride of profession is aroused when any person seeks to evade them by a back exit or blocks their approach with pickets of vulgar detectives. This is not because they are "keyhole sneaks" and "blackguards," as the *Evening Post* implies, but because they are true men, faithful to the interests of the journals they serve.[20]

When the *World* concluded by "insist[ing] that the President is public property," it established a principle that would persist throughout the next century.

The notion that the president (and not the presiden*cy*) constitutes a public property shocked Cleveland, but unwittingly he played a role in this development—even after his honeymoon. With his tariff message, Cleveland tried to shift public attention from his party in the legislature to his presidency, but when the press altered their emphasis, they focused on the person in the presidency, not the institution. In fact, the emerging press preoccupation with personalities might well have helped to shift authority from the legislature to the executive, an institution more conducive to dramatic displays of human strength (and weakness). Whether the press emphasis would also increase presidential power would depend on the nature of the coverage and how it was crafted. When the *World* declared the president had become "public property," the paper provided one of several clues to successful news management, although Cleveland neglected to detect it.

As "interesting news," press coverage of the president's personal life could enhance as well as detract from presidential popularity. News coverage of Cleveland's honeymoon actually boosted his popular image, by highlighting the human, emotional side of a president otherwise viewed as cold and aloof.[21] Rather than use the event to his advantage, however, Cleveland remained appalled by the violation of his privacy. On several occasions, he expressed disgust that the press preferred to focus on his personal life and his family rather than on his ideas and his principles. (According to George Parker, Cleveland's informal press secretary, the president shunned attempts to manipulate the news because he wanted to shape public opinion "by giving it something real and substantial upon which to carry his message laden with ideas and principles.")[22] When Cleveland underwent oral surgery to remove a cancerous tumor, he kept the procedure and his condition secret. (Cleveland's experience in the spring of 1893 provides a sharp contrast to the detailed coverage of Ronald Reagan's surgery for prostate cancer in the summer of 1985!) It never occurred to Cleveland that he could package his personal experience in a way that would win the public's affection or sympathy.

Moreover, as the *World* revealed, reporters "will meet those who favor them with their confidence in a spirit of fairness and candor," but Cleveland's interaction with reporters remained rigid and restricted. The president never took them into his confidence; he granted few interviews and rarely conducted off-the-record discussions. Correspondents had to submit questions in writing through Cleveland's secretaries. When Cleveland issued a formal statement, he made sure the press release went to all news organizations. (The absence of exclusives alienated Pulitzer even before the controversy concerning coverage of Cleveland's honeymoon.) Throughout his first administration, Cleveland's relations with the press became increasingly strained; in his second administration, the loss of public approval made it even more difficult for him to maintain press support. By the end of his presidency, Cleveland had managed to alienate most of his original supporters in the press—a consequence of his policies and his public standing but also a reflection of his refusal to court or accommodate the growing national press corps.

In contrast to Cleveland, Woodrow Wilson appeared to appreciate the advantages a sympathetic press could provide and, initially, he took steps to cultivate their cooperation. Theodore Roosevelt had invited reporters into the White House, and they quickly established permanent residence by forming the White House press corps. Like Roosevelt, Wilson welcomed this development because he expected his guests from the press to provide new means for transmitting his messages directly to the people.

At the same time, the formation of the White House press corps seemed to suit the evolving needs of journalists. As public policy (and the political process) became more extensive and more complex, reporters attempted to explain as well as describe events to their readers. Expository writing required interaction with public officials who could provide insights as well as information. When Wilson announced he would hold regular press conferences, journalists' expectations soared. Twice a week, approximately one hundred newspaper reporters crowded into the East Room of the White House, eager for the opportunity to interact with the president.

Almost immediately, the reporters' high hopes were dashed, as it became clear their expectations and those of the president clashed. Wilson prohibited reporters from quoting him directly and repeatedly evaded their questions. Instead of interacting with the press, the professor-turned-president delivered lectures, expecting reporters to take accurate notes and then print what they learned for the public. When reporters failed to follow his instructions or dared to offer critical comment, the president became enraged, and the relationship turned adversarial. On one occasion when a reporter from the *New York Herald* quoted Wilson, the president barred him from the press conferences and tried to get him fired. (Fortunately for both sides, Wilson's press secretary, Joseph Tumulty, intervened to smooth things over.) In February 1914, concern about Wilson's lack of accessibility and the slow flow of information led reporters to form the White House Correspondents Association to negotiate better terms of their employment, air their complaints, and determine the membership at press conferences. The move made little difference: By the end of the year, Wilson cut the press conferences to once a week and assigned the task of conducting them to one of his aides, usually Tumulty.

Wilson failed at his press conferences for several reasons. He believed he knew the mind of the people better than the reporters did, but he was speaking to professional journalists who had begun to see themselves as guardians of the public interest. Moreover, Wilson hoped that press conferences would resemble question time in the British Parliament (as Wilson understood that practice), but the quality and manner of reporters' questions disappointed him. In particular, the president resented invasions of his family's privacy, and like Cleveland, Wilson expressed disgust "that the interest of the majority was in the personal and the trivial rather than in principles and policies."[23] (Yet, despite his complaints, Wilson managed to escape serious scandal about his presumed extramarital affair.)[24] Finally, contrary to Wilson's expectations, reporters tried to provide more than a mere transmission valve for the president's public pronouncements. When they engaged in exposition, Wilson learned that the medium could alter his message. Once Wilson recognized that the press would constitute an intermediary between the president and the public, he set out to circumvent them.

World War I facilitated Wilson's hasty retreat from his campaign to court the press corps. The president ended his press conferences in the summer of 1915, after the sinking of the *Lusitania,* and following his reelection he cited his busy schedule during the war as an excuse to avoid them. Throughout his entire second term, Wilson held only four official press conferences. The war also gave Wilson the rationale he needed to establish an official government publicity bureau, the Committee on Public Information (CPI). CPI provided an efficient propaganda machine, but the government's steady flow of misinformation exacerbated the distrust reporters had already developed. Finally, according to Wilson, the war rendered sufficient reason to restrict free speech and free press, and he did not hesitate to sign the Espionage Act of 1917 or the Trading with the Enemy Act and the Sedition Act of 1918.

At the Versailles Peace Conference, Wilson joined the other world leaders and agreed to withhold information, except for the announcement of official decisions. After the peace conference, when Wilson declined to discuss specific aspects of the treaty with reporters, he gave the advantage to his political opponents, who seized control of the agenda by selectively leaking information in their favor. Wilson's opponents set the terms of the debate and put the president on the defensive. After Wilson collapsed during his public tour to promote the League of Nations, he tried to conceal information about his stroke, but press speculation eventually forced him to authorize his physician to reveal the details (albeit four months after the event). As Pulitzer had warned Cleveland, each overt attempt to obstruct or deceive the press only inspired the reporters to rebel. Like Cleveland, Wilson started his presidency with the admiration and endorsement of much of the press, but he managed to alienate them by the end of his second term.

After his miserable experience holding regular press conferences, Wilson seized every opportunity to bypass the White House press corps, just as he attempted to go over the heads of legislators when they failed to succumb to his strong will. His speaking tour to promote the league and his appearances before Congress enabled Wilson to gain publicity without the interference of questions from reporters. He might have achieved greater success if he had been able to communicate directly with the people by using radio and television. Nevertheless, when Wilson tried to bypass the White House press corps, he failed to detect the opportunities that new institution could provide. Reagan would demonstrate how to take advantage of those opportunities and satisfy the expectations of most reporters while also escaping the demands of press conferences.

With the formation of the White House press corps, the press and the president became linked institutionally, and this institutional tie appeared to establish a symbiotic relationship between them.[25] The press needed the president for information and insights (often simply to supply "news"), while presidents seemed to need the press to publicize their achievements and cultivate public support. With developments in mass communications and technology, however, the president's dependence on the press diminished. Yet, as Reagan would show, even when presidents do not need to rely on the White House press corps, they can put it to good use.

Reagan and his staff understood that the presence of the press in the White House could enhance the president's agenda-setting capacity. This enhanced capacity matters less to leaders who accept the status quo and seek to preserve the prevailing consensus, but setting the national agenda is the central task of conviction-style leaders. That task becomes easier to achieve when reporters sit in the White House, waiting for the president to make news.[26] In particular, the White House press corps gives the president an advantage relative to members of Congress: Reporters cover Capitol Hill, but legislators must compete with the president (and with each other) as they try to attract media attention. The president automatically commands it. Reagan could have tried to bypass the press corps entirely, as Wilson did, but instead he opted to seize the opportunities the White House press corps provides. In a way that resembled his legislative strategy, Reagan adopted a two-tier approach to media relations: He combined direct communication with the public with skillful management of the press.

Every aspect of press operations in the Reagan White House was designed to highlight the president's leadership strength and focus attention on his priorities.[27] By the time Reagan took office, the White House press corps had grown to more than 1,700 members (although those who regularly attended briefings numbered about 75). As one of their first moves, Reagan's White House officials installed theater row seats for the press briefings, an innovation that established order, facilitated control, and turned the press corps into a captive audience. (Reporters generally welcomed the change, as they acquired more comfortable seats and enjoyed the benefit of reserved spaces.) Although several hundred members of the White House staff engaged in press relations, only a few advisors had major responsibility for news management. Before the first press briefing each day, White House officials Michael Deaver and James Baker met at 8:15 A.M. to prepare a single story or "line of the day" for reporters, a practice that had started in the Nixon White House. Then at approximately 9:00 A.M., "Deputy" Press Secretary Larry Speakes[28] met with the "regulars" to describe the president's schedule—another agenda-setting tool—and later he conducted a second, pre-noon briefing for a larger group of reporters. Reagan held fewer press conferences than any other modern president, but White House officials had frequent contact with reporters and orchestrated "controlled access" to the president. When reporters demanded more press conferences on the grounds that the president was too remote, their argument failed to resonate with a public who heard and saw Reagan virtually every day on television.

While White House officials fed the press a daily ration of carefully crafted stories along with dramatic depictions, Reagan also took his case directly to the people. Following the example of FDR, Reagan delivered radio addresses each week, which also provided the basis for news reports on the evening broadcasts and in the morning papers the following day. Of course, he had an additional, even more useful means to communicate with the public, and television provided yet another agenda-setting mechanism.[29] White House officials took special care to supply visuals for the network news each day, and the president frequently delivered televised addresses to the nation during prime time to promote specific policies or "explain" current events. With few exceptions (notably, barring reporters from Grenada during the U.S. invasion), Reagan packaged his presidency and promoted his policies by relying on a combination of news management and public appeals rather than resorting to censorship or hardball tactics to suppress the press.

His British counterpart managed the news with a heavier hand, but Thatcher also adopted many of Reagan's strategies. Indeed, these two leaders operated in structural settings more similar than generally recognized. In the U.S. and the U.K., media politics evolved in somewhat different ways, but by the late twentieth century presidents and prime ministers had become similarly situated in relation to the press.

Great Britain

As in the U.S., few sources of national news existed in Britain during the first half of the nineteenth century. In 1828 the press gallery started to operate in Parliament, but like their U.S. counterparts in the congressional press gallery, British reporters merely recorded parliamentary debates. Editors of British newspapers favored certain groups and endorsed particular points of view, but mass political parties had not yet formed, and the loyalties of the press shifted along with those of the political elite. Indirectly and perhaps unwittingly, the major source of national news, the *Times,* played a role in the early formation of party organization.

When Sir Robert Peel composed and publicized the first party manifesto, he did so at the suggestion of John Walter, proprietor of the *Times.* Walter had written to James Scarlett (then legal advisor to the *Times*) and suggested that Peel deliver a popular statement of the principles that would guide the policies of his government. With great fanfare, the *Times* published the Tamworth Manifesto and then continued to report (and applaud) Peel's speeches throughout the campaign. During his first, brief government the *Times* consistently and enthusiastically endorsed Peel's premiership. When he resigned in 1835, the paper praised Peel for his independence from the antireform Tories and for the "temper, capacity, and power" of his leadership, which the *Times* elevated to the stature of dynamic leadership practiced by Pitt the Younger.[30]

When Peel's party won the 1841 election, the *Times* declared the result rendered "the spectacle . . . of a triumphant reaction of sound public opinion." According to the paper: "[U]ntil now the world has never known an instance of a party being installed in power expressly by the voice of a great people . . . solely because the nation places confidence in their capacity and disinterestedness, and recognises in them a tone of principle which it feels to be necessary for wise and good government."[31] The paper continued to exert significant influence when it encouraged repeal of the Corn Laws and presented the issue as a matter concerning the national welfare (rather than a partisan struggle). Finally, the *Times* was the first paper to announce Peel's decision to secure repeal, and the paper supported him after the event, while the Tory press condemned him.

Peel had no need to resort to the techniques of news management that Jackson employed. He and many of his successors could rely on their relationships with newspaper owners and editors who operated in the same elite circles. (Both Scarlett and Walter were members of Parliament.) In the years of Peel's premiership, the *Times* occupied a privileged place as one of the few reputable, legitimate sources of news and as the paper with the largest circulation. The *Times* played a significant role in political developments by promoting Peel and then providing even stronger support for William Gladstone during his first government, but changes in the news business would alter both the status of the *Times* and the nature of interaction between politicians and the press.

In the 1860s repeal of the paper duties and use of the telegraph made it cheaper and easier for provincial papers to publish the news, and their numbers rapidly increased. The *Times* soon lost its status as the paper with the largest readership, and by 1864, the circulation of provincial papers was twice that of the London dailies.[32] Press readership also grew as the franchise expanded, and competition among newspapers intensified as the number of papers continued to increase dramatically throughout the second half of the nineteenth century.[33]

By midcentury, the provincial papers had started to send correspondents to London, and many of them established London offices. To present partisan political activity in livelier and more entertaining ways, reporters began to engage in sketch writing, and to write their sketches, they needed the opportunity to observe national politics firsthand. Then, in the 1880s, mass education and increased literacy led the public to demand more accurate and informative reporting, and reporters shifted their activity from creating colorful portraits to rendering factual accounts. (At the same time, the press also became more sensational as newspapers sought to expand their markets.) When news organizations started to report on a wide range of topics and court a more diverse readership, their reporters began to acquire greater expertise and specialization. As in the U.S., commercial incentives fueled the development of professional journalism in Britain.

The new journalism—with its emphasis on accuracy and exposition—led reporters to seek greater access to public officials. To explain both policies and personalities to their readers, editors instructed their correspondents to investigate behind-the-scenes activity at Westminster.[34] In 1884 newspaper correspondents formed the "lobby," a group that derived its name from the place where journalists gained access to politicians—the lobby outside the House of Commons chamber. The lobby provides an institutional parallel to the White House press corps, with one essential difference that reflects systemic differences between the U.S. and the U.K., which mattered a great deal at the time. Meeting at Westminster, lobby correspondents could interact with members of Parliament and cabinet ministers, and not the prime minister alone.

Development of the lobby served the interests of MPs as well as those of reporters. As the franchise expanded, MPs needed new and better ways to communicate with their constituents. Moreover, by the late nineteenth century, the number of reporters who were fiercely partisan declined, as demonstrated by the ease and frequency of their moves between Liberal and Conservative papers.[35] To secure favorable press coverage, politicians needed to court reporters.

Initially, MPs proved somewhat reluctant to welcome reporters into their institution, but members grew to accept the lobby as legitimate when they found that journalists could be trusted to keep their secrets. In Britain, reporters' struggle to gain acceptance even after they secured access might explain why they declined to discuss the private affairs of politicians, except when private matters became public scandals as a result of lawsuits. Certainly their efforts to become "acceptable" made lobby correspondents susceptible to news management. Even now, they must agree to "lobby terms," which include keeping comments off the record and using nonattributable sources. The lobby rules invite politicians to provide information and misinformation, while escaping responsibility or accountability; in other words, the arrangement facilitates leaks.[36]

Gladstone was one of the first prime ministers who complained about the "leakages" coming from his cabinet.[37] To prevent them, the prime minister started to restrict open discussion and often declined to reveal his genuine intentions in cabinet meetings. In general, Gladstone considered the prying press a nuisance, and he shunned direct contact with reporters. Instead, he continued his predecessors' practice and cultivated personal relationships with newspaper editors and proprietors. Yet when the editorial preferences of the major papers started to shift from Liberal to Conservative at the end of the 1870s, Gladstone was forced to innovate.

By taking his case to the country—through pamphlets as well as public speeches—Gladstone found he could avoid press intervention and editorial distortion of his message. When he delivered public speeches, both the Liberal and Conservative newspapers reported his words verbatim. No doubt Gladstone's desire to circumvent the press influenced his decision to embark on his famous oratorical campaign at Midlothian in 1879. Gladstone's public approach also satisfied the growing demand of the newspaper industry for popular stories. Alex Ritchie of the *Leeds Mercury* revealed the shifting focus of the news when he declared to the Press Association, "Gentlemen like to peruse their newspaper at breakfast time, and they will not always care to wade through four or five columns of Parliamentary matter."[38] By 1879, newspapers ceased to report parliamentary debates, which had become more complex and technical and therefore were deemed less interesting to the public.

News coverage of Gladstone's Midlothian campaign reveals a great deal about the "news values" that were beginning to emerge. While the *Times* declared its judgment that "the character of the demagogue has preponderated over that of the statesman," the paper rendered vivid depictions of the masses—ordinary farmers and shopkeepers—eager to absorb what Benjamin Disraeli derided as Gladstone's "drenching rhetoric." According to the *Times*, "[I]f Mr. Gladstone needed inspiration, it must have been afforded by the eager audiences and crowds which have surrounded him."[39] During the campaign, the *Times* observed that Gladstone also accomplished "one of the most extraordinary physical feats on record" as he rendered a dramatic "display of endurance and energy."[40] Finally, the *Times* highlighted the principles of Liberalism Gladstone declared with determination, even as it mocked his presentation of his convictions as the "designs of Providence."[41] Although the *Times* condemned Gladstone's approach as demagogic and ridiculed his oratorical outpouring of passion, those same qualities made the event newsworthy. Other politicians also started to go public, but the nature of Gladstone's leadership and his rhetoric commanded special attention.

In the twentieth century, prime ministers began to employ public relations advisors and strategically leak information to their friends in the news business. Nevertheless, like Gladstone, early innovators in the art of news management overlooked the lobby as a tool that might enable them to craft their public image or publicize their agenda. Even David Lloyd George shunned interaction with the lobby, although—driven by a desperate desire to direct the press—he did adopt other, more extreme, measures in his attempt to determine the nature of the news.

As soon as Lloyd George felt secure in his position as prime minister, he brought several press barons into his government. In 1917 he sent Lord Northcliffe (owner of the *Times* and the *Daily Mail*) to replace Foreign Secretary Balfour as the head of a diplomatic mission in the U.S. (The appointment of such an undiplomatic character as Northcliffe certainly seemed peculiar, but the move accomplished two of Lloyd George's goals: It put Northcliffe in the government, while it also got him out of the country!) Shortly after Northcliffe returned to Britain, Lloyd George made him director of propaganda in enemy countries. In addition, Lord Beaverbrook (owner of the *Daily Express*) directed the Ministry of Information, and Lord Rothermere (owner of the *Daily Mirror* and Northcliffe's brother) became head of the new Air Ministry (after Northcliffe turned down the position). These were not the only appointments drawn from the ranks of the news business, but they did constitute the most prominent and controversial ones.

Even more scandalous, Lloyd George used the honors list to recruit supporters and reward loyalty from the press as well as to build his personal fund. From 1918 to 1922, forty-nine men in the newspaper business secured honors as privy councillors, peers, baronets, and knights. In 1917 Sir Max Aitken became Lord Beaverbrook, and Northcliffe became viscount. In 1919 Rothermere and Burnham (the *Daily Telegraph*) also became viscounts, and Sir Edward Russell (the *Liverpool Daily Post*) became a baron. Two long-time allies, Sir George Riddell *(News of the World)* and Sir Henry Dalziel *(Reynold's News)*, became peers in 1920. (Dalziel was also the nominal owner of the *Daily Chronicle,* which Lloyd George had purchased with money from the Lloyd George Fund in 1918.) Both Lloyd George's predecessors and his successors (notably Thatcher) bestowed honors on prominent figures in the press, but Lloyd George adopted this strategy to enhance his personal stature rather than to advance (even ostensibly) partisan objectives. As a result, his use of the honors list sparked suspicion and scandal, which other premiers have generally managed to escape.

Despite his emphasis on manipulating the press and the extraordinary efforts he made (or perhaps because his motives and means were so transparent), Lloyd George achieved only limited success. By 1922, the three press lords—Northcliffe, Rothermere, and Beaverbrook—all opposed Lloyd George. (Even earlier they organized an "Anti-Waste" campaign against expensive government programs and put forward their own candidates in by-elections.) The *Times* in particular had exalted Lloyd George's leadership and helped propel him into the premiership, but he could not count on its continuous support even when Northcliffe occupied a ministerial post. In fact, press support generally fluctuated with the prime minister's political positions, prospects, and popularity—to a great extent because the proprietors and editors of newspapers maintained their own ideological agendas and pursued their own commercial goals. Furthermore, Lloyd George clearly needed the press more than they needed him. To expand and consolidate his personal following, without a party organization or ample funds, Lloyd George constantly sought to secure favorable publicity. (Most of the Liberal papers remained loyal to Herbert Asquith, although Lloyd George managed to maintain the support of the *Manchester Guardian* and the Unionist press.) Ultimately, Lloyd George reaped few rewards from all his Machiavellian maneuvering, and the only concrete advantages he possessed came from the measures and the machinery of war.

Both government secrecy and censorship greatly increased during World War I. The first Official Secrets Act had passed in 1889 (five years after the formation of the lobby), and anticipating the war, in 1911 Parliament strengthened the original legislation by adding section 2, which made it a criminal offense for any government official to communicate "prohibited" information. During the war, the government also developed its own information system: The Official Press Bureau (briefly the Ministry of Information) lasted only until 1918, but this propaganda machine established a precedent for the release of "official information" that continues today.[42]

The lobby also underwent changes that would enhance the opportunities for prime ministers to manage the news. Even before the start of the war, the lobby began to meet as a single group ("collective lobbying") for press briefings. More significant, during the war lobby correspondents shifted their focus from Parliament to Downing Street and Whitehall, and for the first time "departmental spokespersons" routinely distributed official information to the press. Nevertheless, prime ministers proved slow to detect the advantages inherent in these developments. The first Downing Street press office was not established until the 1930s, and the 1945–50 Labour government was the first to hold press briefings on a regular daily basis. Once these steps were taken, the lobby came to resemble more closely the White House press corps, and prime ministers became more presidential in their approach to media management.

Like President Reagan, Prime Minister Thatcher developed innovative press strategies to highlight and promote her agenda. (At least one of her predecessors, Harold Wilson, had excelled at media management, but the ideological nature of Thatcher's leadership enabled her to maximize the agenda-setting capacity of the new structural arrangements.) Thatcher's press secretary Bernard Ingham formally briefed lobby correspondents twice a day: At 11:00 A.M. he met with mainly the regional and evening press at Number 10 Downing Street; at 4:00 P.M. he spoke to the national media at Westminster. Attendance varied among the 150 members of the lobby, but a core of at least 30 reporters regularly attended lobby briefings.[43] Throughout the day, Ingham also briefed small groups of journalists and held meetings with individual reporters. He always delivered his statements on an off-the-record basis, and therefore his comments remained unattributable. As in the U.S., events could force Downing Street press officers to engage in spin control and damage limitation, but they usually focused their efforts on advancing the prime minister's programs and priorities.

One of Ingham's most successful innovations entailed the secondment of Whitehall press officers. Information officers from the Whitehall departments worked at the Downing Street press office for six weeks and then returned to their departments. Press officers often brought with them extensive knowledge of their departments, but more important, Number 10 Downing Street became "a finishing school for information officers."[44] They took back to their departments the skills and the perspective they acquired at Number 10. As a result, the strategy was both media oriented and administrative: It served to promote the prime minister's agenda in the press and in the civil service.

The development of Downing Street press operations helped to presidentialize the prime minister's role in several ways. The prime minister's press secretary often used briefings to discredit ministers, and the lobby rules prevented reporters from direct attribution. Ministers came to view the prime minister's press office as a powerful weapon that could destroy their careers. Even benign use of the press office served to draw the prime minister away from her parliamentary base and place her in the role of mobilizing public opinion. Moreover, Thatcher's habit of using the royal "we" when she addressed the press revealed her own sense that the prime minister had come to resemble the head of state and invited the media to draw comparisons with the queen. (In one of her most memorable remarks, following the birth of her first grandchild, Thatcher gleefully announced, "We have become a grandmother!") In general, Thatcher's efforts to focus attention on her leadership (rather than her cabinet or party) were greatly enhanced by the increasing importance of television.

With its emphasis on visual depictions, television news finds it easier and more appealing to report on the actions of the prime minister, a single leader, rather than try to capture the activities of a group, the party or the cabinet. Focused on the leader, television broadcasts have even altered the character of parliamentary question time, making it more like a presidential press conference. Indeed, Ingham and Speakes compared notes and concluded that their preparation for both events was strikingly similar.[45] On both sides of the Atlantic, the leaders were coached on how to evade pointed questions and produce, instead, a "sound bite" that would provide the leading line for the news broadcast that day.

Thatcher welcomed such advice and fully appreciated the significance of television as a tool to craft her image.[46] According to her personal consultant, Tim Bell, "She believed propaganda is a necessary part of any campaign, of any government. And you should employ experts to do it. She always listened to the experts. . . . She thinks presentation is very important. And there's an advantage working with women. They are interested in the way they look."[47] Bell worked with other consultants, notably Gordon Reece, and together they advised Thatcher on how to change her voice, alter her appearance, and adjust her image to suit changing circumstances. Above all, Thatcher and her advisors proved adept at manipulating images of "women"—running the gamut from queen to housewife—so that the prime minister could use them to her advantage.[48] Scripted performances and staged photo opportunities were as important to Thatcher as they were to Reagan.

Reagan, Thatcher, and the Modern Media

Significant differences between the press in the U.S. and the U.K. diminished in the late twentieth century, and many distinctions that continue to be drawn between the modern media in the two countries matter less than generally assumed. For example, the British prime minister's press secretary is a civil servant, and, in theory, the tasks of the press secretary are limited to government, not "political," activity. The artificiality of that distinction became vividly apparent during the Thatcher years, when Ingham served as press secretary. The length of his service—eleven years—coupled with his aggressive approach and loyalty to the prime minister made Ingham an extremely controversial figure, a type of conviction-style press secretary.

Other distinctions fade in significance upon close examination. The print media remain partisan in the U.K., but Conservative prime ministers do not automatically win positive publicity. (Thatcher generally earned more favorable media coverage than her successor, John Major, secured.) In addition, between 1945 and 1990, the press became less predictable and less managed by party. Many developments contributed to the decline of partisanship in the press, including commercial considerations—most readers are not party identifiers—and the media's increasing reliance on polls rather than "wishful thinking."[49] Furthermore, the U.K. has public ownership of broadcasting, but radio and television now also have commercial stations that fuel competition, making British broadcasting more closely resemble the media in the U.S.

Finally, the British prime minister's press secretary is always an anonymous source, whereas the U.S. press secretary is usually named and quoted directly. In practice, however, U.S. reporters also use unattributable sources in the White House (e.g., a "senior White House official"). Informal practices exist in both countries, which preserve secrecy, encourage leaks, and discourage accountability. One reporter who has worked in both the U.S. and the U.K. expressed admiration for the adversarial tradition in the U.S. but also remarked that journalistic integrity gets compromised "on the fringes" and "around the edges" by such factors as frequent social interaction between reporters and politicians in Washington, D.C.[50] In focusing on the apparent differences, one can easily overlook the striking similarities.

On the other hand, some essential differences remained during the era of Thatcher and Reagan. Britain has the Official Secrets Act and no First Amendment, factors that fuel a political culture in which government secrecy is more widely accepted than in the U.S. Just as important, in the British context, formal restrictions can be imposed on the media. When Thatcher's news management techniques failed, she could resort to methods of control and suppression unavailable to a U.S. president.

Consider the following examples.[51] Early in Thatcher's first government, she proposed a protection of government information bill that her own parliamentary majority considered too restrictive, but that same year she managed to block the broadcast of a BBC documentary on the Irish Republican Army (IRA). During the Falklands war, her government exercised extensive control and censorship; in the aftermath, her government prosecuted civil servants (under section 2) who released damaging information to the press or to members of Parliament. Thatcher disapproved of the BBC's coverage of the miners' strike and took retaliatory action: She tried to privatize the BBC by imposing high license fees that would have forced it to adopt advertising, but the independent Peacock Commission rescued the corporation by tying its fees to inflation. Thatcher escalated her attack on public broadcasting in

1985–86 (at a time when her approval ratings plunged). She temporarily convinced the Board of Governors to block the airing of a BBC film, *At the Edge of the Union,* on the IRA and Loyalist paramilitaries. During the same period, the police raided the BBC's Glasgow studios, and MI5 vetted the BBC staff. In December 1987, her government secured an injunction to prevent the Radio 4 series *My Country, Right or Wrong.* Also in the same year, Thatcher forced the resignation of Director General Alistair Milne, after the BBC aired the *Panorama* program "Maggie's Militant Tendency." In November 1988, the government banned all radio and television interviews with members of Sinn Fein, the political wing of the IRA. Finally, Thatcher's government changed the Official Secrets Act in 1989 by wiping out section 2 but tightening restrictions on defense, international relations, and crime and security operations.

Thatcher discovered that heavy-handed efforts to control journalists usually fail to enhance a leader's image and that, as a strategy, censorship or circumvention often backfires. (As Pulitzer put it, "To throw obstacles in their way is to spur them to greater efforts.") She proved much more successful when, like Reagan, she attempted to manage rather than suppress the press. And when it came to routine news management, Thatcher and Reagan inherited advantages that earlier conviction-style leaders lacked: structures of interaction conducive to media manipulation. They also derived benefits from the news values that had evolved, which generally serve to highlight essential aspects of conviction politics.

Members of the media often unwittingly enhanced the leadership qualities of Reagan and Thatcher. Reporters insist their place in the political order determines the content of the news. Situated between the president or prime minister and the public, they define their task as twofold: to present the leader to the public and to represent the public. To a great extent, the structure in which reporters operate—the White House press corps or the lobby—affects the presentation of the president or prime minister. In their capacity as "representatives," reporters allow news values to shape the story. During the Reagan and Thatcher years, reporters' two tasks—presenting the leader and representing the public—rarely pulled them in different directions. Both the structure of interaction and news values facilitated the leaders' ability to determine the depiction of their conviction politics.

The Structure of Interaction

The White House press corps or the lobby provides the structural context in which reporters seek the information they need to present the president or prime minister (and their policies) to the public. Both U.S. and British re-porters perceive these structural arrangements as essential to performing their task of presentation. "The White House press corps is a transmission valve," declared one U.S. journalist. "In the White House, our job is to ex-pound the president's message."[52] "To convey information is [the only] power we have," another reporter insisted. "I think our job is always to re-quire presidents to explain their policies."[53] In Britain, reporters express the same view: As lobby correspondents, they strive to describe and explain the prime minister's policies to the public. (British journalists might say "explain the government's policies," but they tend to use "prime minister" and "gov-ernment" interchangeably—as in the phrase "when the government travels abroad.") On both sides of the Atlantic, reporters would often directly trans-mit the images and the messages Reagan and Thatcher wished to convey.

Both British and U.S. journalists have published several critical accounts of official news management, which describe how the structures they work in shape their behavior and craft the content of the news. Their own de-scriptions of the White House press corps and the lobby usually emphasize the element of coercion exercised by presidents and prime ministers and their "spin doctors."[54] On a daily basis, however, these structures facilitate media management in more subtle ways: by bringing reporters close to the leaders, keeping them close together, and establishing routines that shape their habits of "newsgathering."

Their physical proximity to the president or prime minister (and their of-ficial spokespersons)—and their distance from others in their profession—can dull the dose of skepticism journalists generally try to inject into their stories. Reporters in the White House press corps and the lobby become part of the institution they cover, and they can play a role in the spectacle that surrounds the president and prime minister. One British journalist, an out-spoken critic of the lobby system, emphasized the importance of the fact that "lobby correspondents are detached—even from their own news organiza-tions."[55] Lobby correspondents are not separated from their colleagues only when they attend official briefings or work in the press gallery; they even have their own bar in Westminster, where they often spend many hours "waiting for the news to happen."

In the case of the White House press corps, reporters run the risk of be-coming part of the "palace." One reporter for a major television network ad-mitted, "The White House really gets into the game, and of course reporters get into the game too. I've been in the White House for nine years. I enjoy being part of the royal procession and I enjoy the perks. I enjoy the jeering and the cheering. You really have to watch yourself . . . to remember there is a political motive to everything they do."[56] Reporters' experiences in the

Reagan years suggest that it becomes easy to lose sight of yourself (and your professional role) when you work in the presence of the king.

In the environment of the White House press corps (or the lobby), reporters begin to identify with the subject of their reports. Indeed, their status becomes linked to the prestige of the leaders they cover. As another television broadcaster admitted, "Ronald Reagan, for reporters, was like a radar. He lighted up everyone around him. He lighted up reporters—even me. My notoriety came about because of Reagan, not because of me."[57] Reporters also succumbed to the mesmerizing charm that Reagan possessed as a "celebrity." Reagan's press secretary recalled: "Ford used to have cocktail parties and invite a few reporters, so we tried it with Reagan. It was like a rock star. Reporters tried to fly friends and family in. They never ate, despite the spread. There would be a crush around him—pictures with the president—and they would want to hold his hand."[58] Thatcher might have lacked Reagan's background as a movie star, but she apparently cast a similar spell on many British journalists.[59]

Admittedly, the depiction of an enraptured, spellbound press corps fails to fit the popular picture of White House reporters as aggressive watchdogs nipping at the heels of the president. Reporters have good reasons to cultivate the appearance of an adversarial relationship—correcting a president who commits gaffes, for example—while they decline to ask more pointed (and potentially damaging) questions. The adversarial act adds a theatrical dimension to the interaction between a president and the media, especially during televised press conferences. It also creates the impression that reporters are fulfilling their role as representatives and holding the president accountable, without actually alienating their White House sources. The adversarial style of U.S. reporters has misled their public and even fooled some of their British counterparts, who "refer to Washington as a paradigm they would like to copy."[60] One prominent journalist who has worked in both systems insists that the White House press corps "is a far tamer and more deferential group than the lobby."[61] Differences between lobby correspondents and White House reporters are more apparent than real: Separated from their news organizations and placed before the president or the prime minister, in both countries journalists develop an identity that links them to their sources and makes them especially vulnerable to news management.

Their identity is not, however, a "group identity" in the sense that it nurtures or encourages collective action against news management. Reporters remain fiercely competitive, a trait that impedes their ability to resist or rebel against manipulation. When lobby correspondents from three British newspapers—the *Scotsman,* the *Independent,* and the *Guardian*—tried to boycott Ingham's briefings as a way to force him to speak "on the record," the rest of the lobby refused to join them. According to all accounts—Ingham's as well as those of reporters who continued to attend the briefings—reporters from the three rebel organizations resorted to eavesdropping at the door. If the entire lobby had left, Ingham might have been forced to change the conditions of the briefings. Instead, the rebel reporters returned to the ranks and continued to follow the traditional lobby rules.

In the U.S., Speakes encountered similar limited boycotts. On one occasion, reporters from the *New York Times* refused to take a background briefing from Secretary of State George Shultz. Speakes recalled what happened next: "[T]he reporters from the [New York] *Times* could get holier than thou. I went back to my office and I took a copy of the *Times* and marked the off-the-record comments on the front page. I circled them in red and sent a copy to the reporters. And that was the end of the 'boycott.'"[62] Not all *New York Times* reporters insisted on using attributable sources, and even some of those who complained on that occasion were willing to use off-the-record comments when it served their purpose. When reporters act individually and selectively reject the tools of misinformation, they prove unable to exert their collective clout and hold officials accountable.

Paradoxically, the competitive climate within the White House press corps and the Westminster lobby pits reporters against each other, and yet it also fails to produce diversity in news reporting. Reporters work as a group, and often news managers can count on "pack journalism" to ensure the impact of their efforts will be universal. As Deaver explained, "Reporters don't leave the building [to investigate] because they're afraid they'll miss the big story."[63] One reporter adamantly insisted, "We are not lapdogs," but then he admitted that "the Reagan White House was effective in getting its message out." And he explained why:

> The White House press corps is not free to roam around the White House. It's not like Capitol Hill. . . . White House reporters are chained to the pressroom by our news organizations. We are hired to stay there. Any given moment the pope [*sic*] can be shot again. . . . Broadcasters are chained to the pressroom because of the need for instant reporting and the immediate broadcast. The wire services too—because of the need for a flash. It's another way to manage us. We have no time to dig.[64]

Pack journalism produces a ripple effect: Broadcasters and reporters for the wire services are "chained" to the pressroom, and print journalists are expected to cover the same stories. "Editors say, 'Don't be part of the pack,'" according to one journalist, "and then they ask, 'Why haven't you got what the wires have?'"[65] No news organization wants to miss *the* story of the day—and pack journalism ensures there will be only one story.

Lobby correspondents can more freely roam the halls of Westminster. In a parliamentary system, only one group of reporters covers the prime minister, the government, and the opposition, including the backbenches. Yet lobby correspondents usually explore other sources only after they have heard the official view from Number 10, and they tend to limit their "investigation" to the issue presented by the prime minister, often looking to present "the other side." Lobby correspondents rarely show initiative. "The lobby trains you and tames you," insisted one British journalist.[66] They seldom perceive the need to search for a news story when one particular source, the Downing Street press office, consistently supplies a good one. And reporters on both sides of the Atlantic acknowledge that supplying the story provides an effective way to manipulate it.

Deaver summed up the Reagan White House strategy and reporters' reaction to it. As he recalled, "By the time the press got there [the White House], we had the day planned. It became their routine. The agenda was set not by the Congress, the Democrats, the media, but by the White House. Somebody was always thinking about where we wanted to be in a week or two. It's easier for reporters to accept information than challenge it. There are not many hardworking people over there in the White House press corps."[67] One journalist (now a columnist) admitted, "It's easy to be lazy. You've got page one, whether you make phone calls or not."[68] Another one recalled, "In the Reagan years, we struck a devil's bargain with the White House. We gave up the fight for direct access and settled for secondhand backgrounding. There became a kind of weariness."[69] To a great extent, their routine induced passivity, and reporters become habituated to the rhythms of news management.

In fact, when the White House and Number 10 made no efforts to manage the news, reporters expressed their disappointment and their discontent. According to Deaver, "We would get pressure from the anchors for a story, and we would need to create something. If we didn't get it to them, they'd get us. There were many times when we did an event just to satisfy an anchor." (When asked for an example, Deaver replied, "It happened all the time.")[70] Ingham also alleged that when he failed to produce a story for reporters, they accused him of letting them down.[71] In both the White House press corps and the lobby, reporters proved more likely to be roused by the failure to practice news management than by the routine manipulation they experienced.

Most significant, reporters accepted and viewed as legitimate the agenda-setting function of press operations in the White House and Number 10. As Ingham put it, leaders "have to persuade the media to persuade the public,"[72] but Reagan's and Thatcher's attempts to persuade reporters took place on an uneven playing field: The leaders set the agenda and reporters presented it to the public. As one U.S. reporter explained, "The press is the tail wagged by the big dog. Whatever we do, we do not set the agenda. . . . People don't want the press to set the agenda." In response to the question, "Who does set the agenda?" he replied, "Well, it is usually the White House."[73]

Of course, any skillful news managers can use the White House press corps and the lobby as vehicles to set and promote their leader's agenda, but the style of conviction politics enhances the prospects for agenda setting. A conviction-style leader articulates a distinctive, specific agenda and usually renders a simple, straightforward message that lends itself to a "line of the day." Indeed, conviction politics itself automatically narrows the scope of debate and defines the terms. One British journalist described the power Thatcher exercised over the press and the public when he recalled, "The intellectual temper of the argument changed. Radical Thatcher won the argument. The terms of reference, of debate changed."[74] According to one of his U.S. counterparts, "The leadership of Reagan and Thatcher automatically narrows the agenda. In response to a reporter's question, Reagan would say, 'That's not what we came to do.'" The same reporter continued by defining power as the ability "to put something on the agenda and keep it there. That's where you find the intersection between the president and the press. And the president has the advantage. It is the one thing the president can do, and it is important whether he has convictions. If he has strong convictions, he can keep it on the agenda. That was one of the keys obviously for Reagan. They said, 'There's an economic agenda, a social agenda, an international agenda.' But they said, 'Our economic agenda is *the* agenda.'"[75]

Of course, events could spur reporters to attempt to direct discussion away from the set agenda and onto another topic. (According to several U.S. reporters, this is why they learned to shout!) Speakes admitted, in these circumstances, "The challenge was to not talk about their issue. It was a challenge to keep the president from talking."[76] (He also confessed that they shielded Reagan from the press—not because they feared he would say something false, but because they feared he would say something true, which was not part of the planned program for the day.) In the absence of an unusual or sudden event, however, Reagan, like Thatcher, usually stayed "on message."

By reinforcing the agenda-setting capacity of structural arrangements, the consistent and emphatic style of conviction politicians also helped to mold reporters' habits and shape their expectations. Those habits and expectations continued to influence reporters even when they followed the president or prime minister out of the White House or Number 10 and into the country or abroad. The structures of interaction and the leaders' style not only influenced the behavior of reporters but also shaped their consciousness.

To understand why other presidents and prime ministers encounter hostile journalists who report mostly negative news, consider whether those leaders neglect to employ the tools of news management available to modern executives. After President William Clinton took office, he immediately alienated reporters by moving the pressroom farther away from the Oval Office (when, instead, he might have chosen to take reporters under his wing). Furthermore, Clinton's attempts to bypass the press—preferring to hold "town meetings" rather than press briefings—spurred reporters to rebel and encouraged them to engage in investigative reporting. Finally, even when he or his press secretary met with the press, they usually failed to convey a clear message. (The journalist who observed that Reagan would declare, "That's not what we came to do," added, "In Clinton's case, we asked, 'What didn't you come to do?'")[77] Thatcher's immediate successor, John Major, also struggled in a hostile media environment fueled by reporters' perception that "the prime minister is in office, but he is not in power."[78] Reporters tend to read a leader's failure to manage the news and convey a clear message as signs of weak leadership. In that case, the leader who neglects news management will also fail to satisfy news values.

News Values

Two powerful influences—commercial incentives and reporters' representative role—combine to produce the same effect on news values. Commercial pressures force news organizations to cater to popular tastes, while reporters insist they operate free of any such influence. Most journalists would agree with the one who insisted, "Decisions are made on the basis of individual judgment, not to sell papers. They are never made the way people on the outside think they're made."[79] At the same time, however, reporters who see themselves as the unelected representatives of the people believe they should express the views and values of their readers and viewers. Whether the motivation is professional or commercial, journalists and their news organizations usually speak for their public audiences as they speak to them.

In the U.K., reporters from both popular and elite papers agree that they try to reflect and appeal to popular tastes, a task they perceive as part of their professional obligation to represent their readers. One "pop" reporter put it bluntly when he declared, "It's not up to me to decide what is true. I tell the people what they want to hear."[80] At the opposite end of the ideological spectrum, another tabloid reporter explained, "Our readers must be able to identify with the story. I usually think of the *Mirror* reader. . . . I know the *Mirror* audience because my own family members were readers."[81] Representing a more upscale constituency, another journalist expressed a similar view: "I always have in mind a picture of my readers, their livelihood, the information they need to make decisions. . . . I've always been a *Times* reader myself and I always will be. I think I know what interests the *Times* reader—what he or she wants or needs to know."[82] According to yet another reporter for an elite paper, what constitutes news is "whatever interests the readers. Usually, that's the same thing as whatever interests me. If I'm not quite representative of the *Observer* readers, I'm not far off."[83] These reporter-representatives see themselves as delegates who must satisfy the public's wants and respond to its demands.

Just as constituents can constrain elected representatives, the public can limit journalists. "Readers provide a sort of censorship," one British reporter emphasized as he described his representative role. "They are the ones who determine what is newsy."[84] Another reporter expressed frustration at the public's negative reaction to his critical reports during the Falklands war. "Journalists often act on the basis of what the public wants to believe," he explained. At the time of the sinking of the *Belgrano*, "people wanted to believe, 'We were protecting our boys.' If the public wants to believe this, there is little we can do."[85] Journalists insist no amount of facts and figures can dispel the public's myths or shake its firm beliefs.

Reporters in the U.S. expressed similar views on the obligations and constraints imposed by their connection with the public. One network television reporter recalled, "Many people have blamed the media for not holding Reagan to account, but we conveyed the message that Reagan was disengaged, and the public simply didn't care. He had a winning way."[86] A newspaper columnist had the same recollection: "There was a lot of tough stuff about Reagan in the beginning. Nit-picking is the job of print journalists. But Reagan was always charming—and Reagan was winning."[87] "The public don't always want watchdogs," another columnist insisted. "Sometimes they want us to back off."[88] Yet another one agreed, "Part of the immunity [from criticism] Reagan had as an immensely popular figure. The public thought we were being whiny."[89] A popular television journalist summed up the situation when he declared, "Perception is power," and explained, "Reagan had the power because we perceived him as popular. At first, Congress laughed at him, but they underestimated him. Then they got the kind of mail that turned them around—and we turned around."[90] Like members of Congress afraid to vote against a popular president, reporters hesitated to criticize Reagan. Journalists fear that when they criticize popular leaders, they put their own popularity at risk.

To determine what the public wants, reporters rely on many of the same tools that elected representatives employ to assess constituent views. Journalists study public opinion polls and election results, and when they can, they "travel around the country to talk to voters."[91] Members of the public also contact journalists, and during the Reagan presidency they often wrote to instruct the press corps to "stop picking on him!"[92] According to a network news reporter, "When we had the temerity to question him, we would get nasty mail. One time I received a letter from a lady on the Philadelphia mainline. She wrote and said, 'You are a guest in the president's home and you should behave like one.' People acted like he was king."[93] Constituents use the mail to pressure unelected as well as elected representatives.

Any popular leader—consensus or conviction—is likely to secure better press than an unpopular one, and positive publicity can further increase the leader's popularity. As one British reporter described the phenomenon, "Thatcher's style was amplified by the press, and that had an impact on public opinion. Of course, she was also successful, which made her popular, and that had an impact on the press. There was a circularity there."[94] Although that "circularity" applies to popular leaders generally, public support proves even more essential to conviction politicians who attempt to achieve fundamental change. By augmenting the conviction-style leader's popularity when they merely attempt to reflect it, reporters unwittingly play a role in the transformations leaders seek to secure.

Reporter-representatives also see themselves as guardians of the public interest, and occasionally they act as "trustees" rather than delegates. Indeed, the fact that reporters sometimes focus on what the public *should* know and care about—even when it does not—might account for the widely held view that reporters are unrepresentative of the public at large. Nevertheless, one British journalist expressed an opinion that pervades his profession when he insisted, "The public must be told what really goes on. The public ought to know that appearance is not reality."[95] Another one explained, "My job is to analyze the political reality—in every party with a view toward the national interest."[96] Yet another reporter considered it his obligation "to determine whether the individuals [in politics] are serving their own interest or the public interest."[97] Reporters interviewed on both sides of the Atlantic identified their "best story" as one that exposed a scandal or led to an investigation. A journalist in the U.S. summed up the sentiment expressed by many of his colleagues when he instructed the author, "Your concern as a political scientist is with effectiveness in government. Our concern as journalists is with accountability."[98] Reporters perceive their watchdog function as a matter of guardianship, and they tend to boast about that role in a way that dignifies their professional duties.

What happens when the responsibilities of delegate and those of trustee conflict—when what the public "ought to know" differs from what it wants to know? Like the pragmatic politicians whom reporters tend to disparage, journalists often find it difficult to persist in pursuing their loftiest goals. The same journalist who identified accountability as his central concern voluntarily confessed, "Until 1986, there was no accountability in the Reagan White House."[99] He and others admitted that in the Reagan years journalists proved more likely to pander to their publics than instruct or guard them. Most reporters believe what the public generally wants is news that identifies strong leadership, depicts dramatic gestures and passionate rhetoric, and portrays populism at work in politics—news values that served to highlight and enhance the conviction-style leadership of Reagan and Thatcher.

Journalists define "strong leadership" as tough, principled, and consistent, and they tend to view these characteristics in combination. Asked to identify Reagan's media appeal, one television broadcaster responded, "Results mattered, and the fact that the American public was in love with him. That assassination attempt demonstrated that he was John Wayne. He had several things going for him. He was a larger-than-life character. He was tough— 'Stay the course.'" Then the reporter quickly added, "We brought that can-do, John Wayne image to the public,"[100] an acknowledgment that the media's emphasis on strong leadership enhanced Reagan's public appeal.

Strong leaders are also principled people, according to journalists. One columnist described conviction politicians as "real leaders" because they adhere to their principles and, just as significant, because those principles are lofty, moral ones. "A leader's convictions need to be articulated within a larger framework," he explained; "then he will provide real leadership and people will follow. But if [leadership] is just a task, without any sense of morality or any larger framework, he'll fail."[101] Moral principles define leadership and distinguish it from mundane politics, while principles can also help journalists predict the course and consequences of any particular leader. The fact that conviction politicians are unusually consistent also facilitates reporters' ability to predict the character and implications of the politicians' leadership.

Reporters consider consistency another critical component of strong leadership, while they believe that monitoring the consistency of a leader provides a task compatible with their representative role. To maintain their impartiality as they seek to serve their constituents, reporters measure politicians "not against our own ideological positions—but we measure their performance against their rhetoric." When they report on any political leader, according to one journalist, "We measure his words against his past words and his rhetorical stand against his performance."[102] Another insisted, "We look for blatant contradictions between words and deeds"; in the case of Reagan, "He stayed true to his own image. That played well."[103] Reagan's media managers clearly understood which aspects of his image "played well." According to

Deaver, "The [positive] media coverage had a lot to do with his convictions. . . . Reporters like strong leaders and courage in politicians, especially if they stick with it."[104] Reporters insist that politicians set the standards by which they are assessed, and when journalists look for "consistency," they maintain their objectivity, or so they believe. Yet conviction politicians and their media managers understand that the media focus on consistency serves to highlight one of their strengths.

As reporters see it, consistency also leads to clarity, and a consistent leader offers the people a clear choice, which can enhance accountability. (When they examine the consistency of a leader, journalists can manage to meet their obligations as both delegates and trustees.) One columnist applauded Reagan's strong leadership even though he did not personally support the president, and he explained, "Whether you liked him or not, you knew where Reagan stood—on communism, government, taxes. In the campaign, Ronald Reagan understood the need for position taking. . . . He didn't duck and dodge. Nineteen eighty was the last time there was a clear relationship between the campaign and governing. Everyone knew where Reagan stood."[105] One of his colleagues in broadcasting made a similar point about both Reagan and Thatcher: "The character of their leadership was ideological. They had a unifying philosophy. They came to us [the public] after the campaign and told us what to do and how to do it. That's the political strength of any leader with a clear ideology—you know where they stand."[106] Known as a man who practiced what he preached, Reagan had a reputation that fortified his image as a strong leader and enhanced his media appeal.

Perhaps the worst public relations disaster for the Reagan administration—his visit to Bitburg cemetery in May 1985—occurred largely because his actions belied his principles. Before an economic summit scheduled to take place in Bonn, Deaver examined a local cemetery as a potential site for the president and Chancellor Helmut Kohl to hold a ceremony that would honor their nations' veterans and demonstrate the unity of the U.S.-German alliance. Snow covered the grave markers at the time Deaver made his visit, and as a consequence, he failed to observe the graves of forty-nine members of the Waffen SS. When the story broke in mid-April, one month before Reagan's trip, Deaver recalled, "No newscast, no edition of any newspaper, was complete without an interview with a person who had lost someone, or everyone, in the Holocaust."[107] White House officials considered canceling the trip, but Kohl had asked Reagan to carry out his personal commitment. As Deaver considered the options, the president could cancel "or we could ride it out, and hope that by remaining consistent, by once again promoting Reagan as a man of conviction, right or wrong, we could at least gain a 'standoff.'"[108] As part of the damage control, Deaver also arranged to have

General Matthew Ridgeway lay a wreath with Reagan, and the president added a visit to the concentration camp at Bergen-Belsen to his itinerary.

Yet no amount of damage control could turn the story around, precisely because Reagan's visit to Bitburg contradicted his avowed convictions. Reagan consistently extolled the virtues of freedom, promoted individual liberty, and condemned tyranny. His cold war rhetoric frequently drew parallels between the evils of Soviet communism and the atrocities of Nazi Germany. When he took part in a ceremony to honor World War II veterans at a cemetery where SS men were buried, Reagan could hardly claim to act out of conviction. Reporter-representatives proved quick to point out the inconsistency, and their assessment following the event that "the day's predominant tones were those of sorrow and dismay" reflected the disenchantment of the public at large.[109] The case of Bitburg provides the exception that proves the rule: Reagan's reputation for consistently carrying out his convictions supplied an essential element of his media appeal.

Consistent adherence to principle proved just as important to Thatcher's image as a strong leader. According to her press secretary, when it came to dealing with the media, Thatcher's greatest assets were "[h]er conviction style and the fact that it was a woman handbagging men all over the world—refusing to turn as Heath did. 'The lady's not for turning.'"[110] A prominent journalist for an elite London newspaper employed strikingly similar language to describe Thatcher's media appeal. As he recalled, "An aura developed around her and the press reflected it . . . once they got over the fact that she was a woman and she changed her voice. During the Falklands she had been vindicated, and 'the lady's not for turning.' She was a determined woman. She was dominating and domineering. The press is obsessed with powerful leaders."[111] Like Reagan, Thatcher understood that the press "obsession" with powerful leaders could enhance her reputation and prestige.

The way Thatcher wore the label "Iron Lady" shows how she learned to turn even bad publicity into good copy by using her image as a strong leader (and her gender) to maximum advantage. Shortly after Thatcher became party leader, a Soviet newspaper mocked her fierce anticommunism and called her the "Iron Lady." Initially, she tried to shed the label: In 1976, she appealed to her constituents, "I stand before you tonight in my chiffon evening gown, my fair hair gently waved—the Iron Lady of the Western World?" When the label stuck nonetheless, Thatcher followed the advice of Gordon Reece and started to take a different tack. "The Russians said I was an Iron Lady," she told her audiences and then defiantly declared: "They were right. Britain needs an Iron Lady."[112] Thatcher knew she wore the label at some risk—women are supposed to be soft, not hard as iron—but the way she played the game ensured her gamble would pay off.

The media loved the Iron Lady, and the images they transmitted enhanced Thatcher's standing at home and abroad. During the miners' strike as well as the Falklands war, the press focused on her hard line and the fact that she held firm until she defeated her enemies. In the Falklands war, Thatcher managed to convey another powerful image seized by the media: The prime minister with a preference for Victorian values became the heroine of the Victorian era, the ancient Queen Boadicea.[113]

John Wayne and the Iron Lady (or Boadicea) supplied the media with powerful images of strong leadership, while the theatrical dimension of these characters appealed to media values in another way: A cowboy and a warrior queen can easily and frequently yield dramatic displays of heroism and produce passionate rhetoric. News organizations and their reporters believe that to appeal to the public, they need to supply colorful depictions of events, and Reagan and Thatcher gave the media just the material they were looking for.

Simply put, conviction-style leaders prove more likely than consensus politicians to provide the drama and passion that can enliven news stories and engage the interest of the public. According to one journalist, this helps to explain why conviction politicians generally earn better press than consensus politicians do, and he applied his analysis to coverage of the presidency and Congress. As he observed, "Congress—a consensus-building institution—generally gets bad press. Perhaps we crave simple story lines with dramatic events and decisive outcomes. We may want that, while consensus-building accomplishments go unnoticed." Then he added, "Strong leaders employ rhetoric, and we're word people. Conciliators are not good communicators."[114] If print journalists are "word people," television broadcasters are visual people, and conviction-style leaders appeal to them by supplying dramatic visuals to accompany their rhetoric.

As one television broadcaster emphasized, the Reagan officials could manipulate the news because "they were adept at giving us a picture with the story." Along with several other journalists, that broadcaster offered as an example Reagan's "performance on the beaches of Normandy" on the fortieth anniversary of the invasion. For reporters, it was an event that proved "irresistible."[115]

White House officials stage-managed the ceremony in a way that was calculated to highlight the drama of the moment and evoke great emotion from the president as well as the public. Reagan read a letter from Lisa Henn, a woman whose father had served at Normandy, while Henn stood by his side. "I'm going there, Dad, and I'll see the beaches and the barricades and the monuments," Reagan read as his voice cracked. "I'll see the graves and I'll put flowers there just like you wanted to do. I'll never forget what you went through, Dad, nor will I let anyone else forget. And, Dad, I'll always be proud." As Deaver recalled in his memoirs, "The president's eyes brimmed and he had to choke out the final words. Lisa Henn wept openly." Later, Deaver recalled, he learned from Katherine Graham, publisher of the *Washington Post*, that she had "watched a film of the trip, and she cried at the moment when Reagan and the young woman made eye contact during the reading of the letter." Deaver concluded his account by observing that "such moments did bring out the best in Ronald Reagan. At such moments, the world really was his stage."[116] News reports of the event were universally laudatory.[117] If the occasion alone accounted for the drama and emotion, then President Clinton might have received the same (or better) coverage ten years later when he spoke at the fiftieth anniversary in Normandy. Clinton's failure to do so indicates that Reagan possessed traits his successor lacked.

Another media-managed event from the Reagan years illustrates not only the importance of drama and rhetoric but also the way populism figures prominently among news values. On April 26, 1983, a commission appointed by the Department of Education issued its report "A Nation at Risk," which documented the dire state of education in the United States. The media gave the report some coverage when it was released, and the cold war metaphors used by the commission attracted most of the media attention. (Quoting from the report, ABC News White House correspondent Steve Shepard concluded "that as a nation America has been committing unilateral educational disarmament. If an unfriendly foreign power attempted to impose upon America the kind of mediocre educational performance that exists today, we might well have viewed it as an act of war.")[118] The story soon died, but it was resurrected when President Reagan launched a nationwide grassroots education campaign two months later.

Reagan's education campaign provides the only instance when the president allowed the polls to set his agenda, according to his pollster Richard Wirthlin.[119] And Deputy Press Secretary Speakes recalled, "The polls showed the public against us—60 to 40 percent when the report 'America at Risk' was issued. We turned it into a positive. We sent Reagan around the country and put him in the classroom with children. At the end of the period, the percentage flipped, 40 to 60 percent favored the president's policy."[120] Media coverage of Reagan's education tour across the country was extensive and almost entirely without critical comment.

Throughout his tour, Reagan promoted his own views on education, effectively reinterpreting the report issued in April. The president recalled, "[T]he commission's thrust was one of making better use of resources we already have," and he blamed the state of education on federal rules and regulations.[121] When Reagan visited a model school in Whittier, California, he called for "a grass roots campaign for educational renewal."[122] The *New York*

Times tracked the president's journey west through Kentucky and Kansas, and at each stop repeated the message as Reagan delivered it: The federal government is responsible for the "Nation at Risk"; solutions must be found at the state and local levels.[123] In each stump speech he delivered, Reagan exploited the cold war rhetoric originally employed by the authors of the report. As Reagan repeated his themes, the national media echoed them.

In addition to the appeal of his rhetoric and the drama of the president's crusade, the story proved especially newsworthy because the president was cast in the role of one of the people—meeting with them, appealing to them, and tapping their fundamental aspirations. Speakes explained that White House advisors encouraged Reagan to hit the campaign trail because "when the president travels, it's always news. A show on the road would always do well."[124] Typical of the coverage in most news outlets, the *New York Times's* reports satisfied the expectations of Reagan's media managers. "Like the nineteenth century popular adult educators who traveled about the country delivering summertime lectures and holding discussion groups and home meetings," the paper reported, "Mr. Reagan has been conducting a modern-day chautauqua on education itself."[125] Across the country, media reports captured the populist atmosphere created by Reagan's advisors when they designed the nationwide grassroots tour.

In the judgment of reporters and their news organizations, the public wanted to hear their president address the education issue, and Reagan satisfied their desire. The media noted that Reagan's tour followed the commission's report two months earlier, but no journalist questioned the timing or speculated that the president might simply be trying to boost his approval ratings on the education issue in response to the poll results in April. Moreover, Reagan spun the report to suit his ideology, but reporters failed to point out the difference between Reagan's interpretation of the report and the commission's original analysis, which failed to exclude federal funds as a solution to the problem. Furthermore, Reagan took no concrete action (indeed, he campaigned against any federal initiatives). Finally, while conveying the president's message about the importance of state and local initiatives, the reporters nonetheless kept the focus almost entirely on the president.[126] Reporters might have performed their task as delegates by delivering news that people demand, but in this case they made no attempt to exert guardianship or ensure accountability.

While Reagan as "everyman" could easily exploit populism as a media value, Thatcher also learned how to use her populist appeal as a media ploy. Noting that "the press is reflective of something, [though] an imperfect mirror," one British journalist emphasized that Thatcher "was popular in a populist sense, and the press reflected that."[127] Of course, populist leaders need

not be conviction politicians, but conviction-style leaders usually make populist appeals, which enhance their media coverage. When conviction politicians articulate the "general will," they draw on public sentiments and tap
popular emotions while promoting their own solutions. As the media portray this process, the president or the prime minister is one of the people,
speaking to and for the people—and not for special interests—although the
press frequently neglects to report when and how populism can advance the
political interests of the conviction-style leader.

Populism figured prominently in Thatcher's most successful media-managed event, although it was by no means the only feature that made the story
newsworthy. British reporters cited the prime minister's trip to Moscow two
months before the 1987 general election as the greatest of "Bernard's
Coups," and they mentioned her Moscow trip as often as U.S. reporters referred to Normandy. Bernard Ingham also named this as the "best coverage"
Thatcher ever secured because, as he put it, "she looked good—wherever she
went, there were great crowds mobbing her." Years later he recalled that the
event went exactly as he planned it:

> Here was the archenemy of communism—the Iron Lady—allowed
> to meet the people and given license to undermine it by going on tele-
> vision. That was what made it exciting. She went into the flats and su-
> permarkets. . . . She got on with the people terribly well. And she stood
> for freedom. She was uncompromising. That was what the Iron Lady
> was about.
>   . . . [The media responded because of] the visuals—and they decided
> it was a success story. Then it acquired a momentum of its own. It was
> the evidence of their own eyes. There was enthusiasm, exuberance
> among the people.[128]

Just as Speakes described the success of any "show on the road," Ingham insisted, "We [in the press office] know walkabouts are a good story. We had
so many at home." (And he joked, "Our only concern was not dragging all
of Fleet Street through the Moscow flats!") As a public relations effort, the
Moscow trip in 1987 was intended to emphasize Thatcher's world leadership
two months before the general election. But it was also designed to highlight
some of the characteristics that made her a successful leader at home—her
adherence to principle, her passion, and her populism.

From the very start of her Moscow visit, news reports emphasized the
warm response with which Soviet crowds greeted the "Iron Lady." Walkabouts scheduled for the first day produced the photos and the news angles
that media managers had intended. News reports portrayed Thatcher as a

crusader for freedom when she lighted a "Candle for Peace on [her] historic Moscow mission," but the primary press preoccupation focused on the popular response to her visit. Thatcher was "greeted warmly by the crowds" and "mobbed by enthusiastic crowds when she visited a Moscow housing estate." As the *Times* described it, on this day "Russia discovered the 'kind lady' behind the iron image."[129] A popular paper that highlighted the "Flame for Freedom" and described Thatcher as using the visit "to put her most cherished ideals on the line" also declared, "Moscow's going wild about Maggie." News accounts made clear that Thatcher was not only popular but also a populist: On page one, the *Daily Mail* depicted the day as "dominated by a woman whose own gut instincts are shared by a lot of other ordinary people, British or Russian."[130] The report in an elite, left-of-center paper noted that "[t]here were no votes to be won but there were pictures to be taken," but even that newspaper faithfully presented the photos of Thatcher "mobbed by crowds" that Downing Street press officers produced.[131]

The media focus shifted slightly from populism to principled leadership and passionate rhetoric after Thatcher appeared on Soviet television to render a "resolute defense of the nuclear deterrent."[132] While mocking Thatcher's appearance as "glowing, glamorous, gorgeous, girlish," the *Guardian* also ran a commentary that acknowledged, "She has been able to operate here as the conviction politician."[133] As usual, the pops put it more bluntly and dramatically: "Maggie Shakes Russia on Space Missiles," the *Daily Mail* declared.[134] And the next day, the *Mail* quoted a Soviet viewer of Thatcher's broadcast who observed, "Whatever you think of what she said, you have to admire her."[135] Media coverage of Thatcher's television performance emphasized her convictions, her courage, and her commitment, while news reports generally neglected the official purpose of the visit: arms control talks between the British prime minister and Soviet leader Mikhail Gorbachev.

Descriptions of Thatcher's relationships with Gorbachev and with the Soviet people remained largely superficial and often gender-specific. A headline in the *Guardian* announced, "PM shows feminine wiles: Martin Walker describes how Mrs. T and her wardrobe have charmed Muscovites."[136] And the *Daily Mail* emphasized the personal "chemistry" between Thatcher and Gorbachev "that Forged a new Future."[137] Yet even commentaries that focused on Thatcher's "femininity" often served to enhance her image by revealing the soft side of the Iron Lady. (Thatcher understood that women leaders who demonstrate "masculine" leadership traits must walk a fine line or they will tumble below the threshold of acceptable "feminine" behavior.)[138] At other times, the media depicted her female qualities as the basis for a unique arsenal, which the modern warrior queen used to disarm her communist adversaries. "It is possible that only a woman, and perhaps only this woman, would have the affrontery or audacity to use her sex as a weapon quite ruth-lessly," a *Mail* reporter declared. "But she turned it on like an old time Hol-lywood firm star—and they loved it."[139] No one loved it more than the press, for whom the story of Thatcher's trip to Moscow provided principled lead-ership, populist appeals, and perhaps more than one kind of passion.

Finally, another type of news judgment also favors conviction-style leaders. Their pursuit of change and the rare occurrence of conviction in politics make conviction politicians inherently newsworthy. Journalists usually mention these two features as part of a single phenomenon, implying that conviction and change go hand in hand. According to a journalist who was also Reagan's director of communications, "Conviction politicians are just more likely to get good coverage. Politicians usually seem like mealymouthed windbags. Re-porters want to see someone shake up the establishment."[140] A reporter for a major television network admitted, "We favor people who take action rather than preserve the status quo. Most politicians twist in the wind. Reagan didn't. He was an anomaly."[141] According to cynical reporters, conviction in politics constitutes a classic "man bites dog" story—and, as Thatcher learned, the tale grows more interesting when a woman delivers the bite.

Instances of negative publicity were unusual for Reagan and Thatcher, but they did receive bad press during the Iran-Contra and Westland affairs. Of course, the fact that the Iran-Contra scandal broke in the foreign press might attest to the passivity of the White House press corps in the Reagan years. Yet the element of cover-up in those controversies eventually spurred re-porters to rebel, and journalists attempted to uncover what they believed "the public ought to know." Just as significant, the leaders suddenly seemed to lack many of the virtues that had coincided so conveniently with news values. The resignation of a prominent cabinet minister called into question Thatcher's strong leadership, while (at least initially) the press portrayed Rea-gan as weak and out of touch with his own administration. Moreover, the leaders known for their rhetorical skill remained unusually silent as the drama that unfolded proved more tragic than heroic. Despite the negative coverage, media managers and journalists insist that Iran-Contra and West-land provide cases of corrupt politics and flawed policy making, not bad press. In fact, the Iran-Contra and Westland affairs stemmed from phenom-ena the media had unwittingly encouraged: The scandals occurred because strong leaders of great ambition sought to gratify their ruling passions, un-obstructed by any edifice.

Conviction-style leaders generally possess a greater capacity to achieve change than consensus politicians of the same period, but the changing con-text also gave Reagan and Thatcher freer rein than many other conviction politicians enjoyed. In contrast to late-nineteenth-century leaders, Reagan and Thatcher inherited weak political parties that proved responsive to their initiatives and conformed to their convictions. Furthermore, while news values always favored conviction politicians, Reagan and Thatcher also operated in an environment where interaction between leaders and the press proved conducive to news management. Finally, their advantages exceeded the informal factors that shape the politics of presidents and prime ministers. Reagan and Thatcher derived substantial benefits from their predecessors' efforts to control the formal institutions of government and the state, while they adopted innovations of their own that further enhanced the ability of conviction-style leaders to reach their goals.

8

EXECUTIVE AUTHORITY, THE POLITICAL SYSTEM, AND THE STATE

To achieve their ideological goals, conviction-style leaders often discover they must also pursue structural change. Presidents and prime ministers who succeed as conviction politicians manage to alter the structures of leadership and the norms or expectations that reinforce them, while less effective conviction-style leaders fail to remove or circumvent institutional constraints. Admittedly, not all leaders who attempt to increase executive authority are conviction politicians, but all successful conviction politicians try to expand the realm of their power. Just as significant, when conviction-style leaders enhance executive authority, they can change the character of both the political system and the state.

Institutional developments follow distinctive paths in the United States and the United Kingdom, but they lead to similar destinations. In the U.S. a fragmented system characterized by pluralism and separation of powers (with the legislature as the dominant branch) evolves into an executive-centered system that invites presidents to rule by plebiscite. In the U.K. governing authority shifts from Parliament to party and cabinet and then to Number 10 Downing Street. Furthermore, changes in executive authority and the political system coincide with changing notions and functions of the state. Modern conviction-style leaders try to alter the apparatus of the state by transforming the bureaucratic machine into a vehicle specifically designed to advance their convictions. Although the efforts of conviction politicians alone fail to account for these changes, they often play a significant role— and for good reason. In both countries, conditions conducive to conviction politics replace structures designed to create consensus.

Finally, to achieve fundamental structural change, leaders must legitimize their innovations. When conviction-style leaders expand executive authority in ways that reverberate through the political system and the state, they tend to tap democratic aspirations. The president or the prime minister sides with the people against the corrupt interests that have become entrenched in the legislature, the courts, the parties, or the bureaucracy. Conviction politicians insist only they can articulate the general will and pursue the public interest, but to do so they need to escape the constraints that restrain their movement and tame their ambition.

259

The United States

Andrew Jackson was the first president to expand the institutional authority of the executive by tapping popular aspirations. Thomas Jefferson had also viewed his election in 1800 as a "contest of opinion" and derived extra-institutional energy from his popular mandate, but he did not wish to bring about permanent institutional change that would have strengthened the executive. To the contrary, Jefferson interpreted his election and justified his actions as necessary to restore the original meaning of the Constitution by returning to limited government and securing individual rights. Furthermore, President Jefferson struggled to keep his political activities covert and maintain the appearance of statesmanship (although he often failed to do so). Finally, Jefferson repeatedly warned of the dangers of majority rule and the subsequent risks of tyranny. In contrast to Jefferson, Jackson explicitly advocated change, justified his political activities as the pursuit of the public good, and linked his executive authority to majority rule or popular sovereignty.

To make the case for change, Jackson rendered a critique of the system of separation of powers with Congress as the dominant institution, while he also challenged James Madison's notion that a multiplicity of interests would find adequate representation in a large republic. Jackson insisted that the president's authority must equal that of the legislature, but he declined to rely on "checks and balances" as his rationale. Instead, he argued the president must oppose Congress when it fails to represent all interests equally. According to Jackson, when the laws "make the rich richer and the potent more powerful, the humble members of society—the farmers, mechanics, and laborers—who have neither the time nor the means of securing like favors to themselves, have a right to complain of the injustice of their Government."[1] For Jackson, the presidency provides the place for a national leader to voice popular discontent. While he appeared to advocate equality of the three branches of government, Jackson also depicted the president as the only representative of all the people and reminded legislators that the people remain sovereign.[2]

To alter the executive's relationship to the legislature, Jackson changed the nature of the presidential veto. Hoping to end the policy of government aid to private corporations, he exercised his first veto against a bill that authorized the government to invest in the stock of a Kentucky company for a turnpike from Maysville to Lexington.[3] In the Maysville veto message, Jackson appealed to the people as the "highest tribunal." He insisted that the law not only violated federalism but also placed an undue burden on the poor, essentially the argument he would make in opposition to the National Bank. In fact, Jackson cited Maysville in each of his subsequent veto messages, and he often reiterated its reasoning. Ultimately, he used the veto power more often than all his predecessors combined, and after Jackson the threat of a veto became an effective legislative strategy for presidents to pursue.[4]

More significant, Jackson broke new ground when he based his reasoning on political as well as constitutional arguments. In doing so, Jackson created a policy forum intended to rival the legislature. His veto messages, with their passionate, populist rhetoric, were clearly crafted to persuade the public as well as Congress to embrace his convictions. At the same time, Jackson's use of the veto enhanced the limited agenda-setting capacity of the nineteenth-century presidency. During the bank war, for example, President Jackson wanted the bank on the agenda, while he also wanted to knock the tariff and nullification off it. After he issued his veto message, Jackson announced (somewhat prematurely), it "has killed the ultras, both tarifites and nulli-fiers."[5] In general Jackson found, as he declared with delight to Amos Kendall, "the veto works well."[6] By giving the president a new vehicle to persuade and set the agenda, the veto facilitated Jackson's ability to pursue both his ideological and his political goals.

As Jackson strengthened the presidency relative to Congress, he also attempted to appropriate judicial authority by insisting that all three branches were equal as interpreters of the Constitution. In 1832 Jackson sided with the state of Georgia against the Supreme Court decision in *Worcester v. Georgia* and refused to enforce the court's ruling in favor of the Cherokees. The only other president who defied the judiciary in this way was Abraham Lincoln, and war, not popular sovereignty, rendered the rationale for his action. During the bank battle, Daniel Webster alleged that Jackson had effectively struck the judiciary out of the system by reducing constitutional interpretation to a matter of mere opinion. In Webster's view, Jackson's bank veto conveyed the message: "I am the State."[7]

In his second administration, Jackson's actions sparked another dispute concerning the constitutional interpretation of presidential power, and once again, he linked his institutional authority to his political goals and the public's aspirations. When the secretary of the treasury refused to remove the bank deposits, Jackson dismissed him. The Senate then censured the president, and Jackson immediately responded by sending a formal letter of protest in which he defended his action. Jackson declared that the treasury was "wholly an executive department" and the power of removal was "an original executive power." More significant, Jackson insisted that the Senate lacked authority to censure the president, who was the only "direct representative of the people."[8] When Jackson articulated and defended the president's removal power, he interpreted the Constitution and adapted institutions in a way that enabled him to pursue his policy objective, and the democratic nature of his argument enhanced his ability to succeed.[9]

Jackson proved able to frame even his most overt political objectives in terms that tapped popular aspirations. As he described the spoils system, it would provide a check on corruption. According to Jackson, those who held public office "for any length of time" were "apt to acquire a habit of looking with indifference upon the public interests and of tolerating conduct from which an unpracticed man would revolt. . . . Corruption in some and in others a perversion of correct feelings and principles divert government from its legitimate ends and make it an engine for the support of the few at the expense of the many."[10] Moreover, Jackson argued that rotation in office would increase public participation in governing. "No man has any more intrinsic right to official station than another," according to Jackson. In his opinion, ordinary citizens of intelligence were capable of performing the "plain and simple duties" of public service, and the benefit of their participation outweighed the experience of the elite.[11] Of course, Jackson also knew that increased use of his appointment powers would make public officials personally accountable to and dependent on the president. By rendering a new rationale for the maxim "to the victor goes the spoils," Jackson enhanced his influence and facilitated the implementation of his policies. His rationale made the pursuit of his political objectives a matter of public purpose and part of the process of democratization.

Jackson's "kitchen cabinet" provides another case of an institutional innovation that served to enhance presidential authority and autonomy while promoting democratic values. Jackson distrusted national politicians, especially their commitment to radicalism, and as a result, he refused to rely on the advice of officials in his party or cabinet. Instead, Jackson sought confidential counsel by meeting with those whom he did trust in an informal setting. His kitchen cabinet included Martin Van Buren (who was also secretary of state), his friends—William B. Lewis of Tennessee and Andrew Jackson Donelson, his nephew and private secretary—and newspaper reporters Kendall and Francis Blair. Through the use of his kitchen cabinet, the president maintained and highlighted his independence from professional politicians, and Jackson's public distrusted the Washington establishment and political elite as much as he did.

Ultimately, Jackson managed to alter the place of the presidency in the political order and in the public mind. As "representative of all the people," the president could rival the legislature and defy the judiciary. Of course, conditions conducive to structural change were already under way when Jackson took office. Change in presidential selection and extension of the franchise enhanced the legitimacy of his innovations and the credibility of his assertions. The institutional viability of the old political order had already been challenged, creating new opportunities for creative presidential leadership and conviction politics. Yet it was Jackson who rendered the rationale that changed public expectations of executive leadership and legitimized structural change. After Jackson's presidency, executive authority would depend to a much greater extent on the support of a majority in the public, though few nineteenth-century presidents proved able to obtain it.

Grover Cleveland never managed to attract a majority of the electorate, but he did secure pluralities that enabled him to win the popular votes in three consecutive elections. (The only other president to do so was Franklin Delano Roosevelt.) As a Jacksonian, Cleveland tried to cultivate and use his popular support to enhance his authority as president. Yet Cleveland operated in an ideological and institutional context that differed from Jackson's environment. Cleveland embraced Jackson's reasoning and employed many of his predecessor's tools, but he proved unable to build on Jackson's legacy by constructing a new, expanded realm of presidential power.

Like Jackson, Cleveland used the presidential veto more often than all his predecessors combined. (In fact, only FDR exercised the veto more frequently.) When he blocked the Bland (silver) bill, the *New York Times* put President Cleveland in the tradition of Jacksonian presidential leadership: His veto "showed he is the representative, and the sole representative of the whole country," the newspaper announced.[12] As most of Cleveland's vetoes prevented bills that funded pensions, he largely used his constitutional power as a political instrument to combat the corruption and wastefulness of Congress.

Cleveland followed in Jackson's footsteps in another way. In a manner reminiscent of Jackson's battle with the Senate, in 1886 Cleveland challenged the Senate's interpretation of the revised Tenure of Office Act. When Cleveland moved to replace Republican George M. Duskin as U.S. attorney for the Southern District of Alabama with Democrat John D. Burnett, the Senate directed the attorney general to deliver all papers relating to the Alabama office, including those explaining the suspension of Duskin. In response, Cleveland ordered the attorney general to refuse to hand over the papers. When the Senate Judiciary Committee called for the formal censure of the attorney general, Cleveland replied with a message addressed to the Senate but directed to a wider, public audience. He argued that only the president should determine what constitutes "official" papers, and the Senate could not demand an explanation for the dismissal of an executive officer whom the president deemed unsuitable to carry out his administrative orders. Moreover, Cleveland reminded the Senate that the president was accountable only to the people and should not be thwarted by Congress. If Congress thought he behaved unconstitutionally, its only recourse was impeachment.[13] When Congress subsequently repealed the Tenure of Office

Act, it surrendered to the president all discretion in suspending or removing executive branch officials.

Cleveland also took a few steps beyond Jackson's pathbreaking legacy. He certainly exceeded Jackson in interpreting the meaning of the grant of power in article II to "take care that the laws be faithfully executed" when Cleveland ordered federal troops in the Pullman strike. Sending the troops without a request from the state constituted a daring move and an expansive interpretation of presidential power, but in this case Cleveland took a position that pitted him against the people rather than placing him on their side. He also attempted to add to Jackson's innovations by composing single-issue messages to Congress. To focus national attention on his policies and priorities, Cleveland sent separate messages on the Tenure of Office Act, the repeal of the Sherman Silver Purchase Act, the U.K.-Venezuela boundary dispute, and the tariff. In the case of the tariff, Cleveland tried to make his preoccupation the nation's central concern by addressing that issue alone in his annual state of the union message.

As Jackson did in his veto messages, Cleveland in his tariff message emphasized the burden Congress had imposed on the poor. "The people can hardly hope for any consideration in the operation of these selfish schemes [of trusts]," Cleveland declared, and he insisted it was the president's obligation to fight for greater fairness.[14] The press asserted that Cleveland had rendered a message that would "ring in every stump and echo in every work shop"; his bold move "created a profound sensation" throughout the nation.[15] In this, Cleveland's most significant innovation, he linked the exercise of his power to democratic aspirations. Moreover, by focusing national attention on his top priority, he further enhanced the agenda-setting capacity of nineteenth-century presidents. Nevertheless, Cleveland's use of the president's annual message as a political tool proved insufficient to enable him to achieve his policy objective or create fundamental institutional change.

Cleveland also achieved only limited success when he attempted to secure civil service reform. Such reform would loosen what had become a restraint on presidential power: By the late nineteenth century, strong parties had taken away executive discretion in the distribution of spoils. Yet Cleveland endorsed civil service reform primarily as a matter of principle, and initially he pursued the issue as a moral crusade. Cleveland took several concrete actions and attempted to achieve reform largely by executive order. On July 14, 1886, he issued an order that warned officeholders against using their positions to engage in partisan activities. He also urged the Civil Service Commission to correct inconsistencies in qualifications and standards across departments. In his second term, Cleveland adopted additional measures: On May 8, 1893, he announced that he would refuse personal interviews of office seekers and asked members of Congress not to make requests on behalf of constituents and friends. Finally, in 1895–96 Cleveland signed executive orders that revised civil service rules and added forty-four thousand positions to the civil service lists. By the end of his second term, more than 40 percent of the positions held by federal employees had become classified, whereas approximately 10 percent had civil service protection when Cleveland first took office.[16]

Despite these accomplishments and his lofty rhetoric, Cleveland could have done much more, but this otherwise rigid conviction politician proved willing to compromise on civil service reform. To some extent, Cleveland agreed with Jackson that anyone of "reasonable intelligence" could perform government jobs, and he wanted to open the door "for the rich, and the poor alike."[17] (Like Jackson, Cleveland also believed his party better represented the poor than Republicans did.) In this case, the dominant democratic argument in favor of spoils ran counter to institutional change. Moreover, although Cleveland came under heavy pressure from his Mugwump followers to enact sweeping reform, most Democrats resisted change: The party faithful proved indignant at Cleveland's adherence to merit and the appointment of so many Republicans. The president himself believed that spoils served the party more than the public but acknowledged that spoils were essential to maintain the party organization—and parties, Cleveland repeatedly lamented, "seem to be necessary."[18] Compromise on civil service reform constituted one of Cleveland's major concessions to his party.

Cleveland left little legacy of institutional change to his successors. As indicated in chapter 3, he increasingly confronted constraints created by his own convictions, which often placed him at odds with "the people." Just as significant, the structures of the political order—Congress and political parties—proved stronger than Cleveland's willful determination to pursue change. Despite his innovative use of the president's annual message (and its probable impact on public opinion), Cleveland could not convince Congress to revise the tariff in the ways he wanted. Notwithstanding the substantial steps he took toward civil service reform, he proved unable to overcome party constraints. Cleveland might have chosen to emphasize the unfair advantage partisans have over others who seek office, and thereby transformed civil service reform into a democratic cause, but that would have required a frontal assault on political parties during their golden age. Cleveland might also have challenged the functions and legitimacy of the legislature (as well as of the parties) rather than limit his criticisms to the policies that Congress produced. Yet he declined to provide a public critique of the political order—its theoretical foundations or its practices. Indeed, he never tried to alter the norms or expectations of presidential leadership. Instead, Cleveland remained content to repeat but not willing to expand or revise Jackson's reasoning.

Nevertheless, when Woodrow Wilson honored Cleveland's achievements, he credited Cleveland with delivering a critique of the system and rendering a new rationale for presidential leadership. According to Wilson, Cleveland initially held a strict construction of executive responsibilities, but he quickly learned he needed to adopt a more flexible and active approach. As Wilson recalled, Cleveland delivered his tariff message because he was "thoroughly sick of seeing a great party drift and dally," and his battle with Congress to repeal silver coinage in 1893 "would have ended in some weak compromise had not the President stood resolute." To counteract stalemate in the legislature and promote policies based on principle, Cleveland developed "the habit of independent initiative in respect of questions of legislative policy," and as a result, "he felt his personal power grow." "To have a personal following, carry out the real pledges of his party, and make his purpose felt as the nation's spokesman," Cleveland found he must "force partisan leaders, for their own good, to feel his power from without." During Cleveland's administrations, Wilson concluded, "It was singular how politics began at once to center in the President, waiting for his initiative. . . . Power had somehow gone the length of the avenue, and seemed lodged in one man."[19] Wilson tried to convince his audience that Cleveland had managed to transform a fragmented, leaderless system into a structure conducive to conviction-style presidential leadership.

Wilson glossed over Cleveland's failure to secure tariff reform and the problems that plagued his second administration. Nor did Wilson consider what happened when Cleveland's convictions clashed with public sentiment and he could no longer use his "power from without" to pressure party chieftains. In his only critical comment on Cleveland, Wilson referred to the passion "of hatred he has stirred up"; yet even that emotion served to "authenticate his greatness."[20] Rather than render an accurate account of Cleveland's presidency, Wilson wanted to illustrate his own concept of presidential leadership and promote it as the solution to a flawed political order.

Like Jackson, Wilson believed that popular support could legitimize executive authority, but Wilson's critique of the system and his solution differed from Jackson's. According to Wilson, the U.S. system suffered from stalemate, and only strong conviction-style leadership in the presidency could advance progress. In 1908 Wilson declared, "[T]here is but one national voice in the country, and that is the voice of the President," but he moved beyond Jackson when he added, "The nation as a whole has chosen him and is conscious that *it has no other political spokesman*" (emphasis added).[21] For Wilson, public support could place the presidency at the center of the system and give the institution superior authority. Dynamic presidential leadership would make the national government more responsive to the popular will and transform the system into an efficient policy-making machine.

To strengthen presidential leadership and democratize the process of presidential selection, Wilson endorsed the primaries both in theory and in practice. As explained in chapter 6, Wilson envisioned candidate-oriented parties: During the primaries, candidates would campaign on their convictions and cultivate majority support for their policies; then the president-elect would carry a popular mandate into office. In addition, an open contest would alleviate corruption: Principled parties, organized around conviction-style leaders, would replace nineteenth-century organizations, which were "unmitigated nuisances . . . savory with decay and rank with rottenness."[22] Theodore Roosevelt had also promoted primaries through his active participation, but Wilson legitimized change in presidential selection by providing a rationale for reform. Once again, a president's carefully crafted reasoning linked increased executive authority to democratic goals.[23]

President Wilson brought about another institutional change that shifted the place of the presidency in the political order and the public mind when he personally appeared before Congress to deliver his messages. Indeed, he simultaneously advanced his two reforms when, during his first state of the union address, he advocated national legislation that would provide for primaries. Wilson appeared before Congress for each of his annual messages (except in 1919, when he was ill) and on other special occasions to build support for specific legislative measures.

Wilson adopted this practice early in his first term, when he urged Congress to approve the Underwood tariff bill. Echoing the sentiments of Cleveland, President Wilson promoted tariff reform by emphasizing the need for public officials to rise above the interplay of interests in order to serve the public good. Wilson hoped his physical presence in the chamber would enable everyone to see the new, central place of the presidency in the policy-making process. At the same time, he focused the eyes of the public and their representatives on the president personally in the hope that they would start to perceive the person as the embodiment of the institution.

Following his first appearance, Mrs. Wilson commented that it was the sort of thing Roosevelt would have done "if only he had thought of it." "Yes I think I put one over on Teddy," President Wilson declared.[24] Others drew the same comparison: The *New York Times* wondered "that in seven years Theodore Roosevelt never thought of this way of stamping his personality upon his age."[25] Wilson had found a unique way for the president to have a personal impact on public policy and political development.

Of course, the idea was neither new nor Wilson's own invention. Early presidents had adapted the British practice of opening Parliament with a "speech from the throne" by speaking to Congress, but Jefferson abandoned the monarchical ceremony in order "to establish good principles and good practices to fortify republicanism behind as many barriers as possible."[26] Wilson's friend Walter Hines Page, a publisher and editor from North Carolina, encouraged the president to appear before Congress to promote tariff reform, and later, Oliver Newman, chief editorial writer for the *Washington Times*, urged Wilson to deliver his annual messages in person. In his book *The State,* Professor Wilson had speculated that the president's state of the union address might have linked the executive and the legislature. According to Wilson, "Possibly had the President not so closed the matter against new adjustments, this clause of the Constitution might legitimately have been made the foundation for a much more habitual and informal, and yet at the same time *much more public and responsible interchange of opinion between the Executive and Congress*" (emphasis added).[27] President Wilson justified his action as a measure designed to enhance public accountability and executive responsibility as well as a means of increasing presidential influence in the legislative arena. He believed he had discovered a "dignified" way for the president to persuade, and if the practice evoked images of a monarch, it might well serve to enhance presidential prestige.[28]

Although Wilson was pleased with his performance, his first appearance before Congress did spark some initial critical comment in the press. The *World,* for example, endorsed the president's tariff reform but criticized his approach. "The President of the United States cannot afford to take the chance . . . of having his leadership publicly rebuked as private meddling," the paper declared and then advised, "[I]n the matter of consulting with Congressmen [it is] wiser to follow the beaten path of tradition."[29] Nevertheless, to achieve institutional change and win support for his policies, Wilson proved willing to risk his personal influence.

Eight months later, when the president appeared to deliver his annual message, virtually all the newspapers welcomed his move. The *New York Times,* which endorsed both the style and the substance of the president's message, assessed his appearance as "a great personal triumph" that earned "tumultuous" applause. In particular the *New York Times* emphasized the visual effect of his performance: "The scene [had] a strikingly picturesque quality," the paper reported.[30] The *Herald* agreed and declared, "The President's annual address to Congress is most inspiring. It heartens, it animates, it stimulates—it soothes."[31] While praising the president's performance, other newspapers declined to endorse specific proposals on his agenda, but the president's agenda defined the scope of discussion.

Wilson's Republican successors followed his example occasionally in the 1920s, and after Franklin Delano Roosevelt seized upon it, all modern presidents continued the practice. Later, television served to enhance the spectacular effect of the president performing live before an audience that comprised the entire government. Today the state of the union address always commands the special attention of the nation, and the president's script usually defines the legislative agenda for the year.

At the time of Wilson's presidency, conditions proved conducive to reforms that would enhance presidential power and further democratize the political system. Progressive reformers had already advanced a number of measures that weakened the old political parties and challenged the integrity of traditional lawmakers. In addition, changes in the news business made the press receptive to Wilson's efforts to personalize the presidency. Finally, Wilson benefited from the creative leadership practiced by Teddy Roosevelt, although it was Wilson who provided the rationales needed to legitimize structural change and create new norms for presidential leadership. Ultimately, Wilson's innovations produced a rhetorical presidency, in which the president initiates and advocates policies by "going public," and public support can determine presidential success. In the new political order, public opinion empowers (and constrains) presidents, and popular will—articulated and advanced by the president—propels public policy. Wilson reformed the presidency in ways that democratized the political process and created greater opportunities for strong, efficient leadership.

At the same time, however, the expansion of the state that accompanied Wilson's new liberalism threatened to erect new barriers to effective executive leadership—a problem Wilson fully grasped. Long before he advocated his new liberalism or advanced institutional change, Wilson sought to strengthen leadership and increase efficiency in government by promoting the study and science of public administration. As a political scientist he understood that the state is not a liberal concept, and as an advocate, he knew he would need to reconcile any call for greater administrative efficiency with the stringent requirements of democratic accountability. In an 1886 essay that would later shape much of the study and profession of public administration, Wilson proposed a solution by creating a distinction between politics and administration. Politics would remain separate from (while defining the tasks for) administration, according to Wilson, and professional administrators would follow the scientific method to implement public policies in an efficient and objective manner.[32] A quarter of a century later, President Wilson would attempt to put his ideas into practice—when the state building that stemmed from his new liberalism made the need to reform administration even more urgent.[33]

As early as 1886 Professor Wilson insisted that the increasing complexity of government demanded the study of public administration. "It is getting to be harder to run a constitution than to frame one," Wilson declared (rendering a remark that would be quoted frequently in public administration literature throughout the twentieth century). "Seeing every day new things which the state ought to do," he added, "the next thing is to see clearly how it ought to do them." Then Wilson linked his call for the use of "impartial scientific method" in administration to the popular campaign against political corruption. According to Wilson, "The poisonous atmosphere of city government, the crooked secrets of state administration, the confusion, sinecurism, and corruption ever and again discovered in the bureaux at Washington forbid us to believe that any clear conceptions of what constitutes good administration are as yet very widely current in the United States."[34] In their campaign to end spoils, reformers would simply invoke the "politics-administration distinction," but in his essay Wilson needed to develop his argument further in order to convince his readers that the type of state he proposed could be reconciled with liberalism.

Wilson revealed his understanding of the dilemma the state can create for liberalism when he explained why the subject of administration had been neglected in both the U.S. and the U.K. In contrast to countries on the European continent, Wilson explained, the Anglo-American world had shunned centralization and developed complex constitutional systems; the role of "popular assent" and "liberal principles of government" prevented citizens from surrendering authority to a single entity.[35] In particular, both nations remained committed to limiting executive power, whereas expansive executive authority would be needed to command the modern state. As Wilson explained, "The English race, consequently, has long and successfully studied the art of curbing executive power to the constant neglect of the art of perfecting executive methods. It has exercised itself much more in controlling than in energizing government. It has been more concerned to render government just and moderate than to make it facile, well-ordered, and effective. English and American political history has been a history, not of administrative development, but of legislative oversight—not of progress in governmental organization, but of advance in law-making and political criticism."[36] Yet Wilson believed he had found new ways to reconcile the concentrated power necessary for efficient administration with the principles of democratic accountability and popular sovereignty cherished in the Anglo-American tradition.

According to Wilson, popular sovereignty complicates the task of administration because the people "can agree upon nothing simple." "Advance must be made through compromise, by a compounding of differences, by a trimming of plans and a suppression of too straightforward principles," he observed.[37] (Racial and ethnic diversity further obscures opinion in the U.S., Wilson added.) To solve the problems that arise from fragmented public opinion, Wilson recommended conviction-style leadership. As he explained,

"Whoever would effect a change in a modern constitutional government must first educate his fellow-citizens to want some change. That done, he must persuade them to want the particular change he wants. He must first make public opinion willing to listen and then see to it that it listen to the right things. He must stir it up to search for an opinion, and then manage to put the right opinion in its way."[38] Here again, Wilson argued that the public needs strong, principled leadership. If a conviction-style leader can convince the public to embrace the "right opinion," then popular sovereignty will fail to limit executive power or obstruct efficient administration.

In another part of the essay, Wilson resolved the same dilemma in a different way by returning to the politics-administration distinction. The administrative state poses no threat to individual liberty because constitutional principles, not administrative practices, guarantee liberty. "Self-government does not consist in having a hand in everything," and the people should allow a great deal of discretion in administration. After all, Wilson insisted, "large powers and unhampered discretion seem to me the indispensable conditions of responsibility."[39] Moreover, the public need not fear "the creation of a domineering, illiberal officialism:" Civil servants will be "sensitive to public opinion," "thoroughly trained," with "steady, hearty allegiance to the policy of the government they serve."[40] Wilson concluded that the politics-administration distinction makes borrowing the foreign science of administration from continental Europe "safe" for the Anglo-American world.[41] In other words, the U.S. and Britain can adopt administrative methods from illiberal regimes and retain their liberal principles.

The vague, often contradictory nature of Wilson's essay made him somewhat reluctant to publish it, but President Wilson acted on the basis of the politics-administration distinction years later. Racial segregation among public employees, for example, was intended to enhance administrative efficiency, or so Wilson argued. As he explained, "[S]egregation of the colored employees in the several [federal] departments was begun . . . with the idea that the friction, or rather the discontent and uneasiness, which has prevailed in many of the departments would thereby be removed."[42] If racial segregation could keep "politics" out of administration, Wilson was prepared to adopt and endorse this distinctly illiberal practice.

In other respects, Wilson's attempts to implement his ideas on administration produced a valuable legacy, especially in the area of public budgeting. Wilson believed the executive should formulate the federal budget using business principles as a guide: After the legislature approved the budget, the executive would implement it with the aid of career professionals trained in business practices. To achieve such a system, Wilson promoted several specific measures.[43]

Some measures were designed to increase efficiency and economy in government generally. The Federal Reserve Act of 1913 created a system by which the federal government could make monetary policy by acting through a semi-independent board to affect interest rates and determine the money supply. The Underwood bill combined with the Sixteenth Amendment shifted taxation from tariffs to income tax. (Wilson believed tariffs were neither efficient nor economic, whereas the income tax would democratize the structure and, he hoped, provide sufficient revenue.) Finally and most significant, Wilson encouraged and facilitated fundamental change in the executive budget process.

President Wilson quickly endorsed the changes proposed by the Commission on Economy and Efficiency in 1910, which would have created a national budget system. Unfortunately, several factors obstructed his ability to implement the commission's recommendations. First, World War I placed increasing demands on his time and attention. Later, Wilson vetoed the bill he generally wanted because the legislation would have prevented the president from removing the comptroller general, and Wilson believed it infringed on presidential prerogatives (shades of Jackson and Cleveland). Yet when the bill passed again, Wilson's successor, President Warren Harding, signed it. The legislation created the Bureau of the Budget (BOB, later the Office of Management and Budget, or OMB), an organization staffed by career professionals (who were also financial experts) and designed to assist the chief executive in preparing budgets and submitting them to Congress. Despite the delayed passage, the Budget and Accounting Act of 1921 was largely the result of Wilson's efforts and an attempt to institutionalize his ideas. His administrative reforms in general and the creation of BOB in particular were designed to strengthen the executive, increase efficiency, and facilitate economic management untainted by politics.

Wilson created the "institutionalized presidency," but subsequent developments fell short of achieving his goals and called into question his reasoning. For decades, the limits of Wilson's politics-administration distinction have preoccupied students and practitioners of public administration. Most of them agree that civil servants usually fail to fulfill Wilson's high (and naive) expectations, although different explanations for this have been proposed. Critics point out that civil servants maintain their own agendas, develop relationships with organized interests, prove to be "representative" (thereby reflecting the diversity of the public), and/or fall victim to organizational pathologies such as inertia and insularity. Whatever the cause, the bureaucracy that Wilson helped to create quickly came to constrain executive leadership.

As the institutionalized presidency and the executive branch continued to expand, the administrative state increasingly restricted presidential power. At the same time, the general public perceived the growing bureaucracy as an obstruction to its will and as inefficient and costly. Wilson failed to anticipate that the state he envisioned would frustrate presidential leadership and alienate the public. He certainly never imagined that another conviction politician in the presidency would attempt to politicize administration in order to achieve what Wilson sought by separating politics and administration: decisive executive leadership, increased efficiency, and greater economy in government.

When Ronald Reagan inherited Wilson's legacy of political and administrative reforms, he put the political to maximum use, while he reversed the administrative trend Wilson had established. Reagan's presidency was quintessentially rhetorical: The Great Communicator excelled at "going public" and preferred to lead by plebiscite, even though he also employed traditional tools of bargaining.[44] In addition, Reagan attempted to fortify Wilson's presidency-centered system by proposing constitutional changes that would strengthen the executive while ostensibly increasing presidential responsibility and democratic accountability. To combat the influence of interest groups and secure greater economy in public spending, Reagan promoted the line item veto. To allow the public to choose freely in presidential elections and hold accountable the president, Reagan campaigned to abolish the two-term limit on the executive. When he took extraordinary steps to influence the federal judiciary by screening applicants and employing an ideological litmus test, he mustered democratic arguments to justify his strategies. According to Reagan, liberal jurists were out of touch with public sentiment and rendered decisions that served to thwart the popular will. Notwithstanding these bold attempts to expand his influence and augment his authority, Reagan achieved his greatest institutional innovations in the area of administration.

Reagan brought about fundamental change when he politicized administration and centralized the institutional presidency in the White House. Other modern presidents had attempted to achieve greater influence in commanding the bureaucracy, but their efforts always proved unsuccessful. To a great extent, Reagan's predecessors sought to enhance expertise and efficiency, while essentially maintaining the politics-administration distinction.[45] Moreover, they lacked Reagan's ideological fervor and firm convictions: Even if they had wanted to shape administration in their own image, the result would have reflected their pragmatic concerns and partisan preoccupations as much as their policy preferences. The source of change in the Reagan years was not systemic; nor did change flow from historical inevitability.[46] Conviction-style leadership provided the critical causal variable.

Reagan's ideological commitments and clear agenda enabled him to shape administration in ways that would serve his ultimate goals, while he also publicly justified his strategies by supplying rationales for the changes he pursued. From his earliest speeches for General Electric throughout his presidential addresses, Reagan bashed bureaucrats for their incompetence and their extravagance. By the time he campaigned for the presidency, his rhetoric resonated with a public increasingly alert to the "waste, fraud, and abuse" in government and dissatisfied with the lavish spending habits and inefficiency of the welfare state. While he leveled his attacks on the bureaucracy, he also drew a link between its shortcomings and the need to preserve individual liberty: Reversing Wilson's logic, Reagan portrayed the modern state as leviathan. As he politicized the administrative state and deinstitutionalized (by centralizing) the "institutional presidency," Reagan took care to tap democratic aspirations and cultivate public sentiment.

To achieve his administrative goals, Reagan relied primarily on his presidential appointment and removal powers. As members of his transition team carefully screened applicants, they employed loyalty and ideology as the central criteria for selection. Moreover, Reagan extended his influence further into the bureaucracy than his predecessors had attempted to do: The Reagan team paid special attention to appointments at the subcabinet and junior levels.[47] To ensure that they would not be "captured" by their departments or agencies, new appointees underwent a period of socialization or indoctrination conducted by Reagan aides in the White House, not by agency officials. Reagan also replaced careerists with loyalists in the Senior Executive Service. In this regard, he took advantage of the Civil Service Reform Act of 1978, which made 10 percent of the positions open to political appointees. (Reagan interpreted this to mean 10 percent of the positions allocated, not filled.) He further politicized administration when he appointed a staunch conservative, Donald Devine, as director of the Office of Personnel Management (OPM). (Devine cut the number of career officials by 18 percent and increased the number of political appointees by 169 percent.) Finally, by eliminating programs and shifting priorities, Reagan created additional changes in personnel that facilitated the implementation of his agenda.[48]

In the process of evaluating programs and setting priorities, the Office of Management and Budget played a new, central role. During the Reagan presidency, OMB became a central clearinghouse for government programs; budget authority shifted dramatically from the departments and agencies to OMB and the White House. At the same time, OMB and its director, David Stockman, assumed a lobbying function. Stockman and his assistants attended White House meetings as well as Congressional hearings. Whereas BOB was designed to strengthen the executive by providing financial expertise alone, Reagan's OMB director proved to be both a financial wizard and a skillful political strategist.

OMB director Stockman played a critical role in regulatory reform as he did in the budget process. (In fact, through budget cuts, Stockman managed to eliminate many regulations.) On February 17, 1981, Reagan issued Executive Order 12291, which gave OMB extensive powers of intervention and review. Reagan demonstrated his determination to deregulate when he vested clearance powers in a single unit, empowered OMB to develop uniform standards, and subjected regulations to strict quantitative, cost-benefit analysis.[49] As Reagan shifted regulatory authority from executive agencies to OMB and the White House, he benefited from the ideological screening during the appointment process.[50] By the end of Reagan's first year, most government agencies were issuing fewer regulations. Throughout the process of deregulation (and budgeting in general), OMB director Stockman worked closely with White House personnel. Reagan achieved his goals not only by politicizing administration but also by centralizing operations in the White House.

Within the White House, Reagan designed a unique staffing arrangement for his first administration. A group of three advisors—known as the "troika"—provided the core of the White House structure: White House "counsellor" Edwin Meese, Chief of Staff James Baker, and Deputy Chief of Staff Michael Deaver. In general, Meese oversaw the design and coordination of policy; Baker took charge of political strategies; and Deaver guarded the president's time and his image. At least initially, most of the policy making took place in the cabinet and in working subgroups known as cabinet councils, a management technique Meese brought into the Reagan White House from California. Organized around specific policy areas, the cabinet councils linked the White House, the Executive Office, and the cabinet (including agencies and departments). Richard Darman, Baker's aide, also headed an unofficial command center at the White House known as the Legislative Strategy Group (LSG). In sum, Meese and the cabinet councils recommended policies, while Deaver, Baker, and Darman promoted them. The troika provided an arrangement that generally worked well for Reagan in his first term, although many observers at the time perceived the structure as a setting conducive to conflict.

One central source of conflict stemmed from the fact that White House staff appeared to exert greater influence than cabinet secretaries did. When Treasury Secretary Donald Regan described conflict in Reagan's first administration, he emphasized the power struggle that occurred between the White House and the cabinet. According to Regan, "[If you were from the White House,] you'd let the cabinet members talk, and you'd get your own shot later. As soon as the meeting would end, you'd run to the president and tell him why he should not do what his secretary advised. We called them the backbenchers. They were there because it was the place where policies were discussed and settled. So everyone wanted to sit in on the meetings. And I mean everyone—the White House staff, their assistants, everyone."[51] When asked if cabinet members resented his participation in the meetings, Baker responded angrily, "I don't care if [they] resented it or not. You can't divide policy from political considerations. It was an agreement I made with the president when I became chief of staff—that I could attend all meetings."[52] To a great extent, what the press perceived as a tug-of-war between "pragmatists" and "ideologues" more often reflected institutional conflict between the White House and the cabinet, and in cases of conflict, the White House usually won.

Personal factors provided yet another source of conflict. Most people interviewed for this study emphasized the ways personality conflicts obstructed efficient administration in the White House and throughout the executive branch, but such disputes certainly fail to constitute a unique feature of the Reagan presidency. A different kind of personal factor was peculiar to the Reagan administration, however. Advisors held widely divergent views of the president's abilities, and their opinions of the chief divided them on strategy—whether to manage the president with a heavy hand or "let Reagan be Reagan."[53]

More significant, debate concerning the administration's priorities—especially the economy versus national security—created conflict within the White House. While Baker downplayed the perceived conflicts among members of the troika, he emphasized, "[T]he real difficulties were with [National Security Advisor William] 'Judge' Clark. He and Casey were trying to run an independent operation. We tried to prevent them from meeting alone with Reagan. They played to his dark side. Most of the conflicts [in the White House] were with the national security advisor."[54] "My view was to focus 100 percent on the economy," Baker reiterated in a second interview. "Central America was a distraction."[55] Asked about the administration's priorities, Meese recalled, "People in the White House were queasy about Central America. They were afraid it would make him seem too warlike. It was always a number-two topic, second to the tax cut or something."[56] Despite "problems on the national security front," Baker emphasized, "[w]e had control of the legislative agenda. The LSG had control. And we had control of the bully pulpit."[57] Of course, the president also considered economic recovery his top priority, and throughout his first term, Reagan consistently used his own bully pulpit to focus public attention on his economic agenda.

Chief of Staff Baker emphasized the different tasks of policy makers and political aides that fueled tension within the Reagan administration. According to Baker, the nature of the political process gave political aides the advantage. As he explained:

The Legislative Strategy Group won out [over the cabinet] because of the process of implementation of policy. When you involve Congress, it requires give-and-take, and negotiation. The policy could be delivered to the Hill, but you still need to accommodate. Our argument was that the policy side didn't have a realistic view of politics. If success means that you have to shave 20 percent off the policies, that's what Reagan wanted. The political side of the White House had all the levers. The policy side had their seminars, but when policy would touch Congress, it needed to go through the Legislative Strategy Group.[58]

Despite some tension between policy advisors and political aides, Baker insisted that the media misread and magnified the conflict in their reports because "[i]t was easy for the press to understand and depict the ideologues versus the pragmatists."[59] Although they considered these press reports inaccurate and exaggerated, news managers in the White House found no reason to discourage reporters from telling tales of rivalry between ideologues and pragmatists.

Conflict within an administration can often damage the president's reputation, making the chief executive seem weak and indecisive, but Reagan's conviction-style leadership seemed to shield his image. Loyal and ideologically committed appointees never questioned Reagan's direction or commitment. Moreover, members of the press corps (and the public) rarely expressed doubts about where Reagan stood. Ironically, the media's depiction of conflict within the Reagan administration actually worked to the benefit of the president (while it also enhanced the reputation of some staff). Strange as it might seem, the Reagan White House showed that even "bad news" about internal strife could be spun to serve the goals of the administration.

When Reagan did compromise, the press often interpreted the deal as a product of Baker's influence. As a result, Reagan usually maintained his image as a man of conviction, while the press would depict him as a hapless, ill-informed president, duped by his strategists into making concessions. Yet Baker was not with Reagan in California when the governor proved willing to compromise in order to achieve his central objectives. The perceived influence of the so-called pragmatists in the White House concealed Reagan's own political instincts. Like Thatcher's "wets," Reagan's pragmatists brought him closer to achieving his ultimate goals without revealing the leader's own willingness to compromise.[60]

White House political strategists performed another role that resembled the function of moderates in Thatcher's first cabinet. Members of Congress proved eager to work with Baker, Darman, and the LSG staff because they viewed these White House aides as more reasonable than many of Reagan's policy advisors. Few understood that "Reagan was results oriented more than an ideologue," according to Baker, "but his ideological rhetoric served his purpose in negotiations."[61] Members of Congress considered Baker and Darman allies in their struggle to strike a deal, and just as significant, Reagan's rivals perceived any concession as victory, given the president's apparently rigid adherence to conviction.

Finally, conflict in the White House during Reagan's first term provided another benefit: It ensured a degree of debate and the circulation of different ideas. Substantial policy disagreement existed even among the so-called ideologues: between supply-siders, monetarists, and traditional Republican budget balancers, and sometimes within these camps.[62] Rather than resolve conflict among his economic advisors, Reagan often embraced the theoretical contradictions in his collection of convictions. As a result, economic policy often lacked coherence, but the diversity of views expressed guaranteed that no single ideological camp could pursue its beliefs unchecked and unrestrained by countervailing forces.

The problems of centralization in the White House became apparent only in Reagan's second term, when little internal conflict took place. After 1984, Reagan adopted a hierarchical system of staffing with a chief of staff, Don Regan, who became known as the "prime minister." Information was funneled and filtered through Regan; no longer were aides running to the president to rat on their rivals. Furthermore, Iran-Contra showed how a single group of ideologically committed aides could construct and carry out a scheme unchecked by adversaries within the administration and undaunted by constitutional constraints. Indeed, the Iran-Contra affair demonstrates many of the dangers of centralization in the White House: Aides suffered from groupthink and bolstering, personalities became more significant than procedures, expertise was lacking, and corruption followed. Centralization of administration in the White House proved dangerous only when staffing within the White House was also centralized. Then the fears that Wilson tried to dispel—of concentrated power and the subsequent threat to constitutional principles—became reality.

Ultimately, Reagan brought about two fundamental institutional changes in the area of administration. Wilson had shifted responsibility for administration from the legislative to the executive branch, but Reagan concentrated the authority of the executive branch within the White House. Just as significant, Reagan politicized administration, largely by placing loyal and ideologically committed appointees throughout the federal bureaucracy. Of course, several aspects of the environment facilitated Reagan's ability to achieve his administrative goals. His predecessors' efforts to expand their influence with the bureaucracy made Reagan's attempts appear to be the continuation of a trend rather than bold innovations. Moreover, growing public sentiment in favor of more limited government and opposed to government waste provided a favorable climate of expectations. In addition, calls to roll back the state coincided with cries for stronger executive leadership in the aftermath of the failed presidencies of Gerald Ford and Jimmy Carter. Yet it was Reagan who seized the opportunities of the moment, provided rationales for the changes he pursued, and possessed the determination to articulate and promote clear objectives.

The changes Reagan brought about were conducive to conviction politics, and for other presidents to benefit from his innovations, they must practice conviction-style leadership. When President William Clinton formed his administration, his transition team made special efforts to appoint "Friends of Bill," and the president promised the country that he would choose an administration that "looked like America." To achieve Reagan's degree of success, chief executives need to employ ideological or policy-oriented criteria. The presidency today possesses much greater capacity to command the state, but presidents must know what they wish to command and possess the determination to carry it out.

Differences between the structures of government and the constitutions of the U.S. and the U.K. ensured their paths of political development would also differ. While authority in the U.S. shifted from Congress to the presidency, in Britain it moved from Parliament to party and then from cabinet to the office of prime minister. Nevertheless, the blueprints for developments in both nations reveal a common design that linked the expansion of executive authority to the process of democratization and led to the creation of conditions more conducive to conviction politics.

Great Britain

Sir Robert Peel took a critical step in the evolution of modern British institutions when he delivered the first nationally publicized party manifesto in 1835. The substance of his message reflected his belief that preservation of the constitution would sometimes require modifications to it. To protect "ancient rights" (and ward off radical challenges to constitutional principles), Peel believed he and his party needed to embrace moderate reform. At the same time, Peel used the manifesto as a tool designed to craft a modern party that could advance his ideological goals. In the manifesto, Peel rendered an appeal to the new middle-class voters whose views and values he largely shared. He expected the manifesto to provide the foundation for a broad-based national party that would lead to stronger government. According to

Peel's plan, party government would replace the loose configurations of factions that had characterized the prereform Parliament and presented obstacles to strong, effective leadership.[63]

Before the 1832 reform bill, prime ministers and their governments proved constrained by the need to build support among factions for their legislative initiatives. The first sign of modern parties appeared when factions aligned themselves for or against the reform bill. Once Peel brought his party over to the side of reform, he ran the risk that Parliamentary affairs would return to factional politics, and he had no intention of laboring under those constraints as prime minister. "If I do accept office," Peel warned, "it shall be by no unnatural and factious combinations with men."[64] When he designed and publicized the Tamworth Manifesto, Peel hoped to create conditions more conducive to strong, conviction-style leadership.

Parliamentary candidates had delivered similar addresses to their constituents, but Peel was clearly attempting to affect national opinion, not influence voters in his own constituency.[65] To reach a national audience, he used the London press, and his supporters in the press praised the democratic nature of Peel's move as they publicized it. The *Evening Standard* described the Tamworth Manifesto as the "first instance of a minister throwing himself upon the judgment of the public; the first formal acknowledgement that the people, in their collective body, have a right to know before hand, minutely and circumstantially, the principles upon which the government is to be carried on."[66] In substance as well as style, the appeal of the Tamworth Manifesto appeared democratic as Peel paid "the first homage offered to the popular principle of the Reform Bill," according to the *Standard.*

At the start of the manifesto, Peel declared that the reform bill had settled a great constitutional question, and he announced his intention to adhere to its measures and interpret its "spirit," but Peel did not design the manifesto primarily as a forum to articulate his party's new position. In fact Peel wrote to John Wilson Croker (who reviewed the manifesto in the *Quarterly Review*) that Croker had ascribed the address too much to the necessities imposed by the Reform Act. Instead, Peel insisted, "the necessities rather arose from the abruptness of the change in government, and to say the truth, from the policy of aiding our friends at the elections."[67] The Tamworth Manifesto did provide the basis for countless conservative campaign speeches,[68] and throughout the 1830s, Peel along with other Conservatives repeated the manifesto pledge to pursue moderate reform.

When he formed his government in 1841, Peel expected to escape the constraints created by "unnatural alliances" and, instead, lead the type of party Edmund Burke described as "a body of men united by principle." On the other hand, to bring together numerous factions under the umbrella of the Conservative party, Peel had tried to conciliate the neutrals, attract moderates, and avoid offending the ultras. As a result, he acknowledged the principles he articulated in the Tamworth Manifesto were "necessarily vague."[69] As early as 1835, Peel might have foreseen the clash between party and principle that would come in 1846. The Tamworth Manifesto (like most of its successors) proved too vague to unify the parliamentary party, and it certainly failed to facilitate conviction politics.

To reconcile the demands of party building with the practice of principled politics, Peel simultaneously pursued another goal: He wanted to create a party that would share his enthusiasm for the liberal ideas that prevailed among the new middle class. At the time of the Tamworth Manifesto, disagreements had begun to rage within the party about its future direction. Although all sides acknowledged the party would need to expand its base beyond the aristocracy, many traditional Tories took the paternalistic position of advocating an alliance with the working class against the new industrial interests. To Peel, that was impractical—the working class did not have the vote—and, just as significant, Peel endorsed the liberal views and values of the middle class. His strategic goal of attracting the middle class to his party conveniently coincided with his ideological goal of trying to change the party's orthodoxy. It is no accident that the party's label changed from Tory to Conservative under Peel's leadership, although the Peelites would eventually leave and form the basis for the Liberal party, a place where they could remain true to their name.

Peel declined to engage in attempts to build a party organization, although his party established its first election fund in 1835, and he served as one of its trustees. After the Conservatives split, only Peelite candidates received party funds in the 1847 general election. The only organizational initiative adopted was one that identified the party with Peel personally, and it followed him when he left.

Despite the party's fate and the Tamworth Manifesto's limitations, Peel did manage to create the first broad-based national party, and his success in this effort created a second significant institutional change. When Peel became prime minister in 1841, he established the principle that the crown must appoint the person who commands a majority in the House of Commons. Thereafter, the prime minister was accountable to the Commons, not to the Crown. That institutional development certainly increased Peel's influence and enhanced his ability to shape national debate, while it also fundamentally altered the place of the premier in the British political system.

Of course, Peel discovered that he had replaced one context of constraints with another as factional politics moved from Parliament to party. When he declared a precise position on a matter of high principle, his party split. In the case of the Corn Laws, Peel rallied a body of men united on principle only by crossing party lines. As explained in chapter 6, William Gladstone's party-building efforts far exceeded those of Peel, and Gladstone encountered even greater constraints with more dire consequences for the practice of conviction politics. Unlike Peel, Gladstone failed to achieve his major policy objective, while he also declined to challenge the integrity or legitimacy of British political institutions in the Victorian age.

Where Gladstone did score substantial success was in the area of state building. In the 1850s Gladstone actively promoted civil service reform. He initiated and then endorsed the Northcote-Trevelyan report, which documented abuses in the civil service and recommended open competition and examinations, merit-based promotions, and a two-tier service that distinguished between mechanical and intellectual positions. Although the proposed reforms won the support of the Peelites, the proposals encountered fierce opposition from the Whigs, who dominated the cabinet and made up the majority of the parliamentary party. As he promoted civil service reform, Gladstone's reasoning foreshadowed Wilson's logic: Gladstone hoped to create a corps of enlightened, well-educated civil servants, and he linked civil service reform to his campaign to open up the universities.[70] In contrast to Wilson, however, Gladstone emphasized the need for education in the classics rather than professional training in public administration. (Their distinct intellectual legacies help to explain the different character and background of civil servants in the two countries even today.) Later, in his first and most productive government, from 1868 to 1874, Gladstone proved able to enact many of the Northcote-Trevelyan reforms without legislation.

When Prime Minister Gladstone invited his cabinet ministers to choose open competition, all ministries except the Foreign Service did so.[71] At Gladstone's urgent and emphatic request, in 1870 the queen issued an Order in Council that abolished patronage and made competitive examinations compulsory. Finally, a two-grade system was introduced, which would continue to characterize the British civil service in the twentieth century. The achievements of Gladstone's first government firmly established the foundations for the modern British state, and the ramifications extended across the Atlantic when the Northcote-Trevelyan reforms inspired the Pendleton Act of 1883.

In the political arena, Gladstone's major innovation proved more controversial and ultimately less effective than his state-building efforts. Acting on his own, in 1879 Gladstone initiated an oratorical campaign in what would become his constituency of Midlothian. Instead of attending the usual events organized by party managers, Gladstone went directly to the people, speaking to groups of farmers and shopkeepers assembled in marketplaces and city halls. He spoke on a wide range of domestic and foreign policy issues, and for the first time in British history, during parliamentary recess a British party leader (albeit unofficial) urged the public to oust the sitting government.

Before Gladstone embarked on the Midlothian campaign, he wrote to the 2nd Earl Granville and explained his objective: "It seems to me good policy to join on the proceedings of 1876–9 by a continuous process to the Dissolution. Should this happen, which I think likely enough, about March, there will have been no opportunity immediately before it of *stirring the country.* I will not say our defeat in 1874 was owing to the want of such an opportunity, but it was certainly I think much aggravated by that want" (emphasis added).[72] Gladstone knew his oratory would prove more effective in "stirring the country" than any written statements, however widely publicized. He hoped his declarations at Midlothian would put his party in power, but he also wanted his words to shape national sentiment. In addition, he undoubtedly expected the campaign to boost his personal popularity in the country and thereby increase his political influence in Parliament and within his party.

As explained in chapter 7, the press reports attest to Gladstone's success with the public. The *Times* quickly acknowledged, "If Mr. Gladstone needed inspiration, it must have been afforded by the eager audiences and crowds which have surrounded him,"[73] and later the paper remarked that "Englishmen and Scotchmen can appreciate such a display of endurance and energy."[74] Yet press reports also leveled harsh criticisms that echoed the views of many members of the political elite.

While popular with the public, Gladstone's approach ignited fiery comments from his critics. "It must on the whole be said that the character of the demagogue has preponderate over that of the statesman," the *Times* concluded.[75] A few days later, the paper mocked: "[Gladstone] asks whether 'it is in the Design of Providence that, besides the concerns of a vast Empire, over which this little island rules, we should be meddling in the business of every portion of the globe.' The designs of Providence must be left to Mr. Gladstone's own discussion. Other people do not presume to be so familiar with them."[76] Provoked by Gladstone's persistent assault on "Beaconsfieldism" during the campaign, the Earl of Beaconsfield delivered the most devastating depiction of the unofficial Liberal leader. According to Disraeli, at Midlothian Gladstone showed he was "a sophistical rhetoritician inebriated by the exuberance of his own verbosity, and gifted with an egotistical imagination that can at all times command an interminable and inconsistent series of arguments to malign an opponent and to glorify himself."[77] Unfortunately for Gladstone, the press and the opposition were not his only critics.

Gladstone's oratorical campaign created almost as much controversy within the ranks of the Liberal party. The Whigs opposed his approach: They considered Gladstone's campaign unseemly and demagogic, and most

Whigs believed the sitting government should be granted wide discretion on matters of foreign policy. At the same time, Granville and Hartington argued with Gladstone on several points of substance.[78] Clearly no consensus existed within the party on the wide range of domestic and foreign policy issues Gladstone addressed, and conditions did not permit his convictions to fill the void. To members of the public, Gladstone might have been "saluted as the embodiment of Liberalism,"[79] but many Liberals took a different view.

Following the Liberal victory in 1880, Gladstone's enhanced popularity in the country ensured his selection as prime minister, but his oratorical campaigns failed to produce all the benefits he hoped for. In particular, the views Gladstone espoused had not won the support of other Liberals. (A party manifesto might be "necessarily vague," but it is more likely to prove binding than a leader's independent declarations.) Lacking agreement on important policies and having no clear direction, Gladstone's second government was marred by factional conflict and divided loyalties.

Moreover, in the case of the Midlothian campaign and later during his attempts to shape public opinion on home rule, Gladstone practiced plebiscitary leadership without defending it or providing a rationale. To Granville, Gladstone had insisted that he intended to assist his party, not circumvent it. As Cleveland managed to do with his tariff message, Gladstone in his Midlothian campaign addressed ordinary citizens and developed a new vehicle to persuade them, but his ability to set the agenda proved short-lived. Like Cleveland, Gladstone left in place the structures that obstructed his ability to translate popular support into political influence. When home rule met defeat for the fourth time, Gladstone complied with the demands of his cabinet colleagues, who urged him to refrain from another public campaign in which he planned to challenge the legitimacy of the Lords. In doing so, Gladstone left the essential tasks of institutional reform to his successor, David Lloyd George.

Nevertheless, in one respect, Lloyd George owed a great debt to Gladstone: Lloyd George promoted his most significant institutional change while he served as chancellor of the exchequer. By making the budget an essential instrument of public policy, Gladstone had transformed the position of chancellor, and it would maintain its tremendous power and prestige at least until Thatcher's governments. (Her chancellor, Nigel Lawson, greatly admired Gladstone and no doubt longed for the days when the chancellor's authority in economic policy was unrivaled and unchallenged.)[80] As chancellor, Lloyd George designed the famous People's Budget of 1909, which raised revenue by leveling substantial taxes on the land. To combat opposition, Lloyd George took his case to the people, and when the popular plan faced defeat in the House of Lords, he welcomed the opportunity to change that institution. As Lloyd George took each step—from promoting the budget to campaigning against the House of Lords—he carefully crafted his message in a way that was guaranteed to tap popular aspirations and build support for his goals.

During his campaign on behalf of the budget, Lloyd George rendered one of the most memorable and dramatic performances of his career. Speaking at Limehouse in the summer of 1909, he documented the abuses of specific landlords and pleased the crowd when he exclaimed, "Oh, these dukes, how they harass us!"[81] Throughout his stirring speech, Lloyd George defended the central features of the budget, while he also stressed its social purpose. He explained in his conclusion:

> We are placing burdens on the broadest shoulders. Why should I put burdens on the people? I am one of the children of the people. I was brought up amongst them. I know their trials; and God forbid that I should add one grain of trouble to the anxieties which they bear with such patience and fortitude. When the Prime Minister did me the honour of inviting me to take charge of the National Exchequer at the time of great difficulty, I made up my mind, in framing the Budget which was in front of me, that at any rate no cupboard should be barer, no lot should be harder. By that test, I challenge you to judge the Budget.[82]

Clearly Lloyd George hoped the People's Budget would firmly establish his reputation as a man of the people as well as one of its children.

Shortly after he delivered his Limehouse speech, Lloyd George expressed satisfaction with the effect he was having on public opinion, and his success seemed to boost both his courage and his ambition. In August he wrote to his brother: "[There are] startling accounts of the changes effected by the Budget in public opinion. There is undoubtedly a popular rising such as has not been witnessed over a generation. What will happen if [the Lords] throw it out I can conjecture and I rejoice in the prospect. Many a rotten institution, system and law will be submerged by the deluge."[83] Critical comment came from much of the press and the official opposition in the House of Commons, but as Lloyd George predicted, the fatal blow to the budget was delivered not by the opposition leader, Arthur Balfour, but by "Mr. Balfour's poodle," the House of Lords.[84]

When the Lords defeated the budget by a vote of 350 to 75 on November 30, Lloyd George's attack on the landlords exploded into a battle with the landed Lords. Since 1671 Britain had been governed by an unwritten rule that denied the Lords power to veto any money bill, but the peers asserted the 1909 budget constituted a scheme to spark a social revolution.

Lloyd George had not necessarily set out to provoke the wrath of the House of Lords,[85] but when the Lords' call for an election came, he seized the opportunity to turn it into a referendum on their institutional authority. During the campaign, Lloyd George warned:

> Let [the Lords] realize what they are doing. They are forcing a Revolution. The Peers may decree a Revolution, but the People will direct it. If they begin, issues will be raised that they little dream of. Questions will be asked which are now whispered in humble voice, and answers will be demanded with authority. It will be asked why five hundred ordinary men, chosen accidentally from among the unemployed, should override the judgment—the deliberate judgment—of millions of people who are engaged in the industry which makes the wealth of the country. It will be asked who ordained a few should have the land of Britain as a perquisite? Who made ten thousand people owners of the soil, and the rest of us trespassers in the land of our birth? Where did that Table of the Law come from? Whose finger inscribed it?[86]

The Liberals narrowly defeated the Conservatives (by two seats) in the January 1910 general election.[87] To Lloyd George and the Liberals, the result rendered victory on the budget and a mandate for parliamentary reform.

Following the election, the Lords passed the budget, but they resisted any reform to limit their veto power. After a constitutional conference failed to reach agreement and another election took place,[88] Prime Minister Asquith managed to convince King George V to threaten the Tory Lords by creating a flood of new Liberal peers. After the bill passed the House of Commons, the *Times* described the reform as "the most revolutionary measure submitted to Parliament for hundreds of years." According to the paper, "The majority of this House of Commons has sanctioned a scheme of Single-Chamber Government for the land whose two-Chamber Constitution has been the admiration and the model of free peoples of the world."[89] The *Times* opposed the reform, but the paper urged the Lords to pass the bill rather than face the creation of new peers.[90] Finally, the Lords passed the Parliament Act of 1911 by a vote of 131 to 114. The act deprived the House of Lords of their absolute veto;[91] they could delay but no longer obstruct home rule. Gladstone's ideological goal would be achieved only by first securing the structural reform he had been prevented from pursuing.

When Lloyd George first proposed his budget and later campaigned for parliamentary reform, conditions conducive to change were already under way. As in the U.S., reform movements—including the suffragettes and labor—critiqued nineteenth-century notions of representation, while they also challenged the authority and legitimacy of both political institutions and economic arrangements. As Lloyd George declared his convictions and campaigned to carry them out, he could capitalize on the opportunities created by the reform impulse. Later when he became prime minister, he shifted his rationale for pursuing change from the process of democratization to the defense of democracy itself: To win the war, he needed to concentrate power and take bold steps to circumvent institutional constraints.

When he became prime minister in 1916, Lloyd George immediately demonstrated that he preferred to rely on his own associates rather than the formal government apparatus, and the new war cabinet gave him unprecedented authority in decision making. In contrast to his predecessor, who presided over both a War Committee of seven and a cabinet of twenty-three ministers, Lloyd George created one body of five ministers (and only the chancellor ran a department). The smaller size of the war cabinet facilitated Lloyd George's ability to persuade his colleagues, but the new prime minister wanted more than enhanced influence.

Lloyd George also wanted to control the agenda, and a second step helped him to define the scope and limits of cabinet discussions: Lloyd George formalized the Cabinet Secretariat. The secretariat originated with the Committee of Imperial Defense in 1902, but since 1914 it had been attached to the War Committee. In 1916, for the first time, it was institutionalized, under the direction of Sir Maurice Hankey. Hankey and his assistants prepared cabinet agendas, recorded the minutes of meetings, circulated cabinet decisions to the departments for action, arranged for ministers and advisors outside the war cabinet to attend meetings on certain issues, and distributed memoranda from the departments. (Previously British cabinets had functioned without even the aid of minutes.) An institutional innovation designed to link the war cabinet and the departments quickly became a vehicle that greatly enhanced the prime minister's power. Lloyd George personally approved all items on the agenda before the secretariat submitted it to the cabinet.

Obstacles imposed by the bureaucracy had frustrated Lloyd George at the War Office, and he was determined to circumvent Whitehall once he became prime minister. He relied on his own "personal secretariat," which came to be called (derisively) his "garden suburb" because his advisors worked out of huts in the garden on Downing Street. These private advisors provided "a little body of illuminati," according to H. W. Massingham,[92] and essentially served as "an administrative intelligence department for Lloyd George."[93] In addition to producing policy papers, members of the garden suburb maintained contact between the prime minister and the departments of government. (Usually, communication traveled from the top down.) Lloyd George's personal secretariat constitutes the earliest attempt to strengthen the prime minister's hold on central government. As the premier's personal policy-making body, the personal secretariat acquired the reputation of a "kitchen cabinet," although the scope and nature of its policy-making authority far exceeded the advisory capacity of President Jackson's original kitchen cabinet.

Lloyd George's contemporaries and later historians believed his administrative practices signaled significant, fundamental change in the politics and constitution of Britain. "Critics and admirers alike saw in the concatenation of a national crisis and an unorthodox premier the origins of a revolution in government," one historian has recalled, concluding, "Cabinet government gave way to prime ministerial rule; Parliament's role diminished, never to recover; even political parties lost their centrality."[94] Lloyd George's institutional innovations created an office that was "certainly" and "distinctly" presidential.[95] He managed to alter the place and the perception of the prime minister—at least temporarily.

War conditions invited Lloyd George to innovate and buttressed his authoritative position, but after the war his control of the government (and the strength of his leadership) greatly diminished. His successors would search to find new ways to command the cabinet and the state in times of peace. As the size and the scope of the state continued to expand throughout the twentieth century, British prime ministers started to rely more heavily on the resources concentrated within Number 10 Downing Street and less on the formal structures of cabinet and Whitehall. (In this regard, the trend bears a striking resemblance to developments in the U.S., where authority shifted to the White House.) Not until Margaret Thatcher, however, did a peacetime prime minister seek to substitute her own arrangements for those prescribed by the constitution.

Thatcher proved determined to transform the traditional structures of the British government and the state into an arena more conducive to conviction politics. When she held cabinet meetings, several factors—especially her leadership style—enabled her to direct and dominate the discussion. Just as significant, she sought to circumvent the cabinet by shifting decision-making authority to Number 10 Downing Street. Ultimately, the influence and authority of her private advisors challenged and superseded the role of cabinet ministers. At the same time, Thatcher's zeal for structural reform extended beyond the cabinet to Whitehall. She considered the civil service yet another consensus institution in dire need of reform. Like other successful conviction-style leaders, Thatcher took care to link her pursuit of institutional change to popular demands and democratic aspirations.

Thatcher provided several rationales to justify her assault on traditional institutions and the state. In an argument designed to advance her neoliberal ideology, she insisted that the modern welfare state served to thwart individual initiative and obscure responsibility. More often, she leveled her criticisms at the cost and inefficiency of the state, offering arguments that clearly resonated with a public that had endured the winter of discontent. The severe disruption of services in 1979 lowered the public's opinion of the civil service and intensified its call for strong leadership, producing a climate of expectations conducive to the types of change that Thatcher wanted to pursue. Finally, she attacked the structures of the state and government that she believed obstructed the public will. To articulate and implement the "public good," Thatcher insisted she must dismantle an edifice that supported only consensus and, instead, construct a "conviction government."

Before Thatcher took office, she revealed her radical intentions to a newspaper reporter. "When the time comes to form a real Cabinet, I do think I've got to have a Cabinet with equal unity of purpose and a sense of dedication to it," she declared. She explained, "It must be a Cabinet that works on something much more than pragmatism or consensus. It must be a 'conviction' Government. . . . We've got to go in an agreed and clear direction. As Prime Minister I couldn't waste time having any internal arguments."[96] Despite her determination to lead a conviction government, Prime Minister Thatcher soon discovered that she would need to include in her first cabinet many members of her party who reflected diverse interests and conflicting views.

Among her first group of ministers, friends and foes alike expected that "unity of purpose" would emerge from the traditional way the cabinet functions as a consensus-building institution.[97] "Cabinet government is about trying to persuade one another from within," Geoffrey Howe explained in his resignation speech. He recalled, "That was my commitment to government by persuasion, persuading colleagues and the nation."[98] According to another minister, "It is essential that you have unity, but unity comes out of great dispute. That dispute takes place in cabinet. [Ministers] reach a common position. Then they're all bound by the common position."[99] Yet another minister recalled, "She broke the consensus [within cabinet]. She enjoyed breaking the consensus. A compromise would be reached. She'd say fine, then launch out and upset the whole thing. She was breaking the rules, and because of that, her cabinet colleagues found it difficult to work with her."[100] Thatcher's approach to cabinet government challenged the traditional expectations of many of her ministers.

Her conviction-style leadership altered the atmosphere at cabinet meetings. As Patrick Jenkin, a minister in both the Heath and Thatcher governments, explained, "The real secret of her success is the way she handled cabinet. Her ruthless determination to never let anything get past her . . . [s]he would insist—that was the secret. Unlike Heath, who would open it up to discussion. . . . To a minister she would say, 'It's quite obvious you're barking up the wrong tree.' Her single objective was to reinforce the main tenets of her philosophy." Jenkin also recalled Thatcher's reaction to one of his department's recommendations that seemed to require an expanded bureaucracy. As he described it, "There was blood all over the ceiling. Alarmed by the ferocity of her attack, the others remained silent. . . . Ministers started to say, 'I'm not going to take this to her.' And they stopped proposing department recommendations."[101] Jenkin's comments attest to the substantial impact of Thatcher's leadership style, while they also indicate that her willful determination alone served to silence her cabinet ministers.

Yet even when Thatcher did invite open discussion and try to solicit the recommendations of cabinet ministers, they often remained silent. As William Whitelaw (Thatcher's first home secretary) observed, on at least some occasions, "If they wished to exercise collective decision making, cabinet could have done so."[102] To fully understand the dynamics of Thatcher's cabinet, consider another factor that appears to have buttressed her style: Strange as it might seem, the fact that this conviction politician was a woman served to fortify her strong, determined leadership.

In their accounts of cabinet meetings, most ministers described Thatcher as Jenkin did in the passages above: stern and strict, able to exert control through fear and intimidation. They emphasized her "strident" approach and "shrill" voice, while they portrayed her as high-strung and prone to overreaction. According to another minister, Thatcher's aggressive, confrontational style revealed "bad manners. It is bad manners. I thought my mother would never have allowed me to do that."[103] In fact, during my interviews with cabinet ministers, a surprising number mentioned their mothers when discussing Thatcher's style. Perhaps, in the minds of many ministers—educated in British public schools—Thatcher evoked the image of the only other female authority figure they knew: mother (or maybe nanny). Indeed, this particular prime minister seems to have induced almost childlike obedience from most of the members of her cabinet.

Cabinet ministers also made seemingly contradictory assertions about Thatcher's approach to leadership. James Prior observed that "she loved being called the only man in the cabinet," but he added, "She used all the feminine wiles as well as the sort of macho qualities for which she's become famous."[104] Whitelaw insisted, "She knows how to get her way in a woman's way. She need not be pitied for being a woman in a man's world. She uses her feminine charm."[105] These gender-specific descriptions send a mixed message: Was Thatcher ferocious or manipulative? Cruel or coy? Thatcher did attempt to shape her ministers' perceptions of her, but their own backgrounds and prejudices provided the raw material for her creative efforts to mold a distinctive style.

Conviction-style leadership (tinged with gender politics) played a critical role, but other factors might also account for the cabinet's unusual quiescence. Prior admitted that he and Whitelaw failed to rebel at the time of the 1981 budget because "we lacked the courage to do it."[106] Thatcher had defeated both of them in the leadership contest, and the Thatcherite refrain— "There Is No Alternative"—applied to traditional Tories as much as it did to Labour. They seemed to offer no new ideas and promised only a return to the old order. Just as significant, a cabinet revolt might have occurred if ministers feared they would lose an election, but the divided opposition ensured there really was no alternative for the electorate. Furthermore, the longer Thatcher remained in office, the more difficult it became for the cabinet to constrain her. Initially, Thatcher followed the traditional practice of including in her cabinet members from all wings of the party, but increasingly she came to exclude those she considered not "one of us."[107] A special assistant to yet another minister explained why his boss altered his ideology in the Thatcher era: "If you don't accommodate to the leader's views, you'll be on the outside."[108] No minister wished to be banished to the backbenches, and the duration of her premiership threatened to make banishment an eternal exile. Finally, ministers might have feared Thatcher would consult them even less often if she expected to encounter their opposition.

Even with a quiescent cabinet, Thatcher rarely held more than one meeting per week,[109] and in many critical cases, she kept her ministers in the dark while she acted on her own. Without consulting her cabinet, for example, Thatcher decided to allow the use of British bases in the U.S. attack on Libya. In that case, one minister recalled, "By the time senior members were told, it was all over." (And he added, "[M]ost people don't understand, the stress you undergo in public life when you are obliged to publicly support what you privately deplore.")[110] In only one dramatic instance, the Westland affair, did a cabinet member openly rebel when the prime minister refused to discuss a significant issue. Usually, ministers felt bound by the principle of collective responsibility even when no collective decision making took place.

Thatcher took additional steps to circumvent her cabinet. She was not the first prime minister to use cabinet committees instead of the full cabinet, but she relied on them more than her predecessors did. In contrast to her first cabinet, Thatcher staffed these committees with loyal, ideologically compatible supporters. The most significant was the E Committee, which discussed and formulated economic policy and then submitted proposals to the full cabinet. The E Committee's work proved critical to the design and composition of Thatcher's first three (quite radical) budgets.[111] In addition to the E Committee, Misc 62 (otherwise known as the "Star Chamber") resolved differences between the Treasury and other departments. The combined efforts of the

E Committee and Misc 62 enabled Thatcher to design economic policy without the need to water down her proposals to satisfy the "wets."[112] In addition,
she also used ad hoc groups outside the cabinet committee structure, although
here again she continued a trend established by her predecessors.[113]

After her first government, Thatcher used the cabinet committees less often. Following each reelection, her cabinet became more conviction oriented, and she had less need to circumvent it. As Prior recalled, "I have no
doubt in my case in the end she persuaded me to go to Northern Ireland because she said, 'Oh Jim, you can remain in the E Committee of the cabinet.'
She then took away all the powers of the economic committee."[114] Despite
the fact that she started to acquire a conviction cabinet, both cabinet and
cabinet committee activity declined.[115] Emboldened by each reelection,
Thatcher showed she clearly preferred to concentrate decision-making activities at Number 10 Downing Street rather than rely on any form of cabinet
government.

Immediately after the 1983 election, Thatcher greatly diminished the resources of the cabinet when she abolished the Central Policy Review Staff
(CPRS), the think tank that served the full cabinet. Prime Minister Heath
had established CPRS in 1970. It provided "a small multidisciplinary central
policy review staff in the Cabinet office," which was designed to develop a
comprehensive strategy, because "governments are always at the same risk of
losing sight of the need to consider the totality of their current policies in relation to their longer-term objectives."[116] As Heath explained, "What was
most important was for the Cabinet to be in a position to take strategic decisions. I had seen Cabinets which all the time seemed to be dealing with the
day-to-day problems and there was never a real opportunity to deal with
strategy, either from the point of view of the Government or the country.
What I wanted to do was so to change things so that the Cabinet could do
that."[117] At the time, Heath insisted his objective was to strengthen cabinet
government, not institute prime ministerial (or presidential) government.

Thatcher clearly had different intentions when she abolished CPRS in
1983. As Prior recalled, "By this time she had increased her own team of ad-
visers in the Number 10 Policy Unit. Since they gave advice to her and, unlike the Think Tank (CPRS), not to the full Cabinet, this marked yet
another step in the seemingly inexorable growth in the power of the Prime
Minister."[118] The director of studies at the Centre for Policy Studies (CPS)
defended the prime minister's action and explained why Thatcher made this
controversial move. According to David Willetts, "[T]he CPRS seemed to
become more donnish and detached from day-to-day decisions." In addition, it was a "Cabinet Office body serving all of Cabinet. So any major review would get wide circulation" and run the risk of producing leaks. (In

fact, Thatcher abolished CPRS after embarrassing leaks concerning proposed reforms in education and health.) Furthermore, "CPRS papers could divert the conduct of Cabinet and Cabinet committee business in a way unwelcome to other departments as much as to the Prime Minister." And, finally, Willetts insisted, "Prime Ministers all need arrangements around them with which they personally feel comfortable."[119] Prime Minister Thatcher felt personally comfortable only with her own advisors at Number 10.

The policy unit at Number 10 replaced CPRS. In contrast to CPRS, the policy unit served as "a small creative 'think tank'" and an efficient system of advising the prime minister alone. It could more easily "follow up on implementation of policy decisions," raise issues that might not come from departments, and "lubricate relations between No. 10 and the departments." Furthermore, the unit supplied "direct reports," and Willetts observed, "By the time departmental advice reaches the Prime Minister it can sometimes have a strangely generalized, fuzzy, abstract quality." Finally, it provided a "grand suggestions box," although the ideological nature of the staff ensured all their suggestions would be designed to facilitate the fulfillment of the prime minister's convictions.[120] Admittedly, other prime ministers had developed the policy unit to suit their goals, but none had the clear convictions Thatcher possessed, and none sought to substitute the policy unit for the formal apparatus of cabinet government.[121]

Thatcher also tended to use the policy unit as part of her arsenal to combat cabinet opponents. She would often ask a cabinet minister to prepare a paper for her alone, which is apparently one reason why the number of official cabinet papers was so low in the 1980s. When the minister arrived at Downing Street with his team, he would face the prime minister with her array of supporters—from the policy unit as well as from her private office and her personal advisors.[122]

In fact, Thatcher relied on her personal advisors even more than she used the policy unit. Although Willetts insisted that Thatcher failed to presidentialize operations at Number 10, he acknowledged that "[e]conomic policy advice—a crucial role in the earlier Policy Unit—was carried out ably by Sir Alan Walters as the Prime Minister's' economic adviser, a position which was not part of the unit."[123] Walters's authority came to exceed that of the chancellor of the exchequer. At the conclusion of Thatcher's last government, Walters's superior position induced Chancellor Lawson to resign in protest. Conflict also emerged between Howe when he served as foreign secretary and Charles Powell, Thatcher's foreign policy advisor at Number 10. Powell became the prime minister's "foreign affairs private secretary" in 1984, and his role has been compared with that of a national security advisor in the U.S.[124] For Thatcher, the creation of a conviction government required the concentration of authority in the office of prime minister, a place that could be easily staffed by loyal and ideologically committed supporters.

In Thatcher's view, the civil service constituted another consensus institution that would obstruct the practice of conviction politics, and she quickly adopted measures to change it. Immediately after she took office, she banned recruitment, abandoned a plan to add sixteen thousand new positions, and announced a 3 percent cut in positions. Within a few months, she eliminated another thirty-nine thousand positions. In addition, she became actively involved in promotions at the level of permanent secretaries, while she also openly expressed her views on lower-level appointments. (Previously the Civil Service Commission had made personnel decisions without prime ministerial interference.) Moreover, Thatcher abolished the Civil Service Department (CSD), which had been responsible for central management. (According to Thatcher, officials at CSD had negotiated high wage settlements with the unions, defended their departments against her government's proposed cuts, and supplied an unnecessary level of bureaucracy.) Finally, she implemented measures proposed by the Efficiency Unit that she had established in her office. Contained in a report entitled "Improving Management in Government: The Next Steps," the unit's reforms served to reorganize departments by establishing relatively independent executive agencies to deliver services. By 1991, fifty agencies had been created, and by 1992, half of all civil servants were operating in such agencies. (Thatcher hoped these measures would make civil servants more responsive and less susceptible to the values and interests of their departments.) Because reorganization did not require legislation, Thatcher achieved even more than Reagan was able to accomplish.

Despite structural differences between the U.K. and the U.S., Thatcher and Reagan adopted many of the same strategies to achieve similar goals. Both leaders recruited personnel from the private sector and urged them to find ways to introduce management techniques to public administration. To improve management and reduce costs, Thatcher asked Derek Rayner, chief executive officer of Marks and Spencer, to direct her efficiency review of government, and Reagan invited businessman J. Peter Grace to lead his "Private Sector Survey on Cost Control." Increasingly management skill replaced policy expertise as the criterion for excellence in public service. Forced to employ public-choice reasoning and engage in cost-benefit analysis, public administrators became business managers.[125]

By promoting management techniques, Thatcher and Reagan managed to institutionalize their ideas. Cost-conscious and efficiency-driven procedures were more than mere methods; they constituted components of a neoliberal ideology that mandated scaling back the scope of the state.[126] Woodrow Wilson never anticipated that business practices would define public policy or its perimeters. For Wilson, elected officials would design policies in the public interest, and then administrators—skilled in business practices—would decide how to implement the policies in the most effective, efficient manner. For Thatcher and Reagan, process determined policy; the means became the ends. They shared Wilson's goals, to strengthen executive leadership and achieve greater efficiency, but once they achieved their goals, Thatcher and Reagan no longer shared Wilson's concern that the nature of the state could conflict with popular sovereignty. (Any future president or prime minister with a popular mandate at odds with neoliberal ideology will need to alter the apparatus of the state.) Confident in the conviction that their political principles embodied perennial national values, Thatcher and Reagan found no need to separate politics and administration. To the contrary, they intended to combine them.

Thatcher and Reagan managed to politicize the state in several ways. In addition to the introduction of management techniques, both leaders actively intervened in the appointment process by recruiting and promoting ideologically loyal supporters. Perhaps most significant, deregulation and privatization redirected the resources of the state away from domestic welfare and toward stronger defense. After they restructured the state, Thatcher and Reagan left standing an edifice where their policies had become ensconced and their values enshrined.

Ultimately, both leaders also blurred the distinction between the state and the government. This phenomenon was less apparent in the U.S., where the state remains an underdeveloped concept (and frequently an unacknowledged reality) and where the president serves as both head of government and head of state. In the U.K., however, observers immediately recognized that Thatcher seemed to usurp the role of the monarch. Indeed, in the 1980s parents and teachers increasingly needed to explain to children that the queen and the prime minister were two different individuals.[127] Thatcher managed to confound what the British constitution separates: She appeared as both head of government and head of state. To achieve this result, she not only pursued structural change, she also appropriated powerful images from the Victorian era that enabled her leadership to assume symbolic significance. Frequently depicted in the popular press as Boadicea or Britannia, Thatcher seemed to embody her nation's nineteenth-century virtues of righteousness and courage. Yet the late-twentieth-century incarnation of Britannia knew she could not rule the waves (or the skies) alone. She needed to forge a special relationship with her U.S. counterpart that could advance their ideological objectives in the global arena and further expand the scope of executive authority.

9

THE GLOBAL ARENA

When conviction-style leaders tried to pursue their principles in the global arena, they often confronted constraints, but the 1980s provided an ideological and institutional context conducive to the conviction politics of Ronald Reagan and Margaret Thatcher. Their neoliberalism exalted both individual liberty and national greatness, and as a result, they could escape the contradiction other liberal leaders faced when they departed from the principle of self-determination and aggressively pursued their own national interests abroad. Furthermore, domestic considerations tended to limit leaders in international affairs, but Reagan and Thatcher proved able to command or evade domestic institutions, especially when they could justify their actions as effective means to advance freedom abroad. Finally, the last decade of the cold war rendered unusual opportunities for Reagan and Thatcher to display the strength of their convictions, and their ability to facilitate global change was enhanced by the special relationship they forged.

Reagan and Thatcher enjoyed a partnership unlike any earlier relationship between a U.S. president and a British prime minister. Throughout the 1800s, the two nations struggled with an awkward relationship that occasionally erupted into open hostility. In the first half of the century, citizens vividly remembered the Revolutionary War; the two nations battled in 1812; and later Britain sided with the South during the Civil War, a move that revived old animosities and created new resentments. From the Civil War to the Spanish-American War, most U.S. foreign disputes occurred with Britain. During World War I, the interests of the two nations finally became linked, but Woodrow Wilson and David Lloyd George failed to form a personal alliance that might have enabled them to advance their nations' long-term interests or enhance their ideological influence after the war.

Until Reagan and Thatcher, only two sets of presidents and prime ministers shared relationships based on personal compatibility as well as mutual interests.[1] Franklin Delano Roosevelt and Winston Churchill established the first close personal relationship between a U.S. president and a British prime minister. Yet the war effort provided the solid foundation for their alliance, and in most respects their beliefs differed, including their views on domestic policy and their visions of a postwar world. The only other close relationship existed between John F. Kennedy and Harold Macmillan. JFK viewed

Macmillan as a friend and a counselor, although Kennedy did not always heed Macmillan's advice and Macmillan tended to exaggerate his role as advisor to the president. The dynamics of their relationship reflect the changing status of each nation (and foreshadow one aspect of the relationship between Reagan and Thatcher): The partnership proved more significant to the British prime minister than to the U.S. president. In the postwar period, mutual interests, personal compatibility, or similar political perspectives could serve to link leaders across the Atlantic, but in the case of Reagan and Thatcher, all three factors combined to create a truly unique relationship.

First and foremost, Reagan and Thatcher shared a neoliberal ideology, which they intended to promote in the global arena as well as in the domestic sphere. They disagreed on some specific issues—notably, the Strategic Defense Initiative (SDI) and the Siberian pipeline—but generally they adopted and maintained the same worldview. After their first meeting, Thatcher recalled, "Above all, I knew that I was talking to someone who instinctively felt and thought as I did; not just about policies but about a philosophy of government, a view of human nature, all the high ideals and values which lie—or ought to lie—beneath any politician's ambition to lead his country."[2] Of course, other conviction politicians in the liberal tradition promoted similar principles, but in the late twentieth century, personality and interest fortified the ideological link between leaders.

Before Reagan and Thatcher took office, they met twice in London—in April 1975 and November 1978—and they appeared to establish a friendship from the start. Reagan liked Thatcher and clearly admired her style, especially the strength of her convictions. He revealed his first impression to one of Thatcher's biographers and recalled, "She was extremely well informed, but she was firm, decisive, and she had targets in mind of where we should be going."[3] The admiration and affection Reagan would express whenever he mentioned Thatcher led several of his advisors to conclude that the British prime minister was "the only 'other woman' in his life." On the other hand, Thatcher's view of Reagan was considerably more complicated and not always what it seemed. Consider her first impression of the U.S. president: Thatcher recalled, "I had been immediately struck by his warmth, charm and complete lack of affectation—qualities which never altered in the years of leadership which lay ahead. . . . He was a buoyant, self-confident, good-natured American who had risen from poverty to the White House— the American dream in action."[4] The traits she appreciated in Reagan—his warmth, charm, and good nature—supply a contrast to the qualities she generally admired in world leaders.[5]

Reagan and Thatcher were not compatible in every respect. According to many firsthand observers in Britain, differences in their intellectual inclinations and abilities kept them from forging a genuine friendship. One senior minister emphasized the significance of their ideological bond: "Both were charting new territory in economics. Both had great wariness of the Soviet Union—the Iron Lady and the Evil Empire." But he added, "I don't think they ever had a close relationship. No detailed discussion of policy [took place]. I dare say they would have answered a question on an exam paper about the importance of monetary policy in rather different styles."[6] Officials at Number 10 Downing Street expressed the same sentiment in stronger language, although all such remarks were rendered "off the record."

Yet even when Reagan and Thatcher's personalities were incompatible, they often proved to be complementary, and differences between them might have actually enhanced their relationship. As the U.S. president, Reagan was the dominant partner, but he usually seemed willing to defer to Thatcher's knowledge and to benefit from her expertise. One Downing Street official recalled, "I think he liked to listen to what Margaret Thatcher said because I think he recognized her capabilities. And he was a man who always listened to other people."[7] If Reagan liked to listen, Thatcher certainly liked to talk. (And by most accounts, she did not like to listen.) No doubt Reagan often welcomed Thatcher's advice and appreciated the facts and figures she frequently supplied to bolster his position, especially at economic summits. But Reagan, who had a strong ego and certain sense of self, often humored his British counterpart. His self-deprecating humor and his pleasant demeanor probably facilitated interaction with a leader whose reputation abroad (as at home) was one of a dominating and domineering presence.[8]

Prime Minister Thatcher admitted she admired many of Reagan's personal qualities—his ability to communicate[9] as well as his charm—while she also occasionally revealed her envy. From both sides of the Atlantic, officials told the same story about Thatcher and recalled a remark she supposedly made while boarding her plane to depart from the U.S. According to the story, she turned when she reached the top of the stairs and wistfully sighed, "Ah, what I could do with this country!" Even if the story is apocryphal, it reveals the impression Thatcher gave many firsthand observers in the United States and the United Kingdom.

Unable to lead the U.S. herself, Thatcher could nonetheless reap the rewards of a special relationship with its president, and she believed a strong Anglo-American alliance could serve the concrete interests of both nations. According to Bernard Ingham, the special relationship was not based on Thatcher's "slavish devotion" to Reagan as her critics frequently alleged.[10] Instead, the British prime minister cultivated the relationship because "[i]t lifted the status of this country. We counted for nothing in the U.S. in the 1970s. . . . The special relationship [in the 1980s] was based on the recognition of British interests." Furthermore, Ingham added with emphasis, "It underlined her ability."[11] The special relationship elevated the global status of the British premier by placing her center stage with the U.S. president in the global arena. As a result, Thatcher created the impression that she was an international interlocutor and mediator for the superpowers, even though she played a less critical role in U.S.-Soviet relations than she led many observers to believe. (In this respect, like Macmillan, she greatly exaggerated her own impact.) Nevertheless, for the U.S., Thatcher provided a reliable ally in the West, and her support proved essential during the deployment of Cruise and Pershing II missiles throughout Europe in the fall of 1983. Both national and political interests led the two leaders to initiate and nurture their special relationship.

Whether they acted alone or in partnership, the way Reagan and Thatcher conducted international affairs generally enhanced their political goals as well as their ideological objectives. While they attempted to advance their principles, they also appeared to carry out their campaign pledges to make their nations "great again." Both leaders promised prosperity at home and peace "through strength" abroad. They declared they would reverse their nations' apparent decline in global status by fortifying their national defenses and providing strong leadership. Both leaders quickly seized the opportunity to demonstrate their determination in their first term—as the cases of the Falklands war and the invasion of Granada reveal.

Restoring National "Greatness"

The Falklands war illustrates several aspects of the conviction politics Prime Minister Thatcher practiced in the global arena. When she made the decision to wage war, Thatcher declared her commitment to lofty liberal principles—national sovereignty and self-determination—and the outcome seemed to fulfill her promise to restore British "greatness." At the same time, U.S. assistance during the war provided an early indication of the benefits the special relationship could supply. Thatcher's conduct of the war also revealed both the constraints of cabinet government and her determination to circumvent them. To Thatcher, the end of victory justified some questionable means, including deception, misinformation, and even the prosecution of a civil servant who tried to tell the truth. Finally, events during the Falklands war demonstrate how domestic and international politics frequently overlapped in the Thatcher era: Her domestic economic priorities shaped the circumstances that led to war, and ultimately the war enhanced her political fortunes.

Located in the southeast Atlantic off the coast of Argentina, the Falkland Islands were recognized as British territory, but British governments had questioned whether to change the islands' status long before Thatcher took office, and the issue surfaced again shortly after her election. In the fall of 1979 Nicholas Ridley, a junior minister at the foreign office, first proposed that Britain transfer sovereignty of the islands to Argentina in exchange for an immediate, long-term leaseback. One year later, during a House of Commons debate, members of the Conservative right wing as well as Labour and Liberals MPs attacked his proposal. Thatcher herself refused to return the islands to Argentina under any circumstances, but instead of strengthening the defense of the islands, on June 30, 1981, her government announced that it would withdraw the survey ship HMS *Endurance* from the South Atlantic. The foreign office wanted to keep the *Endurance,* but Secretary of State for Defense John Nott favored the cut. (Nott had replaced Tory moderate Francis Pym as defense secretary because Thatcher believed Nott would more firmly resist the pressure exerted by military lobbyists.) Like his prime minister, the new defense secretary put economic priorities ahead of other considerations.

Later when a committee of privy counsellors chaired by Lord Franks investigated the origins of the war, the extent of foreign office opposition to the cut became clear. Published in January 1983, the Franks report showed that Foreign Secretary Lord Carrington sent at least three memoranda to Nott that urged him to reconsider the *Endurance* cut. Carrington feared it would signal to Argentina that the British government had weakened its commitment to protecting the islands. According to the committee's report, after General Galtieri seized control of the junta in December 1981, the government should have heeded the advice of the foreign office that it was "inadvisable" to withdraw the *Endurance.*

The Franks report also presented evidence that the government had neglected to consider the issue fully. Between January 1981 and April 1, 1982, no meeting of the defense committee of the cabinet was held to discuss the Falklands, and no discussion in full cabinet took place until March 25, 1982.[12] True to her style, the prime minister had preferred to handle the matter through informal channels and rely on the advice of those who shared her values and endorsed her views.[13]

When Argentina invaded the islands on April 1, Thatcher immediately prepared a military response, and in a special parliamentary session on April 3, she encountered no substantial opposition to her plans. Instead, even the Labour party leader Michael Foot proclaimed Britain's role as "defender of people's freedom throughout the world" and asserted the "absolute right" of the Falklanders to British protection. Foot demanded that the government "prove by deeds—they will never be able to do it by words—that they are not responsible for the betrayal and cannot be faced with that charge."[14] War fever quickly took hold of Parliament and the country.

After the debate, Lord Carrington resigned, even though he had tried to warn both the Ministry of Defense (MOD) and Downing Street, and Pym became foreign secretary. Pym had been shadow foreign secretary, and as leader of the House, he could make the move to the foreign office without disrupting the administration of other departments. More important, however, the prime minister needed to unify her party after Carrington's resignation, and as a result she was forced to appoint a Tory moderate rather than one of her loyal lieutenants.[15] To counteract the new foreign secretary's influence, Thatcher created a small war cabinet.

In addition to Pym, four other officials—Nott, Deputy Prime Minister William Whitelaw, Party Chairman Cecil Parkinson, and Chief of the Defense Staff Sir Terence Lewin—composed the war cabinet. With the prime minister, they considered at least five peace proposals, but Galtieri and the Argentine junta thwarted or rejected each proposal. In any event, Thatcher herself did not seem interested in a negotiated peace once the conflict began.

On May 2, the war effort escalated when the British submarine *Conqueror* sank the *General Belgrano* and 368 sailors drowned, a move Thatcher's critics alleged she ordered to undermine a Peruvian peace initiative. Thatcher authorized the attack outside the designated exclusion zone around the Falklands. At the time of the sinking, the government created the impression that the submarine captain had made the decision on the spot because the *Belgrano* threatened the British task force. As late as a television interview in 1983, Thatcher still insisted that the *Belgrano* was "not sailing away," despite convincing evidence to the contrary. She also alleged that she was unaware of the Peruvian peace plan at the time. Parkinson contradicted this during an interview on BBC television,[16] but Thatcher continued to stick by her original story.[17] Long after the war ended, Thatcher remained determined to suppress the truth about the *Belgrano*.

The case of Clive Ponting attests to her government's determination to conceal the facts. In 1984, the new defense secretary, Michael Heseltine, faced questions in the House of Commons concerning the *Belgrano*. As a senior civil servant, Ponting witnessed discussions between Heseltine and his officials that were intended to mislead Parliament. Ponting sent confidential papers to Tam Dalyell, a Labour MP and one of the few outspoken critics of the war. The government then prosecuted Ponting under section 2 of the Official Secrets Act, which prohibited the unauthorized disclosure of official information, except to "a person to whom it is in the interest of the state his duty to communicate it." (Note that Ponting leaked the information to a member of Parliament and not to the press.) Ponting did not deny the charges but said he was obligated by a higher duty to "the interests of the state." Attempting to undercut his defense, the presiding judge made the astonishing assertion that the interest of the state was identical with the policies of the government of the day. Fortunately, others agreed with the civil servant that a higher authority prevailed, and the jury acquitted him.[18]

Thatcher otherwise controlled information about the war through skillful news management. Both the prime minister and her press secretary wanted extensive (albeit selective) news coverage, and their desire for favorable publicity was often at odds with the MOD's need for secrecy. When the MOD canceled lobby-style briefings, for example, Downing Street restored them. Press Secretary Ingham also increased the number of reporters accompanying the task force. At the same time, he and the prime minister carried on a campaign of misinformation and heavy-handed censorship, taking special care to sanitize any pictures sent back home.[19] Finally, the prime minister refused to release the Franks report even under conditions of "embargo" until she presented it to the Commons, although her press secretary did leak favorable paragraphs.[20] Persistent efforts at news management throughout the war appear to have paid off.

Before the Falklands war, Thatcher's government had sunk to an all-time low in the public opinion polls, but she recovered by the time the war ended. According to Gallup, in December 1981 support for the Conservatives stood at 23 percent, Labour also had 23 percent, and the Alliance topped the polls with 50 percent. By March 1982, support for the parties was roughly equal. After the war, Conservatives led the polls with 46 percent, Labour placed second with 27 percent, and the Alliance trailed with 24 percent, poll results strikingly similar to the actual outcome of the 1983 general election.[21] Several factors—including changing perceptions of the economy and internal strife within the Alliance—account for the change, and commentators at the time tended to overestimate the direct impact of the war on public opinion.[22] (Thatcher's government had started to regain support even before the war began.) Nevertheless, to a great extent the Falklands factor became the Thatcher factor, and the war enhanced the image of the conviction prime minister.

Victory in the Falklands war seemed to confirm Thatcher's conviction that strong leadership could make Britain "great again." On July 3, 1982, she provided her own assessment of the war's impact when she declared, "What has indeed happened is that now once again Britain is not prepared to be pushed around. We have ceased to be a nation in retreat. We have instead a new-found confidence—born in the economic battles at home and tested and found true 8,000 miles away. That confidence comes from the rediscovery of ourselves, and grows with the recovery of our self-respect. . . . Britain found herself again in the South Atlantic and will not look back from the victory she has won."[23] As a result of victory, according to Thatcher, the British overcame the "Suez syndrome," a phenomenon she compared with the "Vietnam syndrome" in the U.S.[24]

President Reagan agreed with her assessment and applauded her accomplishment. In the last weeks of the war, he delivered a speech to both houses of Parliament, in which he paid special tribute to the liberal principles recently defended by British forces. According to Reagan, "They fight for a cause, for the belief that armed aggression must not be allowed to succeed, and the people must participate in the decisions of government."[25] Like Thatcher, Reagan insisted the war had been conducted to secure fundamental principles, but many observers questioned that judgment.

On both sides of the Atlantic, some wondered if the benefits had justified the costs. One British journalist noted that the death toll reached approximately 1,000, and 1,700 were wounded, for the sake of 1,800 islanders and 600,000 sheep.[26] Initial reaction in the U.S. also revealed some puzzlement at the strange course of events. Secretary of State Alexander Haig described the atmosphere at the State Department, where "in the early hours of the crisis, most of the staff shared the amusement of the press and public over what was perceived as a Gilbert and Sullivan battle over a sheep pasture between a choleric old John Bull and a comic dictator in a gaudy uniform."[27] When the Falklands war started, U.S. support for Britain was far from certain.

For many weeks, while Haig attempted to negotiate a peace agreement, officials in the Reagan administration remained deeply divided. Secretary of Defense Caspar Weinberger wanted the U.S. to support the U.K., but Jeane Kirkpatrick, the ambassador to the United Nations, opposed siding with the British. (Some officials insisted the U.S. needed to protect its "interests" in Latin America and reminded Reagan that Argentina had been training the Nicaraguan Contras in Honduras. In fact, after the Falklands war, Argentina ceased to provide assistance.) Privately, the U.S. provided supplies and intelligence to the British task force from the start, and when negotiations finally failed, the U.S. publicly sided with Britain. In this early test of the special relationship, the U.K. reaped tangible and essential rewards, but the relationship would soon be seriously challenged again, when U.S. forces invaded the Caribbean Island of Grenada on October 25, 1983.

The invasion of Grenada followed on the heels of U.S. military involvement in Lebanon; consequently, the two events need to be considered together. Following the Israeli invasion of Lebanon in June 1982, Philip Habib, special envoy in the Middle East, persuaded Reagan to include U.S. forces in a "peace-keeping mission" designed to oversee the withdrawal of the Palestine Liberation Organization (PLO) from Beirut. The U.S. Marines left the country as soon as they accomplished their goal. Then Christian leader Bashir Gemayel (recently elected president) was killed by a bomb, and Israel invaded West Beirut, breaking the earlier agreement under which the PLO had been evacuated. Israel failed to intervene as Gemayel's militia slaughtered hundreds of Palestinian refugees. The chaos that ensued led to a second deployment of U.S. forces.

Chaos also reigned within the Reagan administration at the time. Disagreements among advisors combined with changes in personnel disrupted the usually reliable system of advising in place during Reagan's first term. The chiefs of staff opposed the second deployment as they had the first. Secretary of State George Shultz, who replaced Haig during the first deployment, favored the second, but Secretary of Defense Weinberger opposed both. To add to the uncertainty among Reagan's advisors, a battle was raging within the White House to replace William Clark as national security advisor. As a consequence of confusion and conflict, Reagan's advisors failed to provide expertise or clear direction when he needed it most. Among other things, the president did not understand that he had placed U.S. troops at serious risk when he ordered the second deployment, and he was genuinely shocked when on October 23 a suicide bomber attacked the U.S. Marine barracks in Beirut and killed 241 marines.

Within twenty-four hours of the explosion in Beirut, Reagan approved the U.S. invasion of Grenada, where a coup had resulted in the murder of its Marxist prime minister, Maurice Bishop. The Organization of Eastern Caribbean States requested U.S. military intervention, and Reagan informed the congressional leadership of his decision to intervene. The invasion took only two days to defeat the greatly outnumbered Cuban forces and evacuate U.S. students who were attending medical school on the island. The relatively small number of casualties and the ease and speed of the operation combined to make the move popular at home.

Nevertheless, the invasion proved unpopular with the British prime minister. According to Thatcher, "The humiliation inflicted on the United States by the Beirut bombing undoubtedly influenced its reaction to the events which were taking place on the island of Grenada in the eastern Caribbean."[28] In her account of the invasion, she recalled, "What precisely happened in Washington, I still do not know, but I find it hard to believe that outrage at the Beirut bombing had nothing to do with it. I am sure that this was not a matter of calculation, but rather of frustrated anger—yet that did not make it any easier for me defend, not least to a British House of Commons in which anti-American feeling on both right and left was increasing. The fact that Grenada was also a Commonwealth member, and that the Queen was Head of State, made it harder still."[29] As soon as she was informed of the decision, Thatcher immediately wrote to Reagan, "This action will be seen as intervention by a western country in the internal affairs of a small independent nation, however unattractive its regime. I ask you to consider this in the context of our wider East-West relations and of the fact that we will be having in the next few days to present to our Parliament and people the siting of Cruise missiles in this country."[30] When she spoke to the president twenty minutes later, he told her, "We are already at ground zero." As she recalled her reaction, "At the time I felt dismayed and let down by what had happened. At best, the British Government had been made to look impotent; at worst we looked deceitful. Only the previous afternoon Geoffrey [Howe] had told the House of Commons that he had no knowledge of any American intention to intervene in Grenada."[31] If the recollections of her ministers are accurate, the account in her memoirs understates the fury she felt at the time of the U.S. invasion.

Thatcher expressed many legitimate concerns. As she told the president, this act of U.S. aggression would complicate her task of persuading Parliament and the public to accept the deployment of cruise missiles in Britain. She also feared the wider ramifications for the propaganda war then being waged against the Soviets: She told many of her close colleagues she feared the invasion of Grenada put the U.S. on the same uncertain moral ground as the Soviet Union after its invasion of Afghanistan. Furthermore, she alleged that she opposed the invasion on principle. As Thatcher told an audience in the U.S. before the invasion of Grenada (with unintentional irony): "The use of force and the threat of force to advance our beliefs are no part of our philosophy." (Thatcher later recalled, "In light of America's response to a political crisis in a small island in the Caribbean, at least that part of the message had not been understood.")[32] Finally, the president's decision had embarrassed her: The fact that he failed to consult her in advance led her senior minister to deny that the U.S. would make such a move. Perhaps most significant, when the U.S. invaded a member country of the Commonwealth without consulting the British prime minister first, the real nature of the Atlantic alliance was exposed, and the U.K. was seen as the junior, subservient partner. In this respect, the U.S. invasion of Grenada seemed to call into question the recently restored "greatness" of Britain.

In the U.S., however, the invasion of Grenada did a great deal to create the impression that the nation was restoring its own military "greatness," and the move succeeded in shifting the spotlight from Lebanon. By the time of the 1984 presidential campaign, the Grenada victory completely overshadowed the Beirut bombing. The image of a returning student kissing the tarmac took the place of any memory of marines buried beneath the rubble of the bombed barracks. In addition to imposing a press blackout during the invasion, the Reagan administration engaged in skillful news management and media manipulation, and like Thatcher in the Falklands war, Reagan reaped the rewards of these efforts at the polls.

Finally, in both Lebanon and Grenada, the president managed to circumvent Congress. Reagan sent the troops to Lebanon without reporting under section 4(a)(1) of the war powers resolution. Instead, he cited the executive's "constitutional authority with respect to the conduct of foreign relations and as Commander-in-Chief of the United States armed forces." In the fall of 1983, Congress passed legislation that made section 4(a)(1) operative as of August 29, 1983, but it extended the sixty- to ninety-day period of the war powers resolution and authorized the military action in Lebanon for eighteen months. A showdown never materialized because Reagan withdrew the troops before the deadline. In the case of Grenada, the president did report to Congress. The House immediately passed legislation that would have required withdrawal of the troops within sixty to ninety days, but before the Senate could act, Reagan announced that all troops would return home before Christmas (less than two months after the invasion).[33] The war powers resolution provided little restraint on executive authority during U.S. military engagements in Lebanon or Grenada.

The Falklands war and the invasion of Grenada illustrate several aspects of the conviction politics Thatcher and Reagan practiced in the global arena. They appeared to promote fundamental principles: In the case of the Falklands, Thatcher said she was seeking to secure sovereignty in the face of authoritarian aggression; in Grenada, Reagan alleged he intended to restore the rule of law and the integrity of governmental institutions. (In reality, the principle there was less clear than in the case of the Falklands.) More significant, both leaders pursued their objectives free of obstruction, virtually unopposed by any institutional obstacles at home. Furthermore, domestic considerations influenced the nature and the timing of these military interventions, and military success brought tangible political rewards. These events seemed to showcase the "virtue" of conviction-style politicians in the global arena: Strong leadership exercised on behalf of the "national interest" could reverse each nation's apparent decline and revive its historic "greatness." Yet the relative ease by which victory was achieved made each of these military engagements somewhat unique. Reagan and Thatcher would confront more considerable challenges when they set out to conquer the "enemy" embodied in international terrorism.

Conviction politicians in the liberal tradition met their match when they encountered international terrorists. In fact, terrorism represents another kind of conviction politics, as Prime Minister Thatcher seems to have understood. Whenever she condemned terrorists, she declined to label them fanatics or criticize their zeal. Writing about her adversaries in the Irish Republican Army (IRA), Thatcher revealed, "It was possible to admire the courage of [Bobby] Sands and the other hunger strikers who died, but not to sympathize with their murderous cause."[34] Thatcher would depict the substance of their cause as "evil," but she knew their style mirrored her own: Terrorists have clear convictions and passionately pursue them.

When Reagan and Thatcher addressed the issue of terrorism, they adhered to their convictions with different degrees of determination. Thatcher utterly refused to compromise or negotiate with anyone she considered a terrorist. In the spring and summer of 1981 she firmly resisted the demands of IRA prisoners on a hunger strike. IRA leader Bobby Sands died from starvation, and nine others followed, but Thatcher never wavered in her determination. Her hard line against terrorism grew even firmer following an explosion at the Grand Hotel in Brighton, where Conservatives were staying for their party conference in October 1984. (The bomb killed five people and injured two cabinet ministers, Norman Tebbit and John Wakeham.) Throughout her premiership, Thatcher repeatedly demonstrated that her battle against terrorism was not merely a war of words, providing a sharp contrast to the uneven efforts of her U.S. counterpart.

With the exception of the U.S. raid on Libya, Reagan spoke but declined to act against terrorism. Consider the following cases, which all took place in June 1985.[35] On June 14, Arab terrorists hijacked TWA flight 847 from Athens to Rome and took the passengers as hostages. The hijackers demanded that Israel release seven hundred Shiites taken in Lebanon. Diplomatic pressure secured the release of the TWA passengers. (Syrian president Hafez Assad intervened; National Security Advisor Robert McFarlane contacted Nabih Berri, leader of Amal, the largest Shiite group; and Hashemi Rafsanjani, speaker of the Iranian Parliament, provided assistance.) The passengers safely returned home, but the hijackers achieved their goals: They got publicity for their cause, and Israel freed the Shiites.

Other acts of terrorism quickly followed. On June 19, Salvadoran guerrillas murdered 13 people, including 4 U.S. Marines at a café in San Salvador. That same day, a bomb exploded at the Frankfurt airport, killing 3 people and wounding 42. On June 23, Sikh terrorists caused the crash of an Air India Boeing 747, and 329 passengers were killed. This series of events prompted the president to deliver a widely publicized speech in which he denounced terrorists as a strange "collection of misfits, loony tunes, and squalid criminals."[36] In every case, however, the Reagan administration spoke loudly but carried no stick. Even worse than Reagan's inaction, his administration's arms initiative with Iran contradicted his publicly stated policy, which barred negotiations with terrorists, and the sale of arms actually led to more hostages being captured than were freed.

In the spring of 1986, the Reagan administration finally found a stick to strike at state-sponsored terrorism. On April 14, 1986, U.S. bombers based in the U.K. hit two Libyan cities—ostensibly in retaliation for the terrorist bombing of a Berlin disco that killed a U.S. serviceman, among others. The U.S. military hit Libyan leader Moammar Qadaffi's barracks, killing his two-year-old daughter and wounding two of his sons. (It was later discovered that Qadaffi himself had been a target, but he escaped serious injury.) The U.S. raid on Libya evoked dramatically different reactions from the public at home and abroad.

In the U.S., Reagan earned his highest approval ratings in May and June 1986, and those ratings would soon yield political rewards. Congress, for example, finally passed his aid package for the Nicaraguan Contras. Some controversy occurred when the public learned that Reagan had condoned a series of public relations announcements designed to deceive Qadaffi. The administration's campaign of misinformation succeeded in misleading the U.S. press as well as the Libyan leader, and State Department spokesman Bernard Kalb resigned in protest. Yet the public and elected officials generally voiced little criticism of the administration's action and instead applauded Reagan's daring move.

Abroad, however, the raid on Libya ignited harsh criticism. France had denied U.S. bombers the use of its airspace and later publicly denounced the attack. After the raid, the United Nations General Assembly passed a Libyan resolution condemning the air strikes. It ordered the U.S. to "refrain from the use or threat of force" against Libya and acknowledged Libya's right to compensation for damages that included approximately one hundred civilian casualties.[37] In the global arena, Reagan's only friend remained Thatcher, who paid a heavy price for her support: Her decision to allow the U.S. to use British bases damaged her standing in her party and in the country.

Even before the raid, anti-U.S. sentiment had been growing in Britain. According to a MORI poll published in the *Sunday Times,* 62 percent thought the U.S. neglected British views, and more than half thought the U.S. posed either a greater threat to peace than the Soviets (20 percent) or an equal threat (34 percent). After the raid, two-thirds of the respondents thought the prime minister was wrong to allow the use of the bases.[38] The raid intensified hostility toward the U.S. and revived British fears that the U.S. viewed the U.K. as an "unsinkable aircraft carrier."[39]

Despite the short-term political costs she incurred, in her memoirs Thatcher concluded her discussion of the raid by emphasizing the benefits. According to Thatcher, "However unpopular, no one could doubt that our action had been strong and decisive. I had set my course and stuck to it. Ministers and disaffected MPs might mutter; but they were muttering now about leadership they did not like, rather than a failure of leadership. I had faced down the anti-Americanism which threatened to poison our relations with our closest and most powerful ally, and not only survived but emerged with greater authority and influence on the world stage: this the critics could not ignore."[40] Like the Falklands war and the U.S. invasion of Grenada, the raid on Libya bolstered the leaders' image of strength and determination.

At the time of the raid, Thatcher's decision sparked substantial speculation about her motives. Earlier in the year, she seemed to oppose such military action when she declared, "I do not believe in retaliatory strikes that are against international law. . . . Once you start to go across borders, then I do not see an end to it. I uphold international law very firmly."[41] Nevertheless, three months later she allowed the U.S. bombers to depart from their British bases. Conventional wisdom contends that the raid on Libya demonstrates how easily and extensively the U.S. could influence British policy.[42] Other commentators believe that Thatcher opposed the raid but felt she needed to show that the allies were not "craven and wimpish."[43] In my interviews with several ministers, two other explanations emerged. Both indicate that in this case Thatcher used the special relationship to pursue what she perceived as her own nation's interests.

Prime Minister Thatcher had independent reasons for wanting to strike at Qadaffi. On April 17, 1984, in St. James's Square, a gunman inside the Libyan People's Bureau shot a British policewoman who was guarding the building from protesters outside.[44] Moreover, her government had substantial evidence that Qadaffi was supplying weapons to the IRA.[45] (During a phone conversation shortly before the raid, Reagan "drew attention to what we knew from intelligence about Libyan direction of terrorist violence," Thatcher has recalled.)[46] The prime minister might have allowed the public—at home and abroad—to think she was playing the role of a good ally in order to protect intelligence sources.[47] For Thatcher, the target of the raid was probably not only Libya but also the IRA. In this, an unusual case of quiet conviction politics, she might well have concealed her genuine motive behind the shield of the special relationship.

The attack on Libya constituted a grand gesture against international terrorism that produced mixed results. U.S. hostage Peter Kilburn, a former librarian at the American University in Beirut, was killed immediately after the raid. On the other hand, the massive retaliation that many critics feared never occurred. Furthermore, the raid on Libya revealed the benefits both nations and their leaders derived from the special relationship. Without the use of the British bases, the U.S. raid would have been considerably more difficult and dangerous. Without the U.S. attack, Thatcher would have missed the opportunity to deliver a blow to a terrorist foe much closer to home. To pursue her long-term objectives, Thatcher was prepared to endure short-term political costs. She also knew that in the long run the special relationship could boost the international standing of her nation as well as enhance her own stature—especially if it lifted her and her country to the level of the superpowers.

The End of the Cold War

In the second half of the twentieth century, communism loomed large as the global "enemy" of liberalism, and conviction politicians Reagan and Thatcher clearly set out to defeat it. They held the same ideological view of communism: namely, that it was evil and immoral because it tried to smother the individual and extinguish liberty. Distinct factors shaped their opinions—reading the works of Alexander Solzhenitsyn influenced Thatcher, and his encounter with communists in Hollywood apparently affected Reagan—but they arrived in the same place. By 1980, Thatcher and Reagan appeared determined to destroy the Evil Empire.

Admittedly, both leaders started to soften and shift their position by 1983.[48] They seem to have done so independently but at roughly the same juncture and for similar reasons. The deployment of cruise and Pershing II missiles had strengthened security in Western Europe. More significant, by 1985 another critical factor fostered change: Mikhail Gorbachev became general secretary. Thatcher met Gorbachev before Reagan did, but they quickly reached the same judgment. As Thatcher put it, Gorbachev was a man they "could do business with."

Whether their positions were firm or flexible, Reagan and Thatcher generally agreed on the strategies the West needed to pursue, although the British prime minister did oppose two fundamental aspects of Reagan's foreign policy: the Strategic Defense Initiative (SDI) and the intermediate-range nuclear forces (INF) treaty. Reagan held several basic convictions that made the reduction of nuclear arms and strategic defense central to his vision. He genuinely feared nuclear war would destroy civilization, and to avoid that destruction, he proposed a reduction of nuclear arms, not a limit in their growth. He viewed the Soviet Union as an evil empire, but he also thought its ambitions might be contained by appealing to the Soviet national interest, and he believed the Soviet economy could not sustain a serious arms race with the U.S.[49] These and other convictions held by Reagan were considered quite radical in the 1980s, and as Thatcher knew, some of his beliefs were rooted in a deeply disturbing source.

Long before he became president, Reagan had acquired a fascination with the biblical account of Armageddon, which he continued to maintain as leader of the free world.[50] Early in his presidency, some of Reagan's critics feared his view of Armageddon would lead him to use nuclear weapons, but the president's belief in the biblical account produced the opposite effect: If the end of the world was approaching, Reagan wanted to provide protection, not launch the first strike. The story of Armageddon appealed to Reagan's adventurous imagination, while it also enriched his vision and fortified his sense of mission.

As a result, Reagan endorsed the Strategic Defense Initiative, or "Star Wars," as it became popularly known.[51] National Security Advisor McFarlane described the relationship between Armageddon and Star Wars when he explained, "[Reagan] sees himself as a romantic, heroic figure who . . . believes that the power of a person and an idea could change the outcome of something as terrible as Armageddon. This was the greatest challenge of all. . . . He didn't see himself as God, but he saw himself as a heroic figure on earth."[52] The development of strategic defense had a long history, but interest in it had languished primarily because of its high cost and questionable feasibility. Reagan revived the issue in his 1976 campaign; it became a plank in the 1980 Republican platform; and ultimately SDI would evolve into one of Reagan's firm convictions.

Many of Reagan's advisors supported the research and development of SDI, although their reasons were not always the same as the president's. Like Reagan, they considered SDI part of an overall strategy of increasing defense at a rate that the Soviet economy could not sustain, but unlike the president, they viewed it as a useful bargaining tool. In contrast to his advisors, Reagan rigidly refused to negotiate on strategic defense, and eventually he even offered to share the technology with the Soviets once it was developed. For Reagan, SDI did not merely provide a convenient strategy. By the time he presented it to the public, it had become one of his fundamental beliefs.[53]

In a nationally televised speech on March 23, 1983, Reagan announced SDI and proposed a $17 billion program for its development. He introduced the subject by promising to provide "a vision of the future which offers hope." Reagan invited the public to consider, "What if a free people could live secure in the knowledge that their security did not rest upon the threat of instant U.S. retaliation to deter a Soviet attack, that we could intercept and destroy strategic ballistic missiles before they reached our own soil or that of our allies?"[54] The president recognized that "defensive systems have limitations and raise certain problems." Specifically, "*If paired with offensive systems,* they can be viewed as fostering an aggressive policy" (emphasis added).[55] Reagan apparently never understood that weapons developed for strategic defense could also be used offensively. His failure to grasp some of the implications of SDI meant that he could never fully comprehend its danger or why it would so deeply disturb both his Soviet adversaries and some of his closest allies.

Prime Minister Thatcher always strongly opposed SDI, although she tried to express her opposition quietly and somewhat surreptitiously. Publicly, she couched her position in terms of opposing strategic defense hardware but not its research. Privately, and following discussions with Gorbachev, in 1984 she told the president that it was not technologically feasible and that it could undermine nuclear deterrence. (Supposedly, she told the president that thanks to her training as a chemist, she *knew* SDI was not feasible.) During a visit to Camp David she managed to persuade Reagan to sign a statement, which included the following four points: First, the West did not seek nuclear superiority (which Reagan had said in his SDI speech); second, research and deployment of SDI would be negotiated; third, SDI was intended to enhance deterrence; and, finally, it would not obstruct arms control negotiations. The British press hailed this Camp David Accord as a diplomatic triumph, one that signaled Thatcher's growing preeminence in global affairs.[56]

It was critical for Thatcher to appear to have an impact on the president and U.S. policy. Her meeting at Camp David followed shortly after her talks with Gorbachev, and she was cultivating her image as "interlocutor between the Superpowers."[57] But the prime minister was walking a fine line: Despite her personal rapport with Gorbachev, her special relationship with Reagan provided the basis for her prominence among the allies and her significance on the world stage. She could not afford to rupture that relationship. In this case, to pursue her conviction, she needed to employ hidden-hand tactics.

On March 15, 1985, Foreign Secretary Howe delivered a critical speech in which he challenged both the feasibility and the concept of SDI. "There would be no advantage," Howe told the Royal United Services Institute, "in creating a new Maginot Line of the twenty-first century."[58] Just as significant, he reminded his audience, "Impressions can be created by words as well as deeds. . . . Words and dreams cannot by themselves justify what the prime minister described to the UN as the perilous pretense that a better system than nuclear deterrence is within reach at the present time."[59] Like his prime minister, Howe wanted to bring the man who dreamed of Star Wars back down to earth.

British journalists interpreted the speech as a sign of dissension in the cabinet because Thatcher had declined to attack SDI in public. Conventional wisdom assumes that Thatcher neglected to read Howe's speech in advance.[60] When asked about the event, Howe alleged that he did not know if she personally read it, but he admitted it was seen in advance at Number 10. (In much of the speech, he reiterated the four points listed in the statement Thatcher negotiated at Camp David.) By allowing her foreign secretary to express her view, Thatcher could convey her conviction without direct personal involvement. If she did so, she devised a clever maneuver that permitted her to pursue her principle but served to safeguard the special relationship.

Contrary to the impression Thatcher created at Camp David, she failed to influence Reagan on SDI or alter his beliefs in any way. Despite the provisions he agreed to in their formal statement, Reagan did see SDI as an alternative to traditional deterrence, and he would not negotiate or compromise it. As he declared when he announced the program, he continued to believe SDI "could pave the way for arms control measures to eliminate [nuclear] weapons." Reagan remained convinced he had found a way of "rendering these nuclear weapons impotent and obsolete."[61]

A nuclear-free world was Reagan's dream but Thatcher's nightmare. When asked about Reagan's "conviction" that nuclear weapons could be eliminated, she objected to the use of the word and defiantly declared, "I would have said it was an aspiration. It cannot be a conviction. It is unrealistic."[62] To Thatcher, Star Wars was a figment of Reagan's childish imagination and its goal—to secure a nuclear-free world—was the product of pure fantasy.

Like SDI, the plan to eliminate nuclear weapons was endorsed by many of Reagan's advisors as a strategic tool and propaganda ploy. Secretary of Defense Weinberger originally came up with "zero option" as a plan the Soviets were certain to reject. The defense secretary actually believed in maintaining the traditional two-track approach—to build up defense while negotiating arms control, a position of critical significance to Thatcher. Yet Reagan embraced the zero option as early as 1981, and, like SDI, it provided no mere strategy but became a critical component of Reagan's core beliefs.

During Reagan's first term, little progress on arms negotiation or contact between the superpowers took place. At least in part this was due to the frequent change in Soviet leadership. Leonid Brezhnev died on November 10, 1982; Yuri Andropov on February 9, 1984; Konstantin Chernenko on March 10, 1985. Finally, in the spring of 1985, Gorbachev became general secretary, four months after he met with Thatcher in London. Thatcher encouraged Reagan to schedule the first summit that took place in Geneva in November 1985. At that meeting, Reagan and Gorbachev disagreed on critical issues, especially SDI, but they did agree to hold future summits, a significant accomplishment at the time.

In October 1986, a second summit was held in Reykjavik, Iceland. Reagan initially viewed the meeting in Reykjavik as an opportunity to set the agenda for the forthcoming summit in Washington, but substantial gains were made in negotiations, especially concerning the elimination of ballistic missiles. At one point, when Gorbachev suggested that both nations eliminate all their nuclear weapons, Reagan seemed to agree. (In contrast to the first summit in Geneva, Reagan was poorly prepared for the meeting in Reykjavik.) Gorbachev insisted, however, that the U.S. limit SDI research to the laboratory, and Reagan walked out when they reached an impasse. At first Reykjavik threatened to produce a public relations disaster, but White House spin control and the Great Communicator's televised address to the nation reversed the effect: Following Reykjavik, 11 percent more thought Reagan was dealing successfully with the Soviets.[63] Reagan's conduct proved less popular with U.S. allies, especially Thatcher, who feared Reagan had been prepared to surrender all the weapons of Western defense. Ironically, in her view SDI had proven useful after all: At least it blocked the president's ability to reach a dangerous agreement that might have left the West defenseless.

In February 1987, Gorbachev removed a critical roadblock when he proposed to separate INF negotiations from the issue of SDI. This paved the way for the INF treaty, which Reagan and Gorbachev signed when the two leaders met in Washington in December 1987. (The document was officially entitled "Treaty Between the United States of America and the Union of Soviet Socialist Republics on the Elimination of Their Intermediate-Range and Shorter-Range Missiles.") Eight hundred fifty-nine U.S. nuclear missiles and 1,836 Soviet nuclear missiles with ranges of 300 to 3,400 miles were scheduled for destruction. Admittedly, this constituted only 4 percent of the superpowers' nuclear arsenals, but it was the first U.S.-Soviet treaty to destroy nuclear weapons and provide for on-site monitoring of their destruction.

Most of the world applauded when Reagan and Gorbachev signed the INF treaty, but Thatcher opposed it and considered it a dangerous departure from the doctrine of deterrence. She remained convinced that Europe should not be denuclearized. Nevertheless, for the most part, she repressed her reservations about INF, perhaps because she knew her opposition would fail to have an impact on either Reagan or Gorbachev. In fact, to publicly oppose them when they signed the treaty might expose her limited role and prevent her from sharing in the glory of their achievement.

Although Reagan and Gorbachev would meet one more time, at Governors Island on December 7, Reagan's visit to Moscow in May 1988 was in many ways his grand finale. The president and the general secretary signed two modest arms control agreements, while SDI blocked further negotiations on strategic arms. Yet Reagan used the summit to focus attention on human rights, an exception to the "quiet diplomacy" he usually practiced on this issue. At Moscow State University, he emphasized the values and benefits of a free society.[64] On the same day, at a lunch with members of the cultural and artistic community, Reagan revealed the relationship between freedom and art when he quoted Soviet filmmaker Sergei Eisenstein: "The most important thing is to have the vision. The next is to grasp and hold it. You must see and feel what you are thinking. You must see it and grasp it. You must hold and fix it in your memory and senses. And you must do it at once."[65] Then Reagan added, "That is the very essence, I believe, of successful leadership not only on the movie set, where I learned about it, but everywhere." To a great extent, in U.S.-Soviet relations, President Reagan had demonstrated what could be achieved when a leader has a vision and sets out to "do it at once."

Reagan claimed credit for the historic global developments that occurred during his presidency. In his farewell address, he proudly declared, "Once you begin a great movement, there's no telling where it will end. We meant to change a nation, and instead we changed a world."[66] Of course, Reagan's foreign policy carried certain costs and entailed high risks. In at least one respect, the defeat of liberalism's enemy proved a Pyrrhic victory: Increased U.S. defense spending forced the Soviets into an arms race their economy could not sustain, but it also put a strain on the U.S. economy and left a legacy of spiraling deficits. Moreover, Reagan's rigid adherence to SDI could have blocked any arms negotiations and triggered a dangerous response from the Soviets. In this respect, it was critical that the Soviet leadership was in the hands of a politician who was also pursuing change.

On the other hand, Reagan deserves credit for negotiating the INF treaty and for facilitating the demise of communism. Very early in his presidency, he recognized that the Soviet economy would eventually collapse, and his defense budgets (including funds allocated for SDI) successfully speeded up the process. Furthermore, he challenged the Soviet leader to extend the reach of his reforms: At the Brandenburg Gate in 1987, it was Reagan who urged Gorbachev to "tear down this wall."[67] Reagan always carried with him the sense he conveyed to the British Parliament in 1982 when he quoted Gladstone: "You cannot fight against the future. Time is on our side."[68]

That speech Reagan delivered at Westminster might well be one of his most revealing. Paying tribute to another British leader, Reagan expressed his admiration for Winston Churchill, who "had that special attribute of great statesmen—the gift of vision, the willingness to see the future based on the experience of the past."[69] Reagan read the past as yielding one significant lesson, which he declared toward the end of his speech: "While we must be cautious about forcing the pace of change, we must not hesitate to declare our ultimate objectives and to take concrete actions to move toward them. We must be staunch in our conviction that freedom is not the sole prerogative of a lucky few, but the inalienable and universal right of all human beings."[70] History taught Reagan that liberal principles were universal and abiding truths, and on this fundamental point Thatcher could easily agree.

Ultimately, their common interests, mutual admiration, and shared goals enabled Reagan and Thatcher to survive the occasional ordeals that arose from their differences. In 1988 at the Royal Institute of International Affairs in London, Reagan saluted the prime minister for advancing "the cause of the Western alliance and human freedom." He extolled her "valor and strength" and graciously gave her credit for "the achievements of the Moscow summit as well as the Geneva and Washington summits."[71] (Notably, he declined to mention Reykjavik.) At the end of Reagan's second term, Thatcher welcomed the final tributes he generously paid to her.

In response to his remarks, Thatcher was quick to shower public praise on the president. She immediately repaid his compliments by gushing, "Your leadership has made America strong and confident again. Thank you Mr. President. Thank you for the summit. Thank you for your testament of belief and God bless America."[72] Later, in an article she authored for the *National Review* upon Reagan's retirement, her eulogy revealed what she herself valued most about leadership. According to Thatcher, Reagan "achieved the most difficult of all tasks: changing attitudes and perceptions about what is possible. From the strong fortress of his convictions, he set out to enlarge freedom the world over at a time when freedom was in retreat—and he succeeded."[73] Victory in the cold war seemed to vindicate the virtues of conviction-style leadership practiced in the global arena.

Neoliberal Economics in the Global Arena

In addition to his vision of a world without nuclear weapons, Reagan also imagined a world without trade barriers. When he announced that he would run for the presidency in 1979, Reagan promised to secure what he called the "North American accord," a campaign pledge he took seriously once in office. Fighting protectionist sentiment in Canada and the U.S., President Reagan and Prime Minister Brian Mulroney negotiated the Canada-U.S. Free Trade Agreement, which was approved by Congress and the Canadian Parliament and signed by the president on January 2, 1988. (Mulroney faced a serious struggle in Canada, combating not only protectionism but also anti-U.S. sentiment.) Furthermore, Reagan managed to secure approval for a "framework agreement" with Mexico, an initiative that paved the way for the North American Free Trade Agreement (NAFTA). Reagan achieved substantial success in promoting the principle of free trade—the enduring, often defining issue for conviction politicians in the liberal tradition.[74]

At global economic summits, Reagan and Thatcher were usually allied (although the British prime minister did join other world leaders when they expressed concern about growing U.S. deficits). Here again, in many ways, Reagan and Thatcher complemented each other: As U.S. president, Reagan commanded greater attention, while Thatcher frequently supplied the facts and figures to support their convictions and advance their goals. Their dependence on each other at global economic summits probably did strengthen their relationship, as many commentators believe.[75]

On one occasion, however, economic considerations threatened to create a rift in the relationship, and in this unusual instance, Thatcher sided with her European allies against the U.S. When martial law was imposed in

Poland in December 1981, the U.S. retaliated by imposing economic sanctions on the Soviet Union. This action revoked licenses for oil and gas equipment, including pipe-layers, and consequently affected a European contract to build a gas pipeline from Siberia to West Germany. Thatcher adamantly opposed the move, in part for its possible economic and financial consequences on Europe. But she objected even more strongly when the U.S. asserted extraterritorial authority and announced that it would impose sanctions on foreign counties that ignored the embargo. Eventually, the Reagan administration lifted the sanctions in November 1982, but the dispute seriously strained the special relationship.

In this case as in so many others, Thatcher needed to guard that relationship. At the time, her connection with Reagan enabled her to secure favorable terms when the U.K. had to renegotiate its purchase of Trident. (The U.S. had upgraded the submarine, and to maintain the independent British deterrent could have been too expensive.) Fortunately for Thatcher, the pipeline dispute did not block negotiations, and the U.S. and the U.K. reached a new agreement in March 1982.

The pipeline conflict provides an unusual case when Thatcher sided with Europe against the U.S., but much more often, she was engaged in a struggle within the European community. Thatcher held a strong conviction that British sovereignty (and autonomy) must be preserved within the community. Moreover, as she pursued her goals, she often practiced the same style of leadership at European meetings as she did at home. (One of her ministers quipped that Thatcher "insist[ed] on treating heads of government as if they were members of her cabinet.")[76] Both the style and the substance of her leadership created controversy within Europe.

During the early years of her premiership, conflict centered on Britain's contribution to the community's funds. Britain's small size in terms of agriculture meant that it received less of the European subsidy than other countries did, but the U.K. paid more in levies and duties on non-European imports. (At one point, Thatcher accused the Common Market of stealing "my money.") For several years she tried to secure a rebate and finally succeeded in 1984. When this conflict was resolved, a more fully integrated European market became possible.

Thatcher appreciated the free-market aspects and advantages of the community, and she endorsed the 1986 "Single Act" legislation that created a single market. Enthusiastic about the extension of free trade, Thatcher believed the economic benefits outweighed any reservations she had about its federalist aspects. In general, Thatcher did not take the threat of federalism seriously—until the president of the European Commission (EC), Jacques Delors, proposed a new plan for the community.

Delors's plan included a "social charter," which introduced a social demo-cratic framework of workers' rights throughout the community and, more significant, proposed "economic and monetary union" (EMU). Thatcher feared the social charter might revive British unions, but she was even more concerned about EMU. In particular, Thatcher opposed tying British ster-ling to the exchange rate mechanism (ERM) of the European monetary sys-tem, whose purpose it was to secure exchange rate stability among member nations. She expressed many objections to the ERM, including her reluc-tance to lose any national control over monetary policy.

In contrast to the prime minister, Chancellor of the Exchequer Nigel Law-son and Foreign Secretary Howe favored the ERM. Lawson informally pegged sterling to the deutsche mark, effectively establishing an exchange rate target for sterling without joining the ERM. Nevertheless, Thatcher re-peatedly voiced her firm opposition to managed exchange rates, a position she made especially clear in a parliamentary response she delivered in March 1988. As soon as the conflict within the cabinet became public, commenta-tors were "drawing parallels with the split over the Corn Laws that kept the Tories out of power for twenty years."[77] Ultimately, the issue would facilitate her demise just as the Corn Laws had ended Peel's leadership.

Pledging only that Britain would join when "the time was ripe," Thatcher continued to add preconditions and delay the nation's entry into the ERM. Lawson and Howe urged her to set a specific date, and in June 1989, before the meeting of the European Council in Madrid, both threatened to resign if she did not adopt a more conciliatory approach. To avoid the resignation of her top two ministers, Thatcher did reaffirm the commitment to join af-ter getting inflation down in Britain.[78] Narrowly escaping a crisis, she promptly removed Howe as foreign secretary, and he became leader of the House and deputy prime minister, a largely ceremonial title. Reflecting on her action, Lawson later concluded, "She had become reckless over Europe, reckless over the Poll Tax, reckless over what she said in public, and reckless over her colleagues."[79] As Lawson's language indicates, the conflict concern-ing exchange rate policy quickly evolved into controversy that centered on the prime minister's style.

At the peak of the conflict, Thatcher publicly opposed her chancellor and sided instead with her private economic advisor, Walters, who had recently returned to Downing Street. In October, Walters leaked to the *Financial Times* excerpts from his forthcoming academic article on the ERM. Walters described the ERM as "half-baked" and insisted the case for sterling joining the ERM had "never attained even a minimum level of plausibility." Accord-ing to Walters, "My advice has been for Britain to retain its system of flexi-ble exchange rates and stay out. . . . So far, Mrs. Thatcher has concurred."[80]

Walters's argument explicitly contradicted the chancellor's position and directly assaulted his authority. Immediately Lawson informed the prime minister that he would resign if she did not dismiss Walters. When Thatcher refused, Lawson turned in his letter of resignation, in which he wrote, "The successful conduct of economic policy is possible only if there is, *and is seen to be,* full agreement between the Prime Minister and the Chancellor of the Exchequer. Recent events have confirmed that this essential requirement cannot be satisfied so long as Alan Walters remains your personal economic advisor."[81] Shortly after Lawson's resignation, Walters also resigned. In the end, she lost both her chancellor and her "guru."[82]

Increasingly isolated, Thatcher also grew more obstinate and independent. At the 1990 European Summit in Rome, she was defeated in a vote that established the timetable for the U.K. to join the ERM. When she returned to Britain and reported to the House of Commons, she attacked EC president Jacques Delors and the notion of economic and monetary union. "No, no, no," shouted the conviction politician to both Delors and his plan. Two days after that report, Howe submitted his resignation, and ten days later, on November 13, he delivered his speech to Parliament.

While explaining the reasons for his resignation, Howe tried to emphasize substantive differences more than matters of style, but he had difficulty separating the two throughout much of his speech. To illustrate the flaws of Thatcher's leadership and their consequences, he recalled, "The point is more sharply put by a British businessman trading in Brussels and elsewhere who wrote to me saying that people throughout Europe see our prime minister finger wagging, hear her passionate 'no, no, no' much more clearly than the content of carefully worded formal texts. It is too easy for people to believe that we all share her attitude, for why else, he asks, has she been our prime minister for so long. This, my correspondent concluded, is a desperately serious situation for our country. Sadly, I have to agree." Howe concluded with a clarion call to his colleagues: "The time has come for others to consider their own response to the tragic conflict of loyalties with which I have myself wrestled for perhaps too long."[83] The next day Michael Heseltine announced his decision to challenge Thatcher for the leadership.

In the fall of 1990 (even before Howe's resignation), Thatcher's government finally decided that sterling would join the ERM. With inflation at 10 percent, John Major as the new chancellor favored the move, and Thatcher could not afford to lose another senior minister. Unpopular in Parliament and in the country (largely due to the poll tax), Thatcher proved unable to continue to resist pressures from the cabinet. Officially, British membership went into effect on October 8, 1990, but the U.K. would withdraw during Major's premiership. In general, the nature and extent of British membership in the European Union would trouble and divide Major's government as it did Thatcher's. Prime Minister Thatcher might have created the impression that Britain had regained its confidence as well as its global "greatness," but when she left office, in many ways the national identity remained uncertain. Britain's insecurity about its changing economic status pervaded political controversies throughout the Thatcher era (and beyond), including the major scandal of her premiership, the Westland affair.

Circumventing Constitutional Constraints

When Thatcher and Reagan practiced conviction politics in the global arena, they often managed to defy the demands of domestic institutions and circumvent constitutional constraints. In the Westland affair, Thatcher bypassed her cabinet and misled the Parliament.[84] In the Iran-Contra scheme, Reagan evaded the Congress and much of the executive branch. Furthermore, in both cases, the leaders engaged in deception and cover-ups, embracing the maxim that the ends justify the means. They suffered short-term political damage but eventually recovered their popular support. Neither constitution nor public opinion served to restrain Thatcher and Reagan during the Westland and Iran-Contra affairs, two cases that vividly illustrate the dangers of conviction-style leadership as practiced in the late twentieth century.

The Westland controversy started in 1985, when Westland, Britain's last helicopter company, no longer seemed viable, and the government needed to decide whether to rescue it by accepting a bid from a U.S. company, Sikorsky, or one from a European consortium. Thatcher's secretary of state for defense, Michael Heseltine, promoted the European bid (of which British Aerospace had become a member); Thatcher and her secretary of state for trade and industry, Leon Brittan, preferred the U.S. company's offer. Members of the E Committee discussed the issue, but Thatcher never called a full cabinet meeting to consider it, and in December, when Heseltine did raise the issue in cabinet, the prime minister cut him off. In her memoirs, Thatcher recalled what happened: "Without any warning Michael raised the issue of Westland in Cabinet on Thursday 12 December. This provoked a short, ill-tempered discussion, which I cut short on the grounds that we could not discuss the issue without papers. Nor was it on the agenda."[85] Thatcher had set the agenda for cabinet, and once again a minister proved unable to alter it. In contrast to the usual quiescent response of her ministers, Heseltine stormed out of the meeting and announced to the press his resignation in terms that emphasized the danger created by her defiance of constitutional norms and procedures.[86]

In the House of Commons in January 1986, Brittan spoke for the prime minister and gave an account of what happened. While addressing one of the many controversial aspects of the event, he denied that anyone had put pressure on British Aerospace to withdraw from the European consortium. In particular, he alleged he did not know about a letter from Sir Austin Pearce, British Aerospace chair, to the prime minister about the Westland affair. That letter dealt with a meeting at which Brittan told Sir Raymond Lygo, the British Aerospace chief executive, that the European bid was "against the national interests." Following full disclosure, Brittan was forced to apologize for having deceived the House of Commons.

The deception of her loyal minister called into question the integrity of the "principled premier"—in the Commons and in the country. By the end of January a Harris poll revealed that 75 percent believed Thatcher was handling the affair badly, and 43 percent favored her retirement before the next general election.[87] Like Reagan after Iran-Contra, Thatcher would recover, but worse was still to come.

For the public (and Parliament), the plot thickened in February. A letter had been leaked from the solicitor general, Sir Patrick Mayhew, to Heseltine that accused the defense secretary of peddling misinformation about Westland. Contrary to the parliamentary convention that prohibits disclosing the advice of law officers, the leak was an obvious attempt to discredit Heseltine. Mayhew and the attorney general demanded an inquiry into the leak. In response, Thatcher authorized setting up an internal investigation. The leak, it turned out, came from Brittan, who asserted that it was a "disclosure" made in the public interest and with the approval of Thatcher's office. Brittan was forced to resign, and Thatcher tried to dismiss it all as a "misunderstanding" between office staffs. In fact, Thatcher herself had learned of her office's involvement and Brittan's ploy before she initiated an official inquiry. At the time, however, she found it convenient to ignore this information.[88] Shielded by the loyalty of her minister, Thatcher used the weapon of "ultimate deniability" to defeat her critics. In contrast to Reagan, however, when Thatcher declared that she was ill-informed, it was a declaration difficult to reconcile with her hands-on management style.

In the final debate in the House of Commons, the prime minister stated that she had delivered the "true facts," and her explanation won the backing of a majority of 160. Even Heseltine rallied to Thatcher's side, announcing that the political battle was over and admitting only that the situation could have been handled better. Quoting Winston Churchill, former Labour leader Michael Foot ridiculed the reformed rebel: "It is all right to rat, but you cannot re-rat." Foot's successor, Neil Kinnock, attacked Thatcher for "dishonesty, duplicity, conniving, and maneuvering," but in his speech he rambled and ranted in a way that undercut the force of his argument. In fact, it was the Social Democratic leader David Owen who stated the case most forcefully against the prime minister, demanding information she continued to conceal. When he confronted Thatcher directly, she simply sat in silence.[89] Despite Owen's revealing interrogation, the humiliated "defendant" survived her trial. Thatcher maintained the support of her party members in the Commons, though she lost the support of the people who put them there. In the national opinion polls, the Conservative party fell to third place, and the prime minister's own approval rating hit its lowest point since before the Falklands war.[90]

To the British public, the Westland affair proved significant for several reasons. The event revealed the dark side of the prime minister's independent leadership style, while it also exposed her dishonesty and duplicity in a way that damaged her reputation as an avowed "conviction politician." Just as significant, the Westland affair challenged the British public to confront their nation's changing status in the world.

Much of the debate during the controversy smacked of xenophobia, sparked by the fact that Britain was about to lose its last helicopter company. In this regard, Thatcher might have been more realistic than some of her opponents were. She understood that Britain needed to encourage foreign investment, and she knew her nation could not compete alone, especially in the defense industry. Of course, when Thatcher sought to strengthen economic ties, she usually looked across the Atlantic, not to Europe. As the Westland affair followed failure to negotiate a deal with Ford or General Motors to purchase British Leyland (BL), she feared U.S. investors would abandon their interest in the U.K.

In the case of BL as well as Westland, Thatcher's opponents voiced strong anti-U.S. sentiments. While she shunned those views, she also failed to grasp their intensity or their source. In her memoirs, Thatcher attributed anti-Americanism to the failure of the British to understand President Reagan.[91] But she overlooked another, more obvious source of resentment: In terms of global status, the U.S. had usurped the U.K.'s position in the world. The British leader who otherwise understood the insecurities endemic to her nation's global decline never seemed to comprehend that those same fears could become expressed as hostility toward the U.S. By her own assessment, "the most damaging effect of the Westland affair was the fuel which had been poured on the flames of anti-Americanism. And that fire, once lit, proved difficult to extinguish."[92] Thatcher carefully cultivated her partnership with Reagan, but she failed to grasp that the special relationship between nations also needed to be nurtured.

In the midst of her account of Westland, Thatcher would name Reagan as the most significant of her "staunch friends who rallied round." As she remembered a phone call from the president: "He said he was furious that anyone had the gall to challenge my integrity. He wanted me to know that 'out here in the colonies' I had a friend. He urged me to go out 'and do my darndest.'"[93] (Note the reversal in status here: Reagan assumed the role of booster and depicted the U.S. as a colony, at least as Thatcher recalled their conversation.) Of course, in a very short time, Thatcher would be the one playing the role of "staunch friend who rallied round" when the president's critics had the gall to challenge his integrity.

Events in the Iran-Contra affair call into question President Reagan's integrity as well as the integrity of late-twentieth-century political institutions. The number of investigations, reports, and books on the subject—each with a different interpretation of events—makes the topic a difficult one to address within a few pages in this book.[94] Nevertheless, a brief review of some established facts reveals the dangerous nature and consequences of the conviction politics Reagan chose to practice in Central America and the Middle East.

Reagan's convictions established the objective for operations in Central America and invited his subordinates to devise any means to achieve his end. In 1979 a Marxist coalition overthrew the dictatorship of Anastasio Somosa in Nicaragua. President Carter initially provided aid to the new Sandinista government, but after the Sandinistas supported a Marxist guerrilla offensive in El Salvador, the Carter administration reversed its policy. Reagan was determined to do more than end aid to the Sandinistas. He wanted to assist those who were trying to overthrow the regime. Early in his first term, Reagan clearly articulated his intention to support the Contras—whom he frequently depicted as "freedom fighters"—in "body and soul."[95] For Reagan, providing assistance to the Contras simply constituted "the right thing to do."[96]

Despite his determination to promote democracy and halt communism in the region, Reagan did not want to commit troops to fight a war that lacked public support.[97] In fact, he doubted that a public consensus on U.S. military involvement in Central America could ever be reached. On this issue, Reagan's own advisors proved deeply divided: Haig and CIA director William Casey exerted pressure for greater involvement, Weinberger opposed any military action, and White House staff—especially Michael Deaver and James Baker—feared that Central America could put Reagan's economic program at risk. In the president's mind, covert activity remained the only viable option.

On December 1, 1981, Reagan signed a "finding" in which he approved covert aid to the Contras, ostensibly to interdict the arms flow from Nicaragua to El Salvador. Throughout 1982, the CIA became increasingly involved in overseeing and supporting the Contra effort. As subsequent events would show, in many respects, covert operations provide the worst option for a conviction-style leader. Conviction politics usually requires bold public pronouncements, but Reagan's decision to pursue his objective through secrecy meant that the Great Communicator could never sell his policy honestly to the public. Indeed, President Reagan declined to make a nationally televised speech on behalf of Contra aid until May 9, 1984, but by then public opinion had formed in opposition to his policy.

During Reagan's first term, Congress repeatedly voiced its opposition to the president's goals in Central America and took concrete steps to thwart his ability to pursue his objectives. In December 1982, the House of Representatives passed the first Boland Amendment, which prohibited the CIA and the Department of Defense from using funds for the purpose of overthrowing the Sandinista government or provoking a military exchange between Nicaragua and Honduras. One year later, House Democrats voted for the first time against aid to the Contras, although Senate Republicans approved it. In conference committee, Congress agreed to cap Contra funding, making a move that essentially left the issue unresolved but encouraged the administration to start its search for alternative sources of funds.

Conflict between the administration and Congress intensified in 1984. In January and February, Reagan approved the CIA's placement of magnetic mines in Nicaraguan harbors, which resulted in damage to several ships, including a Soviet oil tanker. Congress learned about the CIA's move at the same time as the public found out—only after the *Wall Street Journal* broke the story in April. The administration had failed to inform in advance the Senate Select Committee on Intelligence, which by law it was required to do. The committee chair, Barry Goldwater, immediately wrote to Casey: "Mine the harbors of Nicaragua? This is an act violating international law. It is an act of war."[98] Senator Patrick Moynihan resigned from the committee and returned only after Casey apologized and agreed to notify the committee in the future. Moynihan later recalled the mining of Nicaraguan harbors as "the outset of this challenge to American constitutional government" and "the first acts of deception that gradually mutated into a policy of deceit."[99] In October 1984, the House passed Boland II, which prohibited any military or paramilitary support for the Contras, but it ultimately failed to alter the administration's determined efforts to assist Reagan's "freedom fighters."[100]

In the face of persistent congressional opposition, members of the Reagan administration intensified their search for alternative funds. By March 1984, National Security Advisor McFarlane had already begun to solicit money from third countries. Israel turned him down, but Saudi Arabia did not. (Reagan knew about the Saudi contributions, the legality of which was discussed at a June 25, 1984, National Security Planning Group meeting.)[101] Congress had exercised its constitutional authority and attempted to block the administration's efforts, but each legislative effort to restrain

Reagan only spurred his subordinates to devise new means to carry out his convictions.

Admittedly, the role of Reagan's convictions in the Iranian part of the Iran-Contra scheme remains unclear. In 1985 and 1986, the Reagan administration sold antitank and antiaircraft weapons to Iran. The initiative violated Reagan's official policy, which barred the sale of weapons to countries that sponsored terrorism, and, in particular, it violated an embargo on the sale of arms to Iran. The president approved the sales and kept them secret, until a Lebanese magazine published the story in November 1986. Reagan aimed to use Iranian influence to secure the release of U.S. hostages in Lebanon. It might be argued that Reagan's goal of freeing the hostages stemmed from conviction, but that objective seems to reflect sentiment—and perhaps sentimentality—more than principle. On the other hand, the Iranian initiative became connected to the administration's goals in Central America. The Iranians were overcharged, and some of the proceeds were used to fund the Contras. Whether the president knew the details about the diversion of funds has never been definitively determined, but he certainly endorsed the end for which these means were employed.

Investigations of the Iran-Contra affair have documented the extent of Reagan's involvement in the Iranian initiative. In December 1985, Reagan signed a finding that authorized a November transfer of weapons to Iran. (Admiral John Poindexter, the national security advisor, later destroyed this document, but a CIA copy was found.)[102] On January 6, 1986, Reagan signed another finding authorizing the covert action to continue. Throughout this period, Israel had been used as a third party to transfer the weapons, but as Edwin Meese informed Reagan, this method required congressional notification. On January 17, Reagan signed yet another finding, one that appeared to offer alternative means to execute the transfer of weapons. The wording resembled the language in the January 6 finding, but Poindexter drafted a new cover memo, which read, "The objectives of the Israeli plan could be met if the CIA, using an authorized agent as necessary, purchased arms from the Department of Defense under the Economy Act and then transferred them to Iran directly after receiving appropriate payment from Iran."[103] At this juncture, "The United States became a direct supplier of arms to Iran. The President told the [Tower Commission] Board that he understood the plan in this way. That day, President Reagan wrote in his diary: 'I agreed to sell TOWs to Iran.'"[104] There has never been any doubt about Reagan's knowledge of or direct involvement in the sale of arms to Iran.

The direct transfer of arms was executed by an operation that became known as "the Enterprise," essentially a covert network of dummy corporations, Swiss bank accounts, aircraft, and other resources run by a retired air force major general, Richard Secord, and his associate Albert Hakim. Through this network, Secord and Hakim raised almost $48 million and spent almost $35.8 on covert operations. At least $3.8 million went to the Contras, and Secord and his associates kept $4.4 million for themselves.[105] Ultimately, the initiative supplied 2,004 TOW antitank missiles and more than two hundred spare parts for ground-launched HAWK antiaircraft missiles to Iran for its war with Iraq. The unusual way the Reagan administration chose to execute its policy was not its only innovation.

The characters who crafted the policy also marked a departure from the past. The national security advisor—first McFarlane and then Poindexter—and their assistant, Lieutenant Colonel Oliver North, assumed primary responsibility for the design and direction of the operation. By relying on his national security advisor and the National Security Council (NSC) staff, President Reagan managed to circumvent official channels for creating and conducting foreign policy. The NSC staff does not actually work for the NSC; staff members work directly for and are accountable to the national security advisor (who works directly and exclusively for the president). In critical aspects of the operation, members of the White House supplanted officials responsible for national security and subverted the formal policy process. Despite the critical roles played by McFarlane, Poindexter, and North, the independent counsel who later investigated Iran-Contra demonstrated that the affair was not entirely a rogue operation within the White House. Both Secretary of State George Shultz and Secretary of Defense Weinberger knew about the Iranian initiatives, and they later took part in the cover-up.[106]

Nevertheless, knowledge at the top of the departments did not mean that the bureaucracy played its traditional role in the design and implementation of policy. The Departments of State and Defense largely remained outside the policy process. Those who were making decisions functioned without the benefit of the analysis or expertise that the bureaucracy—however politicized—can provide. Ultimately, the Iranian initiatives proved to be unwise as well as possibly illegal. In the arms-for-hostages deal, the terrorists released three U.S. hostages held in Lebanon but immediately took three others. Nor did the outcome provide any evidence that the administration had improved relations with "moderates" in the Iranian government, another rationale rendered by the Reagan administration. The failure of the Iranian policy actually confirmed the wisdom of Reagan's avowed convictions that proscribe dealing with terrorists. The dismal fate of his initiative as well as the contradiction between his words and his deeds made the scheme a hard one to sell when the president was forced to go public.

Reagan's televised speech to the nation on November 13 about the Iranian arms deal proved unconvincing and inaccurate. Among other things, he denied that the deals he authorized constituted an arms-for-hostages swap. An ABC poll revealed the public's immediate response to the president's address: Seventy-nine percent opposed the sale of arms to Iran to secure the release of U.S. hostages, and 72 percent opposed the arms sales to improve relations with moderates in Iran. Respondents in the poll had rejected Reagan's rationales. More significant (and damaging to the president's support), 56 percent said Reagan had abandoned his avowed principles and "has been negotiating with terrorists by supplying Iran with arms." Finally, a survey conducted by the *Los Angeles Times* found only 14 percent believed Reagan's version of events.[107] Such a confidence gap delivered a critical blow to the conviction politician. Like Thatcher during the Westland affair, Reagan during Iran-Contra lost his most essential asset: his credibility.

In the first of several official investigations, a special review board appointed by Reagan studied the procedures and role of the NSC staff in an effort to discover what had gone wrong. Senator John Tower, former secretary of state Edmund Muskie, and former national security advisor Brent Scowcroft made up the board. Its final report placed most of the blame on the president's management style, which "is to put the principal responsibility for policy review and implementation on the shoulders of his advisors,"[108] while the report also criticized the "flawed process" by which Reagan advisors designed and implemented the scheme.[109] In general, the Tower report portrayed the president as a hapless victim of overzealous aides.

The next two investigations failed to yield additional insights or ensure accountability. On the same day the Tower Commission began its work, Attorney General Meese ordered a criminal investigation that focused on the diversion of funds to the Contras. From November 21 through 24, Meese had been conducting his own "fact-finding" expedition that was neither comprehensive nor careful. During the Justice Department investigation (and even earlier), North shredded several critical documents. Congressional committees subsequently held extensive hearings, during which the White House withheld thousands of documents and North and Poindexter lied to the legislature. Both were later convicted, but eventually the lower court decisions were reversed on technicalities.[110]

After an investigation that took seven years, Independent Counsel Lawrence Walsh rendered the most accurate account possible—and the harshest judgment of the Iran-Contra affair. Unable to prove that the president violated any criminal statute, Walsh nonetheless concluded that Reagan "set the stage for the illegal activities of others." According to Walsh, the president "created the conditions which made possible the crimes committed by others by his secret deviations from announced national policy as to Iran and hostages and by his open determination to keep the contras together 'body and soul' despite a statutory ban on contra aid." Following public exposure, Walsh continued, "Reagan officials deliberately deceived the Congress and the public about the level and extent of official knowledge of and support for these operations." According to the independent counsel, impeachment "certainly should have been considered."[111] Yet Walsh proved unable to make the case for impeachment by providing a full account of the events because he encountered countless obstructions, including the decision of Reagan's successor, George Bush, to pardon many of the culprits in the Iran-Contra affair.

Frustrated by Bush's action, Walsh rendered a contrast between Reagan and Bush that actually seemed to legitimize Reagan's behavior. During the press conference at the conclusion of his investigation, the independent counsel labeled President Bush's decision to pardon Weinberger and five other officials "an act of friendship or an act of self protection." (Bush would have had to testify at Weinberger's trial.) Then Walsh explained: "I think President Bush will always have to answer for his pardons. There was no public purpose served by that. . . . *President Reagan, on the other hand, was carrying out policies that he strongly believed in. He may have been willful, but he, at least he thought he was serving the country in what he did, and the fact that he disregarded certain laws and statutes in the course of it was not because of any possibly self-centered purpose*" (emphasis added).[112] Even Walsh unwittingly implied that the ends justified the means.

Both Reagan and Thatcher escaped constitutional constraints on their authority and suffered no lasting political damage. In the case of the Iran-Contra affair, the Reagan administration's efforts to obstruct the investigations succeeded, and many of the details of the scheme remain unknown. Furthermore, Congress cowered in the face of a popular president. (At the time, members of Congress also expressed reluctance to "bring down another president" after the dark days of Watergate—especially the first successful president in many years.) Reagan's popularity took a temporary dip in the polls but recovered before he left office. Admittedly, members of the public found the nature and implications of Iran-Contra difficult to grasp. (It was a bizarre and complicated scheme, and in the clearest cases, the public's attention to foreign affairs generally remains low.) More significant, however, the public perceived economic conditions as promising greater prosperity: A new day had dawned, and it was morning again in America. In the case of the Westland affair, Thatcher at first escaped constraints due to the weakness of the official opposition but later fully recovered as a result of improved economic conditions. She went on to secure her historic third victory and, finally, won the electorate's endorsement of her economic policies. At the conclusion of the twentieth century, constitutional considerations came second to public opinion, and perceptions of the economy largely determined that opinion. The Iran-Contra and Westland affairs sent a message to future presidents and prime ministers that they can violate the law and still maintain their public support when economic prosperity prevails. Even the public seemed to agree that the ends justify the means.

Admittedly, in theory, liberalism imposes fewer constraints on leaders engaged in international affairs than it does in domestic politics. According to Lockean liberalism, nations remain in a state of nature (potentially a state of war) in relation to one another, and consequently, no social contract limits their activity. Federative power, which Locke defined as "the power of war and peace, leagues and alliances, and all the transactions with all persons and communities without the commonwealth," is almost always joined with executive authority,[113] and the liberal regime grants to its executive wide discretion in the conduct of foreign affairs. Indeed, the sole purpose of civil society—to secure individual rights—both restricts leaders at home and empowers them abroad: An omnipotent executive defies the notion of limited government and threatens individual rights, but an executive might need unusual authority to defend the regime and secure the rights of its citizens. In the liberal tradition, leadership is less ambiguous and the citizenry less ambivalent in global politics than in domestic affairs. On the other hand, though the scope of executive authority expands in foreign affairs, no liberal theorist has ever condoned an escape from the constitutional constraints that serve to preserve the regime.

For Reagan and Thatcher, however, the ends of Western liberal democracy justified departures from procedural means. Global politics often enabled them to reinforce the basic tenets of the public philosophy they preached at home. When they could orchestrate events in the global arena, they usually seized the opportunity to enact their neoliberal creed—even at the cost of undermining liberalism itself. Reagan and Thatcher revealed their disregard for procedure by circumventing the political process, engaging in covert activity, and allowing or authorizing cover-ups, and they generally shunned advice produced through traditional bureaucratic channels. Rather than consider other political actors legitimate participants in the process, Reagan and Thatcher viewed them as mere obstacles that needed to be overcome, and public opinion provided a poor substitute for institutional constraints. Members of the public stood in awe as they heard the message roar and watched the messenger soar. To citizens on both sides of the Atlantic, the message and the messenger mattered more than the mode of delivery.

10

CONCLUSION

Presidents and prime ministers who practice conviction politics play a critical role in political development, though they encounter distinct opportunities and constraints at different junctures in history. In general, conviction-style leaders possess greater capacity to effect change than other politicians, and late-twentieth-century leaders operate in a context more conducive to their independent initiative than the environment of their predecessors. On both sides of the Atlantic, conviction-style leaders provide vehicles for change when the public demands it, and they often manage to adapt both ideas and institutions to suit changing circumstances. At the same time, their strong decisive leadership presents risks that can be easily overlooked in light of the rewards.

In the Anglo-American tradition, conviction-style leaders have redefined the dominant ideology of liberalism in ways that sustain its relevance and identify its principles with the pursuit of the "public good." Andrew Jackson and Sir Robert Peel leveled an attack on concentrated power and privilege, and then promoted liberal principles that served to advance democratic objectives. To improve the condition of many marginal groups, Grover Cleveland and William Gladstone advocated classic liberalism, while they tried to defeat reformers who pressed for change that directly challenged liberal principles. Their successors, Woodrow Wilson and David Lloyd George, proved to be more innovative: Advancing a new liberalism, they promoted the modern state as a positive means of fulfilling the liberal promise of equal opportunity. Finally, Ronald Reagan and Margaret Thatcher articulated a neoliberal ideology, which sought to reverse the role of the state in domestic welfare but expand its authority to promote freedom abroad and strengthen security at home. The evolution of liberal ideology indicates that it must adapt to endure and that it requires leadership to do so, and yet each adaptation threatens to dilute the meaning of liberalism and diminish the protections it affords.

To the public, the leaders' style often matters more than the substance of their convictions, but the principles the leaders espouse are important because they can determine executive authority as well as define the political order. Nineteenth-century conviction politicians believed in extremely limited government, which restricted the realm of presidential and prime ministerial power. In the twentieth century, when liberalism came to signify positive state action, conviction-style leaders expanded the scope of their authority and acquired greater legitimacy. Even the late-twentieth-century neoliberal leaders who wanted to roll back the state in domestic affairs continued to strengthen it in other ways, and in the process, they further increased executive power and achieved greater autonomy in decision making. Presidents and prime ministers who operate within the liberal tradition will always encounter some limits on their leadership, but the risks posed by strong leadership increase when liberalism loses much of its original meaning or when leaders promote principles outside the liberal tradition.

Conviction-style leaders also try to change traditional liberal institutions, and their efforts have generally facilitated the transformation of systems designed to produce consensus into mechanisms more conducive to conviction politics. Gladstone and Cleveland provide exceptions: Constrained by their classic liberal convictions, they also struggled in an institutional context that proved weightier than their willful determination to achieve change. Other conviction-style leaders have managed to weaken, transform, or circumvent intermediaries such as political parties, the press, the legislature, and the bureaucracy, and they often succeed by rendering the rationale that the ends justify the means. As they pursue reform, these leaders articulate their goals in ways that tap public frustration with the status quo and attack the structures that support it. Ultimately, they achieve institutional change that expands the scope of executive power, and when combined with the evolution of liberal principles, structural change can make individual rights more susceptible to revision and vulnerable to authority.[1]

In sum, conviction politicians often escape the constraints that a liberal regime places on leadership. Representative government does not lend itself to ideological pursuits, clear direction, or consistent policy making, but conviction-style leaders rarely perceive the need to reconcile their methods with the procedural requirements of liberalism.[2] Rather than mediate among the various interests that flourish in a liberal democratic society, conviction politicians insist strong leaders must seize the initiative, set the national agenda, and then persuade members of the public to follow their lead. When they succeed, they manage to bring about fundamental change without creating a constitutional crisis; yet their leadership does affect the constitution—its role in defining the political order and its place in the public mind. Conviction politicians advise citizens to look to leadership, not to the constitution, for the most effective means to secure their goals.

Furthermore, while most conviction-style leaders in the liberal tradition espouse the virtues of economic independence (individual autonomy, personal industry, and self-reliance), they also encourage political dependency by cultivating the call for strong leadership—and then answering it. Conviction-style leadership not only assumes a floundering followership, it also nurtures it. To halt the growing dependence on leadership requires the revitalization of civic culture, including increased citizen participation and civic education.

Abraham Lincoln looked to the citizenry when he proposed a remedy for the risks that strong leadership can pose to the liberal polity. Recalling the revolutionaries who established the foundations of the U.S. Constitution, Lincoln declared, "They were the pillars of the temple of liberty; and now that they have crumbled away, that temple must fall, unless we, their descendants, supply their places with other pillars, hewn from the solid quarry of sober reason. Passion has helped us; but can do so no more. It will in the future be our enemy. *Reason, cold, calculating, unimpassioned reason, must furnish all the materials for our future support and defence"* (emphasis added). According to Lincoln, reason can serve to preserve what passion threatens to destroy—"general intelligence, sound morality, and, in particular, a reverence for the constitution and laws."[3] Lincoln offered a traditional liberal solution when he relied on reason to revive enlightened regard for liberty and ensure the perpetuation of political institutions.[4]

Neither the United States nor the United Kingdom faces the dire circumstances that Lincoln feared: The rare though recurrent emergence of conviction-style leadership mitigates much of the risk. Most of the time, in both countries, the majority expresses general satisfaction with the existing political order and enjoys a relatively high degree of peace and prosperity. In such conditions, presidents and prime ministers generally seek to preserve the status quo, maintain the national agenda, and practice consensus leadership. Promoting a new political order calls for daring initiative and consistent conviction; maintaining the political order requires conciliation and incrementalism.[5] In normal times, political posturing, partisan bickering, and personal conflict occur, but politicians generally shy away from great ideological battles and shun debate about fundamental principles. Although the precise timing of conviction politics proves difficult to pinpoint, at least in part because leaders help to determine it, conviction politicians appear only at moments when the public becomes dissatisfied with status quo, consensus breaks down, and reformers issue clarion calls for change.

At those moments, reliance on "cold, calculating, unimpassioned reason" alone might prove to be unrealistic as well as undesirable. The history of conviction politics indicates that passion provides a recurrent impulse for leaders and their followers even within the rational, rights-oriented liberal tradition. Passion fuels the desire for change that creates conviction politics, and conviction-style leaders drive political development in new, creative directions. Yet when the call for conviction politics comes again, citizens and their elected officials could engage in rational discourse as they seek to satisfy their longing for lofty purpose and new vision in public affairs. Above all, rational regard for the democratic process might temper the passionate pursuit of principle and safely enable citizens to reap the rewards of presidents and prime ministers who practice conviction politics.

NOTES

1. Introduction

1. Margaret Thatcher, *The Path to Power* (New York: HarperCollins, 1995), p. 448.

2. See James MacGregor Burns, *Roosevelt: The Lion and the Fox* (New York: Harcourt Brace Jovanovich, 1984); and Ann Ruth Willner, *The Spellbinders: Charismatic Political Leadership* (New Haven, Conn.: Yale University Press, 1984).

3. Admittedly, the contexts and ideas of Jackson and Peel differ in many respects (and to a greater extent than in the other three pairs), but their defining issues reveal similar liberal principles. Moreover, Cleveland lacks the stature of the other leaders, and certainly his achievements were not as substantial as those of Gladstone. Yet Cleveland is the prototype of a conviction politician, and his popularity in his own time largely stemmed from his leadership style. (As a pair, Cleveland and Gladstone are perhaps in greater ideological agreement than any of the others.) Finally, the description of Lloyd George as a conviction politician might strike many readers as strange: The "Welsh Wizard" could easily be included in a set of compromisers, but initially his ideas won him a popular following, and his reputation for strong leadership propelled him to the premiership during World War I.

4. See Bert Rockman, "What Didn't We Know and Should We Forget It? Political Science and the Reagan Presidency," *Polity* 21 (Summer 1989): 777–792.

5. Anthony Downs, *An Economic Theory of Democracy* (New York: Harper, 1957), p. 96.

6. Margaret Thatcher, *The Downing Street Years* (New York: HarperCollins, 1993), p. 26.

7. For a text of the speech (and analysis of it), see Paul Erikson, *Reagan Speaks: The Making of an American Myth* (New York: New York University Press, 1985), pp. 124–138 and ch. 2.

8. For a text of the speech, see Nicholas Wapshott and George Brock, *Thatcher* (London: Macdonald and Company, 1983), pp. 276–287, and the discussion on pp. 86–90.

9. Personal interview, Cecil Parkinson, June 11, 1991.

10. Surprisingly little social science literature explores the relationship between social movements and national political institutions, especially the presidency. For an article that does, see W. Douglas Costain and Anne Costain, "The Political Strategies of Social Movements: A Comparison of the Women's and Environmental Movements," *Congress and the Presidency* 19 (Winter 1992): 1–28. The authors conclude that the groups' success depended on the willingness of the mass media and national politicians to provide a forum for their ideas.

11. Personal interview, Tony Benn, June 19, 1991.

12. Harvey C. Mansfield Jr., *Taming the Prince: The Ambivalence of Modern Executive Power* (New York: Free Press, 1989), especially ch. 8.

13. For the classic study on the dominant role of liberalism in the U.S., see Louis Hartz, *The Liberal Tradition in America: An Interpretation of American Political Thought Since the Revolution* (New York: Harcourt Brace Jovanovich, 1955). Hartz contrasts the U.S. and the U.K., but his distinctions might be overdrawn. As several critics of his study have pointed

out, class plays a role in the U.S., although it might be concealed by the language of "special interests." Moreover, even if U.S. citizens are born liberals, as Hartz alleges, liberalism also took root in nineteenth-century Britain. Despite its history of feudalism, Great Britain also has a history of rights-oriented reasoning and legal protections that dates back to the Magna Carta. Furthermore, this study differs from Hartz's in another respect: Hartz assigns no role to leaders in the liberal tradition. The only president who merits Hartz's serious attention is FDR, and in that case "liberalism goes underground." See especially chapter 10 of *The Liberal Tradition*.

14. In some respects, Cleveland and Gladstone blur commonly drawn distinctions between liberalism and republicanism. See chapter 3 of this book. For persuasive arguments that the two traditions are not distinct or mutually exclusive, see Ian Shapiro, *Political Criticism* (Berkeley: University of California Press, 1990), ch. 6; and Isaac Kramnick, "The 'Great National Discussion': The Discourse of Politics in 1787," *William and Mary Quarterly* 45 (January 1988): 3–32.

15. See J. G. A. Pocock, *The Machiavellian Moment: Florentine Political Thought and the Atlantic Republican Tradition* (Princeton, N.J.: Princeton University Press, 1975).

16. James D. Richardson, ed., *A Compilation of the Messages and Papers of the Presidents, 1789–1897* (Washington, D.C.: Government Printing Office, 1896), vol. 2, p. 590.

17. *Speeches of the Late Right Honourable Sir Robert Peel* (London: George Routeledge and Company, 1858), vol. 4, p. 689.

18. Speech at Guildhall, London, 1988. Quoted in K. D. Ewing and C. A. Gearty, *Freedom Under Thatcher: Civil Liberties and Modern Britain* (Oxford: Clarendon Press, 1990), p. 208.

19. Roy P. Basler, ed., *The Collected Works of Abraham Lincoln* (New Brunswick, N.J.: Rutgers University Press, 1953), vol. 1, pp. 113–114.

2. Democratic Liberalism: Andrew Jackson and Sir Robert Peel

1. Jackson's oldest brother, Hugh, died in the Revolutionary War, and his brother Robert died from the smallpox he contracted as a British prisoner. His mother died from the cholera she probably contracted while treating two of her nephews, who were ill aboard a British prison ship.

2. See Michael Bentley, *Politics Without Democracy, Great Britain 1815–1914* (Oxford: Basil Blackwell, 1984).

3. Michel Chevalier, *Society, Manners and Politics in the United States*, ed. J. W. Ward (Garden City, N.Y.: Doubleday, 1961), pp. 174, 177.

4. Marvin Meyers, *The Jacksonian Persuasion: Politics and Beliefs* (Stanford, Calif.: Stanford University Press, 1957), p. 8.

5. See Meyers, esp. pp. 12–14; and John Ashworth, *Agrarians and Aristocrats—Party Political Ideology in the United States, 1837–1846* (London: Royal Historical Society, 1983), esp. pp. 43–47.

6. James Sterling Young, *The Washington Community: 1800–1828* (New York: Harcourt, Brace and World, 1966), esp. pp. 190–191.

7. Arthur Schlesinger, *The Age of Jackson* (Boston: Little, Brown and Company, 1945), p. 45. See also Stephen Skowronek, "Presidential Leadership in Political Time," in Michael Nel-

son, ed., *The Presidency and the Political System,* 3rd ed. (Washington, D.C.: Congressional Quarterly, 1990), esp. p. 121.

8. November 5, 1828.

9. November 19, 1828.

10. November 18, 1828.

11. Schlesinger, esp. pp. 45–47.

12. According to Jackson, federalism "is not the reflection of a day, but belongs to the most deeply rooted convictions of my mind." He made this remark after declaring his position on internal improvements: that surplus revenue should be apportioned to the states according to their ratio of representation. James D. Richardson, ed., *A Compilation of the Messages and Papers of the Presidents, 1789–1897* (Washington, D.C.: Government Printing Office, 1896), vol. 2, p. 452.

13. Richardson, ed., vol. 2, pp. 437–438.

14. Richardson, ed., vol. 2, pp. 449–450.

15. Richardson, ed., vol. 2, pp. 449–450.

16. In his first annual message, Jackson discussed the bank's charter and declared, "I feel that I can not, in justice to the parties interested, too soon present it to the deliberate consideration of the Legislature and the people." Richardson, ed., vol. 2, p. 462.

17. Memo on the bank in Robert Remini, ed., *The Age of Jackson* (Columbia: University of South Carolina Press, 1972), pp. 73–74.

18. Richardson, ed., vol. 2, p. 590.

19. Reprinted in *Niles Register,* June 25, 1832.

20. July 12, 1832.

21. July 23, 1832.

22. *Globe,* July 16, 1832.

23. Schlesinger, p. 92. According to Schlesinger, most newspapers reflected the interests and views of their advertisers.

24. Reprinted in *Niles Register,* July 14, 1832.

25. July 1, 1832.

26. Calvin Colton, ed., *Works of Henry Clay Comprising His Life, Correspondence, and Speeches* (New York: Henry Clay Publishing Co., 1897), vol. 5, pp. 534–535.

27. *Works of Daniel Webster* (Boston: Little, Brown and Company, 1857), vol. 3, p. 446.

28. *National Intelligencer,* October 28, 1832.

29. *Globe,* July 16, 1832.

30. In fact, he considered this. See Jackson's memo in Remini, ed., p. 71.

31. In at least one respect, Jackson's victory appears to have altered the nature of political discourse. The charge that the president is "monarchical" starts to signify a leader who is out of touch and removed from the people, not one who (like Jackson) expands executive authority on the basis of popular support. Consider not only the Whig attacks leveled against the royal manner of Van Buren but also the campaign against President George Bush as "King George," a label used by his intraparty opponent Patrick Buchanan in the 1992 presidential primaries.

32. Van Buren was vulnerable not only because of the depression but also because he had the reputation of being an unprincipled wheeler and dealer. Contrast his nicknames, "the Red Fox" and the "Little Magician," to Jackson's titles, "Old Hickory" and the "Old Hero," and return to the contrast between consensus and conviction politicians.

33. Richardson, ed., vol. 3, p. 91.

34. Richardson, ed., vol. 2, p. 447.

35. Herman Melville, *Moby-Dick* (New York: Bantam, 1981), p. 113.

36. A great deal of historical research has focused on the connection between U.S. Democrats and British Radicals, emphasizing how the U.S. experience provided illustrations and myths for Radical propaganda. For examples, see Frank Thistlethwaite, *The Anglo-American Connection in the Early Nineteenth Century* (1959; New York: Russell and Russell, 1971); and G. D. Lillibridge, *Beacon of Freedom: The Impact of American Democracy upon Great Britain, 1830–1870* (Philadelphia: University of Pennsylvania Press, 1955). But the impact of the U.S. reached beyond the Radicals. See David Paul Crook, *American Democracy in English Politics, 1815–1850* (Oxford: Clarendon Press, 1965), p. 199. My discussion here draws heavily on Crook's analysis, especially concerning the impact of Tocqueville's *Democracy in America.*

37. The same year as the publication of Tocqueville's work, Peel delivered the Tamworth Manifesto, in which he announced that his party would accept the 1832 reform bill as an established constitutional principle and pursue further "moderate reform." See discussion in chapters 6 and 8 of this book.

38. Quoted in Crook, pp. 178, 191.

39. Crook, p. 152.

40. Robert Blake, *The Conservative Party from Peel to Thatcher* (London: Fontana, 1985), pp. 17–18.

41. *Times,* January 1, 1844.

42. Quoted in David Thomson, *England in the Nineteenth Century* (London: Pelican, 1950), p. 42.

43. Several factors combined to provide the catalyst for the formation of the Chartist movement, including the imposition of stamp duties designed to suppress the radical press and passage of the Poor Law Amendment Act of 1834. See Edward Royal, *Chartism.* 2nd ed. (London: Longman, 1986).

44. See Dorothy Thompson, *The Chartists* (London: Temple Smith, 1984); and John W. Derry, *The Radical Tradition: Tom Paine to Lloyd George* (London: Macmillan, 1967). Derry notes that after Chartism the Poor Law was less rigidly enforced, and legislation was passed imposing minimum controls on mines and factories, but "the degree to which this can be credited to Chartists is imprecise and impossible to determine." See p. 181.

45. See Norman McCord, *The Anti–Corn Law League: 1838–1846* (London: George Allen and Unwin, 1958); and Donald Read, *Peel and the Victorians* (Oxford: Basil Blackwell, 1987), esp. p. 315.

46. Peel told the House of Commons, "The name which ought to be, and will be associated with the success of those measures is the name of one who, acting, I believe, from pure and disinterested motives, has, with untiring energy, made appeals to our reason, and has enforced those appeals with an eloquence the more to be admired because it was unaffected and unadorned: the name which ought to be chiefly associated with the success of those measures is the name of Richard Cobden." *Parliamentary Debates, Commons,* 3rd series, vol. 87 (1846), col. 1054.

47. Quoted in Norman Gash, *Peel* (London: Longman, 1976), pp. 206–207.

48. See especially, *Times,* July 5, 1841.

49. July 24, 1841.

50. *Parliamentary Debates, Commons,* 3rd series, vol. 59 (1841), cols. 428–429.

51. See Blake, esp. p. 50; and Gash, p. 214.

52. See Gash, p. 270.

53. *Times,* January 1, 1845.

54. *Speeches of the Late Right Honourable Sir Robert Peel* (London: George Routeledge and Company, 1858), vol. 4, p. 689.

55. *Speeches of Peel,* vol. 4, p. 691.

56. *Speeches of Peel,* vol. 4, pp. 695–696.

57. June 25, 1846.

58. *Speeches of Peel,* vol. 4, pp. 716–717.

59. See Bentley, esp. p. 124; Blake, esp. intro; and Gash, p. 311.

60. See J. B. Conacher, *The Peelites and the Party System: 1846–52* (Devon, U.K.: David and Charles, 1972).

61. June 29, 1846.

62. January 1, 1846.

63. January 1, 1847.

64. See Crook, esp. p. 152.

3. Classic Liberalism: William Gladstone and Grover Cleveland

1. George F. Parker, ed., *The Writings and Speeches of Grover Cleveland* (New York: Cassell, 1970), pp. 280–282. See also discussion below.

2. Quoted in Robert McElroy, *Grover Cleveland: The Man and the Statesman* (New York: Harper, 1923) vol. 1, p. 147.

3. Allan Nevins, ed., *Letters of Grover Cleveland: 1850–1908* (Boston: Houghton Mifflin Company, 1933), p. 575.

4. For an account of the conflict with Canada, see Allan Nevins, *Grover Cleveland: A Study in Courage* (New York: Dodd, Mead and Company, 1934), pp. 410–413.

5. During the 1916 presidential election, Woodrow Wilson was careful to avoid offending the 8 million Americans of German or Austrian descent and the 4.5 million Irish Americans. When Ronald Reagan made a visit to Ireland, he restricted his activity to largely symbolic gestures. Finally, Bill Clinton created tension with John Major and his government when Clinton welcomed Sinn Fein leader Gerry Adams to the White House.

6. Cleveland tried to restore the monarch shortly after U.S. Marines helped to oust her at the end of Benjamin Harrison's administration. What happened in the course of his attempt reveals a great deal about Cleveland as a conviction politician and as a classic liberal. Pursuing liberal means as well as liberal ends, Cleveland wanted Congress to act on the issue: In his Hawaiian message of December 18, 1893, the president asserted that "right and justice should determine the path to be followed." He explained why he had withdrawn the treaty of annexation and urged the legislature to devise a plan to restore the monarchy. Congress failed to act on Cleveland's recommendation, and the provisional government that replaced the monarchy remained. Once again, for Cleveland, liberal means thwarted his liberal goal—in this case, self-determination and sovereignty for the Hawaiian Islands. See Special Message to the Senate and House of Representatives, December 18, 1893, in James D. Richardson, ed., *A Compilation of the Messages and Papers of the Presidents, 1789–1897* (Washington, D.C.: Government Printing Office, 1898) vol. 9, pp. 460–472.

7. Nevins, p. 561.

8. Quoted in Nevins, p. 553.

9. Quoted in Nevins, p. 635.

10. Quoted in Nevins, p. 639.

11. One of the changes Cleveland made on Olney's original draft was to substitute the word "conviction" for the word "faith," resulting in the phrase, "I am, nevertheless, firm in my conviction." In making this and other changes, Cleveland actually strengthened Olney's already provocative message. For the two texts, see Nevins, pp. 640–641.

12. Cleveland received many letters voicing opposition to his position and endorsing British claims, and expressions of sympathy for the British view appeared in the elite American press. Despite the immediate hostility this conflict created, Cleveland's attempt to settle the Venezuelan boundary dispute might have actually laid the basis for the twentieth-century alliance between Britain and the U.S. Nevins concludes that the conflict cleared the air between the two countries and "initiated a virtual entente." See Nevins, p. 648.

13. See Robert Kelley, *The Transatlantic Persuasion: The Liberal-Democratic Mind in the Age of Gladstone* (New York: Knopf, 1969), esp. ch. 1. Kelley compares not only Gladstone and Cleveland but also Peel and Jackson (at least briefly), stating the case for comparison much more strongly than I have in chapter 2.

14. Gladstone initially engaged in this activity as a member of a lay Tractarian brotherhood that required "some regular work of charity." For more extensive treatment of the subject, see H. C. G. Matthew, *Gladstone*, 2 vols. (Oxford: Clarendon Press, 1986, 1995), esp. vol. 1, pp. 90–93, and vol. 2, p. 290.

15. Kelley, esp. pp. 198–199.

16. See Kelley, esp. ch. 1. Kelley depicts ethnic politics as a critical factor in the development of the "transatlantic persuasion."

17. See D. W. Bebbington, *The Nonconformist Conscience: Chapel and Politics, 1870–1914* (London: George Allen and Unwin, 1982), esp. p. 10. Bebbington also describes the Nonconformists' social campaigns against alcohol and prostitution, which Gladstone endorsed.

18. See Charlotte Aull Davies, *Welsh Nationalism in the Twentieth Century: The Ethnic Option and the Modern State* (New York: Praeger, 1989).

19. See K. O. Morgan, "Radicalism and Nationalism," in A. J. Roderick, ed., *Wales Through the Ages*, vol. 2, *Modern Wales* (London: Christopher Davies, 1971), esp. pp. 193–197.

20. See J. L. Hammond and M. R. D. Foot, *Gladstone and Liberalism* (London: English Universities Press, 1966), esp. p. 53, 73–74.

21. *Parliamentary Debates, Commons,* 3rd series, vol. 175 (1864), col. 324.

22. See Hammond and Foot, pp. 77–79.

23. See E. J. Feuchtwanger, *Gladstone* (New York: St. Martin's Press, 1975), esp. p. 133.

24. Assessing the impact of Irish disestablishment, Feuchtwanger writes: "The Liberal combination had not been so united since the days of Palmerston. With Irish Church disestablishment, Gladstone had picked a winner; it united Radicals, Dissenters, Adullamites, and all; it divided the Tories. . . . In nailing his colours to the mast of disestablishment in Ireland, Gladstone acted from deep conviction. At the same time, he had brought off a brilliant Parliamentary coup." See Feuchtwanger, pp. 142–143.

25. November 11, 1868.

26. November 18, 1868.

27. November 19, 1868.

28. December 3, 1868.

29. See Matthew, *Gladstone,* vol. 1, p. 147.

30. H. C. J. Matthew, ed., *The Gladstone Diaries* (Oxford: Oxford University Press, 1978), vol. 6, p. 654.

31. Arthur Tilney Bassett, ed., *Gladstone's Speeches* (London: Methuen, 1916), p. 382.

32. Bassett, ed., p. 392.

33. R. B. McCallum, *The Liberal Party from Earl Grey to Asquith* (London: Victor Gollanez, 1963), p. 84. See also Hammond and Foot, pp. 97–98.

34. According to Hammond and Foot, "The general election of 1874 was the first triumph of the Conservative Central Office." See p. 98.

35. December 31, 1879.

36. *Times,* December 31, 1880.

37. *Times,* April 17, 1880.

38. December 31, 1885.

39. Kelley, pp. 196, 200; and Hammond and Foot, pp. 47–48, 54–55.

40. Feuchtwanger, p. 214.

41. According to the *Times,* several factors reduced the Liberal vote in 1885: Chamberlain's radical agrarian policy, which promised every farmer "three acres and a cow" and his support for church disestablishment in England; the electoral alliance between the Conservatives and Parnellites; and the failure of the Egyptian expedition. See *Times,* December 31, 1885.

42. *Times,* January 1, 1886.

43. January 28, 1886.

44. Bassett, ed., p. 606.

45. Bassett, ed., p. 608.

46. Concerning his second proposal for home rule, which closely resembled the first, the *Times* would ridicule the "mutilated clauses stuffed into the Bill out of the American constitution." See *Times,* September 7, 1893.

47. Bassett, ed., p. 626.

48. Bassett, ed., p. 627.

49. Bassett, ed., p. 630.

50. Bassett, ed., p. 644.

51. See Hammond and Foot, ch. 12, esp. p. 143.

52. *Times,* July 4, 1892.

53. See Hammond and Foot, p. 155.

54. When depression hit in the 1880s, the public and the government remained faithful to free-trade principles. At the turn of the century, Chamberlain's attempt to return to protectionism failed to win much support and created conflict within the Conservative party.

55. James Bryce, *Studies in Contemporary Biography* (New York: Macmillan, 1927), ch. 20, p. 419.

56. Quoted in Feuchtwanger, p. 143.

57. Bryce, p. 419.

58. Quoted in Kelley, p. 203.

59. See David Thomson, *England in the Nineteenth Century* (London: Pelican, 1950), esp. pp. 149–150.

60. Feuchtwanger, p. 141.

61. Bryce, p. 447.

62. Hammond and Foot, p. 146.

63. See Robert E. Welch Jr., *The Presidencies of Grover Cleveland* (Lawrence: University Press of Kansas, 1988), ch. 4, esp. pp. 43–47.

64. Headline in the *New York Times,* October 23, 1884.

65. Quoted in Allan Nevins, *Grover Cleveland: A Study in Courage* (New York: Dodd, Mead, and Company, 1934), p. 321.

66. William Allen White, "Cleveland," *McClure's Magazine* 18 (1902): 324–325. Also quoted in Kelley, pp. 295–296.

67. See Gerald McFarland, *Mugwumps, Morals, and Politics* (Amherst: University of Massachusetts Press, 1975).

68. In fact their impact was probably much more limited than Cleveland thought. See Welch, p. 41.

69. The next line was "Burn this letter!"—a reference to Blaine's incriminating statement in the "Mulligan letters," which were published during the campaign.

70. Paul F. Boller Jr., *Presidential Campaigns* (New York: Oxford University Press, 1984), pp. 148–149.

71. The Pendleton Act required examinations for certain competitive jobs, established a period of probation for all competitive appointments, set up the Civil Service Commission, classified approximately 10 percent of the total positions, and barred solicitation, assessment, subscription, or other contribution for any political purpose from government employees. See David H. Rosenbloom, *Federal Service and the Constitution: The Development of the Public Employment Relationship* (Ithaca, N.Y.: Cornell University Press, 1971), esp. pp. 80–83.

72. Parker, ed., pp. 46–47.

73. Parker, ed., p. 60.

74. Quoted in Nevins, p. 377.

75. Parker, ed., p. 73.

76. Cleveland did not insist that all duties be abolished. According to Cleveland, "The taxation of luxuries presents no features of hardship; but the necessaries of life, used and consumed by all the people, the duty upon which adds to the cost of living in every home, should be greatly cheapened." Parker, ed., p. 85. Cleveland argued only for tariff reduction and refused to advocate free-trade doctrine, declaring that "It is a condition which confronts us— not a theory." Parker, ed., p. 86.

77. Parker, ed., p. 83.

78. Parker, ed., p. 87.

79. Quoted in Nevins, p. 381.

80. December 7, 1887.

81. December 7. 1887.

82. Arthur Link, ed., *The Papers of Woodrow Wilson* (Princeton, N.J.: Princeton University Press, 1979), vol. 10, pp. 110, 112.

83. *New York Times,* June 7, 1888.

84. See, for example, *Boston Journal,* June 7, 1888.

85. June 6, 1888.

86. June 7, 1888.

87. January 1, 1889.

88. See Nevins, p. 381.

89. Parker, ed., pp. 91–98.

90. Quoted in Nevins, p. 468.

91. *New York World,* December 30, 1891.

92. Parker, ed., p. 281.

93. Parker, ed., p. 281.

94. Parker, ed., p. 282.

95. Parker, ed., p. 283.

96. July 24, 1892. After the election, the *New York Times* attributed defections from Republican ranks to "principle and conscience on the tariff." November 4, 1892.

97. June 24, 1892.

98. *New York World.* Quoted in Nevins, p. 548.

99. See Nevins, esp. p. 201.

100. See Kelley, p. 337.

101. Quoted in Kelley, p. 336.

102. See Grover Cleveland, *The Government in the Chicago Strike of 1894* (Princeton, N.J.: Princeton University Press, 1913), esp. p. 13.

103. *The Public Papers of Grover Cleveland: March 4, 1885–March 4, 1889* (Washington, D.C.: Government Printing Office, 1889), pp. 260–261.

4. The New Liberalism: Woodrow Wilson and David Lloyd George

1. For a biography that depicts Lloyd George as a traditional liberal, see Peter Rowland, *David Lloyd George: A Biography* (New York: Macmillan, 1975). For an account that emphasizes Lloyd George's radicalism, see John W. Derry, *The Radical Tradition: Tom Paine to Lloyd George* (London: Macmillan, 1967). The following studies credit Lloyd George with establishing the foundations of the modern welfare state: Charles L. Mowat, *Lloyd George* (London: Oxford University Press, 1964); Martin Pugh, *Lloyd George* (New York: Longman, 1988); and Frank Owen, *Tempestuous Journey: Lloyd George, His Life and Times* (London: Hutchinson, 1954).

2. For different interpretations of Wilson's leadership, see Kendrick A. Clements, *The Presidency of Woodrow Wilson* (Lawrence: University Press of Kansas, 1992), esp. p. xi. For a classic depiction of Wilson as a Progressive reformer, see Arthur S. Link, *Woodrow Wilson and the Progressive Era* (New York: Harper and Row, 1954). Of course, historians have also debated whether the Progressive movement was essentially liberal or conservative. For examples, see Richard Hofstadter, *The Age of Reform* (New York: Alfred A. Knopf, 1955); and Gabriel Kolko, *The Triumph of Conservatism* (New York: Free Press of Glencoe, 1963).

3. Arthur S. Link, ed., *The Papers of Woodrow Wilson* (Princeton, N.J.: Princeton University Press, 1968), vol. 4, p. 287.

4. Link, ed., *Papers,* vol. 4, pp. 287–288.

5. T. H. Vail Motter, ed., *Leaders of Men* (Princeton, N.J.: Princeton University Press, 1952).

6. Motter, ed., p. 23. Here Wilson contrasts Peel's determination to Gladstone's "transparent honesty," for Gladstone frequently adopted a scholarly perspective and "could not help seeing two sides of a question." Elsewhere Wilson showers praise on Gladstone, whom he admires for his oratorical gifts and his ability to understand public sentiment.

7. Motter, ed., p. 48. According to Wilson, only the scholar can afford to be a purist when it comes to principle: "Uncompromising thought is the luxury of the closeted recluse. Untrammelled reasoning is the indulgence of the philosopher, of the dreamer of sweet dreams."

8. Motter, ed., p. 49. Wilson would later express the same sentiment in stronger terms: "Where the individual should be indomitable is in the choice of direction, saying: 'I will not bow down to the golden calf of fashion. I will not bow down to the weak habit of pursuing everything that is popular, everything that belongs to the society to which I belong.' I will insist on telling that society, if I think it is so, that in certain fundamental principles it is wrong. . . . What I do insist upon is, speaking the full truth to it and never letting it forget the truth; speaking the truth again and again and again with every variation of the theme, until men will wake some morning and the theme will sound familiar, and they will say, 'Well, after all, is it not so?'" Link, ed., *Papers,* vol. 19, p. 477.

9. Motter, ed., p. 60.

10. Motter, ed., p. 50.

11. Motter, ed., p. 50.

12. Motter, ed., p. 51.

13. Motter, ed., p. 41.

14. Motter, ed., p. 51.

15. Motter, ed., p. 43.

16. Motter, ed., p. 43. In another context, Wilson wrote that the statesman "must first make public opinion willing to listen and then see to it that it listen to the right things. He must stir it up to search for an opinion, and then manage to put the right opinion in its way." Link, ed., *Papers,* vol. 5, p. 369.

17. Motter, ed., p. 26.

18. Motter, ed., p. 40.

19. Motter, ed., p. 42. See also James W. Ceaser, *Presidential Selection: Theory and Development* (Princeton, N.J.: Princeton University Press, 1979), ch. 4, esp. pp. 193–197.

20. Motter, ed., p. 46.

21. Motter, ed., p. 42.

22. Motter, ed., p. 44.

23. Link, ed., *Papers,* vol. 18, p. 536.

24. Motter, ed., p. 42.

25. Motter, ed., p. 42.

26. Ray Stannard Baker, ed., *Woodrow Wilson: Life and Letters* (Garden City, N.Y.: Doubleday, 1927), vol. 2, p. 100.

27. See Jeffrey K. Tulis, *The Rhetorical Presidency* (Princeton, N.J.: Princeton University Press, 1987), esp. ch. 5.

28. Motter, ed., p. 53.

29. Motter, ed., p. 29. For an account of Wilson's thought that emphasizes the erotic character of his language, see Niels Aage Thorsen, *The Political Thought of Woodrow Wilson, 1875–1910* (Princeton, N.J.: Princeton University Press, 1988).

30. Motter, ed., p. 41.

31. Woodrow Wilson, *Congressional Government: A Study in American Politics,* introduction by Walter Lippmann (Gloucester, Mass.: Peter Smith, 1973).

32. Link, ed., *Papers,* vol. 10, pp. 102–119, esp. p. 119.

33. Ceaser, esp. ch. 4 and chapter 6 of this book.

34. See Tulis, esp. ch. 5, and chapter 8 of this book.

35. Link, ed., *Papers*, vol. 4, p. 287.

36. Woodrow Wilson, *Constitutional Government in the United States* (New York: Columbia University Press, 1908), p. 54.

37. See Arthur Link, *Woodrow Wilson and the Progressive Era* (New York: Harper, 1963), esp. ch. 2.

38. Woodrow Wilson, *The State: Elements of Historical and Practical Politics* (Boston: D. C. Heath and Co., 1889), p. 656.

39. Wilson, *The State*, p. 659.

40. Wilson, *The State*, p. 659.

41. Wilson, *The State*, p. 659. Socialism, as Wilson sees it, constitutes a "revolt from selfish, misguided individualism; and certainly modern individualism has much about it that is hateful, too hateful to last." Wilson continues by leveling an assault on combinations or monopolies, but the fact that he blames individualism for this "modern problem" distinguishes him from earlier liberals and paves the way for policies that would restrict the individual in new ways.

42. Wilson, *The State*, p. 661.

43. Wilson returns to the liberal tradition when he defines the limits to state action. The state should act only when it is "indispensable to the equalization of the conditions of endeavor, indispensable to the maintenance of uniform rules of individual rights and relationships, indispensible because to omit it would inevitably be to hamper or degrade some for the advancement of others in the scale of wealth and social standing." (*The State*, pp. 664–665.) The ends of government include the traditional goal of securing rights, but Wilson also mentions objectives that exceed the aims and expectations of classic liberalism. His declaration that "the State exists for the sake of Society, not Society for the sake of the State" guards against totalitarianism but might invite innovations as expansive as the New Deal. (*The State*, p. 664.)

44. Quoted in Clements, pp. 10–11.

45. For an extended discussion of Wilson's record as governor, see Clements, esp. ch. 1, p. 11.

46. See James W. Davis, *Presidential Primaries—Road to the White House* (Westport, Conn.: Greenwood Press, 1980), p. 131.

47. See Evamarie Socha, ed., *National Party Conventions, 1831–1984* (Washington, D.C.: Congressional Quarterly, 1987), esp. pp. 71–72; and Arthur Link, *Woodrow Wilson: Road to the White House* (Princeton, N.J.: Princeton University Press, 1947), chs. 10–13.

48. *New York Times*, July 3, 1912.

49. One author has gone so far as to assert that Wilson's main ambition in life was to "be a political force like William E. Gladstone . . . whose oratory and political principles reflected his view of God's moral order." See Francis Broderick, *Progressivism at Risk: Electing a President in 1912* (New York: Greenwood Press, 1989), p. 60.

50. *New York Times*, July 3, 1912.

51. *New York Times*, July 3, 1912. See also *Washington Post*, July 3, 1912.

52. See Clements, p. 28.

53. See, for example, *New York Times*, November 4, 1912.

54. *New York Times*, November 6, 1912.

55. The 1896 election was not seen as a "critical" election or realignment by contemporary commentators. From 1884 until 1920, the Democrats won the popular vote in the majority of presidential elections.

56. *New York Times,* November 6, 1912.

57. Link, *Progressive Era,* p. 36. See also the discussion in chapter 6 of this book.

58. See Link, *Progressive Era,* pp. 45–53.

59. See Link, *Progressive Era,* pp. 68–75.

60. Quoted in Link, *Progressive Era,* p. 80.

61. Link, ed., *Papers,* vol. 30, p. 24.

62. See Arthur Link, *Wilson: Confusions and Crises, 1915–1916* (Princeton, N.J.: Princeton University Press, 1964), esp. pp. 346–347.

63. Link, ed., *Papers,* vol. 37, pp. 427–428.

64. Quoted in Link, *Confusions and Crises,* p. 347.

65. Quoted in Link, *Confusions and Crises,* p. 348.

66. *New York Times,* May 8, 1916.

67. *New York Times,* May 22, 1916.

68. See Clements, ch. 4.

69. See Link, *Progressive Era,* pp. 61–63.

70. Quoted in Link, *Progressive Era,* p. 227.

71. In addition to the 1916 labor legislation, Wilson's National War Labor Board—despite its limitations—would serve to inspire the associational movement of the 1920s and much of the New Deal's early recovery programs. See Clements, ch. 5, esp. p. 86.

72. In several cases, Wilson became convinced of the necessity for greater governmental action. For example, he grew to doubt that the Clayton bill and a weak interstate trade commission could sufficiently restrain business. In this respect (and on other issues), the president's friend Louis Brandeis exercised a powerful intellectual influence.

73. In *The State,* Wilson wrote: "By forbidding child labor, by supervising the sanitary conditions of factories, by limiting the employment of women in occupations hurtful to their health, by instituting official tests of the purity or the quality of goods sold, by limiting the hours of labor in certain trades, by a hundred and one limitations of the power of unscrupulous or heartless men to out-do the scrupulous and merciful in trade or industry, government has assisted equity" (p. 663). Wilson was writing about the states, but his rationale would also justify action at the national level.

74. Quoted in Eleanor Flexner, *Century of Struggle: The Woman's Rights Movement in the United States* (Cambridge, Mass.: Harvard University Press, 1959), p. 278.

75. The women's movement was divided in its opinion of Wilson and his motives. The National American Woman Suffrage Association (NAWSA) considered Wilson an ally, but the more radical National Women's Party (NWP) believed that Wilson would support their cause only when and to the extent that he was forced to do so. See Aileen S. Kraditor, *The Ideas of the Woman Suffrage Movement, 1890–1920* (New York: Columbia University Press, 1965), esp. 233–235. A combination of militant action by NWP and persistent persuasion by NAWSA helped to convince Wilson to alter his position. See Steven M. Buechler, *Women's Movements in the United States: Woman Suffrage, Equal Rights, and Beyond* (New Brunswick, N.J.: Rutgers University Press, 1990), esp. p. 208.

76. *New York Times,* November 7, 1916.

77. *New York Times,* December 31, 1916.

78. *New York Times,* December 31, 1916.

79. Shortly after he took office in 1913, Wilson articulated a number of lofty principles, which he pledged to apply to international politics. He declared that he would not encourage U.S. bankers to lend money to China because it could lead to forcible interference if the loans were not repaid. In fact, Wilson withdrew U.S. support for a consortium that was setting up a loan to develop railroads in China. Furthermore, he insisted that the U.S. would not seek special favors from or exert special influence on Latin American countries. He urged Congress to repeal the 1912 law that exempted U.S. ships from the Panama Canal toll because it violated the equal treatment provision of the Hay-Pauncefote Treaty signed with Britain. Finally, his secretary of state, Bryan, negotiated conciliation treaties with more than twenty countries.

80. *New York Times,* December 30, 1917.

81. *New York Times,* January 1, 1919.

82. See Alexander L. George and Juliette L. George, *Woodrow Wilson and Colonel House: A Personality Study* (New York: Dover Publications, 1964), esp. ch. 14.

83. See Clements, ch. 10.

84. Quoted in Clements, p. 223.

85. David Lloyd George, *War Memoirs of David Lloyd George* (London: Odhams Press, 1938), vol. 1, p. 141.

86. A. J. P. Taylor, ed., *Lloyd George: A Diary by Frances Stevenson* (London: Hutchinson, 1971), p. 175. Frances Stevenson also captures the difference between Wilson and Lloyd George in the following anecdote about lunch with the queen of Rumania: "She gave a lengthy description of her purchases in Paris, which included a pink silk chemise. She spoke of meeting President Wilson on his arrival. 'What shall I talk to him about?' she asked. 'The League of Nations or my pink chemise?' 'Begin with the League of Nations,' said Mr. Balfour, 'and finish up with the pink chemise. If you were talking to Mr. Lloyd George, you could begin with the pink chemise!'" p. 171.

87. Link, ed., *Papers,* vol. 40, p. 538.

88. David Lloyd George, *Memoirs of the Peace Conference* (New York: Howard Fertig, 1972), vol. 1, p. 145.

89. Lloyd George, *Peace Conference,* vol. 1, p. 155.

90. Lloyd George concludes his assessment of Wilson by asking, "Was he hero, saint, or martyr? There was something of each in the struggles of the last years of his life and in the circumstances of his death, though not enough to warrant the claim made on his behalf to any of these noble appellations. But that he honestly consecrated an upright character and a fine intellect to the service of mankind, no one will deny who is not afflicted with a party spirit so charged with rancour as to have become an insanity of the soul." Lloyd George, *Peace Conference,* vol. 1, p. 155.

91. Quoted in Martin Pugh, *Lloyd George* (New York: Longman), pp. 93, 118.

92. See George and George, esp. p. 264.

93. Lloyd George, *Peace Conference,* vol. 1, p. 143.

94. Lloyd George, *Peace Conference,* vol. 1, p. 144.

95. In his tribute to Lloyd George, Winston Churchill used language strikingly similar to the words chosen by Lloyd George to describe Wilson. Churchill praised Lloyd George's "dauntless courage, his untiring energy, his oratory, persuasive, provocative, now grave, now gay." Robert Rhodes James, ed., *Winston Churchill: His Complete Speeches, 1897–1963* (New York: Chelsea House Publishers, 1974), vol. 7, p. 7138.

96. Today "the hywl" is used to describe the atmosphere at football matches, suggesting that the stadium has replaced the chapel as the arena in which people experience ecstasy.

97. Watkin Davies, quoted in Peter Rowland, *David Lloyd George: A Biography* (New York: Macmillan, 1975), pp. 146–147.

98. According to one of his biographers, "Lloyd George, though no doctrinaire, was a surprisingly consistent politician; on free trade, on social reform, on imperialism, there is not the weaving and bobbing that many a jaundiced commentator suggests." See Pugh, p. 188.

99. Lloyd George is radical and liberal—both upper- and lowercase. For the sake of consistency, I use only the lowercase, unless I am making a specific reference to the Liberal party or the British Radical tradition.

100. Quoted in Rowland, p. 44.

101. Fydd literally means "to be," and Cymru Fydd is sometimes translated "Wales to Be." The intention was to portray Wales as a young nation with a promising future (and to shed the image of Wales as an old principality tied to and by its past).

102. In the 1892 general election, Lloyd George's opponent questioned whether Gladstone supported the young Liberal in his bid for reelection. Gladstone responded by sending a lukewarm letter of support. In general, Lloyd George disliked Gladstone but admired the Grand Old Man's leadership style and parliamentary skill.

103. According to one historian, Lloyd George was more preoccupied with "the class above him, 'the dukes,' rather than those below." See Bentley Brinkerhoff Gilbert, "David Lloyd George: Land, the Budget, and Social Reform," *American Historical Review* 81 (December 1976): 1059. Like Wilson, Lloyd George aimed for the "destruction of monopoly," although in the context of British politics, the landowners, not the industrialists, were guilty of building "trusts."

104. He did, however, oppose a bill that would have given the vote only to upper-class women, whom he believed would vote Conservative.

105. In addition to these lofty liberal sentiments he expressed, Lloyd George made another type of argument that revealed a darker aspect of his character. He repeatedly expressed reservations about defending the rights of Jews and portrayed the Boers as adhering more closely to the Christian biblical tradition. In this and many other cases in his career, Lloyd George exhibited signs of anti-Semitism, often delicately described by his biographers as his "ambivalence toward the Jews." Like Wilson's view of African Americans, Lloyd George's anti-Semitism provides a reminder that convictions can be low as well as lofty.

106. According to one of his biographers, Lloyd George "consistently defended free trade—indeed he could do no less—though he refused to invest it with a *moral* justification: 'Some of you chaps have got free trade consciences,' he told Charles Masterman, 'now I have not!' For him free trade was to be justified pragmatically in terms of the advantages it secured for Britain, namely cheap imports for consumers, low costs for industry, and through the maximisation of world trade, high invisible earnings from shipping, insurance, and foreign investments. Yet he remained sufficiently open-minded to appreciate that when other states infringed free trade to the detriment of British interests, some intervention was necessary." See Pugh, p. 35.

107. James, ed., vol. 7, p. 7136.

108. Quoted in Charles L. Mowat, *Lloyd George* (London: Oxford University Press, 1964), p. 16.

109. *Parliamentary Debates, Commons,* 4th series, vol. 190 (1908), col. 585 (entire speech cols. 564–586).

110. See Derry, esp. p. 404.

111. In the U.S., there is no position comparable to chancellor of the exchequer, and even in contemporary Britain, chancellors often lack the autonomy and independence that Gladstone and Lloyd George enjoyed. Certainly, Margaret Thatcher's chancellor felt unduly restricted. See Nigel Lawson, *The View from No. 11: Memoirs of a Tory Radical* (London: Bantam, 1992). Indeed, Lloyd George played a role in weakening the chancellor's position when, as prime minister, he shifted a great deal of policy-making authority to his personal advisors at Number 10 Downing Street. See chapter 8 of this book.

112. The old age pensions bill was a modest effort: It provided only five shillings per week to those over the age of seventy and included many exceptions. Nevertheless, some historians view the 1908 pensions bill as the first major step toward the creation of the welfare state. See, for example, Mowat, esp. p. 16.

113. This must be the most frequently quoted remark made by Lloyd George, and it can be found in any biography. See, for example, Frank Owen, *Tempestuous Journey—Lloyd George, His Life and Times* (London: Hutchinson, 1954), p. 164.

114. The bill included the following provisions: If the Lords withhold approval of a money bill for more than a month, the bill becomes law with royal assent; if the House of Commons passes any other bill three times, it also becomes law with royal assent; and finally, the maximum length of any Parliament is reduced from seven to five years.

115. See Derry, esp. p. 379; and Bruce K. Murray, *The People's Budget 1909/10: Lloyd George and Liberal Politics* (Oxford: Clarendon Press, 1980), pp. 10–12.

116. See Bentley Brinkerhoff Gilbert, *David Lloyd George: A Political Life: The Architect of Change, 1863–1912* (Columbus: Ohio State University Press, 1987), ch. 7, esp. p. 443.

117. George Allardice Riddell, *Lord Riddell's War Diary 1914–1918* (London: I. Nicolson and Watson, 1933), pp. 123–124. Also quoted in Rowland, p. 327.

118. See Mowat, esp. p. 34.

119. *Times,* December 2, 1916.

120. *Times,* December 6, 1916.

121. Several of Lloyd George's biographers insist that he wanted only control of the war effort and not necessarily the position of prime minister. See, for example, Rowland, esp. p. 368.

122. See Frances Stevenson's account of the week's events in A. J. P. Taylor, ed., *Lloyd George: A Diary by Frances Stevenson* (London: Hutchinson, 1971), esp. pp. 130–134. She describes Asquith's refusal to reconstitute the cabinet and Conservative leader Bonar Law's refusal to form a government. (Bonar Law did not believe he could gain the support of Liberals and Labour.) She also emphasizes the significance of Lloyd George's popularity. According to Stevenson, "All classes seem ready to accept him as Dictator and to leave the direction of the War to him. Some of the messages he has received are very touching and bring a lump to one's throat" (p. 132).

123. Quoted in Rowland, p. 462.

124. Reformers included Milnerites, Seebohm Rowntree, and Sidney and Beatrice Webb—"all united by their belief in the necessity for state intervention in social welfare." See Pugh, pp. 119–120.

125. *Times,* December 12, 1918.

126. Quoted in Rowland, p. 509.

127. See Mowat, esp. pp. 47, 49, and Pugh, esp. pp. 139–140.

128. Quoted in Chris Wrigley, *Lloyd George and the Challenge of Labour: The Post-war Coalition, 1918–1922* (New York: St. Martin's Press, 1990), p. 299.

129. Quoted in Wrigley, p. 306.

130. George Allardice Riddell, *More Pages from My Diary, 1908–1914* (London: Country Life, 1934), p. 102. Also quoted in Rowland, p. 268.

131. Riddell, *More Pages,* p. 152. Also quoted in Rowland, p. 268.

132. Quoted in Wrigley, pp. 308–309.

133. Quoted in Pugh, p. 167.

134. Derry, p. 395.

135. Quoted in Thomas Jones, *Lloyd George* (Cambridge, Mass.: Harvard University Press, 1951), p. 206.

136. January 1, 1921.

137. January 1, 1923.

138. *Times,* January 1, 1923.

5. Neoliberalism: Margaret Thatcher and Ronald Reagan

1. Admittedly, Britain had gone much farther than the U.S. in its expansion of state authority. Britain developed a corporatist state: Trade unions and industry became parts of the formal structure of power. Whereas Britain nationalized many of its major industries, the U.S. merely regulated them. Britain built a National Health Service to provide universal health care, while the U.S. only adopted social security and, later, medicare and medicaid. These differences in the structure and functions of the welfare state reflect the differences (largely in emphasis) that persist between the political cultures and constitutional traditions of the two countries. Compared with Britain, the U.S. has always been less centralized, and U.S. citizens generally have been more skeptical of central authority than their British counterparts have been. More significant for the purpose of this study, the challenge to the modern welfare state and the attempt to dismantle its edifice posed a much more formidable task in the U.K. than in the U.S.

2. See Andrew Gamble, *The Free Economy and the Strong State: The Politics of Thatcherism* (London: Macmillan, 1988), esp. ch. 2.

3. See Geoffrey Smith, *Reagan and Thatcher* (New York: Norton and Company, 1991), ch. 2; and Dennis Kavanagh, *Thatcherism and British Politics: The End of Consensus?* (Oxford: Oxford University Press, 1987), chs. 3, 4.

4. Margaret Thatcher, *The Path to Power* (New York: HarperCollins, 1995), p. 372. See also discussion in chapter 9 of this book.

5. Quoted in Hugo Young, *One of Us: A Biography of Margaret Thatcher* (London: Macmillan, 1989), p. 4.

6. Thatcher, *Path to Power,* p. 7.

7. See Wendy Webster, *Not a Man to Match Her: The Marketing of a Prime Minister* (London: Women's Press, 1990), ch. 1.

8. Thatcher, *Path to Power,* p. 148.

9. Thatcher, *Path to Power,* pp. 149–150.

10. The legislation attempted to restrict union power in several fundamental ways. It banned the closed shop, pledged to enforce all agreements between employers and unions,

and established an Industrial Court to try cases arising under the act. The court was empowered to order a sixty-day "cooling-off" period when necessary to the national interest, and it could insist that a secret ballot be held before a strike could be called. The legislation sparked a series of legal disputes involving dockers and railway workers. After dockers were jailed for contempt of court, the government managed to have the decision against them reversed on appeal. It quickly became clear that enforcement of the act would transform striking workers into martyrs and increase public sympathy for the unions.

11. Robert Blake, *The Conservative Party from Peel to Thatcher* (London: Fontana, 1985), p. 314.

12. As Blake describes the reaction to Powell's speech, "The 'classes,' to use the categorisation of the 3rd Marquis of Salisbury, were shocked, but the 'masses' were delighted." See Blake, esp. p. 306.

13. Quoted in Peter Clarke, *A Question of Leadership: Gladstone to Thatcher* (London: Hamish Hamilton, 1991), p. 297.

14. Thatcher, *Path to Power*, p. 141.

15. "Escaping the Chrysalis of Statism," interview of Sir Keith Joseph by Anthony Seldon, *Contemporary Record: The Journal of the Institute of Contemporary British History* 1 (Spring 1987): 28.

16. Interview by Anthony Seldon, p. 28.

17. Personal interview (phone), Alfred Sherman, February 4, 1994.

18. Thatcher, *Path to Power*, p. 28.

19. Quoted in Young, p. 406. Thatcher made this announcement to a dining club known as the Conservative Philosophy Group, mostly composed of young right-wing MPs and academics, formed to provide a source of radical new ideas.

20. Interview by Anthony Seldon, p. 29.

21. Thatcher, *Path to Power*, p. 252.

22. Personal interview (phone), Alfred Sherman, February 4, 1994.

23. Samuel H. Beer describes this tradition as "Tory Democracy." See Beer, *Modern British Politics: Parties and Pressure Groups in the Collectivist Age* (New York: W. W. Norton, 1982), esp. pp. 3–8, 91–97.

24. Personal interview, James Prior, June 6, 1991.

25. Personal interview, John Biffen, July 2, 1990. Biffen served as chief secretary to the treasury (1979–81), secretary of state for trade (1981–82), and leader of the House of Commons (1982–87).

26. Personal interview, Timothy Raison, June 18, 1991.

27. Personal interview, Ken Livingstone, June 18, 1991.

28. Personal interview, Tony Benn, June 19, 1991.

29. See Patricia Lee Sykes, *Losing from the Inside: The Cost of Conflict in the British Social Democratic Party*, 2nd ed., (New Brunswick, N.J.: Transaction, 1990), esp. pp. 30–31.

30. See Joel Krieger, *Reagan, Thatcher, and the Politics of Decline* (New York: Oxford University Press, 1986), esp. introduction and ch. 1.

31. Quoted in Krieger, p. 57.

32. See *Telegraph,* December 28, 1978.

33. Excerpt reprinted in Thatcher, *Path to Power*, p. 448.

34. In his analysis of the 1979 election, William Schneider concluded: "It cannot fairly be said that the British electorate resoundingly endorsed [Thatcher's] economic philosophy on

May 3rd. But it can be said that the voters rebelled against the failure of the Labour party's alternative." See William Schneider, "The Mistress of Downing Street: Why She Won," *Public Opinion* 2 (June–July 1979): 54.

35. Schneider, p. 53.

36. See David Butler and Donald Stokes, *Political Change in Britain* (New York: St. Martin's Press, 1976).

37. David Butler and Dennis Kavanagh, *The British General Election of 1979* (London: Macmillan, 1980), p. 350.

38. See Ivor Crewe in Dennis Kavanagh, ed., *The Politics of the Labour Party* (London: George Allen and Unwin, 1982), p. 42.

39. See Bo Sarvik and Ivor Crewe, *Decade of Dealignment* (Cambridge: Cambridge University Press, 1983).

40. Initiatives taken in 1979 paved the way for the British nationality bill in 1981, which established three new categories of "citizenship." See *Times,* December 31, 1981.

41. In January 1979 Prime Minister Callaghan set up a commission to establish comparability between public and private sector employees. Chaired by Hugh Clegg, the commission made recommendations that the Labour government pledged to honor after the election. "Concerned not to lose vital votes," the Conservatives agreed that they would also honor the Clegg Commission's recommendations. Thatcher would later admit that "hard, if distasteful, political calculations had led us to commit ourselves during the election campaign to honour the decisions of the Clegg Commission." See Margaret Thatcher, *Downing Street Years* (New York: HarperCollins, 1993), pp. 32, 44-45 and *Path to Power,* pp. 438–439.

42. Personal interview, Geoffrey Howe, July 3, 1990.

43. The chancellor's proposed enterprise zones became part of the Local Government Planning and Land Act of 1980. For a report that compares enterprise zones in the U.K. and the U.S., see *Enterprise Zone Notes* (Washington, D.C.: U.S. Department of Housing and Urban Development, September 1985), pp. 2–4.

44. See Thatcher, *Downing Street Years,* p. 96.

45. *Times,* December 31, 1980.

46. Personal interview, Geoffrey Howe, July 3, 1990.

47. See Roy Jenkins, *A Life at the Center: Memoirs of a Radical Reformer* (New York: Random House, 1991), ch. 15, esp. p. 261.

48. Reproduced in Thatcher, *Downing Street Years,* p. 122.

49. Quoted in Peter Jenkins, *Mrs. Thatcher's Revolution: The Ending of the Socialist Era* (Cambridge, Mass.: Harvard University Press, 1988), p. 99.

50. As Thatcher describes it, Alan Walters, John Hoskyns, and Alfred Sherman introduced her to Swiss economist Jurg Niehans, who persuaded her to loosen control of the money supply. See Thatcher, *Downing Street Years,* pp. 133–134. Howe also emphasized the importance of "technical obstacles," especially the fact that methods and measures were "crude." Personal interview, Geoffrey Howe, July 3, 1990.

51. Quoted in Young, p. 215.

52. Personal interview, Geoffrey Howe, July 3, 1990.

53. Personal interview, Ian Glimour, June 26, 1991. (Gilmour served under Lord Carrington, the foreign secretary in this period.)

54. See Alan Walters, *The British Renaissance* (Washington, D.C.: American Enterprise Institute, 1983).

55. *Times,* December 31, 1981.

56. Personal interview, Ian Gilmour, June 26, 1991.

57. Support for the parties is based on response to the question, If there were a general election tomorrow, which party would you support? Gallup poll results reprinted in Elizabeth Hann Hastings and Philip K. Hastings, eds., *Index to International Public Opinion, 1981–82* (Westport, Conn.: Greenwood Press, 1983), p. 394.

58. See Sykes, *Losing from the Inside.*

59. Personal interview (phone), Alfred Sherman, February 4, 1994.

60. It is impossible to assess precisely the influence of the Argonauts. Many of the ministers whom I interviewed stressed the significance of the group. Sherman certainly believed that the Argonauts convinced cabinet ministers and fortified the resolve of representatives from industry. He also alleged that "[a] major early success of the Argonauts in collaboration with the CPS was the ouster of Jim Prior from the Department of Employment, his position of leading challenger of Margaret Thatcher on behalf of the Butskellite tendency." Letter to the author, February 1994. Sherman tended to exaggerate, but in this case his assertion is supported by Thatcher. Throughout her memoirs, she emphasizes the opposition to Prior that came from many who were also Argonauts, although she never mentions the Argonauts or the Luncheon Club by name.

61. Thatcher, *Downing Street Years,* p. 141.

62. Personal interview, James Prior, June 28, 1990.

63. See Thatcher's account in *Path to Power,* esp. pp. 420–423.

64. See also James Prior, *A Balance of Power* (London: Hamish Hamilton, 1986), esp. ch. 9.

65. Personal interview, James Prior, June 28, 1990.

66. As Prior explained, "Quite often during the passage of the bill through the House, the right wing of the Conservative party would put down an amendment which I would resist. And when it came to the vote, the bulk of the Conservative party had to go into the lobby to vote down the amendment in conjunction with the Labour party."

67. Personal interview, Norman Tebbit, June 27, 1990.

68. Personal interview, Norman Tebbit, June 27, 1990.

69. *Parliamentary Debates, Commons,* 6th series, vol. 17 (1982), col. 814. See also Sykes, *Losing from the Inside,* pp. 52–53.

70. Gallup poll results reprinted in Hastings and Hastings, eds., *Index to International Public Opinion, 1981–82,* p. 394; and in Elizabeth Hann Hastings and Philip K. Hastings, eds., *Index to International Public Opinion, 1982–83* (Westport, Conn.: Greenwood Press, 1984), p. 425.

71. See Marina Warner, *Monuments and Maidens: The Allegory of the Female Form* (London: Picador, 1987), esp. pp. 49–51. See also chapter 9 in this book.

72. MORI poll results reprinted in Elizabeth Hann Hastings and Philip K. Hastings, eds., *Index to International Public Opinion, 1980–81* (Westport, Conn.: Greenwood Press, 1982), pp. 314–315; Hastings and Hastings, eds., *Index to International Public Opinion, 1986–87* (Westport, Conn.: Greenwood Press, 1988), p. 390; and Hastings and Hastings, eds., *Index to International Public Opinion, 1989–90* (Westport, Conn.: Greenwood Press, 1991), p. 381.

73. Gallup poll results reprinted in Elizabeth Hann Hastings and Philip K. Hastings, eds., *Index to International Public Opinion, 1984–85* (Westport, Conn.: Greenwood Press, 1986), pp. 430–431.

74. Gallup poll results reprinted in Hastings and Hastings, eds., *Index to International Public Opinion, 1985–86* (Westport, Conn.: Greenwood Press, 1987), p. 376; Hastings and Hastings, eds., *Index to International Opinion 1986–87*, pp. 386, 391; and Hastings and Hastings, eds., *Index to International Public Opinion, 1988–89* (Westport, Conn.: Greenwood Press, 1990), p. 342.

75. Gallup poll results reprinted in Hastings and Hastings, eds., *Index to International Public Opinion, 1986–87*, p. 390; and Hastings and Hastings, eds., *Index to International Public Opinion, 1988–89*, p. 341.

76. Gallup poll results reprinted in Hastings and Hastings, eds., *Index to International Public Opinion, 1980–81*, p. 313.

77. See *Times,* June 2, 1983.

78. Kinnock made this remark on TV South's program *The South Decides* in response to a member of the audience who said, "At least Mrs. Thatcher has got guts." Kinnock replied, "And it's a pity that people had to leave theirs on the ground at Goose Green in order to prove it." See *Times,* June 7, 1983.

79. MORI, *Public Opinion* 6 (June–July 1983): 23.

80. MORI, *Public Opinion* 6 (June–July 1983): 23.

81. See David Butler and Dennis Kavanagh, *The British General Election of 1983* (New York: St. Martin's Press, 1984), esp. p. 119.

82. Ivor Crewe, "Why Labour Lost the British Elections," *Public Opinion* 6 (June–July 1983): 7–9, 56–60.

83. Crewe, "Why Labour Lost," pp. 8–9.

84. *Sunday Times,* June 12, 1983.

85. Personal interview, Peter Walker, July 2, 1990.

86. Thatcher, *Downing Street Years,* p. 348.

87. See Peter Jenkins, pp. 224–234.

88. Thatcher attacked the miners as "the enemy within" in two speeches in 1984: in July while speaking to the 1922 Committee and in November at the Carlton Club. See her own account in Thatcher, *Downing Street Years,* p. 370.

89. Personal interview, John Biffen, July 2, 1990.

90. Thatcher clashed with the Anglican Church on several occasions. One of the most dramatic, public confrontations took place in 1984 after the archbishop of Canterbury criticized the government's policies as divisive and mean-spirited. On another occasion, members of Thatcher's government attacked the archbishop's report, "Faith in the Inner City," as "Marxist." In general, Thatcher tended to view the Anglican Church as part of the postwar welfare state establishment and therefore attempted to undermine its influence. As one scholar has concluded, "The [Thatcher] government has shown more interest in religious matters than almost any since Gladstone's." See David Martin, "The Churches: Pink Bishops and the Iron Lady," in Dennis Kavanagh and Anthony Seldon, eds., *The Thatcher Effect: A Decade of Change* (Oxford: Clarendon Press, 1989), esp. p. 355.

91. See Nigel Lawson, *The View from No. 11: Memoirs of a Tory Radical* (London: Bantam, 1992), p. 333, and in general, chs. 27 and 28.

92. Personal interview, Norman Tebbit, June 27, 1990.

93. John Wakeham replaced Cecil Parkinson before plans to privatize electricity were completed and there is some dispute about which minister contributed more to the plans. Many of those whom I interviewed gave credit to Wakeham, whereas Thatcher herself credits Parkinson. (Her choice is not surprising, given their close relationship.) See *Downing Street Years,* p. 683.

94. Personal interview, Cecil Parkinson, June 11, 1991. It should be noted that in this conflict (concerning CEGB's control of the "national grid"), Marshall backed down, although he later resigned when the board lost control of the nuclear power plants.

95. See Thatcher, *Downing Street Years*, pp. 682–685.

96. Anthony Heath, Roger Jowell, and John Curtice, *How Britain Votes* (Oxford: Pergamon Press, 1985), p. 133.

97. Highlighting Kinnock's personal background and leadership appeal, the party election broadcast included shots of the leader and his wife, Glenys, holding hands while taking a stroll. The striking similarity led news broadcasters to show clips from both the Kinnock and Reagan commercials, with at least one commenting that Glenys and Nancy appeared to be wearing the same red sweater. The following year in the 1988 presidential primaries, Senator Joseph Biden stole some of Kinnock's lines from a speech reproduced and featured in the 1987 party election broadcast. In effect, Biden lifted lines from Kinnock in a commercial that copied Reagan's!

98. In a television interview on May 24, David Frost asked Kinnock how a nonnuclear Britain could defend itself against a nuclear aggressor. Kinnock simply replied, "[You have to use] the resources you've got to make any occupation totally untenable." Quoted in *Times,* May 27, 1987.

99. Personal interview, John Banks, June 19, 1991.

100. Statement made on May 11. See *Economist,* June 13, 1987.

101. *Observer,* June 7, 1987.

102. *Times,* June 11, 1987.

103. Ivor Crewe, "What's Left for Labour: An Analysis of Thatcher's Victory," *Public Opinion* 10 (July–August 1987): 52–56. See especially data on pp. 53, 55–56.

104. See Anthony Heath, John Curtice, Roger Jowell, Geoff Evans, Julia Field, and Sharon Witherspoon, *Understanding Political Change: The British Voter 1964–1987* (Oxford: Pergamon Press, 1991), esp. chs. 5–7.

105. Crewe, "What's Left," p. 54.

106. Crewe, "What's Left," p. 56.

107. See illustration 2E in David Butler and Dennis Kavanagh, *The British General Election of 1987* (New York: St. Martin's Press, 1988).

108. See J. R. G. Tomlinson, "The Schools," in Kavanagh and Seldon, eds., ch. 14, esp. p. 183.

109. See Tomlinson, esp. p. 185. According to Tomlinson, "Underlying these processes were deeper objectives of the neoliberal political programme of removing or neutralizing institutions and power groupings which intervene between the state and the individual, notably the breaking of the power of the teacher trade unions (over pay, conditions of service, and curriculum), a considerable reduction in the powers of local government and its realignment towards being an agency of central government, and an orchestrated denigration of the profession."

110. The groundwork for the 1988 act was laid by Keith Joseph in his 1985 White Paper, "Better Schools." See Tomlinson, p. 190.

111. See Tomlinson, esp. pp. 185, 194.

112. See *Times,* December 30, 1988.

113. Even after passage of the health service and community service bill, the government revised its schedule for implementation in order to blunt its impact before the next general election. See "Treatment Suspended," *Economist,* June 16, 1990.

114. According to one critical account of health care reform, "[T]he Thatcherite Tories,

enthralled by the Reaganites, turned to the United States for inspiration. They found Alain Enthoven, business professor at Stanford University (and today, a leading proponent of 'managed competition' in US Health policy), who in 1985 had advocated the introduction of an 'internal market' to the health service." See Anna Coote, "What Thatcher Did to British Health Care," *Dissent* 41 (Winter 1994): 53.

115. See Thatcher, *Downing Street Years,* pp. 606–617; Lawson, pp. 612–619; and Charles Webster, "The Health Service," in Kavanagh and Seldon, eds., ch. 13, pp. 166–182.

116. Thatcher, *Downing Street Years,* p. 648.

117. Lawson, p. 574. According to the chancellor, "It was the most strongly worded attack I launched on any policy proposal throughout my time in Government." See p. 573.

118. Personal interview, Anthony Meyer, August 5, 1990.

119. Lawson, p. 1001.

120. Personal interview, James Prior, June 28, 1990.

121. Personal interview, John Biffen, July 2, 1990.

122. See Helmut Norpoth, *Confidence Regained: Economics, Mrs. Thatcher, and the British Voter* (Ann Arbor: University of Michigan Press, 1992).

123. A poll conducted by Market and Opinion Research International in June 1988 identified some of the limits of public support for Thatcher's policies, especially overwhelming opposition to privatization of water and electricity, education and health reform, and the poll tax. Furthermore, although a majority viewed Britain as "Thatcherite," they also agreed that this was not the ideal society and preferred one that was more "caring." See *Sunday Times,* June 12, 1988. See also Ivor Crewe, "Values: The Crusade That Failed," in Kavanagh and Seldon, eds., ch. 18, pp. 239–250.

124. Personal interview, Chris Patten, June 24, 1991.

125. In particular, the trade unions lost their bloc vote at conference and the party abandoned clause four, which contained its commitment to public ownership of the means of production, distribution, and exchange.

126. Personal interview, Tony Benn, June 19, 1991.

127. Perhaps one of the most bizarre manifestations of Thatcher's image and appeal in the U.S. is provided by her advertised participation in Peter Lowe's "Success 1996," a seminar that promises to teach participants "the latest strategies for business and personal success." As advertised, the seminar announced that Lady Thatcher would appear with actor Christopher Reeve and football star Joe Montana. See *Lawrence Journal,* September 24, 1996.

128. Reagan used this phrase in the standard speech he delivered as the GE spokesman and included it in his nationally televised speech on behalf of Barry Goldwater, "A Time for Choosing," October 27, 1964. Reagan told viewers, "You and I have a rendezvous with destiny." In his speech accepting the Democratic nomination on June 27, 1936, FDR said, "There is a mysterious cycle in human events. . . . This generation of Americans has a rendezvous with destiny." *Official Report of the Proceedings of the Democratic National Convention* (Philadelphia, 1936), p. 342.

129. In his speeches, Reagan frequently drew examples from movie plots and presented the stories as factual accounts. See Michael Paul Rogin, *Ronald Reagan, the Movie, and Other Episodes in Political Demonology* (Berkeley: University of California Press, 1987).

130. See Lou Cannon, *Reagan* (New York: Putnam, 1982), esp. pp. 54–55.

131. Quoted in Rowland Evans and Robert Novak, *The Reagan Revolution* (New York: E. P. Dutton, 1981), p. 26.

132. Reagan testified before the House Committee on Un-American Activities. He refused to name names, but he also declined to oppose the Hollywood blacklist. To the committee, Reagan delivered the following statement: "In opposing [communists], the best thing to do is make democracy work. . . . I never as a citizen want to see our country become urged, by either fear or resentment of [communists], that we ever compromise with any of our democratic principles through that fear or resentment. I still think that democracy can do it." Testimony delivered on October 23, 1947. Reprinted in Eric Bentley, ed., *Thirty Years of Treason (Excerpts from Hearings Before the House Committee on Un-American Activities)* (New York: Viking, 1971), pp. 146–147.

133. According to Reagan, he "saw firsthand how the welfare state sapped incentive to work from many people in a wonderful and dynamic country." See Ronald Reagan, *An American Life* (New York: Simon and Schuster, 1990), p. 119.

134. See Reagan, *American Life,* pp. 119–120.

135. Reagan, *American Life,* pp. 138–139.

136. Barry Goldwater, Speech Accepting the Republican Presidential Nomination. Text reprinted in *New York Times,* July 17, 1964.

137. See Karl O'Lessker, "Pyrrhic Defeat: Barry Goldwater Lost by a Landslide in 1964. But His Legacy Changed the Terms of the National Debate," *Policy Review* 29 (Summer 1984): 52–55.

138. In general, the Ford team conducted a vicious campaign against Reagan during the 1976 primary season. Ironically, the Ford campaign ran a negative ad in California that was strikingly similar to the "girl with a daisy" ad from LBJ's campaign against Goldwater in 1964. The Ford ad warned: "Governor Reagan couldn't start a war; President Reagan could." See Lyn Nofziger, *Nofziger* (Washington, D.C.: Regnery Gateway, 1992), pp. 190–192.

139. Personal interview, Lyn Nofziger, May 20, 1993.

140. In his autobiography, Goldwater recalls his conflicts with Reagan but tends to downplay their significance. Instead, Goldwater concludes his account with a laudatory assessment of the Reagan legacy. See Barry M. Goldwater with Jack Casserly, *Goldwater* (New York: Doubleday, 1988), esp. pp. 388–393.

141. See Lou Cannon, *Ronnie and Jesse: A Political Odyssey* (Garden City, N.Y.: Doubleday, 1969).

142. See Cannon, *Reagan,* pp. 132–138.

143. William A. Rusher, publisher of the *National Review,* proposed the idea of forming a third party that would join conservative Democrats and dissatisfied Republicans. According to Cannon, Reagan seriously considered leading the new party, but Holmes P. Tuttle—the same man who persuaded Reagan to deliver "A Time for Choosing"—convinced him to stay with the Republicans. See Cannon, *Reagan,* p. 197.

144. With the exception of John Connally and Philip Crane, the candidates came from the traditional or moderate wing of the Republican party. They were George Bush, Senators Howard H. Baker Jr. and Robert Dole, and Representative John B. Anderson.

145. *New York Times,* December 17, 1980. See also "When the Democrats Ran Dry," *Washington Post,* December 14, 1980.

146. *New York Times,* December 30, 1979.

147. Seymour Martin Lipset and William Schneider, "The Confidence Gap During the Reagan Years, 1981–1987," *Political Science Quarterly* 102 (Spring 1987): 1–23, esp. 1.

148. See "1980 Election One of Most Unusual," *Gallup Opinion Index,* Report No. 183 (December 1980): 29–30.

149. "Opinion Roundup," *Public Opinion* 3 (December–January 1981): 30.

150. This might well have been a "hyperbolic" interpretation adopted by macro economists and the media, as Frank Levy has argued. In fact, unique circumstances in California can account for the success of Proposition 13, and there was substantial diversity among the seventeen states that voted on fiscal initiatives in the November 1978 elections. See Frank Levy, "On Understanding Proposition 13," *Public Interest* 56 (Summer 1979): 66–89.

151. Reagan, *American Life*, p. 207.

152. As governor of California, Reagan endorsed Proposition 1: It would have limited public expenditures from tax revenues to the 1973 percentage of personal income (approximately 8 percent at the time) and then lowered it by one-tenth of 1 percent per year until it reached 7 percent. Proposition 1 required a two-thirds vote of the legislature to institute any new tax and imposed tax limits on cities and counties that could be overturned only by popular vote. Reagan called his proposition "the taxpayers' bill of rights," but it sparked fierce opposition from organized interests, especially the State Employees and Teachers Association, and voters defeated it on the November 1973 ballot.

153. See Elton Rayack, *Not So Free to Choose: The Political Economy of Milton Friedman and Ronald Reagan* (New York: Praeger, 1987).

154. According to what might well be an apocryphal account, in 1974 Laffer drew a curve on a napkin while having drinks with Richard Cheney, then White House chief of staff. The "Laffer curve" became a simple illustration of how supply-side economics should work. Although the simplicity of supply-side economics and its emphasis on tax cuts appealed to Reagan, Cannon makes a convincing case that Proposition 13 was much more important. See Cannon, *Reagan*, esp. pp. 235–236.

155. Self-described neoconservatives include prominent intellectuals such as Irving Kristol, Norman Podhoretz, Charles Krauthammer, Jeane Kirkpatrick, and Daniel Patrick Moynihan. Many neoconservatives are former Democrats or cold war liberals who grew disenchanted with the social welfare policies of the 1960s and, more important, became increasingly concerned to reverse what they perceived as global decline. For a survey of the range of neoconservative ideas and their institutions, see Christopher Bright, "Commentary in the Public Interest," *World Affairs* 153 (Fall 1990): 53–59.

156. See Gillian Peele, "The Agenda of the New Right," in Dilys M. Hill, Raymond A. Moore and Phil Williams, eds., *The Reagan Presidency: An Incomplete Revolution?* (New York: St. Martin's Press, 1990), esp. pp. 31–32.

157. Jeane Kirkpatrick, "Dictatorships and Double Standards," *Commentary* (November 1979): 34–45.

158. Kirkpatrick first met Reagan at a dinner party at the home of columnist George Will. After the event, she learned that Reagan had requested a seat next to her so that they could discuss foreign affairs. Personal interview, Jeane Kirkpatrick, January 7, 1993.

159. Quoted in Dan Himmelfarb, "Conservative Splits," *Commentary* 85 (May 1988): 56.

160. Intellectuals identified as "paleoconservative" could be viewed as the elite advocates of the Religious Right. Himmelfarb distinguishes between neoconservatives and paleoconservatives and explains: "[N]eoconservatives belong to the tradition of liberal-democratic modernity, the tradition of Montesquieu, Madison, and Tocqueville; paleoconservatives are the heirs to the Christian and aristocratic Middle Ages, to Augustine, Aquinas, and Hooker. The principles of neoconservatism are individual liberty, self-government, and equality of op-

portunity; those of paleoconservatism are religious—particularly Christian—belief, hierarchy, and prescription." See Himmelfarb, p. 56.

161. The 1980 Republican platform included the following plank: "We will halt the unconstitutional regulatory vendetta launched by Mr. Carter's IRS commissioner against independent schools." Studies of the Religious Right also cite Carter's National Conference on American Families as a catalyst for organized opposition. When they arrived, conservative Christians were shocked to discover that gays and lesbians had been invited to take part in a conference devoted to family issues. See William Martin, *With God on Our Side: The Rise of the Religious Right in America* (New York: Broadway Books, 1996), esp. pp. 178–191.

162. Bruce Nesmith, *The New Republican Coalition: The Reagan Campaigns and White Evangelicals* (New York: Lang Publishing, 1994), esp. p. 77.

163. Martin, esp. p. 209.

164. See Matthew Moen, *The Transformation of the Christian Right* (Tuscaloosa: University of Alabama Press, 1992).

165. Martin Anderson, *Revolution: The Reagan Legacy* (Stanford, Calif.: Hoover Institution Press, 1990), p. 114.

166. Personal interview, Edwin Meese, July 7, 1992.

167. There are striking similarities—in style and format—between FDR's first inaugural address and Reagan's, which suggest that Reagan and his speechwriter probably used Roosevelt's speech as a blueprint. In addition to the psychological dimension that runs through both speeches, they follow a common outline: beginning with a description of dire economic circumstances, then calling for immediate action, and emphasizing the importance of vision. Not surprisingly, there are also significant differences in the substance of the messages, some of which are noted below. See Franklin Delano Roosevelt, First Inaugural Address, in John Gabriel Hunt, ed., *The Inaugural Addresses of the Presidents* (New York: Gramercy Books, 1995), pp. 377–382.

168. *The Public Papers of Ronald Reagan* (Washington, D.C.: Government Printing Office, 1982), vol. 1, p. 1.

169. Reagan, *Public Papers,* vol. 1, p. 1.

170. Reagan, *Public Papers,* vol. 1, p. 1.

171. Reagan, *Public Papers,* vol. 1, pp. 1–2.

172. Reagan, *Public Papers,* vol. 1, p. 2.

173. Reagan, *Public Papers,* vol. 1, p. 2.

174. Reagan, *Public Papers,* vol. 1, p. 2.

175. Reagan, *Public Papers,* vol. 1, p. 4.

176. In FDR's first inaugural, he also mentions the importance of vision. Adapting a phrase from the Book of Proverbs, FDR declared, "[W]hen there is no vision, the people perish." Ironically, FDR was referring to the "unscrupulous money changers" when he delivered this statement and said, "They know only the rules of a generation of self-seekers. They have no vision" (Hunt, ed., pp. 178–179), whereas Reagan found in the business community examples of those who dream "heroic dreams."

177. There is another difference between the inaugural addresses of Reagan and FDR: Roosevelt concluded by asking for additional authority so that he can provide the leadership the nation needs, whereas Reagan told citizens that they are all heroes who can help themselves and their communities. The difference seems to stem from their distinct beliefs about government; in practice both presidents concentrated power in the executive.

178. See Anderson, esp. pp. 112–114.

179. Stockman entitled his memo "On the Danger of a GOP Economic Dunkirk." See David A. Stockman, *The Triumph of Politics* (New York: Harper and Row, 1986), pp. 71–73.

180. Personal interview, Richard Wirthlin, September 24, 1992.

181. Reagan, *Public Papers,* vol. 1, p. 81.

182. Reagan, *Public Papers,* vol. 1, pp. 82–83.

183. Reagan, *Public Papers,* vol. 1, p. 83.

184. Personal interview, Senator Paul Laxalt, March 24, 1993.

185. This is the percentage of respondents answering "approve" to the question "Do you approve or disapprove of the way Ronald Reagan is handling his job as president?" Unless otherwise noted, approval ratings in this chapter are taken from Gallup Political Barometers.

186. Quoted in Cannon, *Reagan,* p. 404.

187. Quoted in Cannon, *Reagan,* p. 414.

188. See Elizabeth Sanders, "The Presidency and the Bureaucratic State," in Michael Nelson, ed., *The Presidency and the Political System,* 2nd ed. (Washington, D.C.: Congressional Quarterly, 1988), ch. 17, esp. pp. 379–382.

189. Reagan, *Public Papers,* vol. 1, p. 668.

190. Stockman, p. 348.

191. See Paul E. Peterson and Mark Rom, "Lower Taxes, More Spending, and Budget Deficits," in Charles O. Jones, ed., *The Reagan Legacy: Promise and Performance* (Chatham, N.J.: Chatham House Publishers, 1988), ch. 7, pp. 213–240.

192. Reagan, *Public Papers,* vol. 1, p. 687.

193. Personal interview, Michael Deaver, April 13, 1993.

194. Reagan, *American Life,* p. 283.

195. Personal interview, Richard Wirthlin, September 24, 1992.

196. *New York Times,* December 19, 1981.

197. *Washington Post,* December 17, 1981.

198. William Greider, "The Education of David Stockman," *Atlantic* 248 (December 1981): 27–54.

199. Personal interview (phone), Caspar Weinberger, July 22, 1992.

200. *New York Times,* December 25, 1982.

201. *Washington Post,* December 22, 1982.

202. See Martha Derthick and Paul Quirk, *The Politics of Deregulation* (Washington, D.C.: Brookings Institution, 1985), esp. pp. 30–33, 212–218.

203. *Washington Post,* November 11, 1983.

204. *Washington Post,* November 20, 1983.

205. *New York Times,* October 14, 1984.

206. See Gerald Pomper, "The Presidential Election," in Gerald Pomper, ed., *The Election of 1984* (Chatham, N.J.: Chatham House Publishers, 1985), ch. 3, esp. p. 70.

207. See Benjamin Ginsberg and Martin Shefter, "Ronald Reagan and the Reconstitution of American Politics: Creating a Supply Side Society" (paper presented at the Annual Meeting of the American Political Science Association, 1986).

208. See Krieger, ch. 6, esp. p. 153.

209. Eventually, Reagan retreated, and the Supreme Court settled the issue in an 8-1 ruling that made it legal for the IRS to deny tax exemptions to schools found guilty of racial discrimination.

210. Congress was responding to a 1984 Supreme Court decision *(Grove City College v. Bell)*, which limited antidiscrimination laws to specific programs that received federal money.

211. "Opinion Roundup," *Public Opinion* 7 (December–January 1985): 37.

212. See Pomper, "Presidential Election," p. 84; and Scott Keeter, "Public Opinion in 1984," in Pomper, ed., ch. 4, esp. p. 93.

213. See "Character of Reagan Support Markedly Different Than In '80," *Gallup Report*, 230 (November 1984): 10–11.

214. See Thomas Ferguson and Joel Rogers, *Right Turn* (New York: Hill and Wang, 1986), ch. 1, esp. p. 19. Another study identifies the start of these trends in the late 1970s and therefore concludes that Reagan secured a policy mandate as early as the 1980 election. See William G. Mayer, *The Changing American Mind* (Ann Arbor: University of Michigan Press, 1992), part 1. However, even if conservative trends in public opinion emerged before Reagan's first election, few voters supported Reagan in 1980 because he was a conservative, but many more did so in 1984.

215. Keeter, "Public Opinion," p. 98. See also Gregory B. Markus, "The Impact of Personal and National Economic Conditions on the Presidential Vote: A Pooled Cross-Sectional Analysis," *American Journal of Political Science* 32 (Winter 1988): 137–154; and Roderick Kiewiet, *Macroeconomics and Micropolitics: The Electoral Effects of Economic Issues* (Chicago: University of Chicago Press, 1983).

216. Keeter, "Public Opinion," p. 91.

217. Keeter, "Public Opinion," p. 95.

218. Reagan, *Public Papers, 1985,* book 2, p. 682.

219. Personal interview, James Baker, May 11, 1993.

220. Personal interview, Donald Regan, August 27, 1992.

221. Personal interview, Jeffrey Birnbaum, February 2, 1994. Birnbaum also coauthored the definitive study of the 1986 tax reform. See Jeffrey H. Birnbaum and Alan S. Murray, *Showdown at Gucci Gulch: Lawmakers, Lobbyists, and the Unlikely Triumph of Tax Reform* (New York: Random House, 1987).

222. Personal interview, Donald Regan, August 27, 1992.

223. Personal interview, James Baker, May 11, 1993.

224. *New York Times,* December 22, 1985.

225. Personal interview, Jeffrey Birnbaum, February 2, 1994. See also Birnbaum and Murray, esp. p. 22.

226. Reagan, *Public Papers, 1986,* book 2, p. 1415.

227. Headline of the *Washington Post.* Quoted by Reagan, *Public Papers, 1986,* book 2, p. 1414.

228. *Washington Post,* October 19, 1986.

229. See *New York Times,* December 23, 1987, and December 27, 1987; *Washington Post,* December 23, 1987.

230. *New York Times,* October 24, 1988.

231. *Washington Post,* October 23, 1988.

232. This was the conclusion of one study based on content analysis of Reagan's state of the union addresses. See Matthew C. Moen, "Ronald Reagan and the Social Issues: Rhetorical Support for the Christian Right," *Social Science Journal* 27 (1990): 199–207, esp. p. 205. Journalists frequently observed that Reagan's rhetoric had the effect of legitimizing the New Right. For example, see Sidney Blumenthal, "The Righteous Empire," *New Republic,* October 22, 1984, pp. 18–24.

233. For a discussion of Reagan's selection process, see John Anthony Maltese, "The Presidency and the Judiciary," in Michael Nelson, ed., *The Presidency and the Political System,* 4th ed. (Washington, D.C.: Congressional Quarterly, 1995), pp. 468–495. For an analysis of the nature of Reagan's appointments, see David M. O'Brien, "The Reagan Judges: His Most Enduring Legacy?" in Jones, ed., pp. 60–101.

234. See Nancy E. Marion, *A History of Federal Crime Control Initiatives, 1960–1993* (Westport, Conn.: Praeger, 1994), ch. 7.

235. See Lipset and Schneider, esp. p. 10.

236. See Mayer, esp. chs. 3–5.

237. Reagan, *Public Papers,* vol. 1, p. 81.

238. See Samuel Beer, "Ronald Reagan: New Deal Conservative?" *Society* 20 (January–February 1983): 40–47.

239. The Reagan presidency produced more ethics violations than any other administration in the twentieth century. Consider the following examples: Attorney General Meese assisted a friend, E. Robert Wallach, in securing a government contract for what became known as the Wedtech Corporation. Under Anne Gorsuch Burford, the EPA was investigated for granting political favors and general mismanagement. Deputy Secretary of Defense Paul Thayer passed insider trading information to friends, and Thomas Reed of the NSC also engaged in insider trading. Under Samuel Pierce, HUD was investigated for influence peddling, favoritism, abuse, fraud, and embezzlement. After they left the White House, Deaver and Nofziger were prosecuted for lobbying their former employers (Deaver was convicted for perjury, and Nofziger's conviction was reversed on appeal). Others accused of ethics violations include Secretary of Labor Raymond J. Donovan, National Security Advisor Allen, and Secretary of Interior James Watts. Finally, see the discussion on Iran-Contra in chapter 9 of this book.

240. See Lipset and Schneider, pp. 1–23.

241. "Text of the State of the Union Address," *Washington Post,* January 24, 1996.

6. The Pursuit of Principle and Party Constraints

1. See David Butler, "American Myths About British Parties," *Virginia Quarterly Review* 31 (Winter 1955): 46–58.

2. See Samuel H. Beer, *Modern British Politics: Parties and Pressure Groups in the Collectivist Age* (New York: W. W. Norton, 1982); and J. D. Stewart, *British Pressure Groups* (Oxford: Clarendon Press, 1958).

3. See R. T. McKenzie, *British Political Parties* (London: Heinemann, 1955).

4. Richard Rose, "Parties, Factions and Tendencies in Britain," *Political Studies* 12, no. 1 (1964): pp. 33–46.

5. See James Ceaser, *Presidential Selection: Theory and Development* (Princeton, N.J.: Princeton University, 1979), esp. ch. 4.

6. Wilson's priorities might explain his focus on Gladstone's leadership (and neglect of the Liberal party). The leader occupied the central place in Wilson's vision. Parties proved significant only in relation to leadership: In Wilson's words, parties must be made to realize they are mere "servants." Wilson's failure to consider the context of Gladstone's leadership might also have been a deliberate omission. As a political scientist, Wilson was prone to sacrifice ac-

curacy for the sake of argument. Known for his gifts as a great orator, Gladstone provided the type of leader Wilson wanted in the U.S., and so he "found" him in the U.K.

7. In addition to the overview included in chapter 4, see the following writings of Wilson: For his early view that the U.S. system required reforms modeled after the British parliamentary system, see *Congressional Government* (Cleveland: World Publishing, 1885); and "Cabinet Government in the United States," *International Review* 7 (August 1879): 146–163. For Wilson's later view that the U.S. presidency could provide the popular leadership necessary for coherent and efficient government, see "Mr. Cleveland as President," January 15, 1897, reprinted in Arthur Link, ed., *The Papers of Woodrow Wilson* (Princeton, N.J.: Princeton University Press, 1979), vol. 10, esp. p. 119; and T. H. Vail Motter, ed., *Leaders of Men* (Princeton, N.J.: Princeton University Press, 1952).

8. Herbert Croly, *Progressive Democracy* (New York: Macmillan, 1914), pp. 345–346.

9. In 1950, the American Political Science Association's report *Toward a More Responsible Two Party System* harked back to President Wilson's statements as the basis for many of its reform proposals. The report quoted Wilson three times, citing only statements he made as president, and it referred to his presidency twice but neglected to mention his scholarship. See *Toward a More Responsible Two Party System* (New York: Rinehart, 1950). For a brief intellectual history of responsible-parties theory (and its interpretation of Wilson), see Patricia Sykes, "Party Constraints on Leaders in Pursuit of Change," *Studies in American Political Development* 7 (Spring 1993): 151–176 (esp. pp. 151–156).

10. *National Intelligencer,* October 28, 1832.

11. See Arthur M. Schlesinger Jr., *The Age of Jackson* (Boston: Little, Brown and Company, 1946), esp. p. 206; and Harold C. Syrett, *Andrew Jackson: His Contribution to the American Tradition* (Westport, Conn.: Greenwood Press, 1953), esp. pp. 31–32.

12. See Stephen Skowronek, "Presidential Leadership in Political Time," in Michael Nelson, ed., *The Presidency and the Political System,* 2nd ed. (Washington, D.C.: Congressional Quarterly, 1988), p. 123.

13. Robert V. Remini, *Andrew Jackson* (New York: Harper and Row, 1966), p. 167.

14. Robert V. Remini, *Andrew Jackson and the Course of American Freedom: 1822–32* (New York: Harper and Row, 1981) vol. 2, esp. pp. 356, 358.

15. *Telegraph,* May 24, 1932.

16. James D. Richardson, ed., *A Compilation of the Messages and Papers of Presidents, 1789–1897* (Washington, D.C.: Government Printing Office, 1896), vol. 2, p. 448.

17. Richardson, ed., vol. 2, p. 448.

18. In addition to Jackson's first annual message, see Ceaser, esp. pp. 160–161.

19. Richardson, ed., vol. 2, p. 448.

20. See Robert Blake, *The Conservative Party from Peel to Thatcher* (London: Fontana, 1985), especially ch. 1.

21. See the text of the Tamworth Manifesto in the *Memoirs by the Right Honourable Sir Robert Peel* (London: John Murray, 1856), pp. 58–67.

22. Initially, *Times* owner John Walter suggested to Sir James Scarlett that Peel deliver a "popular declaration," and Scarlett sent the letter to Peel. See *The History of the Times* (London: Kraus Reprint, 1935), vol. 1, pp. 58–67.

23. Norman Gash, ed., *Documents of Modern History: The Age of Peel* (London: Edward Arnold, 1968), pp. 79–80.

24. See *Times,* 1841, esp. July 15, 24, 26.

25. On the last night of the Whig Parliament Peel revealed: "If I could be induced to believe that an alteration in the Corn Laws would be an effective remedy for [social and economic distress] . . . I would earnestly advise a relaxation, an alteration, nay, if necessary a repeal of the Corn Laws." *Parliamentary Debates, Commons,* 3rd series, vol. 59 (1841), col. 413.

26. Gash, ed., pp. 86–88.

27. Gash, ed., p. 128.

28. Gash, ed., p. 129.

29. *Parliamentary Debates, Commons,* 3rd series, vol. 87 (1846), col. 1054.

30. *Speeches of the Late Right Honourable Sir Robert Peel* (London: George Routledge and Company, 1858), vol. 4, pp. 716–717.

31. Blake, ch. 2, esp. p. 52.

32. *New York Times,* October 23, 1884.

33. July 12, 1884.

34. July 11, 1884.

35. When Cleveland accepted the Democratic nomination for mayor in 1881, he declared that he believed public officials were the "trustees of the people." His advisors later transformed this statement into the catchier phrase "A public office is a public trust," which became the slogan for his subsequent campaigns. See Robert E. Welch Jr., *The Presidencies of Grover Cleveland* (Lawrence: University Press of Kansas, 1988), p. 24.

36. *New York Times,* October 23, 1884.

37. The platform read: "Knowing full well . . . that legislation affecting the operations of the people should be cautious and conservative in method, not in advance of public opinion, but responsive to its demands, the Democratic party is pledged to revise the tariff in a spirit of fairness to all interests. But in making reduction in taxes, it is not proposed to injure any domestic industries, but rather to promote their healthy growth." George Thomas Kurian, ed., *The Encyclopedia of the Democratic Party* (Armonk, N.Y.: Sharpe Reference, 1997), p. 469.

38. George F. Parker, ed., *The Writings and Speeches of Grover Cleveland* (New York: Cassell, 1970), pp. 83, 85.

39. *Boston Journal,* December 7, 1887.

40. *New York Times,* December 8, 1887.

41. *New York Times,* November 4, 1892.

42. Quoted in Allan Nevins, *Grover Cleveland: A Study in Courage* (New York: Dodd, Mead and Company, 1934), p. 510.

43. *New York Times,* August 11, 1893.

44. March 16, 1894.

45. *New York Times,* March 25, 1894.

46. See Welch, p. 124–125.

47. Factors often cited to explain the 1896 "realignment" are the panic of 1893 and Bryan's candidacy, but the role of Cleveland's leadership is generally neglected. Cleveland's response to the panic alienated the groups he had attracted in 1892 (see chapter 3), and his position on the currency split the Democratic party. Cleveland handed the Republicans an opportunity to revive their electoral fortunes, and they seized it. For classic examples of realignment theory, including accounts of the 1896 election, see Walter Dean Burnham, *Critical Elections and the Mainsprings of American Politics* (New York: Norton, 1970); and James L. Sundquist, *Dynamics of the Party System* (Washington, D.C.: Brookings Institution, 1973).

48. November 16, 1868.

49. *Times,* December 5, 1868.

50. *Times,* March 27, 1880.

51. April 14, 1880.

52. See especially Erik Eyck, *Gladstone* (Frank Cass and Company, 1966), p. 336; and E. J. Feuchtwanger, *Gladstone* (New York: St. Martin's Press, 1975), p. 213.

53. See Roy Jenkins, *Gladstone* (London: Macmillan, 1995), esp. p. 520.

54. *Times,* January 6, 1886.

55. W. E. Gladstone, *Midlothian Speeches* (Leicester, U.K.: Leicester University Press, 1971), p. 212.

56. March 20, 1886. With the exception of its disapproval of the Midlothian campaign, the *Times* was generally sympathetic to Gladstone and supported the Liberal party. But the paper's editors adamantly opposed Gladstone's positions on Irish issues. During the 1880s, its coverage of Gladstone became increasingly critical. See *The History of the Times: The Tradition Established 1841–1884* (London: Kraus Reprint, 1971), esp. ch. 24.

57. March 22, 1886.

58. *Times,* March 22, 1886.

59. *Times,* March 27, 1886.

60. April 5, 1886.

61. *Times,* August 12, 1892. Many theories exist about why and how the Labour party came to replace the Liberal party, but the most widely accepted view emphasizes the Liberals' failure to integrate the working class and the trade union movement. As in the U.S., leadership—both Gladstone's and Lloyd George's—played a critical role in the "realignment." For an overview of the literature on the Liberal party's decline, see Arthur Cyr, *Liberal Politics in Britain* (New Brunswick, N.J.: Transaction, 1988). For a study that emphasizes the role of Gladstone's home rule campaign (and, to a lesser degree, Lloyd George's participation in the coalition government), see Michael Bentley, *British Liberalism in Theory and Practice 1868–1918* (London: Edward Arnold, 1987).

62. Link, ed., *Papers,* vol. 10, p. 119.

63. *Times,* November 2, 1912.

64. *New York Times,* November 6, 1912.

65. *New York Times,* November 6, 1912.

66. Ray Stannard Baker, ed., *Woodrow Wilson, Life and Letters—President 1913–1914* (New York: Greenwood, 1968), vol. 4, p. 99.

67. Shortly after he took office, Wilson had declared, "I shall not be acting in a partisan spirit when I nominate progressives—and only progressives. I shall be acting as a representative of the people of this great country." Baker, ed., vol. 4, p. 100.

68. Baker, ed., vol. 4, p. 112.

69. Baker, ed., vol. 4, p. 118.

70. Baker, ed., vol. 4, p. 121.

71. Quoted in John Braeman, ed., *Wilson* (Englewood Cliffs, N.J.: Prentice Hall, 1972), p. 51.

72. Arthur Link, *Wilson: Campaigns for Progressivism and Peace, 1916–1917* (Princeton, N.J.: Princeton University Press, 1965), p. 8; William Crotty and John S. Jackson, *Presidential Primaries and Nominations* (Washington, D.C.: Congressional Quarterly, 1985), esp. table on p. 205.

73. *New York Times,* June 16, 1916.

74. Quoted in Link, *Progressivism and Peace,* p. 102.

75. *New York Times,* October 10, 1916. See also Arthur Link, *Woodrow Wilson and the Progressive Era* (New York: Harper, 1963), esp. p. 239. According to Link, "Wilson's bold championship of labor's supreme objective and of the cause of social justice stood out in vivid contrast to the equivocation of the Republican platform and Hughes' evasive declarations."

76. *New York Times,* November 7, 1916.

77. *Times,* December 1, 1916.

78. *Times,* December 6, 1916.

79. *Times,* December 7, 1916.

80. David Lloyd George, *War Memoirs of David Lloyd George,* 2nd ed. (London: Odhams Press, 1938), vol. 1, pp. 620, 623, 625.

81. Lloyd George, vol. 1, p. 626; see also A. J. P. Taylor, ed., *Lloyd George: A Diary by Frances Stevenson* (London: Hutchinson, 1971), p. 134.

82. Quoted in Peter Rowland, *David Lloyd George: A Biography* (New York: Macmillan, 1975), pp. 447–448.

83. *Times,* November 18, 1918.

84. *Times,* November 14, 1918.

85. *Times,* December 12, 1918.

86. Lord Beaverbrook, *The Decline and Fall of Lloyd George* (London: Collins, 1963), p. 9.

87. The experience of the Labour government might well have influenced the postwar generation of responsible-party theorists in the U.S. The 1945–50 government did carry out virtually all its manifesto commitments and produced substantial programmatic change. To a great extent, however, Labour acted on the basis of a bipartisan consensus that had developed. In addition, there was little intraparty democracy in this period: Both the extraparliamentary party and the parliamentary Labour party showed greater deference to the government than they did at any time before or since. Moreover, the prime minister, Clement Attlee, was not a strong leader or one with firm convictions. Instead, Attlee acted as a chairman of the board who allowed his talented ministers (many of whom were conviction politicians) to initiate new programs.

88. Personal interview, John Sears, June 30, 1992.

89. Personal interview, John Sears, June 30, 1992.

90. Personal interview, John Sears, June 30, 1992.

91. Personal interview, John Sears, June 30, 1992.

92. Personal interview, Lyn Nofziger, May 20, 1993.

93. Personal interview, Lyn Nofziger, May 20, 1993.

94. Personal interview, Lyn Nofziger, May 20, 1993.

95. Personal interview, Frank Fahrenkopf, July 6, 1992.

96. The op-ed page of the *Washington Post* captured the Republican party's dilemma after the 1992 election by printing two articles side by side under the banner "What Does the GOP Have to Do?" In one article, William J. Bennett argued that the GOP needs to "Become a 'Conviction' Party Once Again" as it was under Reagan. In the other article, Senator Nancy Kassebaum urged the GOP to "Reinvent Itself" by returning to the principle of "limited government," but to do so it must abandon the "topsy-turvy thinking evident in the divisive debate regarding abortion." See *Washington Post,* November 10, 1992.

97. The boll weevil is a beetle in the southern U.S. whose destructive larvae hatch in and

damage the cotton bolls. Although the term was originally applied to Southern Democrats in a disparaging way, the Boll Weevils embraced the label and wore it as a badge of honor.

98. A gypsy moth is a native of the Old World; its caterpillars feed on foliage and destroy trees. Liberal Republicans acquired this label after the Southern Democrats became known as Boll Weevils.

99. Personal interview, Senator Paul Laxalt, March 24, 1993.

100. Personal interview, James Baker, May 11, 1993.

101. Personal interview, Kenneth Duberstein, March 5, 1993.

102. See Samuel Kernell, *Going Public: New Strategies of Presidential Leadership* (Washington, D.C.: Congressional Quarterly, 1986).

103. *The Public Papers of Ronald Reagan* (Washington, D.C.: Government Printing Office, 1982), vol. 1, p. 665.

104. Personal interview, Frank Fahrenkopf, July 6, 1992.

105. David Rohde argues that Reagan's extreme policy views made it easier for Democrats to compromise and achieve consensus within their party. See *Parties and Leaders in the Postreform House* (Chicago: University of Chicago Press, 1991). Barbara Sinclair argues that conflict with a conservative, confrontational president forced Democratic representatives to support stronger leadership in the House of Representatives. See "The Emergence of Strong Leadership in the 1980s House of Representatives," *Journal of Politics* 54 (August 1992): 657–684; and "Agenda Control and Policy Success: Ronald Reagan and the 97th House," *Legislative Studies Quarterly* 10 (August 1985): 291–314.

106. See Jon R. Bond and Richard Fleisher, *The President in the Legislative Arena* (Chicago: University of Chicago Press, 1990), especially ch. 4.

107. Social security provides the exception: On this issue, Congressional Republicans resisted Reagan's proposed reforms, but they did so because the proposals lacked popular support. See discussion in chapter 5 of this book.

108. See David R. Mayhew, *Divided We Govern: Party Control, Lawmaking, and Investigations 1946–1990* (New Haven, Conn.: Yale University Press, 1991), esp. p. 189.

109. Jeffrey K. Tulis, *The Rhetorical Presidency* (Princeton, N.J.: Princeton University, 1987).

110. See McKenzie, especially ch. 2.

111. At the same time, however, the second ballot became open to contestants who had not entered the first round. If no one wins the second ballot, a third is held—a runoff between the top three candidates, using a single transferable vote.

112. The final vote was Thatcher 146; Whitelaw 79; Prior 19; Howe 19; and Peyton 16. See Robert Blake, *The Conservative Party from Peel to Thatcher* (London: Fontana, 1985), pp. 316–320.

113. See Wendy Webster, *Not a Man to Match Her: The Marketing of a Prime Minister* (London: Women's Press, 1990), especially chs. 3, 4, and 6.

114. Robert Behrens, *The Conservative Party from Heath to Thatcher* (London: Saxon House, 1980), ch. 3, esp. p. 40.

115. February 12, 1975.

116. Behrens, p. 25.

117. Jim Prior, *A Balance of Power* (London: Hamish Hamilton, 1986), p. 118.

118. Anthony Heath, Roger Jowell, and John Curtice, *How Britain Votes* (New York: Pergamon Press, 1985). See also discussion of general elections in chapter 5 of this book.

119. Personal interview, James Prior, June 28, 1990.

120. Bruce Cain, John A. Ferejohn, and Morris Fiorina, "The Constituency Service Basis of the Personal Vote for U.S. Representatives and British Members of Parliament," *American Political Science Review* 78 (March 1984): 110–125.

121. Personal interview, Norman Tebbit, June 27, 1990.

122. Elizabeth Hann Hastings and Philip K. Hastings, eds., *Index to International Public Opinion, 1985–86* (Westport, Conn.: Greenwood Press, 1987), p. 427.

123. Peter Jenkins, *Mrs. Thatcher's Revolution: The Ending of the Socialist Era* (Cambridge, Mass.: Harvard University Press, 1988), p. 207.

124. Reported in the *Times,* April 17, 1986.

125. Personal interview, Cecil Parkinson, June 11, 1991.

126. Personal interview, Peter Jenkins, June 19, 1991.

127. Personal interview, Ian Gilmour, June 26, 1991.

128. Quoted in Norman Gash, *Peel* (London: Longman, 1976), p. 141.

129. Lloyd George, preface to vol. 1, p. vii.

130. Link, ed., *Papers,* vol. 1, pp. 109–110.

131. *Toward a More Responsible Two Party System,* p. 14.

132. *Toward a More Responsible Two Party System,* pp. 89–90.

7. The Depiction of Conviction: Presidents, Prime Ministers, and the Press

1. See Frank L. Mott, *American Journalism—A History: 1690–1960* (New York: Macmillan, 1962).

2. Quoted in John Tebbel and Sarah Miles Watts, *The Press and the Presidency* (New York: Oxford University Press, 1985), p. 77.

3. Keith Melder, "The Whistlestop: A History of the Partisan Press," *Campaigns and Elections* 6 (Spring 1985): 62.

4. Clearly, the contemporary media emphasis on scandal is not unique to the post-Watergate and post-Vietnam era, as many scholars imply. For examples, see Larry Sabato, *Feeding Frenzy: How Attack Journalism Has Transformed American Politics* (New York: Free Press, 1991); and Thomas E. Patterson, *Out of Order* (New York: Vintage Books, 1994).

5. Quoted in Tebbel and Watts, p. 79.

6, Quoted in Michael Nelson, "Presidents and the News Media," in *Congressional Quarterly's Guide to the Presidency* (Washington, D.C.: Congressional Quarterly Press, 1989), p. 718.

7. Quoted in Tebbel and Watts, p. 81.

8. Quoted in Tebbel and Watts, p. 85.

9. See Tebbel and Watts, p. 87.

10. January 22, 1831.

11. See Melder, esp. p. 61.

12. Mott, p. 412.

13. See Gerald Baldasty, "The Nineteenth Century Origins of Modern American Journalism," in *Three Hundred Years of the American Newspaper* (Worcester, Mass.: American Antiquarian Society, 1991), esp. p. 409.

14. Mott, p. 389.

15. See Mott, esp. p. 405.

16. Mott, p. 413.

17. Quoted in Tebbel and Watts, p. 267.

18. See Mott, pp. 510–511.

19. *New York Evening Post,* June 4, 1886.

20. *New York World,* June 5, 1886.

21. See Allan Nevins, *Grover Cleveland: A Study in Courage* (New York: Dodd, Mead, and Company, 1934), ch. 18.

22. Quoted in Tebbel and Watts, p. 271.

23. To George Creel, head of the Committee on Public Information, quoted in Tebbel and Watts, p. 375.

24. Scholars disagree about whether Wilson's friendship with Mary Peck (also known as Mary Allen Hulbert) was an extramarital affair. Tebbel and Watts refer to Wilson's "extramarital affair with the fascinating Mrs. Mary Peck" as if it were established fact. Tebbel and Watts, p. 365. Clements skirts the issue by noting that "his romantic letters to Mary Peck suggest that he was at least severely tempted outside of marriage." Kendrick A. Clements, *The Presidency of Woodrow Wilson* (Lawrence: University Press of Kansas, 1992), p. 2. Alexander George and Juliette George insist that "no one who understands the role friendship played in Wilson's life, who knows his devotion to Mrs. Wilson, his religious scruples and the equally intimate tone of his correspondence with male friends, can give credence to the scandalous imputations made in connection with his letters to Mrs. Hulbert." Alexander George and Juliette George, *Woodrow Wilson and Colonel House: A Personality Study* (New York: Dover, 1964), p. 32.

25. See Michael Baruch Grossman and Martha Joynt Kumar, *Portraying the President: The White House and the News Media* (Baltimore: Johns Hopkins University Press, 1981).

26. See Grossman and Kumar, esp. ch. 3.

27. For a comprehensive and insightful overview of the news management techniques employed by the Reagan White House from the perspective of a journalist, see David Broder, *The Front Page* (New York: Simon and Schuster, 1987), esp. ch. 5.

28. Larry Speakes took the place but not the title of Press Secretary James Brady after Brady was seriously wounded during the assassination attempt on Reagan.

29. Research on the media has long assumed and recently demonstrated the agenda-setting capacity of the press, supporting the notion that the media "do not tell us what to think, but do tell us what to think about." See Bernard Cohen, *The Press and Foreign Policy* (Princeton, N.J.: Princeton University Press, 1963); and Shanto Iyengar and Donald Kinder, *News That Matters: Television and American Opinion* (Chicago: University of Chicago Press, 1987). Even more recently, some evidence suggests that the media might also tell us what to think. See Shanto Iyengar, *Is Anyone Responsible? How Television Frames Political Issues* (Chicago: University of Chicago Press, 1991).

30. See Norman Gash, *Sir Robert Peel: The Life of Sir Robert Peel After 1830* (Totowa, N.J.: Rowman and Littlefield, 1972), p. 121.

31. *Times,* July 27, 1841.

32. Gladstone proposed the repeal of paper duties in his 1860 budget. See Roy Jenkins, *Gladstone* (London: Macmillan, 1995), pp. 225–226.

33. There were 131 newspapers in 1851; 456 after 1900. For an account of this expansion, see E. A. Smith, *A History of the Press* (London: Ginn and Company, 1970).

34. Colin Seymour-Ure, *The Press, Politics, and the Public* (London: Methuen, 1968), p. 196. On the development of the lobby, see also Jeremy Turnstall, *The Westminster Lobby Correspondents: A Sociological Study of National Political Journalism* (London: Routledge and Kegan Paul, 1970).

35. Alan J. Lee, *The Origins of the Popular Press 1855–1914* (London: Croom Helm, 1976), esp. pp. 197–211.

36. One of Gladstone's biographers (and the editor of his diaries) refers to the formation of the lobby as "that peculiar British institutionalization of the 'leak' which began in 1884." See H. C. G. Matthew, *Gladstone* (Oxford: Clarendon Press, 1995), vol. 2, p. 115.

37. Michael Cockerell, Peter Hennessy, and David Walker, *Sources Close to the Prime Minister: Inside the Hidden World of News Manipulators* (London: Macmillan, 1984), pp. 31–33.

38. Quoted in Matthew, vol. 2, pp. 44–45.

39. *Times,* November 29, 1879.

40. *Times,* December 3, 1979.

41. *Times,* December 3, 1879.

42. See Cockerell, Hennessy, and Walker, esp. ch. 2.

43. See Bernard Ingham, *Kill the Messinger* (London: HarperCollins, 1991), esp. chs. 13 and 14.

44. Personal interview, Bernard Ingham, June 20, 1991.

45. Personal interviews, Bernard Ingham, June 20, 1991, and Larry Speakes, March 5, 1993.

46. See Michael Cockerell, *Live from Number 10: The Inside Story of Prime Ministers and Television* (London: Faber and Faber, 1989).

47. Personal interview, Tim Bell, June 26, 1991.

48. See Wendy Webster, *Not a Man to Match Her: The Marketing of a Prime Minister* (London: Women's Press, 1990), esp. chs. 4 and 5.

49. See Colin Seymour-Ure, *The British Press and Broadcasting Since 1945* (Oxford: Basil Blackwell, 1991), p. 200.

50. Personal interview, Jurek Martin, June 11, 1993.

51. For a more complete overview, see Alastair Hetherington, "The Mass Media," in Dennis Kavanagh and Anthony Seldon, eds., *The Thatcher Effect* (Oxford: Clarendon Press, 1989), ch. 22.

52. Personal interview, David Broder, July 7, 1993.

53. Personal interview, Sam Donaldson, July 1, 1993.

54. See, for examples, Mark Hertsgaard, *On Bended Knee: The Press and the Reagan Presidency* (New York: Farrar, Straus and Giroux, 1988); and Cockerell, Hennessy, and Walker.

55. Personal interview, Anthony Howard, June 13, 1984.

56. Personal interview, Bill Plante, February 9, 1994.

57. Personal interview, Sam Donaldson, July 1, 1993.

58. Personal interview, Larry Speakes, March 5, 1993.

59. See, for example, Michael Elliott, "My Girl: Postcard from London," *New Republic,* May 29, 1989.

60. See Adam Raphael's review of Cockerell, Hennessy, and Walker in *Observer,* June 17, 1984.

61. *Observer,* June 17, 1984. Also, personal interview, Adam Raphael, June 21, 1984.

62. Personal interview, Larry Speakes, March 5, 1993.

63. Personal interview, Michael Deaver, April 13, 1993.

64. Personal interview, Sam Donaldson, July 1, 1993.

65. Personal interview, Clarence Page, June 9, 1993.

66. Personal interview, Anthony Howard, June 13, 1984.

67. Personal interview, Michael Deaver, April 13, 1993.

68. Personal interview, Jack Germond, June 10, 1993.

69. Personal interview, David Broder, July 7, 1993.

70. Personal interview, Michael Deaver, April 13, 1993.

71. See Ingham, p. 268.

72. Personal interview, Bernard Ingham, June 20, 1991.

73. Personal interview, Sam Donaldson, July 1, 1993.

74. Personal interview, Peter Jenkins, June 19, 1991.

75. Personal interview, David Broder, July 7, 1993.

76. Personal interview, Larry Speakes, March 5, 1993.

77. Personal interview, David Broder, July 7, 1993.

78. Personal interview, Jurek Martin, June 11, 1993. Martin alleged that he was quoting Major's chancellor of the exchequer, Norman Lamont.

79. Personal interview, Jack Germond, June 10, 1993.

80. Personal interview, Gordon Greig, June 6, 1984.

81. Personal interview, Chris Hampson, June 14, 1984.

82. Personal interview, Julian Haviland, June 11, 1984.

83. Personal interview, Adam Raphael, June 21, 1984.

84. Personal interview, Paul Keel, June 8, 1984.

85. Personal interview, Anthony Bevins, June 28, 1983.

86. Personal interview, Bill Plante, February 9, 1994.

87. Personal interview, Jack Germond, June 10, 1993.

88. Personal interview, Clarence Page, June 9, 1993.

89. Personal interview, David Broder, July 7, 1993.

90. Personal interview, Sam Donaldson, July 1, 1993.

91. In personal interviews, two columnists, David Broder and Jack Germond, used the same language "travel around the country to talk to voters." In general, both British and U.S. columnists emphasized the importance of traveling, and, of course, they enjoy greater freedom than reporters who work inside the White House press corps or the Westminster lobby.

92. Personal interview, Jack Germond, June 10, 1993.

93. Personal interview, Bill Plante, February 9, 1994.

94. Personal interview (phone), Peter Riddell, August 2, 1993.

95. Personal interview, Anthony Howard, June 13, 1984.

96. Personal interview, Geoffrey Smith, June 3, 1984.

97. Personal interview, Julian Haviland, June 13, 1984.

98. Personal interview, David Broder, July 7, 1993.

99. Personal interview, David Broder, July 7, 1993.

100. Personal interview, Sam Donaldson, July 1, 1993.

101. Personal interview, Clarence Page, June 9, 1993.

102. Personal interview, David Broder, July 7, 1993.

103. Personal interview, Bill Plante, February 9, 1994.

104. Personal interview, Michael Deaver, April 13, 1993.

105. Personal interview, Jack Germond, June 10, 1993.

106. Personal interview, Sam Donaldson, July 1, 1993.

107. Michael Deaver with Mickey Herskowitz, *Behind the Scenes* (New York: William Morrow and Company, 1987), p. 181.

108. Deaver, p. 183.

109. *New York Times,* May 6, 1985. The *New York Times*'s coverage was typical. Page one was almost entirely devoted to the event, and the three main articles were titled "Demonstration for Soviet Jews Jams Fifth Avenue," "For Bitburg, Day of Anger Ends Quietly," and "Reagan Joins Kohl in Brief Memorial at Bitburg Graves: Visit Stirs Wide Protests."

110. Personal interview, Bernard Ingham, June 20, 1991.

111. Personal interview, Peter Jenkins, June 19, 1991.

112. Cockerell, p. 234.

113. Marina Warner, *Monuments and Maidens: The Allegory of the Female Form* (London: Picador, 1987), pp. 49–51.

114. Personal interview, David Broder, July 7, 1993.

115. Personal interview, Sam Donaldson, July 1, 1993. Most reporters and White House officials interviewed for this study mentioned Normandy when asked, "What was the best coverage Reagan ever got?" Similarly, British reporters and Downing Street officials cited Thatcher's trip to Moscow.

116. Deaver, pp. 175–176.

117. See, for example, the report in *New York Times,* June 7, 1984, which takes note of Reagan kissing Henn and his voice cracking.

118. Transcript provided by ABC News (television), aired April 26, 1983.

119. Personal interview, Richard Wirthlin, September 24, 1992.

120. Personal interview, Larry Speakes, March 5, 1993.

121. *Los Angeles Times,* June 26, 1983.

122. *Los Angeles Times,* June 30, 1983.

123. See *New York Times,* June 26 and 30 and July 1, 1983.

124. Personal interview, Larry Speakes, March 5, 1993.

125. *New York Times,* July 1, 1983.

126. In his book, *Front Page,* David Broder recalls: "The President's 'education offensive' got massive coverage. The *Post* carried fifteen stories, totaling 438 column-inches during the nine weeks at the height of his campaign. Almost without exception, the network news shows carried shots of the President at every stop. By contrast, the state governments which were supposed to take the lead in meeting this challenge got short shrift. . . . The upshot of this pattern of coverage—and the exaltation of the presidency that it reflects—was that Reagan was credited with responding to the education issue, while the work was done by others." Broder, pp. 203–204.

127. Personal interview, Peter Jenkins, June 19, 1991.

128. Personal interview, Bernard Ingham, August 4, 1993.

129. *Times,* March 30, 1987.

130. *Daily Mail,* March 30, 1987.

131. *Guardian,* March 30, 1987.

132. *Times,* April 1, 1987.

133. *Guardian,* April 1, 1987.

134. *Daily Mail,* April 1, 1987.

135. *Daily Mail,* April 2, 1987.

136. *Guardian,* April 2, 1987.

137. *Daily Mail,* April 2, 1987.

138. See Patricia Lee Sykes, "Iron Ladies, Green Goddesses, the Mouth of Marilyn Monroe: When Women of Conviction Enter the Politics of Consensus," *International Issues* 40 (December 1997): 50–71.

139. *Daily Mail,* April 2, 1987.

140. Personal interview, David Gergen, March 31, 1993.

141. Personal interview, Bill Plante, February 9, 1994.

8. Executive Authority, the Political System, and the State

1. James D. Richardson, ed., *A Compilation of the Messages and Papers of the Presidents, 1789–1897* (Washington, D.C.: Government Printing Office, 1896), vol. 2, p. 590.

2. See Patricia Lee Sykes, "The President as Legislator: A 'Superepresenator,'" *Presidential Studies Quarterly* XIX (Spring 1989): 301–315.

3. Richardson, ed., vol. 2, pp. 483–493. Jackson's Maysville veto has been compared with Ronald Reagan's March 1987 veto of the highway authorization bill. See David Resnick and Norman C. Thomas, "Reagan and Jackson: Parallels in Political Time," *Journal of Policy History* 1, no. 2 (1989): 181–205.

4. See Robert V. Remini, *Andrew Jackson and the Bank War: A Study in the Growth of Presidential Power* (New York: W. W. Norton and Company, 1967).

5. John Spencer Bassett, ed., *The Correspondence of Andrew Jackson* (Washington, D.C.: Carnegie Institution of Washington, 1929), vol. 4, p. 462.

6. Jackson made this statement with reference to his use of the veto to block internal improvements. See Bassett, ed., vol. 4, p. 465.

7. Edward Everett, ed., *Works of Daniel Webster* (Boston: Little, Brown and Company, 1857), vol. 3, p. 435.

8. Richardson, ed., vol. 3, p. 91.

9. According to Schlesinger, many of Jackson's contemporaries believed that he would put the bank issue behind him after the 1832 election, but "These calculations omitted General Jackson, who cared less for his popularity than for his program." Jackson's emphasis on his role as the "direct representative of the people" during the controversy indicates that he cared a great deal about his popularity and his program—and understood the link between the two. See Arthur Schlesinger, *The Age of Jackson* (Boston: Little, Brown and Company, 1945), p. 97.

10. Richardson, ed., vol. 2, pp. 448–449.

11. Richardson, ed., vol. 2, pp. 448–449.

12. *New York Times,* March 26, 1894.

13. *Public Papers of Grover Cleveland* (Washington, D.C.: Government Printing Office, 1889), pp. 59–67.

14. George F. Parker, ed., *The Writings and Speeches of Grover Cleveland* (New York: Cassell, 1970), p. 83.

15. See *Philadelphia Press,* December 7, 1887, and *New York World,* December 7, 1887.

16. Robert McElroy, *Grover Cleveland: The Man and the Statesman* (New York: Harper, 1923), vol. 1, esp. ch. 6. See also Welch, esp. pp. 61–62; and Stephen Skowronek, *Building*

a New American State: The Expansion of National Administrative Capacities 1877–1920 (Cambridge: Cambridge University Press, 1982).

17. Parker, ed., p. 45.

18. Parker, ed., p. 47. See also pp. 39–43.

19. Arthur Link, ed., *The Papers of Woodrow Wilson* (Princeton, N.J.: Princeton University Press, 1979), vol. 10, pp. 110–114.

20. Link, ed., *Papers,* vol. 10, p. 119.

21. Woodrow Wilson, *Constitutional Government in the United States* (New York: Columbia University Press, 1908), p. 202.

22. Link, ed., *Papers,* vol. 1, pp. 109–110.

23. See Jeffrey K. Tulis, *The Rhetorical Presidency* (Princeton, N.J.: Princeton University Press, 1987); and James Ceaser, *Presidential Selection: Theory and Development* (Princeton, N.J.: Princeton University Press, 1979).

24. Ray Stannard Baker, ed., *Woodrow Wilson—Life and Letters* (New York: Greenwood, 1968), vol. 4, p. 109.

25. *New York Times,* April 9, 1913.

26. Quoted in Arthur Schlesinger, "Preface" to Fred L. Israel, ed., *The State of the Union Messages of the Presidents 1790–1966,* vol. 3 (New York: Chelsea House, 1966), p. xiii.

27. Woodrow Wilson, *The State—Elements of Historical and Practical Politics* (Boston: D. C. Heath and Company, 1889), p. 566.

28. On April 8, 1913, Wilson wrote to a friend, "Today I break another precedent by reading my message to Congress in person. The town is agog about it. . . . The President has not addressed Congress in person since John Adams's day—and yet what [could be] more natural and dignified?" Quoted in Schlesinger, in Israel, ed., vol. 3, p. xvii.

29. *New York World,* April 10, 1913.

30. *New York Times,* December 3, 1913.

31. *New York Herald,* December 3, 1913.

32. Link, ed., *Papers,* vol. 5, pp. 359–380.

33. Wilson's policies centralized and increased the scope of the state, especially his regulatory policies, domestic assistance policies, and administration of grant-in-aid programs. See Larry Walker and Jeremy Plant, "Woodrow Wilson and the Federal System," in Jack Rabin and James S. Bowman, eds., *Politics and Administration: Woodrow Wilson and American Public Administration* (New York: Marcel Dekker, 1984), ch. 7.

34. Link, ed., *Papers,* vol. 5, pp. 362–363.

35. Link, ed., *Papers,* vol. 5, p. 364.

36. Link, ed., *Papers,* vol. 5, p. 367.

37. Link, ed., *Papers,* vol. 5, p. 368.

38. Link, ed., *Papers,* vol. 5, p. 369.

39. Link, ed., *Papers,* vol. 5, pp. 373–374.

40. Link, ed., *Papers,* vol. 5, p. 376.

41. Link, ed., *Papers,* vol. 5, p. 379.

42. Quoted in Arthur Link, *Wilson: The New Freedom* (Princeton, N.J.: Princeton University Press, 1956), p. 251. See also David H. Rosenbloom, *Public Administration and Law* (New York: M. Dekker, 1997), pp. 104–105.

43. See Thomas Lynch and Maurice Rahimi, "Woodrow Wilson and the Revolution in Public Budgeting," in Rabin and Bowman, eds., chapter 5.

44. See Samuel Kernell, *Going Public: New Strategies of Presidential Leadership,* 3rd ed. (Washington, D.C.: Congressional Quarterly Press, 1997), esp. ch. 5.

45. In his essay "White House and Whitehall," Richard Neustadt compared White House staff with British civil servants. Neustadt suggested that presidents increasingly use their White House staff to provide the expertise and objective analysis that U.S. civil servants fail to provide. His essay was written long before the Reagan presidency and was based largely on his experience in the Kennedy administration. See Richard Neustadt, "White House and Whitehall," in Anthony King, ed., *The British Prime Minister,* 2nd ed. (London: Macmillan, 1983). See also Terry M. Moe, "The Politicized Presidency," in John E. Chubb and Paul E. Peterson, eds., *The New Direction in American Politics* (Washington, D.C.: Brookings Institution, 1985), ch. 9.

46. For the view that change in the Reagan years was "inevitable," see Moe, "Politicized Presidency," in Chubb and Peterson, eds. Moe argues that all modern presidents moved in these directions because the structures of "neutral competence" proved incompatible with presidential leadership goals. He interprets the Reagan presidency as "a consummate expression of the historical drive toward congruence" between existing structures and the president's incentives and resources (p. 263). Nevertheless, Moe concedes that Reagan's success places him "in a pivotal historical position, and could well establish him as the most administratively influential president of the modern period" (p. 271).

47. See Richard P. Nathan, *The Administrative Presidency* (New York: Macmillan, 1983), ch. 5.

48. See Elizabeth Sanders, "The Presidency and the Bureaucratic State," in Michael Nelson, ed., *The Presidency and the Political System,* 2nd ed. (Washington, D.C.: Congressional Quarterly, 1988), ch. 17.

49. See Sanders in Nelson, ed., esp. pp. 382–389.

50. See Martha Derthick and Paul Quirk, *The Politics of Deregulation* (Washington, D.C.: Brookings Institution, 1985), esp. pp. 216–217. Derthick and Quirk contrast Reagan to Carter, whose agency heads worked to obstruct his regulatory efforts.

51. Personal interview, Donald Regan, August 27, 1992.

52. Personal interview, James Baker, June 28, 1993.

53. Advisors' opinions of Reagan's ability tended to reflect the intensity of their ideological commitment. In interviews, the more ideological advisors discussed accomplishments as Reagan's own, whereas the more pragmatic advisors tended to say "we" did this or that. This was most striking in the case of Baker, who rarely mentioned Reagan's name in the course of two separate interviews. Perhaps those who shared Reagan's beliefs considered him intelligent, whereas those who remained skeptical about some of his convictions viewed success in terms of political skill (often theirs).

54. Personal interview, James Baker, May 11, 1993.

55. Personal interview, James Baker, June 28, 1993.

56. Personal interview, Edwin Meese, July 7, 1992.

57. Personal interview, James Baker, June 28, 1993.

58. Personal interview, James Baker, May 11, 1993.

59. Personal interview, James Baker, May 11, 1993.

60. To a great extent, Reagan and Thatcher reverse what Fred Greenstein has called "hidden-hand" leadership. They attempt to appear overtly ideological even when they are conciliatory. See Fred I. Greenstein, *The Hidden-Hand Presidency* (New York: Basic Books, 1982).

61. Personal interview, James Baker, June 28, 1993.

62. See Martin Anderson, *Revolution: The Reagan Legacy* (Stanford, Calif.: Hoover Institution Press, 1990), esp. ch. 13. David Stockman's memoirs also include numerous accounts of conflicts among and within various groups of economists. See David Stockman, *The Triumph of Politics* (New York: Harper and Row, 1986).

63. See Michael Bentley, *Politics Without Democracy, Great Britain 1815–1914: Perception and Preoccupation in British Government* (Oxford: Basil Blackwell, 1984), esp. pp. 96, 126.

64. *Parliamentary Debates, Commons,* 3rd series, vol. 59 (1841), col. 428.

65. See Donald Read, *Peel and the Victorians* (New York: Basil Blackwell, 1987), esp. pp. 12, 69.

66. *Evening Standard,* December 18, 1835.

67. Quoted in Norman Gash, *Peel* (London: Longman, 1976), p. 168.

68. See Read, esp. p. 71.

69. *Memoirs by the Right Honourable Sir Robert Peel* (London: J. Murray, 1858), part 2, p. 62.

70. See Roy Jenkins, *Gladstone* (London: Macmillan, 1995), esp. pp. 164–167.

71. E.J. Feuchtwanger, *Gladstone* (New York: St. Martin's Press, 1975), pp. 163–164.

72. Quoted in Feuchtwanger, p. 190.

73. *Times,* November 29, 1879.

74. *Times,* December 3, 1879.

75. *Times,* November 29, 1879.

76. *Times,* December 3, 1879.

77. Quoted in *Times,* November 29, 1879.

78. See J. L. Hammond and M. R. D. Foot, *Gladstone and Liberalism* (London: English Universities Press, 1966), p. 103.

79. *Times,* November 25, 1879.

80. See Nigel Lawson, *The View from No. 11: Memoirs of a Tory Radical* (London: Bantam, 1992), p. 279.

81. Speech delivered on July 30, 1909. Reprinted in David Lloyd George, *Better Times* (London: Hodder and Stoughton, 1910), p. 152.

82. Lloyd George, p. 156.

83. Quoted in Peter Rowland, *David Lloyd George: A Biography* (New York: Macmillan, 1975), pp. 146–147.

84. In 1907, during a debate on an early proposal to reform the House of Lords, Lloyd George addressed the Conservatives' contention that the Lords were the watchdogs of the constitution. According to Lloyd George, the upper chamber was merely "Balfour's poodle": "[I]t fetches and carries for him and barks and bites anybody he sets it on to." Quoted in Rowland, p. 189.

85. See Martin Pugh, *Lloyd George* (New York: Longman, 1988), p. 48; and Kenneth O. Morgan, *The Age of Lloyd George* (London: George Allen and Unwin, 1971), pp. 46–47.

86. Quoted in Frank Owen, *Tempestuous Journey—Lloyd George, His Life and Times* (London: Hutchinson, 1954), p. 183.

87. The results were Liberals, 275 seats; Unionists, 273; Irish Nationalists, 82; Labour, 40.

88. The December election results were Liberals, 272 seats; Unionists, 272; Irish Nationalists, 84; Labour, 42.

89. *Times,* May 16, 1911.

90. *Times,* August 9, 1911.

91. The bill included the following provisions: If the Lords withhold approval of a money bill for more than a month, the bill becomes law with royal assent; if the House of Commons passes any other bill three times, it also becomes law with royal assent; and finally, the maximum length of any Parliament is reduced from seven to five years.

92. Quoted in Pugh, p. 104.

93. John Turner, *Lloyd George's Secretariat* (Cambridge: Cambridge University Press, 1980), p. 1 and ch. 1 in general.

94. Pugh, p. 100.

95. John Grigg, *Lloyd George: From Peace to War, 1912–1916* (London: Methuen, 1985), p. 500; Pugh, p. 121.

96. Quoted in Kenneth Harris, *Thatcher* (Boston: Little, Brown and Company, 1988), p. 86.

97. Richard Neustadt compares a prime minister's need to build consensus within the cabinet with a president's need to build support in Congress. See Neustadt in King, ed., pp. 131–147.

98. Speech reprinted in *Times,* November 14, 1990.

99. Personal interview, John Biffen, July 2, 1990.

100. Personal interview, Timothy Raison, June 18, 1991.

101. Personal interview, Patrick Jenkin, 18 June 1991.

102. Personal interview, William Whitelaw, June 20, 1991.

103. Personal interview, John Biffen, July 2, 1990.

104. Personal interview, James Prior, June 28, 1990.

105. Personal interview, William Whitelaw, June 20, 1991.

106. Personal interview, James Prior, June 28, 1990.

107. Her tendency to ask the question "Is he one of us?" produced the title for one popular biography. See Hugo Young, *One of Us: A Biography of Margaret Thatcher* (London: Macmillan, 1989).

108. Personal interview, Tony Kerpel, special assistant to Kenneth Baker, June 12, 1991.

109. Peter Hennessy, "The Prime Minister, the Cabinet and the Thatcher Personality," in Kenneth Minogue and Michael Biddis, eds., *Thatcherism: Personality and Politics* (New York: St. Martin's Press, 1987), p. 60.

110. Personal interview, John Biffen, July 2, 1990.

111. Kenneth Harris, *Thatcher* (Boston: Little, Brown and Company, 1988), pp. 88–89. According to Harris, "It was the existence of the Committees, above all the E Committee, which was to lead to Mrs. Thatcher being accused of neglecting to govern through the Cabinet and resorting to 'Presidential politics.' To the undiscerning eye the new Government was going to be run by a Cabinet in which a wide spectrum of views could be expressed. In fact, as soon became clear, it would be run by a small group of E Committee Thatcherites whose control of economic policy, the key to everything Mrs. Thatcher wanted to change in British society, gave them control of the Cabinet."

112. Harris, p. 101. Again, Harris observes, "It was a pattern of government that might have made for forthright leadership, but which could border on the dictatorial."

113. Hennessy, in Minogue and Biddis, eds., pp. 62–63.

114. Personal interview, James Prior, June 28, 1990.

115. Peter Hennessy, *Cabinet* (Oxford: Basil Blackwell, 1986), p. 110.

116. Report quoted in Hennessy, *Cabinet,* p. 75.

117. Quoted in Hennessy, *Cabinet,* p. 76.

118. Jim Prior, *A Balance of Power* (London: Hamish Hamilton, 1986), p. 137.

119. David Willetts, "The Role of the Prime Minister's Policy Unit," *Public Administration* 65 (Winter 1987): 445. Also, personal interview, July 2, 1990.

120. Willetts, pp. 450–452. Despite the centralization he describes, Willetts insists the policy unit is not "presidential." To support this assertion, he emphasizes only the contrast in the sizes of the staffs at Number 10 and in the White House.

121. See Bernard Donoughue, *Prime Minister: The Conduct of Policy Under Harold Wilson and James Callaghan* (London: Jonathan Cape, 1987).

122. Hennessy, in Minogue and Biddis, eds., p. 63.

123. Willetts, p. 444.

124. Bruce Anderson, *John Major: The Making of the Prime Minister* (London: Fourth Estate, 1991), p. 45.

125. Donald J. Savoie, *Thatcher Reagan Mulroney: In Search of a New Bureaucracy* (Pittsburgh: University of Pittsburgh Press, 1994).

126. Savoie seems to overlook this when he concludes that by transforming senior civil servants from administrators/policy advisors to managers, Reagan and Thatcher restored the politics-administration distinction—in his words, the "politics-management-dichotomy." See Savoie, pp. 12, 282–283.

127. Marina Warner, *Monuments and Maidens: The Allegory of the Female Form* (London: Picador, 1985), p. 44. In general, see Warner, pp. 38–52.

9. The Global Arena

1. See Geoffrey Smith, *Reagan and Thatcher* (New York: Norton, 1991), ch. 3, esp. pp. 29–37.

2. Margaret Thatcher, *The Downing Street Years* (New York: HarperCollins, 1993), p. 157.

3. Quoted in Hugo Young, *One of Us: A Biography of Margaret Thatcher* (London: Macmillan, 1989), p. 250. Note Reagan's use of the word "but." He seems surprised to discover that someone who is well informed can also have firm convictions.

4. Thatcher, *Downing Street Years,* p. 157.

5. On Helmut Schmidt, for example, Thatcher writes, "Although I had had serious disagreements with him, I always had the highest regard for Helmut Schmidt's wisdom, straightforwardness, and grasp of international economics." See Thatcher, *Downing Street Years,* p. 257.

6. Personal interview, Geoffrey Howe, July 3, 1990.

7. Personal interview, Terry Perks (deputy press secretary), June 27, 1990.

8. Consider the following story Reagan tells about a dinner held during the Williamsburg summit in 1983. He addressed Thatcher and said, "Margaret, if one of your predecessors had been a little more clever . . ." She cut him off and delivered the punch line: "I know, I would have been hosting this gathering." As Smith observes, it is revealing that Reagan recalls this story with pleasure—"To steal the punch line of a world leader is not always a sure path to his affections." Smith, p. 107.

9. Consider, for example, her comments on Reagan's speech to both houses of Parliament at the Palace of Westminster: "I was full of admiration that he seemed to have delivered it without a single note. 'I congratulate you on your actor's memory,' I said. He replied, 'I read the whole speech from those two perspex screens'—referring to what we had taken to be some security device. 'Don't you know it? It's a British invention.' And so it was that I made my first acquaintance with Autocue." Thatcher, *Downing Street Years*, p. 258. Notice the subtext here: A British invention, not his "actor's memory," is responsible for Reagan's stunning performance.

10. Bernard Ingham, *Kill the Messenger* (London: HarperCollins, 1991), p. 255.

11. Personal interview, Bernard Ingham, June 20, 1991.

12. In general, the Franks report detailed the government's errors but declined to draw the logical conclusion. Instead, the committee declared, "[W]e would not be justified in attaching any criticism or blame to the present Government for the Argentine Junta's decision to commit its act of unprovoked aggression in the invasion of the Falkland Islands on 2 April 1982." (The committee included Lord Franks, Lord Barber, Lord Lever of Manchester, Sir Patrick Nairne, Merlyn Rees, and Lord Watkinson.) See *The Franks Report: Falkland Islands Review* (1983; London: Pimlico Press, 1992), p. xvi.

13. Commenting on the Franks report, the *Economist* observed, "Despite the prime minister's glancing attention to the issue throughout the month of March, it was never thrashed out by ministers collectively. The limitations of her favoured technique of bilateral meetings and flurries of paper are much in evidence." *Economist*, January 22, 1983.

14. Quoted in Peter Jenkins, *Mrs. Thatcher's Revolution: The Ending of the Socialist Era* (Cambridge, Mass.: Harvard University Press, 1988), p. 161.

15. Thatcher recalled in her memoirs, "Francis is in many ways the quintessential old style Tory: a country gentleman and a soldier, a good tactician, but no strategist. He is a proud pragmatist and an enemy of ideology; the sort of man of whom people used to say that he would be 'just right in a crisis.' I was to have reason to question that judgement. Francis's appointment undoubtedly united the Party. But it heralded serious difficulties for the conduct of the campaign itself." Thatcher, *Downing Street Years*, p. 187.

16. See Young, p. 286.

17. Even in her memoirs, Thatcher insisted, "The decision to sink the Belgrano was taken for strictly military not political reasons: the claim that we were trying to undermine a promising peace initiative from Peru will not bear scrutiny. Those of us who took the decision at Chequers did not at that time know anything about the Peruvian proposals, which in any case closely resembled the Haig plan rejected by the Argentinians only days before. There was a clear military threat which we could not responsibly ignore." Thatcher, *Downing Street Years*, p. 215.

18. See K. D. Ewing and C. A. Gearty, *Freedom Under Thatcher: Civil Liberties and Modern Britain* (Oxford: Clarendon Press, 1990), pp. 143–147.

19. Technological developments now make this type of news management impossible. Reporters can carry their own satellite equipment and send pictures directly back to their news organizations. For the impact of television reporters (and the images they convey) on policy makers in the case of Bosnia, see, for example, Michael Dobbs, "The Amanpour Factor," *Washington Post*, July 23, 1995.

20. See Michael Cockerell, Peter Hennessy, and David Walker, *Sources Close to the Prime Minister: Inside the Hidden World of the News Manipulators* (London: Macmillan, 1984), ch. 8. Also, personal interviews, Bernard Ingham, June 20, 1991, and August 4, 1993.

21. See Jenkins, p. 160.

22. David Sanders, Hugh Ward, and David Marsh, "Government Popularity and the Falklands War: A Reassessment," *British Journal of Political Science* 17 (July 1987): 281–313.

23. Thatcher, *Downing Street Years*, p. 235.

24. According to Thatcher, "Whatever the details of [the Suez] defeat, it entered the British soul and distorted our perspective on Britain's place in the world. We developed what might be called the 'Suez syndrome': having previously exaggerated our power, we now exaggerated our impotence. . . . The truth—that Britain was a middle-ranking power, given unusual influence by virtue of its historical distinction, skilled diplomacy and versatile military forces, but greatly weakened by economic decline—seemed too complex for sophisticated people to grasp. They were determined to think themselves much weaker and more contemptible than was in fact the case, and refused all comfort to the contrary." Thatcher, *Downing Street Years*, esp. pp. 8–9.

25. *The Public Papers of the Presidents of the United States: Ronald Reagan 1982* (Washington: Government Printing Office, 1983), book 1, p. 745.

26. Jenkins, p. 162.

27. Alexander M. Haig, *Caveat: Realism, Reagan and Foreign Policy* (New York: Macmillan, 1984), p. 266.

28. Thatcher, *Downing Street Years*, p. 328.

29. Thatcher, *Downing Street Years*, p. 330.

30. Thatcher, *Downing Street Years*, p. 331. Thatcher observes that Chancellor Kohl of Germany was also "worried about the impact of the American action on European public opinion in the run-up to the deployment of Cruise and Pershing missiles later that month" (p. 335).

31. Thatcher, *Downing Street Years*, p. 332. She also recalled that when Reagan phoned after the invasion, "I was not in the sunniest of moods. The President began by saying, in that disarming way of his, that if he was in London and dropped in to see me he would be careful to throw his hat through the door first."

32. Thatcher, *Downing Street Years*, p. 325.

33. Louis Fisher, *Presidential War Powers* (Lawrence: University Press of Kansas, 1995), pp. 140–142.

34. Thatcher, *Downing Street Years*, p. 391.

35. See Lou Cannon, *President Reagan: The Role of a Lifetime* (New York: Simon and Schuster, 1991), pp. 605–608.

36. Reagan, *Public Papers 1985*, book 2, p. 898.

37. *Washington Post*, November 21, 1986.

38. Jenkins, p. 207.

39. See Duncan Campbell, *The Unsinkable Aircraft Carrier: American Military Power in Britain* (London: Macmillan, 1984).

40. Thatcher, *Downing Street Years*, p. 449.

41. Quoted in Young, p. 475.

42. See, for example, Young, esp. pp. 475–479.

43. Jenkins, p. 211.

44. This is the reason Thatcher gives for her support of the raid in an article published in the *National Review*, December 30, 1988, p. 23.

45. In her memoirs, Thatcher makes several references to the fact that Qadaffi was supplying arms to the IRA. See *Downing Street Years*, pp. 384, 401, 405–406, 413. Furthermore,

when she assesses the benefits of the attack, she notes, "The Extradition Treaty, which we regarded as vital in bringing IRA terrorists back from America, was to receive stronger Administration support against filibustering opposition" (p. 449). Finally, she reveals that Qadaffi also raised money for Arthur Scargill during the miners' strike. See pp. 351, 368–369.

46. Thatcher, *Downing Street Years*, p. 444.

47. During her discussion of the raid, she expresses her reluctance to reveal intelligence information. *Downing Street Years*, p. 446.

48. Personal interview, Geoffrey Howe, July 3, 1990. See also Smith, ch. 10.

49. For a discussion of Reagan's central convictions in foreign affairs, see Martin Anderson, *Revolution* (Stanford, Calif.: Hoover Institution Press, 1990), esp. pp. 72–75.

50. According to Lou Cannon, Reagan's first interest in Armageddon can be traced to an encounter in 1968: His pastor, Donn Moomaw of the Bel-Air Presbyterian Church, and Billy Graham discussed biblical prophecies with Reagan while he was in the hospital recovering from minor surgery. Later, in 1971, Reagan told California Senate president James Mills, "For the first time ever, everything is in place for the battle of Armageddon and the second coming of Christ." In 1980, on Jim Bakker's television show, Reagan declared, "We may be the generation that sees Armageddon." Finally, as late as 1989, Reagan discussed Armageddon with Cannon. See Cannon, p. 289.

51. Senator Edward Kennedy first used "Star Wars" to ridicule Reagan's proposal, but as Martin Anderson observes, "Those who thought to damage the effort by calling it by the apparently pejorative name Star Wars forgot the moral of the famous movie from whence the name came. In the movie Star Wars, the forces of evil are arranged against the forces of good. And, in the end, the forces of good prevail, armed with the latest and swiftest new space technology." See Martin Anderson, p. 77.

52. Quoted in Cannon, p. 290. According to Garry Wills, SDI "fulfills Reagan's narrative requirement that a single hero [or hero-nation] save the day by a decisive act." See Wills, *Reagan's America* (New York: Penguin, 1988), p. 427.

53. See also Wills, p. 465.

54. Reagan, *Public Papers 1983,* book 1, p. 442.

55. Reagan, *Public Papers 1983,* book 1, p. 443.

56. See, for example, Young, 398–399. He (with many others) exaggerates the significance of this statement. There are no indications that Reagan ever intended to be bound by it.

57. Young gives Thatcher this designation. See p. 394.

58. Sir Geoffrey Howe, "Defense and Security in the Nuclear Age," *Atlantic Community Quarterly* 23 (Spring 1985): 38.

59. Howe, p. 41.

60. See, for examples, Smith, p. 159, and Young, p. 398.

61. *Public Papers: Reagan 1983,* book 1, p. 443.

62. Quoted in Smith, p. 58.

63. Cannon, p. 770.

64. Reagan, *Public Papers 1988,* book 2, pp. 683–692.

65. Reagan, *Public Papers 1988,* book 2, p. 681.

66. Reagan, *Public Papers 1988–89,* book 2, p. 1720.

67. Reagan, *Public Papers 1987,* book 1, p. 635.

68. Reagan, *Public Papers 1982,* book 1, p. 743.

69. Reagan, *Public Papers 1982,* book 1, p. 743.

70. Reagan, *Public Papers 1982,* book 1, p. 746.

71. Reagan, *Public Papers 1988,* book 1, p. 717.

72. Quoted in *Times,* June 4, 1988.

73. Margaret Thatcher, "Reagan's Leadership, America's Recovery," *National Review,* December 30, 1988, p. 24.

74. Improving trade relations with Japan proved considerably more difficult. Strategic military considerations restricted Reagan's ability to exert pressure on Japan in the economic arena as they had limited the influence of other cold war presidents. Reagan said a great deal about Japanese trade policy but did little to affect it.

75. See especially Smith, who gives an extensive account of each economic summit.

76. Ian Gilmour, quoted in Bruce Anderson, *John Major: The Making of a Prime Minister* (London: Fourth Estate, 1991), p. 23.

77. Bruce Anderson, p. 29.

78. See Nigel Lawson, *The View from No. 11: Memoirs of a Tory Radical* (London: Bantam, 1992), pp. 933–934.

79. Lawson, p. 936.

80. Quoted in Lawson, p. 955.

81. Lawson, p. 964.

82. Lawson, p. 967.

83. Text reprinted in *Times,* November 14, 1990.

84. Two aspects of the Westland affair made it a global matter: First, the issue arose as a consequence of the failure of Britain's last helicopter company, which reflects the nation's changing status and place in the global economy. Second, the controversy was inextricably linked to discussions about Britain's relationship to Europe and to the U.S.

85. Thatcher, *Downing Street Years,* p. 430.

86. Thatcher has confessed what upset her most about Heseltine's behavior: "Cabinet collective responsibility was being ignored and *my own authority as Prime Minister was being publicly flouted*" (emphasis added). *Downing Street Years,* p. 431.

87. *Observer,* January 26, 1986, p. 1.

88. In her memoirs, Thatcher says she did not know about the leak at the time but does not say when she learned about it. See *Downing Street Years,* p. 434.

89. *Parliamentary Debates, Commons,* 6th series, vol. 90 (1986), pp. 340–342.

90. Gallup poll results reprinted in Elizabeth Hann Hastings and Philip K. Hastings, eds., *Index to International Public Opinion, 1985–86* (Westport, Conn.: Greenwood Press, 1987), p. 427.

91. Thatcher writes, "The British people by and large did not understand or properly appreciate President Reagan." *Downing Street Years,* p. 437.

92. Thatcher, *Downing Street Years,* p. 436.

93. Thatcher, *Downing Street Years,* p. 435.

94. For official reports, see *The Tower Commission Report* (New York: Bantam and Times Books, 1987); *The Report of the Congressional Committees Investigating the Iran-Contra Affair* (New York: Times Books, 1988); Lawrence E. Walsh (independent counsel), *Iran-Contra: The Final Report* (New York: Times Books, 1994). See also Theodore Draper, *A Very Thin Line: The Iran-Contra Affairs* (New York: Hill and Wang, 1991). After studying more than fifty thousand pages of documents and testimony, Draper produced a lengthy study of the subject, but his book was published before the independent counsel's final report. The most compre-

hensive account emerges in the independent counsel's book, *Firewall: The Iran-Contra Conspiracy and Cover-Up* (New York: Norton, 1997).

95. Reagan used these words when he told his national security advisor, Robert McFarlane, that he intended to continue his support for the Contra forces. See Draper, pp. 25–26, and ch. 2.

96. Quoted in Cannon, p. 388.

97. In response to pressure from the Republican right wing, Reagan remarked to Kenneth Duberstein, "Those sons-of-bitches won't be happy until we have 25,000 troops in Managua and I'm not going to do it." Personal interview, Kenneth Duberstein, March 5, 1993; also quoted in Cannon, p. 337.

98. Quoted in Draper, p. 21.

99. Quoted in Draper, p. 22.

100. Members of the Reagan administration would later argue that Boland II did not apply to the National Security staff because it is not an "intelligence agency." Of course, the National Security staff is not authorized to *conduct* any military operations. Furthermore, as in the case of Boland I, the second amendment was attached to an appropriations bill and therefore in effect for only one year. Consequently, the administration continued to try to sustain its support for the Contras, hoping Congress would reverse its decision the following year.

101. *Report of the Congressional Committees Investigating the Iran-Contra Affair,* pp. 48–49.

102. See Draper, p. 501.

103. Quoted in Cannon, p. 638.

104. *The Tower Commission Report,* p. 38.

105. See Cannon's description on p. 593.

106. Independent Counsel Lawrence Walsh found that both the secretary of state and the secretary of defense became implicated in efforts to cover up the affair and concealed important information. Weinberger hid his notes and took part in an attempted cover-up of the possibly illegal November 1985 shipment of Hawk missiles to Iran. Schultz also withheld information pertaining to the sale of arms to Iran. See *Washington Post,* January 19, 1994; for a complete account, see *Iran-Contra: The Final Report.*

107. Cannon, p. 685.

108. *Tower Commission Report,* p. 79.

109. According to the report, "Established procedures for making national security decisions were ignored. Reviews of the initiatives by all the NSC principals were too infrequent. The initiatives were not adequately vetted below the cabinet level. Intelligence sources were underutilized. Applicable legal constraints were not adequately addressed. . . . In all of this process, Congress was never notified." See *Tower Commission Report,* pp. 62–63.

110. At the beginning of the independent counsel's report, Walsh provides a "summary of prosecutions." See *Iran-Contra: The Final Report,* pp. xxiii–xxv.

111. *Iran-Contra: The Final Report,* pp. xiv–xviii.

112. Quoted in *Washington Post,* January 19, 1994.

113. John Locke, *Second Treatise,* sections 146–148.

10. Conclusion

1. During and after the leadership of Thatcher and Reagan, the U.K. and the U.S. placed greater restrictions on the rights of free speech and press, freedom of assembly, and the

rights of the accused. Parliament restricted individual rights more quickly and extensively than Congress did. Without a written constitution or bill of rights, freedom more easily became a residual category—that which had not been legislated against. See K. D. Ewing and C. A. Gearty, *Freedom Under Thatcher: Civil Liberties and Modern Britain* (Oxford: Claredon Press, 1990). Yet in Britain legislative restrictions sparked a battle between judges and politicians, and the courts began to exercise judicial review to preserve civil liberties. See Joshua Rozenberg, *Trial of Strength* (London: Richard Cohen, 1997). In the U.S., judges (largely Reagan appointed) took the lead in efforts to roll back civil liberties safeguards, while Congress followed by passing crime and antiterrorist bills that also served to erode individual rights. Whether the "war on crime" or the "war against terrorism" provided the ostensible goal, at the conclusion of the twentieth century, both countries adopted measures that weakened constitutional safeguards for the individual, and citizens proved willing to sacrifice their rights for the sake of more tangible benefits such as security.

2. Bert Rockman presents this as the fundamental "leadership question"—namely, how to reconcile the need for direction with the requirements of representative government. See *The Leadership Question: The Presidency and the American System* (New York: Praeger, 1984).

3. Roy P. Basler, ed., *The Collected Works of Abraham Lincoln* (New Brunswick, N.J.: Rutgers University Press, 1953), vol. 1, p. 115.

4. In the 1980s many scholars concluded their studies on leadership by issuing calls for renewed emphasis on reason and rational discourse. The author of a book on the U.S. civil rights leader Jesse Jackson recommended an expansion of "rational-discursive" components of the "democratic project in the black community." By "enhancing rational civic culture," ordinary citizens might guard against having their "collective aspirations . . . subsumed into elite agendas." See Adolph L. Reed Jr., *The Jesse Jackson Phenomenon: The Crisis of Purpose in Afro-American Politics* (New Haven, Conn.: Yale University Press, 1986), pp. 135–136. Another scholar concluded his study of Reagan and Thatcher by attributing much of their success to "the manipulation of fears" and "the assimilation of hopes in unlikely guises." See Joel Krieger, *Reagan, Thatcher, and the Politics of Decline* (New York: Oxford University Press, 1986), p. 189. Somewhat surprisingly, these critics who speak from and for the left echo some of the sentiments that Lincoln expressed in his 1838 speech on the "perpetuation of our political institutions."

5. Stephen Skowronek, *The Politics Presidents Make: Leadership from John Adams to George Bush* (Cambridge, Mass.: Harvard University Press, 1993). Skowronek argues that regime-builders have leadership opportunities that their successors lack. Regime-maintainers must struggle with institutional and political constraints, which they inherit from the regime-builders. The difference between his study and my own is largely one of emphasis: This study of conviction-style leaders explores when and how leaders can shape their environment rather than always be shaped by it.

INDEX

AARP (American Association of Retired People), 169

Abortion, 157, 162

Adams, John Quincy, 24, 192, 221, 222, 223

Adamson Act (1916), 88, 89

Addison, Christopher, 104

Advertising, 224, 225

Affirmative action, 176

Afghanistan, 161

AFL (American Federation of Labor), 79

African Americans, and civil rights, 78, 176–177

Agrarian interests, 20, 25, 37, 57, 79, 84, 182

Agriculture, Department of, Bureau of Roads, 87

AIDS, 185

Air India crash (1985), 307

Air traffic controllers, 169–170

Aitken, Max. *See* Beaverbrook, Lord

Allen, Richard, 161–162, 362(n239)

Alliance. *See* Liberal party, and SDP

Amal (Shiite group), 307

American Association for Labor Legislation, 87

American Association of Retired People (AARP), 169

American Enterprise Institute, 117

American Federation of Labor (AFL), 79

American Railway Union, 67

American Rural Credits Association, 86

Amnesty for draft dodgers, 158

Anarchists, 104

Anderson, E. Ellery, 64

Anderson, John, 160

Anderson, Martin, 163

Anglican Church. *See* Church of England

"Anglo-American Gold Trust," 66

Anglo-American relations
  and communications, 30
  democratic ethos and aristocratic tendencies, 20, 22, 27, 296
  and Hawaii, 41
  and Irish and Irish Americans, 339(n5)
  and media, 238–239
  and neoliberalism, 117
  and political development, 2, 19–20, 42, 71, 186, 279
  popular sentiment, 40–41, 322
  trade, 19, 42, 322
  and Venezuela, 41–42
  and World War I, 71, 94–95, 296

See also Conviction politicians

Annual message to Congress, 267, 268–269

Anti–Corn Law League, 33, 34

Anti-imperialism, 98

Anti-Tithe League, 96

Antitrust laws, 79, 84

Argentina, 135, 300, 303

Argonauts, 131–132, 353(n60)

Argyll, Duke of, 54

Asquith, Herbert, 99, 100, 102, 105, 106, 110, 206, 236, 286

Assad, Hafez, 307

Attlee, Clement, 2, 113

Aviation Act (1980), 142

Baker, James, 178, 179, 213, 231, 275, 276–278, 323

Balanced budget, 165

Balance-of-payments deficit (1976), 124

Baldwin, Stanley, 112

Balfour, Arthur, 101, 205

Ballot Act (1872), 49

Bank Charter Act (1844) (Great Britain), 35

Banks, John, 144

Baptists, 44

Bauer, Peter, 121

BBC (British Broadcasting Corporation), 239–240

Beaconsfield, Earl of, 283

Beaverbrook, Lord (Max Aitken), 208, 235, 236

Bell, Tim, 144, 215, 216, 238

Bellamy, Edward, 80

Benn, Tony, 123, 124, 152

Bennett, James Gordon, Sr., 222, 224

Bentinck, George, 195

Berri, Nabih, 307

Beveridge, William, 113

Biddle, Nicholas, 26

Biffen, John, 122

Billings, Bob, 163

"Billion-Dollar Congress," 63

Birkenhead, Frederick, 208

Birnbaum, Jeffrey, 179, 180

Bishop, Maurice, 304

Bitburg cemetery, 250–251

BL (British Leyland), 217, 322

Blaine, James G., 58, 225

Blair, Francis, 222, 262

385